READING
THE AMERICAN
PAST

FIFTH EDITION

Selected Historical Documents
Volume 1: To 1877

MICHAEL P. JOHNSON
Johns Hopkins University

Bedford/St. Martin's   **Boston** ◆ **New York**

For Bedford/St. Martin's

Publisher for History: Mary Dougherty
Executive Editor for History: William J. Lombardo
Director for Development for History: Jane Knetzger
Developmental Editor: Jennifer Jovin
Assistant Production Manager: Joe Ford
Senior Marketing Manager for U.S. History: Amy Whitaker
Project Management: DeMasi Design and Publishing Services
Permissions Manager: Kalina K. Ingham
Cover Designer: Billy Boardman
Cover Art: *Stump Speaking* (oil on canvas), 19th century, George Caleb Bingham (1811–79) © Private Collection/The Bridgeman Art Library International.
Composition: Jeff Miller Book Design
Printing and Binding: RR Donnelley and Sons

President: Joan E. Feinberg
Editorial Director: Denise B. Wydra
Director of Marketing: Karen R. Soeltz
Director of Production: Susan W. Brown
Associate Director, Editorial Production: Elise S. Kaiser
Manager, Publishing Services: Andrea Cava

Library of Congress Control Number: 2011936216

Copyright © 2012, 2009, 2005, 2002 by Bedford/St. Martin's

Manufactured in the United States of America.

6 5
l k j i h

For information, write: Bedford/St. Martin's, 75 Arlington Street, Boston, MA 02116   (617-399-4000)

ISBN: 978-0-312-56413-1

Acknowledgments
Acknowledgments and copyrights appear at the back of the book on pages 328–29, which constitute an extension of the copyright page.

Preface for Instructors

R*eading the American Past* is a collection of compelling documents that represent political, social, and cultural experiences critical to students' understanding of the scope and diversity of United States history. Created by people who shaped American history in ways both large and small, these primary sources reveal the views of the authors, the historical context in which they were written, and the major developments and controversies of their era. The documents give depth, breadth, and variety to textbook discussions of important developments in our nation's past. Organized chapter by chapter to parallel *The American Promise: A History of the United States* in all its editions — full-length, value, compact, and brief, this wide-ranging set of documents offers teachers many pedagogical choices for discussion, analysis, writing assignments, and examinations. Above all, *Reading the American Past* seeks to ignite the sparks of historical imagination that every teacher hopes to see in students' eyes.

Reading a textbook discussion of Columbus's arrival in the New World, for example, gives students basic, up-to-date information that has been collected, sorted out, and synthesized over the past five hundred years. But reading the words Columbus wrote in his log shortly after he stepped ashore in the Western Hemisphere recaptures as no textbook can that moment of profound, mutual surprise when fifteenth-century Europeans and the people they called Indians first encountered one another. As every historian knows, primary sources bridge the gap from the present, when they are read, to the past, when they were written. They encourage students to venture across that span connecting present and past and to risk discovering a captivating and unexpected world.

FEATURES OF THIS BOOK

Three basic principles guided my selection of documents. First and foremost, the sources highlight major events and significant perspectives of a given historical era. Second, I chose and edited documents to be accessible, interesting, and often surprising to students. Third, I sought sources that lend themselves to analysis in classroom discussion and writing assignments — documents that vividly portray controversies marking a particular historical moment and that offer multiple avenues of interpretation.

User-friendly editorial features help students read and interpret the sources. Introductory headnotes and follow-up questions to aid students' reading and discussion accompany each document. Unfamiliar words are defined when they are necessary to understand a document. Editorial intrusions have been kept brief, providing just enough information to allow students to explore the sources and make their own discoveries. By minimizing editorial interventions, I hope to encourage students to focus on the documents and to become astonished, perplexed, and invigorated by what they read.

Documents new to the fifth edition. This new edition incorporates the insights and suggestions of teachers who have used *Reading the American Past*. Guided by their classroom experiences, I have replaced one document per chapter (and two in the last chapter) in order to diversify the historical voices from each era and to give students and teachers fresh choices for investigating major developments.

In all, thirty-two new documents provide greater attention to the global context of American history, as well as offer more coverage of the viewpoints of ordinary Americans — women and men, immigrants and natives, minorities and majorities, workers and bosses. A Native American participant in the Pueblo Revolt of 1680 in New Mexico explains why it happened (Document 3–5). A woman captured by the Seneca during the Seven Years' War describes her life in captivity (Document 6–1). A South Carolina planter's wife reports her encounters with slave women on her husband's rice plantation (Document 13–3). A homesteader's wife describes her new life on the Nebraskan prairie (Document 17–2). A suffragist ridicules arguments used by opponents of voting by women (Document 21–4). A Vietnam veteran denounces the Vietnam War (Document 29–5). And many more.

Diverse perspectives and sources. The documents assembled here provide students a generous cross-section of the diverse experiences that comprise the American past. The reflections of politicians and thieves, generals and privates, reformers and reprobates can be found here, along with those of the nation's countless ethnic and religious minorities. Barack Obama's 2010 speech in Cairo (Document 31–5) joins classic sources such as John Winthrop's *Arbella* sermon (Document 4–1), George Washington's Farewell Address (Document 9–5), and George Kennan's "Long Telegram" (Document 26–2), which disclose the perspectives of influential leaders. The no-less-significant views of common people are revealed by such documents as the memoir of an Englishwoman who became an indentured servant in eighteenth-century New York (Document 5–1), the letter from a slave to President Thomas Jefferson demanding that the president live up to his criticisms of slavery (Document 10–3), twentieth-century letters from American soldiers at war (Documents 22–3 and 25–4), and an interview with a Mexican American migrant farmworker (Document 24–4). Diaries and court cases convey the immediacy of history as lived experience. Reminiscences and oral histories illuminate the past with memories of participants. Speeches, manifestos, congressional testimony, and White House tape recordings spotlight the ends and means of political power. Essays, addresses, and passages from books offer the considered opinions of cultural leaders, whether captains of industry, novelists, or social critics.

Classroom flexibility. The selections in *Reading the American Past* allow instructors to choose documents that best serve their teaching needs. Teachers might, for example, ask students to read documents in preparation for lectures, then refer to the assigned selections as they explain, say, the encounter between Europeans and Native Americans, the tensions that led to the Civil War, or the origins and consequences of the Cold War. An instructor might devote a class to explicating a single source, such as Richard Frethorne's letter describing his life as an indentured servant at Jamestown, Virginia (Document 3–1), or Walter Wyckoff's observations about socialists and anarchists in 1890s Chicago (Document 19–4), or Joseph Stiglitz's article that blamed the economic meltdown of 2008 on the deregulation of the financial system since the Reagan years (Document 31–4).

All the documents are ideally suited for provoking discussions during lecture sessions or in section meetings. Students can be asked to adopt and defend the viewpoint of a given source, to attack it from the perspective of a historical contemporary, to dissect its assumptions and evasions, or to compare and contrast it with other sources. Selections might also be used for quizzes, brief writing assignments, longer papers, or examinations. The documents open these and many other avenues for inspiring students to investigate the American past.

Tips for reading documents. A short introduction for students at the outset of each volume explains the significance of documents for understanding history and outlines the basic questions that students should ask themselves in order to decipher any primary source. It encourages students to consider the historical context, author, date, audience, and language of the sources they are about to read.

Just the right amount of context. A brief paragraph begins each chapter, setting the documents in the larger historical context detailed in the corresponding chapter of the textbook. A headnote precedes every document, identifying its source, explaining when and by whom it was produced, and highlighting why it presents a revealing point of view. Rather than cluttering documents with numerous explanatory notes, I have assumed that students will — and they should — refer to a textbook for basic information about the people and events that appear in the sources, though notes are provided for more obscure words and people.

Thought-provoking questions. To guide students toward key passages and central ideas, "Questions for Reading and Discussion" follow each document. They are intended to help students identify fundamental points, analyze what a document means, and think about its larger historical significance. "Comparative Questions" at the end of each chapter ask students to ponder some of the similarities and differences among the chapter's documents, and to consider how the ideas, observations, and viewpoints expressed reveal the major historical developments of the time.

To see more clearly along the many angles of historical vision offered by the documents, students rely on the guidance, insight, and wisdom of their teachers. *Reading the American Past* gives instructors numerous opportunities to entice students to become active collaborators in the study of American history. Ideally, these documents will help persuade students that the American past is neither frozen in time nor entombed in books, but instead shapes their present and prefigures their future. Ideally, they will come to see that they do not simply read American history; they live it.

ACKNOWLEDGMENTS

For help with this edition of *Reading the American Past* I am indebted to many people, but to none more than the following historians who have shared their professional insights and classroom experiences to suggest ways to make the documents more useful and informative for students and teachers throughout the country: James Barrera, South Texas College; Kevin Brown, Lansing Community College; Tonia M. Compton, Columbia College; Luke E. Harlow, Oakland University; Matthew Harper, University of Central Arkansas; Diana K. Honey, Kennesaw State University; Arlene Lazarowitz, California State University, Long Beach; Matthew Mason, Brigham Young University; Brian Jeffrey Maxson, East Tennessee State University; Suzanne L. McFadden, Austin Community College; Sandy Moats, University of Wisconsin-Parkside; Jeffrey P. Moran, University of Kansas; Maureen Murphy Nutting, North Seattle Community College; Robert O'Brien, Lone Star College-CyFair; Thomas Sabatini, Kent State University at Trumbull; Donald J. Schwegler, SUNY Orange; Jeffrey

Smith, Lindenwood University; Judith Spraul-Schmidt, University of Cincinnati; T.J. Tomlin, University of Northern Colorado; and Janet A. Wiita, Embry-Riddle Aeronautical University.

I have also relied, as usual, on my coauthors of *The American Promise* — James L. Roark, Patricia Cline Cohen, Sarah Stage, and Susan M. Hartmann — for advice and suggestions. Although I have benefited from the support of all of these colleagues, I am nonetheless solely responsible for the final selection of documents and edited passages in this volume.

Many others contributed their energy and creativity to this project. From the outset, Joan Feinberg and Chuck Christensen have enthusiastically supported the publication of a collection of American history documents that aspired to the high standards readers have come to expect from Bedford/St. Martin's. As always, Mary Dougherty, Bill Lombardo, and Jane Knetzger brought their benevolent and constructive stewardship to the project. Jennifer Jovin combined enthusiasm and good editorial judgment to digest reviewers' comments and improve this edition throughout. Andrea Cava, Joe Ford, and Linda DeMasi skillfully steered the book through the production process, while Kalina Ingham and Carolyn Evans handled permissions.

Overall, this book represents the constructive efforts of teachers, students, colleagues, editors, and publishers, all enlisted in the common cause of helping students better understand our collective history. I am the grateful beneficiary of their generosity, intelligence, and insight.

Introduction for Students

Historical documents allow us to peer into the past and learn what happened and what did not happen — crucial beginning points for understanding how and why the present came to be. They record bits of history and preserve the momentary ideas and experiences of individuals and groups. But how can you, a twenty-first-century student, read and truly comprehend a letter from a seventeenth-century indentured servant or a nineteenth-century woman on the frontier, full of irregular spelling and contemporary references? How can you determine the historical value and accuracy of documents recorded years or even centuries ago? How can you read documents to figure out what *really* happened in the past?

FLAWS OF MEMORY

It would be convenient if we did not need documents, if we could depend instead on our memory to tell us what happened. Unfortunately, memory is far from perfect, as we are reminded every time we misplace our keys. We not only forget things that did happen, but we also remember things that never occurred, such as erroneously thinking we put those keys right there on that shelf. Mark Twain once quipped, "When I was younger I could remember anything, whether it happened or not; but my faculties are decaying now, and soon I shall be so [old] I cannot remember any but the things that never happened."

Twain's witticism points to another important property of memory: It changes over time. Every good trial lawyer knows that memory is fragile, volatile, and subject to manipulation by our desires, intentions, and fears. Our memory is constantly reshaped to serve the needs of the present. Compounding the unreliability of memory are two stubborn realities: Most of the people who might remember something about what happened are dead, their memories erased forever; and no person, no single memory, ever knew all there is to know about what happened.

DOCUMENTS AS HISTORICAL SNAPSHOTS

These flaws of memory might cause us to shrug wearily and conclude that it is impossible to determine what happened. But documents make it possible to learn a great deal — although not every last thing — about what really happened. Because documents are created by humans, they are subject to all the frailties of memory, with one vital exception: Documents do not change. Unlike memory, documents freeze words at a moment in time. Ideas, perceptions, emotions, and assumptions expressed in a document allow us to learn now about what happened then. In effect, documents are a bridge from the present to the past. They allow us to cross over and to discover how we got from there to here.

Today you can stand where the audience stood in 1863 to listen to Abraham Lincoln's famous speech at the dedication of the cemetery for the Union soldiers killed at the battle of Gettysburg. Of course you can't hear Lincoln's voice, but you can read his words because the Gettysburg Address exists as a historical document; you can literally read this portion of the American past. The address transports the reader back to that crisp November day almost a century and a half ago, the outcome of the war very much in doubt, when the president and commander in chief of more than a million men in blue uniforms explained in a few words his view of the meaning of the war for the nation and the world. The address captured Lincoln's thoughts at that moment and preserved them, much like a historical snapshot. All documents have this property of stopping time, of indelibly recording somebody's views at a specific moment in the past.

The documents in *Reading the American Past* allow you to travel back in time without getting up from your chair. You can accompany a slave owner as he visits his former slaves for the first time after the Civil War and emancipation. You can listen to a young woman describe her life on the Great Plains frontier to her relatives back East. You can read the letters of soldiers during World War II who recount their part in the global maelstrom. You can witness the confession of the self-professed mastermind of the 9/11 terrorist attacks. These and the many other documents in this book bring the past alive in the words of the people who lived it.

DOCUMENTS CAPTURE DIVERSE VOICES AND EXPERIENCES

Documents record far more than the ideas of presidents. They disclose, for instance, Pueblo Indians' views of conquering Spaniards in the sixteenth century, Native American grievances against New Englanders who precipitated King Philip's War in the seventeenth century, a woman's passionate argument for equality of the sexes in the eighteenth century, the confessions of slave insurrectionists in the nineteenth century, the views

of Vietnam War veterans in the twentieth century, an economist's explanation of the Great Recession in the twenty-first century, and much, much
more. These views and many others are recorded by the documents in this
collection. They permit you to read the American past from the diversity
of perspectives that contributed to the making of America: women and
men, workers and bosses, newcomers and natives, slaves and masters,
voters and politicians, conservatives and radicals, activists and reaction-
aries, westerners and easterners, northerners and southerners, farmers
and urbanites, the famous and the forgotten. These people created historical documents when they stole a spare moment to write a letter or
record thoughts in a diary, when they talked to a scribbling friend or
stranger, when they appeared in court or made a will, and when they
delivered a sermon, gave a speech, or penned a manifesto. Examples of
all these kinds of documents are included in *Reading the American Past*.
Together, they make it possible for you to learn a great deal about what
really happened.

DOCUMENTS BRING YOU FACE-TO-FACE WITH THE PAST

From the almost limitless historical record, I chose documents that clearly
and vividly express an important perspective about a major event or a
widespread point of view during a certain historical era. I selected documents that are not only revealing but also often surprising, controversial,
or troubling. My goal is to bring you face-to-face with the past through
the eyes of the people who lived it.

   Reading the American Past is designed to accompany *The American
Promise: A History of the United States*. Each chapter in this volume paral-
lels a chapter in *The American Promise*. The documents provide eyewitness
accounts that broaden and deepen the textbook narrative. Chapter 16, for
example, supplements the textbook discussion of Reconstruction with
selections from five documents: a report on the attitudes of whites in the
former Confederacy in the summer of 1865; the Mississippi Black Code;
advertisements of former slaves seeking lost family members; a plantation owner's journal entry about his first visit with his former slaves after
they became free following the Civil War; and testimony of an African
American Republican before the congressional committee investigating
the Ku Klux Klan in 1871. Each selection is long enough to convey the
central message of the author, but short enough to be read for the first
time in ten minutes or so. In general, each chapter in this book contains
five documents of roughly similar length.

READING AND UNDERSTANDING DOCUMENTS

To help you read and understand the documents, a brief paragraph at the
beginning of each chapter sketches the larger historical context, which
your textbook explains in more detail. A headnote precedes each document

and identifies its source, explains who produced it and when, and suggests why it is revealing. Questions to aid your reading and discussion follow each selection and point you toward key passages and fundamental ideas and ask you to consider both what a document says and what it means. More questions at the end of each chapter encourage you to compare and find connections among the different documents.

While reading the documents in this book, it's important to keep in mind the historical context; the author, date, and audience; and the meanings of the words themselves. Below are some guidelines and questions to consider while reading any primary document.

ESTABLISH THE HISTORICAL CONTEXT

Getting the most out of these documents requires reading with care and imagination. Historians are interested in what a document says and what it reveals about the historical reality that is only partly disclosed by the document itself. A document might be likened to a window that permits us to glimpse features of the past. A document challenges us to read and understand the words on the page as a way to look through the window and learn about the larger historical context.

Lincoln's Gettysburg Address, for example, hints that he believed many loyal Americans wondered whether the war was worth the effort, whether all those soldiers, as he said, "have died in vain." Lincoln's words do not explicitly say that many people thought the human tragedy of the war was too great, but that seems to be one of their meanings. His address attempted to answer such doubts by proclaiming the larger meaning of the war and the soldiers' deaths. His public statement of the noble ideals of the Union war effort hint at his private perception that many Americans had come to doubt whether the war had any meaning beyond the maiming or death of their loved ones.

To see such unstated historical reality in and through a document, readers must remain alert to exactly what the document says. The first step is to learn something about the era in which the document was written by reading *The American Promise* or another textbook of American history.

IDENTIFY AUTHOR, DATE, AND AUDIENCE

The next step in deciphering a document is to consider three important questions: Who wrote the document? When was it written? Who was the intended audience? These questions will help you understand the information in the brief headnote and answer the questions that accompany each document, as well as the concluding comparative questions that draw attention to similarities and differences among the documents in the chapter. While these editorial features will aid your investigation of the documents, you should always proceed by asking who wrote each document, when, and for what audience.

Author. Obviously, a document expresses the viewpoint of its author. Different people had different views about the same event. At Gettysburg, for example, the Confederacy suffered a painful defeat that weakened their ability to maintain their independence and to defend slavery. If Jefferson Davis, the president of the Confederacy, had delivered a Gettysburg Address, it would have been very different from Lincoln's. Documents also often convey their authors' opinions of the viewpoints of other people, including those who agree with them and those who don't. You should always ask, then: What does a document say about the viewpoint of the author? What does it say about the author's opinion about the views of other people? Does the document suggest the author's point of view was confined to a few others, shared by a substantial minority, or embraced by a great many people? What motivated the author to express his or her point of view in the first place? If the document has been translated or transcribed by another person, what relationship did that person have with the author, and can we trust that the document accurately represents the author's thoughts?

Date. A document conveys valuable information about the era when it was composed as well as about the author's point of view. Since a person's perspective often changes over time, it is critical to know exactly when a document was written in order to understand its meaning. When Lincoln delivered the Gettysburg Address, the outcome of the Civil War remained in doubt; seventeen months later, in April 1865, he was certain of northern victory. The address expresses the urgency and uncertainty of the wartime crisis of 1863 rather than the relief and confidence of 1865. As you read every document, you should ask: How does the document reflect the era when the author wrote it? What does it say about the events under way at the time? What does it suggest about how that particular time was perceived by the author and by other people? How did the times shape the author's thoughts and actions?

Audience. In addition to considering who wrote a document and when, you should think about the author's intended audience. A politician may say one thing in a campaign speech and something quite different in a private letter to a friend. An immigrant might send a rosy account of life in America to family members in the Old Country — an account at odds with the features of life in the New World he or she describes in a diary. The intended audience shapes the message an author seeks to send. The author's expectation of what the audience wants to hear contributes to what a document says, how it is said, and what is left unsaid. Lincoln knew that his audience at Gettysburg included many family members mourning the death of loved ones who "gave the last full measure of devotion" on the battlefield. He hoped his remarks would soothe the heartache of the survivors by ennobling the Union and those who died in its defense. To decipher any document, you should always ask: Who is the intended audience? How did the audience shape what the author says? Did consideration of the audience lead the author to emphasize some things and downplay or ignore others? How would the intended audience be likely to read the document? How would people who were not among the intended audience be likely to read it?

It is particularly important to consider the audience when reading interviews, since both the interviewer and interviewee can have different expectations of the same audience. If the interviewer's questions are provided, how do they guide and shape the responses of the interviewee? What is the interviewer's motivation for conducting the interview, and what is the interviewee's motivation for giving it?

DECIPHER THE LANGUAGE

The meanings of words, like the viewpoints of individuals, also reflect their historical moment. For the most part, the documents in this collection were written in English and the authors' original spelling has been preserved (unless stated otherwise), even if it fails to conform to common usage today. Numerous documents have been translated into English from Spanish, Portuguese, Latin, German, Swedish, or one of several Native American languages. But even documents originally written in English require you to translate the meaning of English words at the time the document was written into the meaning of English words today.

Readers must guard against imputing today's meanings to yesterday's words. When Lincoln said "this nation" in the Gettysburg Address, he referred to the United States in 1863, a vastly different nation from the one founded four score and seven years earlier and from the one that exists today, a century and a half later. The word is the same, but the meaning varies greatly.

Although the meaning of many words remains relatively constant, if you are on the lookout for key words whose meanings have changed, you will discover otherwise hidden insights into the documents. You can benefit simply from exercising your historical imagination about the changing meaning of words. To Lincoln, the phrase "all men are created equal" did not have the same meaning that it did for women's rights leaders at the time, or for slaves or slave owners.

You should always pay attention to the words used in a document and ask a final set of questions: How do the words in the document reflect the author, the time, and the intended audience? Would the same words have different meanings to other people at that time? Does the author's choice of words reveal covert assumptions and blind spots along with an overt message?

THE VALUE OF DOCUMENTS

Historical documents not only provide readers with indelible markers of historical changes that have occurred, they also illuminate the role human beings played in making those changes. Documents instruct us about the achievements and limitations of the past as they inspire and caution us for the future. Documents also instill in us a strong sense of historical humility. Americans in the past were not less good or more evil, less right or more wrong, than we are today. Their ideas, their experiences, and their times were different from ours in many respects, but they made the nation we inhabit. Ideally, the documents in *Reading the American Past* will give you an appreciation of what it took, and will continue to take, to make American history happen.

Contents

1 Ancient America

Before 1492

For millennia, ancient Americans and other human beings have explained who they were and how they came to be with stories, shaped and reshaped in countless tellings. The narratives of human origins that were eventually written down and still survive differed greatly, but they all express a sense of the meaning and mystery of human existence. Native Americans shared some of their origin stories with European settlers who came to the New World in the fifteenth, sixteenth, and seventeenth centuries. Professional anthropologists and their Native American informants recorded many others in the nineteenth and twentieth centuries. Those stories, polished and modified over the centuries, are as close as we will ever get to understanding what ancient Americans believed about their origins. The Europeans who encountered ancient Americans had their own notions of human origins created by ancient peoples in Europe, the Middle East, and North Africa. Christians believed the creation stories in Genesis, the first book of the Bible. As Christianity spread throughout Europe, there was always debate and contention—among Christians themselves, and between Christians and followers of Judaism, Islam, and other ancient beliefs, including those of ancient Greek philosophers such as Aristotle. The following excerpts from Native American origin narratives as well as from the Bible and Aristotle reveal more than contrasting views of the prehistoric origins of the world. They also disclose a great deal about the distinctive worldviews of the people whose encounters in the New World after 1492 did so much to shape American history.

DOCUMENT 1–1

A Taino Origin Story

Friar Ramón Pané was the first European to record an origin narrative of Native Americans. Pané, a Franciscan priest, accompanied Christopher Columbus on his second voyage to the New World and lived among the Taino Indians on the island of Hispaniola, site of the present-day Dominican Republic and Haiti. The following excerpt from Pané's report to Columbus in 1498 reveals the views of Pané's Taino informants as well as Pané's own perspective as a Catholic priest and a Spaniard.

Ramón Pané

On Taino Religious Practices

When in 1492 Christopher Columbus discovered the island of Hispaniola, among the other things reported was that the people of that island did not worship anything other than the heavens, planets, and stars. But after living there and learning the [Taino] language, they became familiar with those people and observed that they had various ceremonies and customs, as did the hermit friar, Ramón [Pané] . . . [who came] from Rome to that island in order to instruct and convert the islanders to our Christian faith. He composed a book about their customs, many of which will be related in this letter.

First, they say that there appear at night on that island certain phantasms and visions of which they senselessly make certain simulacra [idols] which they gather together to worship; seated on the ground on blankets of cotton-wool they carve certain good demons, just as among us there are sculptors. The simulacra are called zemis, and they worship them as eternal gods; they say that there are two, that is, one called Iocauna, and the other elder one, Guamaonocon. These are said to have five mothers. . . .

There is a region of that island which is called Caunana, where they say humankind first issued from grottos in two mountains, that is, the greater part from the larger cave, and the lesser part from the smaller cave. . . . The first to issue from that [smaller] cavern was called Machochael, who guarded the opening every night. He once went out a short distance and saw the sun at dawn, and since he was unable to endure that light, was transformed into a stone. In the same way many others who went out at night from that cavern to go fishing and who were unable to return before the sun rose, upon seeing that light, as punishment since they were not permitted to see it, were immediately transformed into those trees which yield plums. These grow spontaneously on that island in great quantity, without being planted.

They also tell of a ruler named Vaguoniona, who sent his servant out of that cavern to go fishing; that servant, since he was unable to return before the sun rose, was transformed into a nightingale. Ever since then, during the night and in the same season in which he was transformed into a bird, he sings and laments his bad fortune and asks for help from his master Vaguoniona. It is for this reason that they say the nightingale sings at night.

Afterwards Vaguoniona, who greatly loved his servant, left the cave, bringing forth only the females with their nursing children; they went to an island not far from there which is called Matinino; there he left the females and brought back with him the little children. Afterwards, having been abandoned near a little river, they began to cry, uttering "toa, toa," that is, "mamma, mamma," so that they were changed into frogs. This is the reason they say that in the spring those frogs begin to sing.

They say that men came out of those caverns in this way and spread throughout Hispaniola, without their women. They also say that Vaguoniona wandered

---

From Geoffrey Symcox and Luciano Formisano, eds., *Italian Reports on America, 1492–1522: Accounts by Contemporary Observers*, trans. Theodore J. Cachey Jr. and John C. McLucas, Repertorium Columbianum 12 (Turnhout, Belgium: Brepols, 2002), 63–68.

about among different places and, by special grace, was never transformed, except by a beautiful female whom he saw in the sea. He descended into the sea and received from her certain marble pebbles which they call *cibas*, as well as certain little golden tablets which are called *guaninos*. These gems, to this day associated with their kings, are held in reverence as sacred things.

The men who had remained in the cave without their females came out during the night, after washing themselves in ditches where a large amount of rainwater had gathered (and still today they use those baths). As soon as they had come out, it is said, they raced to the plum trees, upon which an infinite number of ants had gathered; they grasped them [the ants] with their hands, as if they were so many females, and when they squeezed them they slipped out of their hands like eels. They went to seek counsel from elderly counselors, and they went to see if there were any men who might have scabies[1] or leprosy or who might have calloused, rough hands with which they could easily hold the ants. Those men are called *caracaracoles*; thus they went to hunt them, and although they captured many [*caracaracoles*], they were nevertheless unable to keep more than four, which they used as females. They say they had no genitals, and for this reason it is said they returned to the elders for counsel; consequently they sent them the woodpecker, who, with his sharp beak, opened the genitals between the thighs of those females, and the others descended from there. . . .

Thus, in this way, their wise men, with gravity and reputation, from bowers and eminent places, instruct these simple islanders and persuade them to believe such things as these to be sacred and true.

Concerning the origins of the sea, they say there was a very powerful man named Iaia, on that island, who killed his only son, whom he placed in a gourd instead of in a fabricated tomb. Later, this Iaia, after having passed many months troubled by the death of his son, returned to that gourd and opened it, and a great whale issued forth. . . . Drawn by the report of this, four youths, born of a single birth, in the hopes of obtaining the fish within the gourd, took it in their hands. Iaia, who had enclosed the bones in the gourd, came upon them; the youths, frightened at their sacrilege, and to avoid being accused of that robbery by Iaia, tried to flee. The gourd, because of its great weight, fell upon the ground and broke, and the sea escaped through the cracks. The sea flowed down the valleys and across the great plains nearly filling them, except for the peaks of mountains and high places that were left uncovered, which created the islands which can presently be seen.

They also say that those brothers, for fear of Iaia, fled to different places and were dying of hunger, for they did not have the courage to stop. They went to knock at the door of a baker, asking for cassava, that is, bread. Entering the house, they spat at the baker a deadly spit that killed him. Those brothers, after a discussion, opened him up with a sharp stone, and out of that wound a female was born, and those brothers slept with her together, and both males and females were the result.

In addition to these things, they say there is a cave which is called Iovanaboina . . . which is for them a more religious place than Santiago de Compostela[2]

---

[1]**scabies**: A skin disease.

[2]**Santiago de Compostela**: A holy shrine for Christian pilgrims in Spain.

is for us. It is adorned with many different paintings and has two doors sculpted to represent their demons, the zemis, one of which they call Bintaitalle, the other Marochum. When we asked them why they worship that cave with such devotion, they said that the sun and moon issued forth from there to illuminate the world. These senseless men affirm these things with great gravity, and there is as great an affluence of people coming and going from that cave as there is in our churches and at the great pilgrimage places. . . .

When they were asked by our men where they learn those vain customs (which are a pestilence among them), they answer that they have been handed down from their ancestors; and that it is not permitted to teach such things . . . except to the sons of the kings; and that they never had writing among them and everything is preserved by memory.

QUESTIONS FOR READING AND DISCUSSION

1. According to Pané's account, how did the acts of Machochael and the men who left the cave alter the world? Why were zemis important?

2. Pané says the Taino told him that men left the caves "without their women." How did women come to populate the earth? Does the narrative suggest that men and women were created more or less as equals?

3. This Taino origin story emphasizes that human beings were "transformed" in numerous ways to shape the world. Why did these transformations occur, according to the narrative? How did these transformations influence humans who were not transformed?

4. In what ways is Pané's religion evident in his account of Taino origins? Do you think Pané was a reliable recorder of Taino beliefs? What parts of Pané's account, if any, seem credible to you? Why?

5. Since Tainos "never had writing among them and everything is preserved by memory," do you think the stories the Taino told Pané were credible accounts of ancient beliefs? What evidence suggests the Taino believed these stories? Is there evidence that their origin narrative had ancient roots? On the other hand, is there evidence that they might have invented the narrative to please or satisfy Pané?

DOCUMENT 1–2

A Penobscot Origin Narrative

In 1893, Joseph Nicolar, an elder of the Penobscot people of Maine, published an account of stories which, he wrote, "have been handed down from the beginning of the red man's world to the present time." Nicolar was the descendant of well-known Penobscot leaders who summarized the story of Klose-kur-beh, The Man from Nothing, after "forty years of search and study." According to Nicolar, Klose-kur-beh "was claimed by all the children of the red man, to be the first person who came upon the earth." The excerpt below introduces Klose-kur-beh, recounts the sacrifice of the first mother, and describes her gift of love for all, as interpreted by Klose-kur-beh.

Joseph Nicolar
The Life and Traditions of the Red Men, 1893

Klose-kur-beh, "The Man from Nothing" . . . [came] into the world when the world contained no other man, in the flesh, but himself. When he opened his eyes lying on his back in the dust, his head [pointed] toward the rising of the sun and his feet toward the setting of the sun. . . . Having no strength to move any part of his body, yet the brightness of the day revealed to him all the glories of the whole world. . . . [H]e saw the land, the sea, mountains, lakes, rivers, and the motion of the waters, and in it he saw the fishes. On the land were the animals and beasts, and in the air the birds. . . .

While the body clung to the dust he was without mind, and the flesh without feeling. At that moment the heavens were lit up, with all kinds of bright colors most beautiful . . . and soon all the colors intermingled, forming a beautiful bright-ness in the center of the heavens over the front of his face. Nearer and nearer came the brightness toward his body until it got almost to a touching distance, and a feeling came into his flesh, he felt the warmth of the approaching brightness, and he fell into a deep sleep. The wind of the heavens fanned his brow, and the sense of seeing returned unto him, but he saw not the brightness he beheld before, but . . . a person like unto himself, standing at his right hand, and the person's face was toward the rising of the sun. . . . The first thought that came unto him was, that he believed the person was able to bring strength unto him, and the "Great Being" answered his thought saying these words: "Thou doest well believing in me, I am the head of all that thou beholdest, and as thou believest, arise from thy bed of dust, and stand on thy feet, let the dust be under thy feet, and as thou believest, thou shalt have strength to walk." Immediately strength came unto him, and he rose to his feet and stood beside the "Great Being."

After this the "Great Being" . . . turned . . . facing the sun. Lifting both hands and looking up he said: "Go thy way!" and immediately the whole heavens obeyed. The sun, moon and all the stars moved towards the setting of the sun. The night coming slowly toward their standing, when the Great Being sending up his voice, saying: "Let us make man in our own image[.]" . . . [T]he Great Being said unto [Klose-kur-beh] . . . "go thy way, toward thy right hand and seek thy com-panions! I will be thy teacher and you will be their teacher"; and [Klose-kur-beh] obeyed his command. . . .

As soon as the news of the return of Klose-kur-beh reached the ears of the first mother of the people, she became very much agitated and her action gave much alarm; nothing seemed to give her relief, and she showed a discontented mind day after day. . . . [S]even little children came and stood . . . looking into the wom-an's face saying, "We are in hunger and the night will soon come; where is the food?" Upon hearing this, water came from the woman's eyes seven drops came and dropped upon the earth. . . . [T]he woman said to the little ones, "hold your peace little ones, in seven moons you shall be filled and shall hunger no more." . . . [T]he woman turned her pleading eyes to [her husband] saying, "Take the stone implement, [and] with it slay me unto death[.]" . . .

From Joseph Nicolar, *The Life and Traditions of the Red Men* (Bangor, ME: C. H. Glass, Printers, 1893), 7–11, 57–67.

[S]he gave directions as to what should be done. She told the man [her husband] after he had slain her, to get twisted branches of the small trees and tie the branches around her neck and drag her body to a large open space of land and to drag it all over the open space, and when the flesh was worn away to the bones turn it and wear away the other side, and after he had dragged her body all over the land to bury her bones in the middle of it and then come away, and in seven moons to go and gather all he found on the land,—gather and eat, but not all of it—save some to put in the land again. Let seven moons pass before you put my flesh in the ground again; put it under the ground so the birds will not devour it. . . . [T]he man did slay the woman and he dragged her body over a large open land and did bury her bones in the center of it as directed. . . .

When the seven moons had passed the man went to the place where his wife's bones lay, and when he came to the place he beheld the place filled with tall plants but not green because the sun had faded them to a yellow shade, and upon examining the stock found substance in them which he tasted and it was sweet, and he called it "Skar-moo-nal"—Corn, and upon reaching the place where the bones lay he found a plant, large, with broad leaves, without substance; because it was bitter in taste he called it "Ootar-Mur-wa-yeh"—Tobacco. Upon his return to the people and made known what he had found[,] there was great rejoicing among them and all went to help the man in the harvest; all the corn and tobacco were properly taken care of. And here corn and tobacco raising began.

The man whose heart had been so heavy with sorrow since slaying his wife, began to be cheerful when seeing such a general rejoicing and happiness so universal. He began to see that granting the request of his wife was for the good of all, and he no longer lay sorrow to his heart. The only perplexity to him was how to dispose of the fruits of the great event. He saw that something must be done and that in the future some wholesome management would be needed. As he was not able to come to a just conclusion of it, he called together seven young maidens and sent them to the north part of the country to get Klose-kur-beh to come among them and tell them what to do with the harvest which was then in the peoples hands. . . .

[W]hen the time arrived, which was appointed by the young maidens, all the people gathered to welcome them home, and when the sun began to cast its shadows toward the setting of the sun the maidens appeared and said, "Klose-kur-beh will come immediately." When the sun was highest, Klose-kur-beh came and immediately the people began to show him the harvest. Upon seeing the great store before him Klose-kur-beh showed signs of joy and said, "There was one thing the Great Spirit did not mention to me, therefore we must be careful in our minds what we do with it. And because this has come from the good of a woman's heart I must first give thanks to the Great Spirit in the name of the seven young maidens who brought the message to me. . . .["]

[T]hen he began to speak to the people, saying: ["]The first words of the first mother, have come to pass. When she first came she claimed her origin from the beautiful blade of the plant and that her power shall be great and it shall be felt all over the world; that she was all love,—even the beast will steal her body—for the love of it. And now that she has gone into the substance, which every living being will love we must take care that the second seed of the first mother be always with you, because this is her flesh. When you are filled with it, it gives strength; her bones also have been left behind for your good. These also are the blades of the plant. This blade will not give strength to the body, but will give strength to the mind; burn it and inhale the smoke it will bring freshness to the mind and your heart will be contented while the smoke of it be in you. These two things must always bring memory to your minds, when you eat remember her, and do the same when the smoke of her bones rises before you; yea more, whatever your work be, stop in your labor until the smoke has all gone to the Great Spirit. And as we are all brothers, divide among you the flesh and bone of the first mother, and let all shares be alike, and then the love of your first mother will have been fully carried out.

A little more I wish to say for your good. By the change made in your first mother, other changes in the world shall follow. There shall be weeping and shedding of tears, and there shall be rejoicing causing the body to move to suit the joy. There shall be a season to put the seed in the ground, and a season for it to grow and then the harvest shall come. There shall be a season for heat and a season for cold, so prepare yourself for all these, that when each one comes you may be ready for it. I shall leave you and shall hearken no more to your calling, but shall wait the calling of the Great Spirit. Strange things shall happen, but those who bring about the changes will tell you all about them so you may understand them." Here Klose-kur-beh took leave of his people to come no more.

QUESTIONS FOR READING AND DISCUSSION

1. How did Klose-kur-beh obtain life from the Great Being? What traits of the Great Being did Klose-kur-beh share and what traits did he lack?
2. Why did the "first mother" ask her husband to kill her and drag her body "all over the land" and "bury her bones in the middle of it"?
3. According to Klose-kur-beh, what was the origin of the first mother and how did she show she "was all love"? How did the powers of the first mother compare to those of the Great Spirit?
4. What does the story of the first mother suggest about the significance of corn, tobacco, and motherhood among the Penobscot?

DOCUMENT 1–3

Genesis: The Christian Origin Narrative

The Bible in use during the fifteenth century was usually written in Latin, which the Christian church adopted as its official language, known only by a tiny educated elite— mostly priests and scholars. Because most Europeans could not read, priests tried to teach the doctrines of Christianity orally and with images in paint, glass, or sculpture like those still found in churches today. Although few of the Europeans who first encountered Native Americans in the New World could read Genesis, most of them were familiar with the main features of the biblical story of the origins of the world. The following passage from Genesis is taken from the famous English translation of the Bible authorized by King James I, initially published in 1611 as England's colonizing of the New World was just beginning. It discloses powerful, commonly held views not only about God but also about the relations between men and women and between human beings and the natural world.

"In the Beginning"

In the beginning God created the heaven and the earth. And the earth was without form, and void; and darkness was upon the face of the deep. And the Spirit of God moved upon the face of the waters. And God said, Let there be light: and there was light. And God saw the light, that it was good: and God divided the light from darkness. And God called the light Day, and the darkness he called Night. And the evening and the morning were the first day. . . .

And God said, Let the waters under the heaven be gathered together unto one place, and let the dry land appear; and it was so. And God called the dry land Earth; and the gathering together of the waters called he Seas: and God saw that it was good. And God said, Let the earth bring forth grass, the herb yielding seed, and the fruit tree yielding fruit after his kind, whose seed is in itself, upon the earth: and it was so. And the earth brought forth grass, and herb yielding seed after his kind, and the tree yielding fruit, whose seed was in itself, after his kind: and God saw that it was good. And the evening and the morning were the third day.

And God said, Let there be lights in the firmament of the heaven to divide the day from the night; and let them be for signs, and for seasons, and for days, and years: And let them be for lights in the firmament of the heaven to give light upon the earth: and it was so. And God made two great lights; the greater light to rule the day, and the lesser light to rule the night: he made the stars also. And God set them in the firmament of the heaven to give light upon the earth, And to rule over the day and over the night, and to divide the light from the darkness: and God saw that it was good. And the evening and the morning were the fourth day.

And God said, Let the waters bring forth abundantly the moving creature that hath life, and fowl that may fly above the earth in the open firmament of heaven. And God created great whales, and every living creature that moveth, which the waters brought forth abundantly after their kind, and every winged fowl after his kind: and God saw that it was good. And God blessed them, saying, Be fruitful, and multiply, and fill the waters in the seas, and let the fowl multiply in the earth. And the evening and the morning were the fifth day.

And God said, Let the earth bring forth the living creature after his kind, cattle, and creeping thing, and beast of the earth after his kind: and it was so. And God made the beast of the earth after his kind, and cattle after their kind, and every thing that creepeth upon the earth after his kind: and God saw that it was good.

And God said, Let us make man in our image, after our likeness: and let them have dominion over the fish of the seas, and over the fowl of the air, and over the cattle, and over all the earth, and over every creeping thing that creepeth upon the earth. So God created man in his own image, in the image of God created he him; male and female created he them. And God blessed them, and God said unto them, Be fruitful, and multiply, and replenish the earth, and subdue it: and have dominion over the fish of the sea, and over the fowl of the air, and over every living thing that moveth upon the earth.

And God said, Behold, I have given you every herb bearing seed, which is upon the face of all the earth, and every tree, in the which is the fruit of a tree yielding seed; to you it shall be for meat. And to every beast of the earth, and to

From *The Holy Bible*, King James Version, Genesis 1–3.

every fowl of the air, and to every thing that creepeth upon the earth, wherein there is life, I have given every green herb for meat: and it was so. And God saw everything that he had made, and behold, it was very good. And the evening and the morning were the sixth day.

Thus the heavens and the earth were finished, and all the host of them. And on the seventh day God ended his work which he had made; and he rested on the seventh day from all his work which he had made. And God blessed the seventh day, and sanctified it: because that in it he had rested from all his work which God created and made.

These are the generations of the heavens and of the earth when they were created, in the day that the Lord God made the earth and the heavens, And every plant of the field before it was in the earth, and every herb of the field before it grew: for the Lord God had not caused it to rain upon the earth, and there was not a man to till the ground. But there went up a mist from the earth, and watered the whole face of the ground. And the Lord God formed man of the dust of the ground, and breathed into his nostrils the breath of life; and man became a living soul.

And the Lord God planted a garden eastward in Eden; and there he put the man whom he had formed. And out of the ground made the Lord God to grow every tree that is pleasant to the sight, and good for food; the tree of life also in the midst of the garden, and the tree of knowledge of good and evil. And a river went out of Eden to water the garden; . . . And the Lord God took the man, and put him into the garden of Eden to dress it and to keep it. And the Lord God commanded the man, saying, Of every tree of the garden thou mayest freely eat: But of the tree of the knowledge of good and evil, thou shalt not eat of it: for in the day that thou eatest thereof thou shalt surely die.

And the Lord God said, It is not good that the man shall be alone; I will make him an help meet[1] for him. And out of the ground the Lord God formed every beast of the field, and every fowl of the air; and brought them unto Adam to see what he would call them: and whatsoever Adam called every living creature, that was the name thereof. And Adam gave names to all cattle, and to the fowl of the air, and to every beast of the field: but for Adam there was not an help meet for him. And the Lord God caused a deep sleep to fall upon Adam, and he slept: and he took one of his ribs, and closed up the flesh instead thereof; And the rib, which the Lord God had taken from man, made he a woman, and brought her unto the man. And Adam said, This is now bone of my bones, and flesh of my flesh: she shall be called Woman, because she was taken out of Man. Therefore shall a man leave his father and his mother, and shall cleave unto his wife: and they shall be one flesh. And they were both naked, the man and his wife, and were not ashamed.

Now the serpent was more subtil than any beast of the field which the Lord God had made. And he said unto the woman, Yea, hath God said, Ye shall not eat of every tree of the garden? And the woman said unto the serpent, We may eat of the fruit of the trees of the garden: But of the fruit of the tree which is in the midst of the garden, God hath said, Ye shall not eat of it, neither shall ye touch it, lest ye die. And the serpent said unto the woman, Ye shall not surely die: For God doth know that in the day ye eat thereof, then your eyes shall be opened, and ye shall be as gods, knowing good and evil. And when the woman saw that the tree was

---

[1]**help meet**: Companion, helper; in this case, a wife.

good for food, and that it was pleasant to the eyes, and a tree to be desired to make one wise, she took of the fruit thereof, and did eat, and gave also unto her husband with her; and he did eat. And the eyes of them both were opened, and they knew that they were naked; and they sewed fig leaves together, and made themselves aprons. And they heard the voice of the Lord God walking in the garden in the cool of the day: and Adam and his wife hid themselves from the presence of the Lord God amongst the trees of the garden. And the Lord God called unto Adam, and said unto him, Where art thou? And he said, I heard thy voice in the garden, and I was afraid, because I was naked; and I hid myself. And he said, Who told thee that thou wast naked? Hast thou eaten of the tree, whereof I commanded thee that thou shouldest not eat? And the man said, The woman whom thou gavest to be with me, she gave me of the tree, and I did eat. And the Lord God said unto the woman, What is this that thou hast done? And the woman said, The serpent beguiled me, and I did eat. And the Lord God said unto the serpent, Because thou hast done this, thou art cursed above all the cattle, and above every beast of the field; upon thy belly shalt thou go, and dust shalt thou eat all the days of thy life: And I will put enmity between thee and the woman and between thy seed and her seed; it shall bruise thy head, and thou shalt bruise his heel. Unto the woman he said, I will greatly multiply thy sorrow and thy conception; in sorrow thou shalt bring forth children; and thy desire shall be to thy husband, and he shall rule over thee. And unto Adam he said, Because thou has hearkened unto the voice of thy wife, and hast eaten of the tree, of which I commanded thee, saying, Thou shalt not eat of it: cursed is the ground for thy sake; in sorrow shalt thou eat of it all the days of thy life; Thorns also and thistles shall it bring forth to thee; and thou shalt eat the herb of the field; In the sweat of thy face shalt thou eat bread, till thou return unto the ground; for out of it wast thou taken; for dust thou art, and unto dust shalt thou return. And Adam called his wife's name Eve; because she was the mother of all living. Unto Adam also and to his wife did the Lord God make coats of skins, and clothed them.

And the Lord God said, Behold, the man is become as one of us, to know good and evil: and now, lest he put forth his hand, and take also of the tree of life, and eat, and live for ever: Therefore the Lord God sent him forth from the garden of Eden, to till the ground from whence he was taken. So he drove out the man; and he placed at the east of the garden of Eden Cherubims [angels], and a flaming sword which turned every way, to keep the way of the tree of life.

QUESTIONS FOR READING AND DISCUSSION

1. According to Genesis, how and why did God create the world?
2. Were plants, animals, and human beings in this account more or less equal in God's eyes?
3. Why did God command human beings to "Be fruitful, and multiply, and replenish the earth, and subdue it: and have dominion . . . over every living thing that moveth upon the earth"?
4. Did God make different demands on men and women? Why?
5. Why did God forbid Adam and Eve to eat from the tree of the knowledge of good and evil? Why did they disobey God? How did God punish them?
6. How might the Genesis account of human origins have influenced Europeans as they encountered peoples in Africa and the New World?

DOCUMENT 1–4

Aristotle on Masters and Slaves

The Greek philosopher Aristotle (384–322 BP) sought to discover the first principles of knowledge using observation, logic, and argument. He headed a famous school in Athens beginning in 335 BP, and after his death his students wrote down versions of his lectures they had heard, the source of this selection from The Politics. *Although relatively few Europeans who encountered Native Americans had actually read Aristotle, his ideas strongly influenced medieval Christianity and were widely diffused by the church. The following excerpt on masters and slaves describes ideas most Europeans in the sixteenth and seventeenth centuries considered common knowledge.*

The Politics, ca. 300 BP

First of all, there must necessarily be a union or pairing of those who cannot exist without one another. Male and female must unite for the reproduction of the species—not from deliberate intention, but from the natural impulse, which exists in animals generally as it also exists in plants, to leave behind them something of the same nature as themselves. Next, there must necessarily be a union of the naturally ruling element with the element which is naturally ruled, for the preservation of both. The element which is able, by virtue of its intelligence, to exercise forethought, is naturally a ruling and master element; the element which is able, by virtue of its bodily power, to do the physical work, is a ruled element, which is naturally in a state of slavery; and master and slave have accordingly a common interest.

The female and the slave are naturally distinguished from one another.... Among barbarians, however, the female and the slave occupy the same position—the reason being that no naturally ruling element exists among them, and conjugal union thus comes to be a union of a female who is a slave with a male who is also a slave. This is why our poets have said, "Meet it is that barbarous peoples should be governed by the Greeks," the assumption being that barbarian and slave are by nature one and the same....

The first form of association naturally instituted for the satisfaction of daily recurrent needs is thus the family.... A complete household consists of slaves and freemen. But every subject of inquiry should first be examined in its simplest elements; and the primary and simplest elements of the household are the connection of master and slave, that of the husband and wife, and that of parents and children....

Property is part of the household and the art of acquiring property is part of household management, for it is impossible to live well, or indeed at all, unless the necessary conditions are present.... Each article of property is thus an instrument for the purpose of life, property in general is a quantity of such instruments, [and] the slave is an animate article of property, and subordinates, or servants, in general may be described as instruments....

From Aristotle, *The Politics*, trans. Ernest Barker; rev. R. F. Stalley (New York: Oxford University Press, 1995), 8–20.

The term "article of property" is used in the same way in which the term "part" is also used. A part is not only a part of something other than itself: it also belongs entirely to that other thing. It is the same with an article of property. Accordingly, while the master is merely the master of the slave, and does not belong to him, the slave is not only the slave of his master; he also belongs entirely to him.

From these considerations, we can see clearly what is the nature of the slave and what is his capacity: anybody who by nature is not his own man, but another's, is by his nature a slave; anybody who, being a man, is an article of property is another's man; an article of property is an instrument intended for the purpose of action and separable from its possessor. . . .

We have next to consider whether . . . there are some people for whom slavery is the better and just condition, or whether the reverse is the case and all slavery is contrary to nature. The issue is not difficult, whether we study it philosophically in the light of reason, or consider it empirically on the basis of actual facts. The relation of ruler and ruled is one of those things which are not only necessary, but also beneficial; and there are species in which a distinction is already marked, immediately at birth, between those of its members who are intended for being ruled and those who are intended to rule. . . .

Animate beings are composed, in the first place, of soul and body, with the former naturally ruling and the latter naturally ruled. . . . It is possible . . . to observe first in animate beings the presence of a ruling authority, both of the sort exercised by a master over slaves and of the sort exercised by a statesman over fellow citizens. The soul rules the body with the authority of a master: reason rules the appetite with the authority of a statesman or a monarch. In this sphere it is clearly natural and beneficial to the body that it should be ruled by the soul, and again it is natural and beneficial to the affective part of the soul that it should be ruled by the reason and the rational part; whereas the equality of the two elements, or their reverse relation, is always detrimental. The same principle is true of the relation of man to other animals. Tame animals have a better nature than wild, and it is better for all such animals that they should be ruled by man because they then get the benefit of preservation. Again, the relation of male to female is naturally that of the superior to the inferior, of the ruling to the ruled. This general principle must similarly hold good of all human beings generally.

We may thus conclude that all men who differ from others as much as the body differs from the soul, or an animal from a man (and this is the case with all those whose function is bodily service, and who produce their best when they supply such service)—all such are by nature slaves. In their case, as in the other cases just mentioned, it is better to be ruled by a master. Someone is thus a slave by nature if he is capable of becoming the property of another (and for those reasons does actually become another's property) and if he participates in reason to the extent of apprehending it in another, though destitute of it himself. Other animals do not apprehend reason, but obey their instincts. Even so there is little divergence in the way they are used; both of them (slaves and tame animals) provide bodily assistance in satisfying essential needs.

It is nature's intention also to erect a physical difference between the bodies of freemen and those of the slaves, giving the latter strength for the menial duties of life, but making the former upright in carriage and (though useless for physical labour) useful for the various purposes of civic life—a life which tends, as it develops, to be divided into military service and the occupations of peace. . . .

It is thus clear that, just as some are by nature free, so others are by nature slaves, and for these latter the condition of slavery is both beneficial and just. . . .

But it is easy to see that those who hold an opposite view are also in a way correct. "Slavery" and "slave" are terms which are used in two different senses; for there is also a kind of slave, and of slavery, which owes its existence to law. (The law in question is a kind of understanding that those vanquished in war are held to belong to the victors.) That slavery can be justified by such a convention is a principle against which a number of jurists bring an "indictment of illegality." . . . They regard it as a destestable notion that someone who is subjugated by force should become the slave and subject of one who has the capacity to subjugate him, and is his superior in power. Even among men of judgment there are some who accept this [view] and some who do not. The cause of this divergence of view . . . is to be found in the following consideration. There is a sense in which good qualities, when they are furnished with the right resources, have the greatest power to subjugate; and a victor is always pre-eminent in respect of some sort of good. It thus appears that "power never goes without good qualities" . . . [and] no other argument has any cogency, or even plausibility, against the view that one who is superior in goodness ought to rule over, and be the master of, his inferiors.

There are some who, clinging, as they think, to a sort of justice (for law is a sort of justice), assume that slavery in war is just. Simultaneously, however, they contradict that assumption; for in the first place it is possible that the original cause of the war may not be just, and in the second place no one would ever say that someone who does not deserve to be in a condition of slavery is really a slave. If such a view were accepted, the result would be that men reputed to be of the highest rank would be turned into slaves or the children of slaves, if they [or their parents] happened to be captured and sold into slavery. This is the reason why they do not like to call such people slaves, but prefer to confine the term to barbarians. But by this use of terms they are, in reality, only seeking to express that same idea of a natural slave which we began by mentioning. They are driven, in effect, to admit that there are some who are everywhere slaves, and others who are everywhere free. The same line of thought is followed in regard to good birth. Greeks regard themselves as well born not only in their own country, but absolutely and in all places; but they regard barbarians as well born only in their own country—thus assuming that there is one sort of good birth and freedom which is absolute, and another which is only relative. . . .

It is thus clear that . . . it is not true that . . . [when men of the highest rank are enslaved as a result of war, then they] are natural slaves and the [victors are] natural freemen. It is also clear that there are cases where such a distinction exists, and that here it is beneficial and just that the former should actually be a slave and the latter a master—the one being ruled, and the other exercising the kind of rule for which he is naturally intended and therefore acting as a master. But a wrong exercise of his rule by a master is a thing which is disadvantageous for both master and slave. The part and the whole, like the body and the soul, have an identical interest; and the slave is a part of the master, in the sense of being a living but separate part of his body. There is thus a community of interest, and a relation of friendship, between master and slave, when both of them naturally merit the position in which they stand. But the reverse is true, when matters are otherwise and slavery rests merely on legal and superior power. . . .

The argument makes it clear that the rule of the master and that of the statesman are different from one another, and that it is not the case that all kinds of rule are, as some thinkers hold, identical. One kind of rule is exercised over those who are naturally free; the other over slaves; and again the rule exercised over a household by its head is that of a monarch (for all households are monarchically governed), while the rule of the statesman is rule over freemen and equals.

QUESTIONS FOR READING AND DISCUSSION

1. According to Aristotle, why were some people "natural slaves"? Who were these people? Why was slavery for them natural? Why was slavery "beneficial and just" for them?

2. How would you argue against Aristotle's defense of natural slavery? Did he make false assumptions? Were his arguments illogical? Can you argue against his view starting from his assumptions? How?

3. To what extent did Aristotle believe that it was good and just for victors in war to enslave their captives? Was slavery for Aristotle anything other than the superior power of the master over the slave? What arguments did Aristotle make against the claim that "all slavery is contrary to nature"? Do you find his arguments convincing? Why or why not?

4. How did the relation of master to slave differ from that of man to woman, husband to wife, parent to children, and statesman to citizens, according to Aristotle? In what sense were "all households . . . monarchically governed"? Since Aristotle argued that "the relation of male to female is naturally that of the superior to the inferior, of the ruling to the ruled," would he claim that women were natural slaves?

COMPARATIVE QUESTIONS

1. What are the major differences and similarities among these creation myths? How do their views of human beings compare to Aristotle's?

2. The creation narratives describe a world before humans existed. To what extent were humans a force for good in the world? How did humans' power compare to that of nature or zemis or the creator? Did Aristotle's views differ? If so, how and why?

3. How do the views of women and men in the creation myths compare to Aristotle's views? What do they reveal about gender roles and expectations among Native Americans and Europeans?

4. Because the creation narratives originated in oral rather than written communication, to what extent can these documents be accepted as expressions of the views of common folk among the Taino, the Penobscot, and Christians? How might the prevalent beliefs in Europe at the time the creation myths were first written down have influenced the accounts?

5. To what extent might the creation myths and Aristotle's views about masters and slaves have influenced the behavior of Native Americans and Europeans when they encountered one another?

2 Europeans Encounter the New World

1492–1600

D uring the fifteenth and sixteenth centuries, European explorers, traders, and soldiers repeatedly encountered non-Europeans, first in Africa and, beginning in 1492, in the New World. Portuguese mariners venturing down the west coast of Africa inaugurated a thriving trade in African goods, including, most fatefully, slaves. The arrival of Christopher Columbus in the Caribbean launched an unremitting series of encounters between Europeans and Native Americans in the Western Hemisphere. These early encounters around the rim of the Atlantic world informed each group about the other and established patterns of communication, miscommunication, and violence that lasted long into the future. The documents that follow illustrate the varied forms of these encounters between strangers and reveal their many-layered novelty and complexity.

DOCUMENT 2–1

The King of the Congo Writes to the King of Portugal

In 1481, a Portuguese explorer happened upon the mouth of the enormous Congo River, and within a decade Portuguese soldiers, traders, and missionaries had made their way inland to Mbanza Congo, the capital of the powerful Kingdom of Congo, establishing a European presence that persisted for centuries. The king of the Congo welcomed the Portuguese intruders who traded European items of all kinds—particularly guns—for such local goods as ivory and, especially, slaves. Portuguese missionaries converted some young Congolese to Christianity, including Mzinga Mbemba Afonso, who became king in 1506 and ruled the Congo for almost forty years. In 1526, concerned about the disastrous consequences of Portuguese trade for both his kingdom and his rule, Afonso wrote King João III of Portugal. Afonso's letters, excerpted here in an English translation of the original Portuguese, are among the very few surviving documents written by an African in the sixteenth century. The letters reveal Afonso's difficult dilemma: how to take advantage of certain features of contact with the Portuguese while avoiding the undesirable—and ultimately destructive—consequences.

King Afonso to King João III
Correspondence, 1526

Mbanza Congo, July 6, 1526

My Lord,

On June 26 we heard of the arrival in our harbor of one of Your Highness' ships. This made us truly glad for it had been a long time since any of your ships had docked in our kingdom bringing with it news of Your Highness which, as one would expect, we had often desired to hear. Moreover we are almost entirely lacking wine and flour for the holy sacrifice. . . .

My Lord, Your Highness must know that our kingdom's end is drawing near, so much so that we must find the appropriate remedy to this situation. What causes so much looseness is the fact that the head of your mission and your officers grant merchants the authorization to establish themselves in this kingdom, to open shops and to sell goods, even those [such as guns] which we forbid. They spread them across our kingdoms and provinces in such great amounts that many of our vassals which, until now, obeyed us are beginning to claim their independence. These days they are able to acquire, in larger quantities than us, those very things with which we kept them subdued and satisfied with our vassalage and governance. This causes great loss for God's service as well as for the safety and peace of our kingdoms and ourselves.

We are not even able to measure the extent of this loss because of the merchants constantly taking away our subjects, children of this land, sons of nobles and vassals, even members of our family. Those thieves and remorseless men take them to trade on the country's wealth which they covet. They kidnap them and sell them. This corruption and depravity are so common that our land is entirely deserted. Your Highness must not consider this favorable neither in itself nor for his service. To avoid this abuse this kingdom only needs priests and some people to teach in schools and not goods with the exception of wine and flour for the holy sacrifice. That is why we ask Your Highness to help us and grant us our wish to demand from the heads of your missions that they no longer send goods and merchants here. It is indeed our wish that this kingdom be neither a place of trade nor a place of transit for slaves for the reasons I just explained.

Once again we ask Your Highness to make it so because we do not have any other means of preventing such obvious damages.

May the Lord in His mercy always protect Your Highness and allow you to serve Him. I kiss your hands many times.

King Afonso to King João III

Mbanza Congo, August 25, 1526

My Lord,

. . . We often spend five to six months without any mass or sacrament because Your Highness' officers wish it so; this hinders God's service and causes great

From Louis Jadin and Mireille Decorato, *Correspondance de Dom Afonso, roi du Congo, 1506–1543* (Brussels: Académie Royale des Sciences d'Outre-Mer, 1974), 154–62, 166–69. English translation by Marianna Dantas.

confusion among our subjects. Some say that Your Highness no longer remembers us or christianity which your father, God bless his soul, had kept for so long in these regions thanks to all the visits he requested, and thanks to his exhortations and encouragement which brought constancy and faith to all and great comfort to us.

Now Your Highness is putting all of this in jeopardy by showing so little interest in us. The [Portuguese ship] pilots' disregard for us is clear when they leave, as they often do, without even waiting for our messages. They pretend to be obeying the orders of Your Highness' officers. When our letters arrive at the harbor they have already left. Then they accuse us of being careless to cover their own errors and to put us in a unfavorable position with regards to Your Highness. Thus they give you an excuse to forget us completely. We beg you not to believe these liars and these men whose sole purpose is to make profit and sell their ill-gotten goods. Through this trade of theirs, they damage and corrupt our kingdom as well as christianity which has been flourishing here for so many years and which cost so much to your ancestors. Yet it is a very precious treasure. The most christian and most catholic kings and princes like Your Highness strive to attract and maintain new peoples into God's service for the increase of the holy catholic faith, to which we all have held on. One can do a lot of damage with so many goods and through such anarchic means. These goods prove themselves so attractive to the simple minded and the ignorant folks that they forget to believe in God in order to believe in them. We must remedy this situation for it is a trick of the devil which could lead to the damnation of all. In addition to this, my Lord, our people fall victim of a monstrous greed which causes them to act like thieves and take their own relatives as well as ours, even christian ones, to trade them and sell them as captives. This corruption is such that our troops are no longer able to put an end to it without frequently conducting numerous and large scale executions[1] among our subjects. This way the innocent will die for the sinner.

It would not be so, my Lord, if Your Highness cared to help us and grant us the favor of sending spiritual medicine, as your father, the King, had done. We cannot do without many priests to celebrate the sacrifice, to conduct preaching, religious education, and confessions. They should visit in pairs all the regions of our kingdom, which is very large and populated. Together with the bishop, our son, we would command them to plant the word of God in the hearts of our subjects. This way, it would remain so deeply engrained that even if they attempted to practice devilish deeds for their damnation the virtue of such remedies would cure them.

My Lord, avoid sending us merchants who engage in vicious trade as well as evil goods. This impedes the salvation of the souls and spoils the good results we had obtained. . . .

Furthermore, we need three or four good grammarians to complete the instruction of our subjects who have begun their education. We have with us many of your and our subjects who can teach reading and writing, but we need men capable of showing and explaining the truths of the holy faith and of judging on thorny matters, which our other subjects generally cannot do. Yet it is very necessary.

Moreover, my Lord, some churches have already been started. We would need five or six masons and ten carpenters to finish them for the service and praise

---

[1]**executions**: Punitive war expeditions [translator's note].

of God, our Lord. This is mainly about [the church] Our Lady of Victory. We have started it in a very dense forest where, according to pagan customs, kings used to be buried. We have cut down the trees of this forest which was very difficult as much due to the roughness of the terrain as to the important men of our kingdom; we feared that they would not even agree to it. However, they were so prompt to accept it and be helpful that they cut down tall and large trees with their own hands and brought construction stones on their own backs. This indeed seems to be a consequence of the divine grace. . . .

Therefore, we ask Your Highness, for the love of Jesus Christ, to be so good as to help us and grant us all that we have said and all that we have often requested. It is as much for the service of God as it is for yours and everything relies on your conscience; as for us, we cannot do much more than what we continuously do. As far as the remedies that we can provide without external help are concerned, we have done our part. But for what we cannot achieve without Your Highness' help and assistance, we ask you for the cure as one rightfully entitled to it. We should not request this either from the king of Castile, or the king of France, or any other Christian king, and we do not wish to be obliged to them due to the numerous reasons we were given. This duty is not their responsibility particularly due to the little contact they have with this kingdom. This kingdom is as Portuguese and loyal to your service as the one Your Highness rightfully inherited and, moreover, there is no room among us for ingratitude. At this very moment we are aware of the great spiritual and temporal benefits we were granted. These will not be forgotten so as to take more into consideration the flaws of our true mother than the deceitful caresses of a stepmother, even though we all are under the same law and faith. I will say no more for Your Highness is aware of what he can expect from us and it is certain that our kingdoms and provinces will always serve you. . . .

May Our Lord, through his holy mercy, always protect Your Highness and may he bless you with a long life and the strengthening of your royal possessions for his holy service.

King Afonso to King João III

Mbanza Congo, October 18, 1526

My Lord,

Your Highness wrote to have us ask him in our letters everything that we need. He would provide us with everything. The peace and well-being of our kingdoms lie, after God, on our life. However we are old already and we have often been affected by various diseases which weaken us to our last resources. The same diseases also strike our sons, relatives and countrymen. Yet in this kingdom we have neither doctors nor surgeons who would know how to administer the appropriate treatment to such infirmities. Also, we have neither pharmacies nor the most efficient medicines. Thus, because we have nothing, many of those who are already educated in the truths of Our Lord Jesus Christ's holy faith die! Most of the inhabitants cure themselves with herbs and various woods or turn to traditional rites. If they survive their faith in those herbs and rites grows and if they die they believe that they are saved which does not favor God's service.

To prevent such damageable erring, since, after God, it is from Your Highness that we receive in our kingdoms all the cures for health, we ask Your Highness to send here two doctors, two pharmacists and one surgeon. Let them come and stay in our kingdoms with all their medicines and tools for we need each of them very much. We shall grant them many favors, because they will be sent by Your Highness; should Your Highness agree to have them work here. We beg Your Highness in urgency to accept to send them to us because this matter is not simply about granting a particular favor but also about serving God for all the reasons we just gave you.

There is, my Lord, yet another great obstacle to the service of God in our kingdoms. Many of our subjects greatly covet the goods which your men bring in our kingdoms from Portugal. To quench this uncontrolled thirst they kidnap many of our free or freed black subjects even nobles, sons of noblemen and even our relatives. They sell them to the white men who are in our kingdom after having delivered their prisoners in secret or during the night in order not to be recognized. As soon as the captives are under the white men's power they are branded. This is how they are found by our guards when they board the ships. The white men then explain that they were bought but they cannot say from whom. Yet it is our duty, as the prisoners claim, to do justice and set them free. To prevent such incidents we have decreed that all white men buying slaves in our kingdoms, however it may happen, should first inform three noblemen and officers of our court to whom I entrusted this control. . . . They will check whether the slaves are not actually free men. If they are found to be slaves nothing will prevent anyone from having them and taking them on board. However, should the opposite be true, the captives will be taken away from the white men. We gave our consent to this favor and these services because of Your Highness' participation in this trade. Indeed we know that it is for your service that these slaves are taken from our kingdoms. If it were not so, we would not agree to it for the reasons we have already given you.

We inform Your Highness of all this so that your subjects will not come to you and say it is otherwise. Indeed they tell Your Highness many lies to keep your mind from remembering the obligations you have towards us and our kingdom for God's service. It seems to us that it would be a great favor if you could let us know through one of your letters what you think of these dispositions.

We kiss Your Highness' hands many times my Lord.

QUESTIONS FOR READING AND DISCUSSION

1. What did Afonso want the Portuguese king to do?
2. Why, according to Afonso, were his "vassals . . . beginning to claim their independence"? What does his statement suggest about his authority over his kingdom and the relations between his people and the Portuguese?
3. According to Afonso, what was wrong with trade with the Portuguese? What special wrongs accompanied the slave trade?
4. Why did the Congolese king believe Christianity was valuable? How did he compare Christianity to common religious beliefs among his people?
5. What meanings are suggested by Afonso's statement that his "kingdom is as Portuguese and loyal to your service as the one Your Highness rightfully inherited"?
6. What hints do these letters contain about why Afonso did not demand an end to the slave trade and insist that the Portuguese leave and never come back?

DOCUMENT 2–2

Columbus Describes His First Encounter with "Indians"

Columbus kept a diary or log of his first voyage to the New World. He used the diary to record details of navigation and, once he arrived in the Caribbean, to note the people and places he observed. When Columbus returned to Spain, he presented his diary as a gift to King Ferdinand and Queen Isabella. The monarchs arranged to have a copy made of the diary. The original diary disappeared, but in the 1530s a priest had access to the copy, which he transcribed, summarized, and occasionally quoted. The copy then vanished as well, but the priest's manuscript has survived. In the quoted passage from the priest's manuscript, excerpted here, Columbus describes his first encounters with indigenous Americans. Columbus's remarks illustrate the understandings and misunderstandings as Europeans and Native Americans "discovered" one another.

The Diario of Christopher Columbus's First Voyage to America, 1492–1493

Thursday, 11 October. . . . What follows are the very words of the Admiral [Christopher Columbus] in his book about his first voyage to, and discovery of, these Indies. I, he says, in order that they would be friendly to us—because I recognized that they were people who would be better freed [from error] and converted to our Holy Faith by love than by force—to some of them I gave red caps, and glass beads which they put on their chests, and many other things of small value, in which they took so much pleasure and became so much our friends that it was a marvel. Later they came swimming to the ships' launches where we were and brought us parrots and cotton thread in balls and javelins and many other things, and they traded them to us for other things which we gave them, such as small glass beads and bells. In sum, they took everything and gave of what they had very willingly. But it seemed to me that they were a people very poor in everything. All of them go around as naked as their mothers bore them; and the women also, although I did not see more than one quite young girl. And all those that I saw were young people, for none did I see of more than 30 years of age. They are very well formed, with handsome bodies and good faces. Their hair [is] coarse—almost like the tail of a horse—and short. They wear their hair down over their eyebrows except for a little in the back which they wear long and never cut. Some of them paint themselves with black, and they are of the color of the Canarians, neither black nor white; and some of them paint themselves with white, and some of them with red, and some of them with whatever they find. And some of them paint their faces, and some of them the whole body, and some of them only the eyes, and some of them only the nose. They do not carry arms nor are they acquainted with them, because I showed them swords and they took them by the edge and through ignorance cut themselves. They have no iron. Their

From Oliver Dunn and James E. Kelley Jr., eds. and trans., *The Diario of Christopher Columbus's First Voyage to America, 1492–1493*, American Exploration and Traveler Series, vol. 70 (Norman: University of Oklahoma Press, 1989), 65–109.

javelins are shafts without iron and some of them have at the end a fish tooth and others of other things. All of them alike are of good-sized stature and carry themselves well. I saw some who had marks of wounds on their bodies and I made signs to them asking what they were; and they showed me how people from other islands nearby came there and tried to take them, and how they defended themselves; and I believed and believe that they come here from tierra firme[1] to take them captive. They should be good and intelligent servants, for I see that they say very quickly everything that is said to them; and I believe that they would become Christians very easily, for it seemed to me that they had no religion. Our Lord pleasing, at the time of my departure I will take six of them from here to Your Highnesses in order that they may learn to speak. No animal of any kind did I see on this island except parrots. All are the Admiral's words.

Saturday 13 October As soon as it dawned, many of these people came to the beach—all young as I have said, and all of good stature—very handsome people, with hair not curly but straight and coarse, like horsehair; and all of them very wide in the forehead and head, more so than any other race that I have seen so far. And their eyes are very handsome and not small; and none of them are black, but of the color of the Canary Islanders. . . . All alike have straight legs and no belly but are very well formed. They came to the ship with dugouts that are made from the trunk of one tree, like a long boat, and all of one piece, and worked marvelously in the fashion of the land, and so big that in some of them 40 and 45 men came. And others smaller, down to some in which came one man alone. They row with a paddle like that of a baker and go marvelously. And if it capsizes on them they then throw themselves in the water, and they right and empty it with calabashes[2] that they carry. They brought balls of spun cotton and parrots and javelins and other little things that it would be tiresome to write down, and they gave everything for anything that was given to them. I was attentive and labored to find out if there was any gold; and I saw that some of them wore a little piece hung in a hole that they have in their noses. And by signs I was able to understand that, going to the south or rounding the island to the south, there was there a king who had large vessels of it and had very much gold. I strove to get them to go there and later saw that they had no intention of going. I decided to wait until the afternoon of the morrow and then depart for the southwest, for, as many of them showed me, they said there was land to the south and to the southwest and to the northwest and that these people from the northwest came to fight them many times. And so I will go to the southwest to seek gold and precious stones. . . . And these people are very gentle, and because of their desire to have some of our things, and believing that nothing will be given to them without their giving something, and not having anything, they take what they can and then throw themselves into the water to swim. But everything they have they give for anything given to them, for they traded even for pieces of bowls and broken glass cups. . . . And also the gold that they wear hung in their noses originates here; but in order not to lose time I want to go to see if I can find the island of Cipango [Japan]. Now, since night had come, all the Indians went ashore in their dugouts.

---

[1]**tierra firme**: Dry land.
[2]**calabashes**: Gourds hollowed out and dried to use as containers.

Sunday 14 October As soon as it dawned I ordered the ship's boat and the launches of the caravels made ready and went north-northeast along the island in order to see what there was in the other part, which was the eastern part. And also to see the villages, and I soon saw two or three, as well as people, who all came to the beach calling to us and giving thanks to God. Some of them brought us water; others, other things to eat; others, when they saw that I did not care to go ashore, threw themselves into the sea swimming and came to us, and we understood that they were asking us if we had come from the heavens. And one old man got into the ship's boat, and others in loud voices called to all the men and women: Come see the men who came from the heavens. Bring them something to eat and drink. Many men came, and many women, each one with something, giving thanks to God, throwing themselves on the ground; and they raised their hands to heaven, and afterward they called to us in loud voices to come ashore. . . . [T]hese people are very naive about weapons, as Your Highnesses will see from the seven that I caused to be taken in order to carry them away to you and to learn our language and to return them. Except that, whenever Your Highnesses may command, all of them can be taken to Castile or held captive in this same island; because with 50 men all of them could be held in subjection and can be made to do whatever one might wish. . . . I . . . returned to the ship and set sail, and I saw so many islands that I did not know how to decide which one I would go to first. And those men whom I had taken told me by signs that they were so very many that they were numberless. . . .

Tuesday and Wednesday 16 October. . . . I came to a village where I anchored and to which had come that man whom I found mid-sea yesterday in that dugout. He had given so many good reports about us that during the whole night there was no lack of dugouts alongside the ship, to which they brought us water and of what they had. I ordered something given to each one, that is to say ten or twelve little glass beads on a thread, and some brass jingles of the sort that in Castile are worth a maravedi[3] each, and some metal lace-ends, all of which they considered of the greatest excellence. And also I ordered them given food, in order that they might eat when they came to the ship, and molasses. And later . . . I sent the ship's boat to shore for water. And the natives very willingly showed my people where the water was, and they themselves brought the filled barrels to the boat and delighted in pleasing us. This island is exceedingly large and I have decided to sail around it, because according to my understanding, on or near it there is a gold mine. . . . These people are like those of the . . . [other] islands in speech and customs except that these now appear somewhat more civilized and given to commerce and more astute. Because I see that they have brought cotton here to the ship and other little things for which they know better how to bargain payment than the others did. And in this island I even saw cotton cloths made like small cloaks, and the people are more intelligent, and the women wear in front of their bodies a little thing of cotton that scarcely covers their genitals. . . . I do not detect in them any religion and I believe that they would become Christians very quickly because they are of very good understanding. . . .

Monday 22 October All this night and today I stayed waiting [to see] if the king of this place or other persons would bring gold or something else of substance;

---

[3]**maravedi**: A Spanish coin equal to about two-thirds of a cent.

and there came many of these people, like the others of the other islands, naked and painted, some of them with white, some with red, some with black, and so on in many fashions. They brought javelins and balls of cotton to barter, which they traded here with some sailors for pieces of broken glass cups and for pieces of clay bowls. Some of them were wearing pieces of gold hanging from their noses, and they willingly gave it for a bell of the sort [put] on the foot of a sparrow hawk and for small glass beads; but it is so little that it is nothing. For it is true that any little thing given to them, as well as our coming, they considered great marvels; and they believed that we had come from the heavens.

QUESTIONS FOR READING AND DISCUSSION

1. What features of Native Americans did Columbus notice? How did he believe they compared with Europeans? Why did he conclude that "they were a people very poor in everything"?

2. Why did Columbus think Indians were friendly? Can you detect hints of what the Indians might have thought about Columbus and his men? How did the two groups communicate with each other?

3. What did Indians believe, as far as Columbus could tell? Why did he assume that Indians thought he and his men came from the heavens?

4. If a diary had been kept by one of the Indians who came aboard Columbus's ship, what might it have said about the Europeans?

DOCUMENT 2–3

A Conquistador Arrives in Mexico, 1519–1520

Bernal Díaz del Castillo, born in Spain in 1492, came to the New World at the age of twenty-two to seek his fortune. After five disappointing years, he joined Hernán Cortés's expedition to Mexico. A battle-hardened conquistador, Díaz participated in all the major events of the conquest. Afterwards, when he read slanted, inaccurate, and fabricated stories of the conquest, he decided to write his own eyewitness account. After working on his manuscript for almost thirty years, he sent a copy to the king of Spain in 1575. It lay buried in Spanish archives until it was published in 1632 as The True History of the Conquest of New Spain. *In this selection (translated from Spanish), Díaz describes what he saw when he and the other Spaniards first arrived in Mexico.*

Bernal Díaz del Castillo
The Conquest of New Spain, 1632

Next morning . . . when we saw all those cities and villages built in the water, and other great towns on dry land, and that straight and level causeway leading to Mexico, we were astounded. These great towns and cues [temples] and buildings rising from the water, all made of stone, seemed like an enchanted vision. . . .

From Bernal Díaz del Castillo, *The Conquest of New Spain*, trans. J. M. Cohen (London: Viking Penguin, Penguin Classics, 1963), 214–35.

Indeed, some of our soldiers asked whether it was not all a dream. . . . It was all so wonderful that I do not know how to describe this first glimpse of things never heard of, seen or dreamed of before. . . . I say again that I stood looking at it, and thought that no land like it would ever be discovered in the whole world. . . . But today all that I then saw is overthrown and destroyed; nothing is left standing. . . .

So, with luck on our side, we boldly entered the city of Tenochtitlán or Mexico on 8 November in the year of our Lord 1519. . . .

The great Montezuma was about forty years old, of good height, well proportioned, spare and slight, and not very dark, though of the usual Indian complexion. He did not wear his hair long but just over his ears, and he had a short black beard, well-shaped and thin. His face was rather long and cheerful, he had fine eyes, and in his appearance and manner could express geniality or, when necessary, a serious composure. He was very neat and clean, and took a bath every afternoon. He had many women as his mistresses, the daughters of chieftains, but two legitimate wives who were Caciques [rulers] in their own right, and when he had intercourse with any of them it was so secret that only some of his servants knew of it. He was quite free from sodomy. The clothes he wore one day he did not wear again till three or four days later. He had a guard of two hundred chieftains lodged in rooms beside his own, only some of whom were permitted to speak to him. . . . For each meal his servants prepared him more than thirty dishes cooked in their native style, which they put over small earthenware braziers to prevent them from getting cold. They cooked more than three hundred plates of the food the great Montezuma was going to eat, and more than a thousand more for the guard. I have heard that they used to cook him the flesh of young boys. But as he had such a variety of dishes, made of so many different ingredients, we could not tell whether a dish was of human flesh or anything else, since every day they cooked fowls, turkeys, pheasants, local partridges, quail, tame and wild duck, venison, wild boar, marsh birds, pigeons, hares and rabbits, also many other kinds of birds and beasts native to their country, so numerous that I cannot quickly name them all. . . .

Montezuma had two houses stocked with every sort of weapon; many of them were richly adorned with gold and precious stones. There were shields large and small, and a sort of broadsword, and two-handed swords set with flint blades that cut much better than our swords, and lances longer than ours, with five-foot blades consisting of many knives. Even when these are driven at a buckler or a shield they are not deflected. In fact they cut like razors, and the Indians can shave their heads with them. They had very good bows and arrows, and double and single-pointed javelins as well as their throwingsticks and many slings and round stones shaped by hand, and another sort of shield that can be rolled up when they are not fighting, so that it does not get in the way, but which can be opened when they need it in battle and covers their bodies from head to foot. There was also a great deal of cotton armour richly worked on the outside with different coloured feathers, which they used as devices and distinguishing marks, and they had casques[1] and helmets made of wood and bone which were also highly decorated with feathers on the outside. They had other arms of different kinds . . . and workmen skilled in the manufacture of such things, and stewards who were in charge of these arms.

---

[1]**casques:** Helmetlike headgear.

Let us pass on to the aviary. I cannot possibly enumerate every kind of bird that was in it or describe its characteristics. There was everything from the royal eagle, smaller kinds of eagles, and other large birds, down to multi-coloured little birds, and those from which they take the fine green feathers they use in their featherwork. . . .

I have already described the manner of their sacrifices. They strike open the wretched Indian's chest with flint knives and hastily tear out the palpitating heart which, with the blood, they present to the idols in whose name they have performed the sacrifice. Then they cut off the arms, thighs, and head, eating the arms and thighs at their ceremonial banquets. The head they hang up on a beam, and the body of the sacrificed man is not eaten but given to the beasts of prey. They also had many vipers in this accursed house, and poisonous snakes which have something that sounds like a bell in their tails. These, which are the deadliest snakes of all, they kept in jars and great pottery vessels full of feathers, in which they laid their eggs and reared their young. They were fed on the bodies of sacrificed Indians and the flesh of the dogs that they bred. We know for certain, too, that when they drove us out of Mexico and killed over eight hundred and fifty of our soldiers, they fed those beasts and snakes on their bodies for many days, as I shall relate in due course. These snakes and wild beasts were dedicated to their fierce idols, and kept them company. As for the horrible noise when the lions and tigers roared, and the jackals and foxes howled, and the serpents hissed, it was so appalling that one seemed to be in hell.

I must now speak of the skilled workmen whom Montezuma employed in all the crafts they practised, beginning with the jewellers and workers in silver and gold and various kinds of hollowed objects, which excited the admiration of our great silversmiths at home. . . . There were other skilled craftsmen who worked with precious stones . . . and specialists in featherwork, and very fine painters and carvers. We can form some judgement of what they did then from what we can see of their work today. . . .

Let us go on to the women, the weavers and sempstresses, who made such a huge quantity of fine robes with very elaborate feather designs. . . . In Montezuma's own palaces very fine cloths were woven by those chieftains' daughters whom he kept as mistresses; and the daughters of other dignitaries, who lived in a kind of retirement like nuns in some houses close to the great cue of Huichilobos, wore robes entirely of featherwork. Out of devotion for that god and a female deity who was said to preside over marriage, their fathers would place them in religious retirement until they found husbands. They would then take them out to be married.

Now to speak of the great number of performers whom Montezuma kept to entertain him. There were dancers and stilt-walkers, and some who seemed to fly as they leapt through the air, and men rather like clowns to make him laugh. There was a whole quarter full of these people who had no other occupation. He had as many workmen as he needed, too, stonecutters, masons, and carpenters, to keep his houses in repair.

We must not forget the gardens with their many varieties of flowers and sweet-scented trees planted in order, and their ponds and tanks of fresh water into which a stream flowed at one end and out of which it flowed at the other, and the baths he had there, and the variety of small birds that nested in the branches, and the medicinal and useful herbs that grew there. His gardens were a wonderful sight, and required many gardeners to take care of them. . . .

When we had already been in Mexico for four days, and neither our Captain nor anyone else had left our quarters except to visit these houses and gardens, Cortés said it would be a good thing to visit the large [market] square of Tlatelolco. . . . On reaching the market-place, escorted by the many Caciques whom Montezuma had assigned to us, we were astounded at the great number of people and the quantities of merchandise, and at the orderliness and good arrangements that prevailed, for we had never seen such a thing before. The chieftains who accompanied us pointed everything out. Every kind of merchandise was kept separate and had its fixed place marked for it.

Let us begin with the dealers in gold, silver, and precious stones, feathers, cloaks, and embroidered goods, and male and female slaves who are also sold there. They bring as many slaves to be sold in that market as the Portuguese bring Negroes from Guinea. Some are brought there attached to long poles by means of collars round their necks to prevent them from escaping, but others are left loose. Next there were those who sold coarser cloth, and cotton goods and fabrics made of twisted thread, and there were chocolate merchants with their chocolate. In this way you could see every kind of merchandise to be found anywhere in New Spain, laid out in the same way as goods are laid out in my own district of Medina del Campo, a centre for fairs, where each line of stalls has its own particular sort. . . . There were sellers of kidney-beans and sage and other vegetables and herbs in another place, and in yet another they were selling fowls, and birds with great dewlaps,[2] also rabbits, hares, deer, young ducks, little dogs, and other such creatures. Then there were the fruiterers; and the women who sold cooked food, flour and honey cake, and tripe, had their part of the market. Then came pottery of all kinds, from big water-jars to little jugs, displayed in its own place, also honey, honey-paste, and other sweets like nougat. Elsewhere they sold timber too, boards, cradles, beams, blocks, and benches, all in a quarter of their own.

Then there were the sellers of pitch-pine for torches, and other things of that kind, and I must also mention, with all apologies, that they sold many canoe-loads of human excrement, which they kept in the creeks near the market. This was for the manufacture of salt and the curing of skins, which they say cannot be done without it. I know that many gentlemen will laugh at this, but I assure them it is true. I may add that on all the roads they have shelters made of reeds or straw or grass so that they can retire when they wish to do so, and purge their bowels unseen by passersby, and also in order that their excrement shall not be lost.

But why waste so many words on the goods in their great market? If I describe everything in detail I shall never be done. . . . They have a building there also in which three judges sit, and there are officials like constables who examine the merchandise. I am forgetting the sellers of salt and the makers of flint knives, and how they split them off the stone itself, and the fisherwomen and the men who sell small cakes made from a sort of weed which they get out of the great lake, which curdles and forms a kind of bread which tastes rather like cheese. They sell axes too, made of bronze and copper and tin, and gourds and brightly painted wooden jars.

We went on to the great cue, and as we approached its wide courts, before leaving the market-place itself, we saw many more merchants who, so I was told, brought gold to sell in grains, just as they extract it from the mines. This gold is placed in the thin quills of the large geese of that country, which are so white as to be transparent. They used to reckon their accounts with one another by the

---

[2]**dewlaps**: Loose skin hanging under the neck, as among turkeys.

length and thickness of these little quills, how much so many cloaks or so many gourds of chocolate or so many slaves were worth, or anything else they were bartering. . . .

Having examined and considered all that we had seen, we turned back to the great market and the swarm of people buying and selling. The mere murmur of their voices talking was loud enough to be heard more than three miles away. Some of our soldiers who had been in many parts of the world, in Constantinople, in Rome, and all over Italy, said that they had never seen a market so well laid out, so large, so orderly, and so full of people.

QUESTIONS FOR READING AND DISCUSSION

1. How did Mexico compare to Europe, according to Díaz? To what extent did Mexico differ from what Díaz expected to find?
2. Why did Díaz find Mexico astounding, like "an enchanted vision"? What might have shaped his expectations and his sense of wonder?
3. Did Díaz consider Mexico civilized? Why or why not? What did Díaz think about Mexican practices of human sacrifice?
4. In what ways was Montezuma different from other Mexicans, according to Díaz? Did such differences strike Díaz as bizarre or conventional?
5. Since Díaz wrote this description of his entry into Mexico many years after it happened, how reliable is it? How might the passage of time and Díaz's hindsight have distorted his memory of this decisive moment?

DOCUMENT 2–4

A Mexican Description of the Conquest of Mexico

This remarkable account comes from the Florentine Codex, a massive cultural encyclopedia of the native people of Mexico that was compiled in the mid-sixteenth century under the direction of Bernardino de Sahagún, a Franciscan missionary. Beginning about 1547, Sahagún trained a group of Mexican men to interview prominent elders and to record their words in Nahuatl, their native language. Sahagún's informants had a vivid memory of the conquest of Mexico, which had occurred only a generation earlier. Sahagún published their account, in both Nahuatl and Spanish, in Book 12 of the Codex—the source of the following selection, which was translated from Nahuatl. This account reveals Mexican perspectives on the events of conquest.

Mexican Accounts of Conquest from the Florentine Codex

The Spaniards . . . set out in this direction, about to enter Mexico here. Then they all dressed and equipped themselves for war. They girded themselves, tying their battle gear tightly on themselves and then on their horses. Then they arranged themselves in rows, files, ranks.

From James Lockhart, ed. and trans., *We People Here: Nahuatl Accounts of the Conquest of Mexico* (Berkeley and Los Angeles: University of California Press, 1993).

Four horse[men] came ahead, going first, staying ahead, leading. They kept turning about as they went, facing people, looking this way and that, looking sideways, gazing everywhere between the houses, examining things, looking up at the roofs.

Also the dogs, their dogs, came ahead, sniffing at things and constantly panting.

By himself came marching ahead, all alone, the one who bore the standard on his shoulder. He came waving it about, making it spin, tossing it here and there. It came stiffening, rising up like a warrior, twisting and turning.

Following him came those with iron swords. Their iron swords came bare and gleaming. On their shoulders they bore their shields, of wood or leather.

The second contingent and file were horses carrying people, each with his cotton cuirass,[1] his leather shield, his iron lance, and his iron sword hanging down from the horse's neck. They came with bells on, jingling or rattling. The horses, the deer, neighed, there was much neighing, and they would sweat a great deal; water seemed to fall from them. And their flecks of foam splatted on the ground, like soapsuds splatting. As they went they made a beating, throbbing, and hoof-pounding like throwing stones. . . .

The third file were those with iron crossbows, the crossbowmen. As they came, the iron crossbows lay in their arms. They came along testing them out, brandishing them, aiming them. But some carried them on their shoulders, came shouldering the crossbows. Their quivers[2] went hanging at their sides, passed under their armpits, well filled, packed with arrows, with iron bolts. Their cotton upper armor reached to their knees, very thick, firmly sewn, and dense, like stone. And their heads were wrapped in the same cotton armor, and on their heads plumes stood up, parting and spreading.

The fourth file were likewise horse[men]; their outfits were the same as has been said.

The fifth group were those with harquebuses,[3] the harquebusiers, shouldering their harquebuses; some held them [level]. And when they went into the great palace, the residence of the ruler, they repeatedly shot off their harquebuses. They exploded, sputtered, discharged, thundered, disgorged. Smoke spread, it grew dark with smoke, everyplace filled with smoke. The fetid smell made people dizzy and faint.

And last, bringing up the rear, went the war leader, thought to be the ruler and director in battle. . . . Gathered and massed about him, going at his side, accompanying him, enclosing him were his warriors, those with devices, his [aides]. . . .

Then all those from the various altepetl[4] on the other side of the mountains, the Tlaxcalans[5] [and others] . . . came following behind. They came outfitted for war with their cotton upper armor, shields, and bows, their quivers full and packed with feathered arrows, some barbed, some blunted, some with obsidian

---

[1]**cotton cuirass**: Vest of armor.

[2]**quivers**: Cylindrical containers for arrows.

[3]**harquebuses**: Spaniards' firearms—a small-caliber long gun.

[4]**altepetl**: Realms.

[5]**Tlaxcalans**: A powerful group of Indians hostile to Mexicans and allied with the Spaniards.

points. They went crouching, hitting their mouths with their hands and yelling, singing . . . , whistling, shaking their heads.

Some bore burdens and provisions on their backs; some used [straps around] their foreheads, some [bands around] their chests, some carrying frames, some board cages, some deep baskets. Some made bundles, perhaps putting the bundles on their backs. Some dragged the large cannons, which went resting on wooden wheels, making a clamor as they came. . . .

Moteucçoma [Montezuma] went in peace and quiet to meet the Spaniards. . . .

Moteucçoma dressed and prepared himself for a meeting, along with other great rulers and high nobles, his rulers and nobles. Then they went to the meeting. On gourd bases they set out different precious flowers; in the midst of the shield flowers and heart flowers stood popcorn flowers, yellow tobacco flowers, cacao flowers, [made into] wreaths for the head, wreaths to be girded around. And they carried golden necklaces, necklaces with pendants, wide necklaces.

And when Moteucçoma went out to meet them . . . , he gave various things to the war leader, the commander of the warriors; he gave him flowers, he put necklaces on him, he put flower necklaces on him, he girded him with flowers, he put flower wreaths on his head. Then he laid before him the golden necklaces, all the different things for greeting people. He ended by putting some of the necklaces on him.

Then [Cortés] said in reply to Moteucçoma, "Is it not you? Is it not you then? Moteucçoma?"

Moteucçoma said, "Yes, it is me." Thereupon he stood up straight, he stood up with their faces meeting. He bowed down deeply to him. He stretched as far as he could, standing stiffly. Addressing him, he said to him,

"O our lord, be doubly welcomed on your arrival in this land; you have come to satisfy your curiosity about your altepetl of Mexico, you have come to sit on your seat of authority, which I have kept a while for you, where I have been in charge for you, for your agents the [previous] rulers[6] . . . have gone, who for a very short time came to be in charge for you, to govern the altepetl of Mexico. It is after them that your poor vassal [myself] came. Will they come back to the place of their absence? If only one of them could see and behold what has now happened in my time, what I now see after our lords are gone! For I am not just dreaming, not just sleepwalking, not just seeing it in my sleep. I am not just dreaming that I have seen you, have looked upon your face. For a time I have been concerned, looking toward the mysterious place from which you have come, among clouds and mist. It is so that the rulers on departing said that you would come in order to acquaint yourself with your altepetl and sit upon your seat of authority. And now it has come true, you have come. Be doubly welcomed, enter the land, go to enjoy your palace; rest your body. May our lords be arrived in the land."

And when the speech that Moteucçoma directed to [Cortés] . . . had concluded, Marina [an Indian woman who accompanied Cortés and who could speak Nahuatl and Spanish] reported it to him, interpreting it for him. And when [Cortés] . . . had heard what Moteucçoma had said, he spoke to Marina in return, babbling back to them, replying in his babbling tongue,

"Let Moteucçoma be at ease, let him not be afraid, for we greatly esteem him. Now we are truly satisfied to see him in person and hear him, for until now we

---

[6]Evidently, Montezuma and other Mexicans initially believed the Spaniards were ancient Mexican gods who had returned to rule over their empire.

have greatly desired to see him and look upon his face. Well, now we have seen him, we have come to his homeland of Mexico. Bit by bit he will hear what we have to say."

Thereupon [the Spaniards] took [Moteucçoma] by the hand. They came along with him, stroking his hair to show their good feeling. And the Spaniards looked at him, each of them giving him a close look. They would start along walking, then mount, then dismount again in order to see him. . . .

[T]he Spaniards went with Moteucçoma to enter the great palace. . . .

And when they had reached the palace and gone in, immediately they seized Moteucçoma and kept close watch over him, not letting him out of their sight. . . . And when this had happened, then the various guns were fired. It seemed that everything became confused; people went this way and that, scattering and darting about. It was as though everyone's tongue were out, everyone were preoccupied, everyone had been taking mushrooms, as though who knows what had been shown to everyone. Fear reigned, as though everyone had swallowed his heart. It was still that way at night; everyone was terrified, taken aback, thunderstruck, stunned.

And when it dawned, everything [the Spaniards] needed was proclaimed: white tortillas, roast turkeys, eggs, fresh water, wood, firewood, charcoal, earthen tubs, polished bowls, waterjars, large clay pitchers, vessels for frying, all kinds of earthenware. Moteucçoma himself ordered it. But when he summoned the noblemen, they would no longer obey him, but grew angry. They no longer performed their duty to him, no longer went to him; no longer was he heeded. But he was not therefore forsaken; he was given all he needed to eat and drink, and water and deer fodder [for the Spaniards].

And when [the Spaniards] were well settled, right away they interrogated Moteucçoma about all the stored treasure of the altepetl, the devices and shields. They greatly prodded him, they eagerly sought gold as a thing of esteem. And then Moteucçoma went along leading the Spaniards. They gathered around him, bunched around him; he went in their midst, leading the way. They went along taking hold of him, grasping him. And when they reached the storehouse . . . then all the shining things were brought out: the quetzal-feather head fan, the devices, the shields, the golden disks, the necklaces of the devils, the golden nose crescents, the golden leg bands, the golden arm bands, the golden sheets for the forehead.

Thereupon the gold on the shields and on all the devices was taken off. And when all the gold had been detached, right away they set on fire, set fire to, ignited all the different precious things, they all burned. And the Spaniards made the gold into bricks. And they took as much of the green-stone as pleased them; as to the rest of the green-stone, the Tlaxcalans just snatched it up. And [the Spaniards] went everywhere, scratching about in the hiding places, storehouses, places of storage all around. They took everything they saw that pleased them. . . .

[T]he Spaniards killed and annihilated the Mexica who were celebrating the feast of Huitzilopochtli[7] at what they call the . . . [Divine Courtyard, Courtyard of the Gods, temple courtyard].

When things were already going on, when the festivity was being observed and there was dancing and singing, with voices raised in song, the singing was

---

[7]**Huitzilopochtli:** The god of war and the chief god in the Mexican pantheon.

like the noise of waves breaking against the rocks. When it was time, when the moment had come for the Spaniards to do the killing, they came out equipped for battle. They came and closed off each of the places where people went in and out. . . . And when they had closed these exits, they stationed themselves in each, and no one could come out any more.

When this had been done, they went into the temple courtyard to kill people. Those whose assignment it was to do the killing just went on foot, each with his metal sword and his leather shield, some of them iron-studded. Then they surrounded those who were dancing, going among the cylindrical drums. They struck a drummer's arms; both of his hands were severed. Then they struck his neck; his head landed far away. Then they stabbed everyone with iron lances and struck them with iron swords. They stuck some in the belly, and then their entrails came spilling out. They split open the heads of some, they really cut their skulls to pieces, their skulls were cut up into little bits. And some they hit on the shoulders; their bodies broke open and ripped. Some they hacked on the calves, some on the thighs, some on their bellies, and then all their entrails would spill out. And if someone still tried to run it was useless; he just dragged his intestines along. There was a stench as if of sulfur. Those who tried to escape could go nowhere. When anyone tried to go out, at the entryways they struck and stabbed him. . . .

And when it became known [what was happening], everyone cried out, "Mexica warriors, come running, get outfitted with devices, shields, and arrows, hurry, come running, the warriors are dying; they have died, perished, been annihilated, o Mexica warriors!" Thereupon there were war cries, shouting, and beating of hands against lips. The warriors quickly came outfitted, bunched together, carrying arrows and shields. Then the fighting began; they shot at them with barbed darts, spears, and tridents, and they hurled darts with broad obsidian points at them. A cloud of yellow reeds spread over the Spaniards. . . .

[A]t the time the Spaniards left Mexico, there came an illness of pustules of which many local people died; it was called "the great rash."[8]

Before the Spaniards appeared to us, first an epidemic broke out, a sickness of pustules. . . . Large bumps spread on people; some were entirely covered. They spread everywhere, on the face, the head, the chest, etc. [The disease] brought great desolation; a great many died of it. They could no longer walk about, but lay in their dwellings and sleeping places, no longer able to move or stir. They were unable to change position, to stretch out on their sides or face down, or raise their heads. And when they made a motion, they called out loudly. The pustules that covered people caused great desolation; very many people died of them, and many just starved to death; starvation reigned, and no one took care of others any longer.

On some people, the pustules appeared only far apart, and they did not suffer greatly, nor did many of them die of it. But many people's faces were spoiled by it, their faces and noses were made rough. Some lost an eye or were blinded.

This disease of pustules lasted a full sixty days; after sixty days it abated and ended. When people were convalescing and reviving, the pustules disease began to move in the direction of Chalco. And many were disabled or paralyzed by it, but they were not disabled forever. . . . The Mexica warriors were greatly weakened by it.

---

[8]**the great rash**: Smallpox.

And when things were in this state, the Spaniards came [back], moving toward us. . . .

And all the common people suffered greatly. There was famine; many died of hunger. They no longer drank good, pure water, but the water they drank was salty. Many people died of it, and because of it many got dysentery and died. Everything was eaten: lizards, swallows, maize straw, grass that grows on salt flats. And they chewed at coloring wood, glue flowers, plaster, leather, and deer-skin, which they roasted, baked, and toasted so that they could eat them, and they ground up medicinal herbs and adobe bricks. There had never been the like of such suffering. The siege was frightening, and great numbers died of hunger. And bit by bit they came pressing us back against the wall, herding us together. . . .

And along every stretch [of road] the Spaniards took things from people by force. They were looking for gold; they cared nothing for green-stone, precious feathers, or turquoise. They looked everywhere with the women, on their abdomens, under their skirts. And they looked everywhere with the men, under their loincloths and in their mouths. And [the Spaniards] took, picked out the beautiful women, with yellow bodies. And how some women got loose was that they covered their faces with mud and put on ragged blouses and skirts, clothing themselves all in rags. And some men were picked out, those who were strong and in the prime of life, and those who were barely youths, to run errands for them and be their errand boys, called their [priests, acolytes]. Then they burned some of them on the mouth; some they branded on the cheeks, some on the mouth.

QUESTIONS FOR READING AND DISCUSSION

1. What did the Mexicans notice about the Spaniards on their entry into Tenoch-titlán? How did their impressions of the Spaniards change, and what happened to change those impressions?

2. Why did Montezuma welcome Cortés, saying "you have come to sit on your seat of authority"?

3. What comparisons did the Mexicans make between themselves and the Span-iards? Did the Mexicans consider the Spaniards civilized? To what extent did the Mexicans perceive the Spaniards as the Spaniards perceived themselves? By what standards did the Mexicans judge the Spaniards?

4. Since this account was collected a generation after the conquest, to what extent might post-conquest Mexican experiences have shaped this narrative?

DOCUMENT 2–5

Cabeza de Vaca Describes His Captivity among Native Americans in Texas and the Southwest, 1528–1536

In April 1528, the experienced conquistador Pánfilo de Narváez led a disastrous expedition to explore and conquer the vast region from present-day Florida to Texas and beyond. Only four of the expedition's 300 members survived, living for eight years as slaves of native Americans in Texas, the American Southwest, and northern Mexico. One of the survivors, Alvar Núñez Cabeza de Vaca, described their ordeal in his Narrative, published in 1542.

The Narrative *offers the first detailed, eyewitness account of life among native Americans in the present-day United States. Cabeza de Vaca wrote from the rare perspective of a Spaniard who expected to become a rich conqueror and instead became a naked and famished slave of the people he came to conquer. Much of the* Narrative *describes his suffering, but in the excerpt below Cabeza de Vaca describes how, after years of captivity, he and his companions earned the respect of their captors by healing their wounds and curing their illnesses. These healing episodes helped the Spaniards survive until 1536 when they stumbled upon a few Spanish soldiers hunting for Indian slaves, who rescued Cabeza de Vaca and his companions and brought them back to Mexico. As you read the passage below, try to decipher what the healings meant for both the Native Americans and their Spanish captives.*

Cabeza de Vaca
Narrative, 1542

On the island I have spoken of they wanted to make medicine men of us without any examination or asking for our diplomas, because they cure diseases by breathing on the sick, and with that breath and their hands they drive the ailment away. So they summoned us to do the same in order to be at least of some use. We laughed, taking it for a jest, and said that we did not understand how to cure.

Thereupon they withheld our food to compel us to do what they wanted. . . .

At last we found ourselves in such stress as to have to do it, without risking any punishment. Their manner of curing is as follows: When one is ill they call in a medicine man, and after they are well again not only do they give him all they have, but even things they strive to obtain from their relatives. All the medicine man does is to make a few cuts where the pain is located and then suck the skin around the incisions. They cauterize with fire, thinking it very effective, and I found it to be so by my own experience. Then they breathe on the spot where the pain is and believe that with this the disease goes away.

The way we treated the sick was to make over them the sign of the cross while breathing on them, recite a Pater noster and Ave Maria, and pray to God, Our Lord, as best we could to give them good health and inspire them to do us some favors. Thanks to His will and the mercy He had upon us, all those for whom we prayed, as soon as we crossed them, told the others that they were cured and felt well again. For this they gave us good cheer, and would rather be without food themselves so as to give it to us. . . . So great was the lack of food then that I often remained without eating anything whatsoever for three days, and they were in the same plight, so that it seemed to me impossible for life to last, although I afterwards suffered still greater privations and much more distress, as I shall tell further on. . . .

Therefore the Indians told me to go and perform the cure. They liked me, remembering that I had relieved them while they were out gathering nuts, for which they had given us nuts and hides. . . .

From Ad. F. Bandelier, ed. and trans. *The Journey of Alvar Núñez Cabeza de Vaca and His Companions from Florida to the Pacific 1528–1536* (New York: Allerton Book Co., 1922), pp. 68–71, 106–8, 129–32, 136–38, 142–44.

When I came close to their ranches I saw that the dying man we had been called to cure was dead, for there were many people around him weeping and his lodge was torn down, which is a sign that the owner has died. I found the Indian with eyes upturned, without pulse and with all the marks of lifelessness. . . . I removed a mat with which he was covered, and as best I could prayed to Our Lord to restore his health, as well as that of all the others who might be in need of it, and after having made the sign of the cross and breathed on him many times they brought his bow and presented it to me, and a basket of ground tunas [prickly pears], and took me to many others who were suffering from vertigo. They gave me two more baskets of tunas, which I left to the Indians that had come with us. Then we returned to our quarters.

Our Indians to whom I had given the tunas remained there, and at night returned telling, that the dead man whom I attended to in their presence had resuscitated, rising from his bed, had walked about, eaten and talked to them, and that all those treated by me were well and in very good spirits. This caused great surprise and awe, and all over the land nothing else was spoken of. All who heard it came to us that we might cure them and bless their children, and when the Indians in our company had to return to their country, before parting they offered us all the tunas they had for their journey, not keeping a single one, and gave us flint stones as long as one and a-half palms, with which they cut and that are greatly prized among them. They begged us to remember them and pray to God to keep them always healthy, which we promised to do, and so they left, the happiest people upon earth, having given us the very best they had. . . .

During that time they came for us from many places and said that verily we were children of the sun. . . . We never treated anyone that did not afterwards say he was well, and they had such confidence in our skill as to believe that none of them would die as long as we were among them. . . .

At sunset we reached a hundred Indian huts and, as we approached, the people came out to receive us, shouting frightfully, and slapping their thighs. They carried perforated gourds filled with pebbles, which are ceremonial objects of great importance. They only use them at dances, or as medicine, to cure, and nobody dares touch them but themselves. . . .

So great was their excitement and eagerness to touch us that, every one wanting to be first, they nearly squeezed us to death, and, without suffering our feet to touch the ground, carried us to their abodes. . . .

[A]nd the next morning they brought us every living soul of that village to be touched by us and to have the cross made over them, as with the others. . . . The next day we went on, and all the people of that village with us, and when we came to other Indians were as well received as anywhere in the past. . . . Among these we saw a new custom. Those who were with us took away from those people who came to get cured their bows and arrows, their shoes and beads, if they wore any, and placed them before us to induce us to cure the sick. As soon as these had been treated they went away contented and saying they felt well. . . .

After we left those we went to many other lodges, but thence on there prevailed a new custom. While we were received very well everywhere, those who came with us would treat those who received us badly, taking away their belongings and plundering their homes, without leaving them anything. It grieved us very much to see how those who were so good to us were abused. Besides, we dreaded lest this behavior might cause trouble and strife. But as we could not venture to interfere or punish the transgressors, we had to wait until we might have more authority over them. Furthermore, the sufferers themselves, noticing how we felt, comforted us by saying we should not worry; that they were so happy at seeing us as to gladly lose their own, considering it to be well employed, and besides, that further on they would repay themselves from other Indians who were very rich. On that whole journey we were much worried by the number of people following us. We could not escape them, although we tried, because they were so anxious to touch us[.] . . .

We reached a village of about twenty lodges, where they received us with tears and deep sorrow. They already knew that, wherever we arrived, the people would be robbed and plundered by those in our company. . . .

In consolation, the robbers told them that we were children of the sun, and had the power to cure or kill, and other lies, bigger even than those which they invent to suit their purposes. They also enjoined them to treat us with great reverence, and be careful not to arouse our wrath; to give us all they had and guide us to where there were many people, and that wherever we should come to they should steal and rob everything the others had, such being the custom.

After giving these instructions, and teaching the people how to behave, they returned, and left us with these Indians, who, mindful of what the others had said, began to treat us with the same respect and awe, and we travelled in their company for three days. They took us to where there were many Indians, and went ahead to tell them of our coming, repeating what they had heard and adding much more to it, for all these Indians are great gossipers and liars, particularly when they think it to be to their benefit. . . . Our companions sacked the dwellings, but as there were many and they only few in number, they could not carry away all they took, so that more than half was left to waste. . . .

After leaving these people we travelled among so many different tribes and languages that nobody's memory can recall them all, and always they robbed each other; but those who lost and those who gained were equally content. The number of our companions became so large that we could no longer control them. . . .

[W]hen at night they came back it was . . . with birds, quails, and other game; in short, all those people could kill they set before us, without ever daring to touch anything, even if dying of hunger, unless we blessed it first. Such was their custom from the time they joined us. . . .

We partook of everything a little, giving the rest to the principal man among those who had come with us for distribution among all. Every one then came with the share he had received for us to breathe on it and bless it, without which they left it untouched. Often we had with us three to four thousand persons. And it was very tiresome to have to breathe on and make the sign of the cross over every morsel they ate or drank. For many other things which they wanted to do they would come to ask our permission. . . .

QUESTIONS FOR READING AND DISCUSSION

1. How did the cures administered by Cabeza de Vaca differ from those of an Indian "physician"?
2. Did Cabeza de Vaca continue to consider his cures "a mockery"? What did he believe were the sources of his healing powers?
3. Cabeza de Vaca describes the "great wonder and fear" and the "fear and agitation" that Indians experienced. Why did he believe they were afraid? What was the significance of the Indians calling him and his companions "children of the sun"?

4. According to Cabeza de Vaca, how did Indians react to his cures? What rituals did they perform? Can you speculate about what those rituals meant to the Indians?

5. Cabeza de Vaca described the Indians as "very deceitful, particularly when they are pursuing some gain." Do you think he believed he and his companions were more virtuous? Why or why not?

COMPARATIVE QUESTIONS

1. How did religion influence the perceptions and expectations of the individuals in these different encounters between Europeans and the inhabitants of the New World?

2. How did Afonso's relations with the Portuguese compare to Mexicans' relations with Spaniards?

3. How did Columbus's reactions to Native Americans compare with Díaz's?

4. How did the responses of the people Columbus first encountered compare with the reception the Mexicans gave to the conquistadors? How do they compare to Cabeza de Vaca's experiences with Indians in Texas and the Southwest? What might account for the differences?

5. How did Europeans' expectations shape their understanding of the New World? How did Native Americans' expectations influence their perception of Europeans? How did New World experiences of both Europeans and Native Americans change their expectations about each other?

6. What did Europeans and non-Europeans seek from each other, according to these accounts? To what extent did each group gain (or lose) from the encounters, according to these documents?

3 The Southern Colonies in the Seventeenth Century

1601–1700

Native Americans, tobacco planters, servants, and slaves peopled the world of the seventeenth-century southern British colonies. Spanish New Mexico and Florida had few tobacco planters, but many more Indians and priests. Few of these people jotted down their activities, their thoughts, or their longings. Their experiences can nevertheless be glimpsed in rare private letters and more common official reports, court testimony, and political announcements. The documents that follow disclose tensions, conflicts, and pleasures of daily life in the seventeenth-century southern colonies.

DOCUMENT 3–1

Richard Frethorne Describes Indentured Servitude in Virginia

Indentured servant Richard Frethorne arrived in Virginia in late December 1622. Just three months later he wrote the following letter to his parents in England begging them to rescue him from what he called "this bondage." Frethorne's letter vividly portrays a servant's perspective on the deadly challenges English colonists confronted fourteen years after the first settlement at Jamestown. His spelling and punctuation were common among seventeenth-century Englishmen but differ from usages today. The best way to decipher the words and layers of meaning in Frethorne's letter is to read it aloud.

Letter to Father and Mother, March 20, April 2, 3, 1623

Loveing and kind father and mother my most humble duty re⸍
you hopeing in God of yo[u]r good health, as I my selfe am at ᵗ⸍
this is to let you understand that I yor Child am in a most ⸍

From *The Records of the Virginia Company, 1606–1626*, vol. 4, ed
bury (Washington, DC: Government Printing Office, 1935), 58–62.

of the nature of the Country is such that it Causeth much sicknes, as the scurvie and the bloody flix [dysentery], and divers other diseases, wch maketh the bodie very poore, and Weake, and when wee are sicke there is nothing to Comfort us; for since I came out of the ship, I never at[e] anie thing but pease [porridge], and loblollie (that is water gruell) as for deare or venison I never saw anie since I came into this land, ther is indeed some foule, but Wee are not allowed to goe, and get [it], but must Worke hard both earelie, and late for a messe of water gruell, and a mouthfull of bread, and beife, a mouthfull of bread for a pennie loafe must serve for 4 men wch is most pitifull if you did know as much as I, when people crie out day, and night, Oh that they were in England without their lymbes and would not care to lose anie lymbe to bee in England againe, yea though they beg from doore to doore, for wee live in feare of the Enimy evrie hower [hour], yet wee have had a Combate with them on the Sunday before Shrovetyde,[1] and wee tooke two alive, and make slaves of them, but it was by pollicie, for wee are in great danger, for o[u]r Plantac[i]on is very weake, by reason of the dearth, and sicknes, of o[u]r Companie, for wee came but Twentie for the marchaunts, and they are halfe dead Just; and wee looke everie hower When two more should goe, yet there came some fo[u]r other men yet to lyve with us, of which ther is but one alive, and our L[ieutenant] is dead, and his ffather, and his brother, and there was some 5 or 6 of the last yeares 20 of wch there is but 3 left, so that wee are faine to get other men to plant with us, and yet wee are but 32 to fight against 3000 if they should Come, and the nighest helpe that Wee have is ten miles of us, and when the rogues over-came this place last, they slew 80 Persons how then shall wee doe for wee lye even in their teeth, they may easilie take us but that God is mercifull, and can save with few as well as with many; as he shewed to Gylead and like Gileads Souldiers if they lapt water,[2] wee drinkee water wch is Weake,[3] and I have nothing to Comfort me, nor ther is nothing to be gotten here but sicknes, and death, except that one had money to lay out in some thinges for profit; But I have nothing at all, no not a shirt to my backe, but two Ragges nor no Clothes, but one poore suite, nor but one paire of shooes, but one paire of stockins, but one Capp, but two bands [col-lars], my Cloke is stollen by one of my owne fellowes, and to his dying hower would not tell mee what he did with it but some of my fellows saw him have but-ter and beife out of a ship, wch my Cloke I doubt [not] paid for, so that I have not a penny, nor a penny Worth to helpe me to either spice, or sugar, or strong Waters,[4] without the wch one cannot live here, for as strong beare in England doth fatten and strengthen them so water here doth wash and weaken the[se] here, onelie keepe life and soule togeather. but I am not halfe a quarter so strong as I was in England, and all is for want of victualls, ffor I doe protest unto you, that I have eaten more in [a] day at home th[a]n I have allowed me here for a Weeke. you have given more th[a]n my dayes allowance to a beggar at the doore; and if Mr Jackson had not relieved me, I should bee in a poore Case, but he like a ffather and shee

---

[1]**Shrovetyde**: The days immediately preceding Lent in the Christian calendar.

[2]**they may easilie take us . . . water**: In the book of Judges in the Old Testament, God directed Gideon to reduce the size of his army so that his enemies would be sure to attribute his victory to God's guidance. Gideon kept the three hundred soldiers who cupped water from the river in their hands and lapped it and left those who knelt to 'rink.

[3]**Weake**: Without added alcohol.

[4]**strong Waters**: Alcoholic drink; strong beer.

like a loveing mother doth still helpe me, for when wee goe up to James Towne that is 10 myles of us, there lie all the ships that Come to the land, and there they must deliver their goods, and when wee went up to Towne as it may bee on Moonedaye [Monday], at noone, and come there by night, then load the next day by noone, and goe homes in the afternoone, and unload, and then away againe in the night, and bee up about midnight, then if it rayned, or blowed never so hard wee must lye in the boate on the water, and have nothing but alitle bread, for when wee go into the boate wee have a loafe allowed to two men, and it is all if we staid there 2 dayes, wch is hard, and must lye all that while the boate, but that Goodman Jackson pityed me & made me a Cabbin to lye in always when I come up, and he would give me some poore Jacks [fish] home with me wch Comforted mee more than pease, or water gruell. Oh they bee verie godlie folkes, and love me verie well, and will doe anie thing for me, and he much marvailed that you would send me a servaunt to the [Virginia] Companie, he saith I had been better knockd on the head, and Indeede so I fynd it now to my greate greife and miserie, and saith, that if you love me you will redeeme me suddenlie, for wch I doe Intreate and begg, and if you cannot get the marchaunts to redeeme me for some litle money then for Gods sake get a gathering or intreat some good folks to lay out some little Sum of moneye, in meale, and Cheese and butter, and beife, anie eating meate will yeald great profit, oile and vyniger is verie good, but ffather ther is greate losse in leakinge, but for Gods sake send beife and Cheese and butter or the more of one sort and none of another, but if you send Cheese it must bee very old Cheese, and at the Chesmongers you may buy good Cheese for twopence farthing or halfepenny that will be liked verie well, but if you send Cheese you must have a Care how you packe it in barrells, and you must put Coopers Chips[5] between evrie Cheese, or els the heat of the hold [of the ship] will rott them, and looke whasoever you send me be it nev[e]r so much looke what I make of yt I will deale trulie with you I will send it ov[e]r, and begg the profit to redeeme me, and if I die before it Come I have intreated Goodman Jackson to send you the worth of it, who hath promised he will; If you send you must direct yo[u]r letters to Goodman Jackson, at James Towne a Gunsmith. (you must sett downe his frayt[6]) because there bee more of his name there; good ffather doe not forget me, but have mercie and pittye my miserable Case. I know if you did but see me you would weepe to see me, for I have but one suite, but it is a strange one, it is very well guarded, wherefore for Gods sake pittie me, I pray you to remember my love my love [*sic*] to all my ffreinds, and kindred, I hope all my Brothers and Sisters are in good health, and as for my part I have set downe my resoluc[i]on that certainelie Wilbe, that is, that the Answeare of this letter wilbee life or death to me, therefore good ffather send as soone as you can, and if you send me anie thing let this be the marke.   ROT

Richard Ffrethorne
Martyn's Hundred.

[Here are t]he names of them that bee dead of the Companie came ov[e]r with us to serve under our L[ieutenants] . . . [a list of twenty names: seventeen men, two women, and a child] All theis died out of my m[aster's] house since I came, and

---

[5]**Coopers Chips**: Chips of wood.
[6]**sett downe his frayt**: Pay for the shipment.

wee came in but at Christmas, and this is the 20th day of March and the Saylers say that ther is two thirds of the 150 dead already and thus I end prayeing to God to send me good successe that I may be redeemed out of Egipt.[7] So vale in Christo.[8]

Loveing ffather I pray you to use this man [who delivers this letter] verie exceeding kindly for he hath done much for me, both on my Journy and since, I intreate you not to forget me, but by anie meanes redeeme me, for this day we heare that there is 26 of English men slayne by the Indians, and they have taken a Pinnace[9] of Mr Pountis, and have gotten peeces [muskets], Armour, swords, all thinges fitt for Warre, so that they may now steale upon us (and wee Cannot know them from English, till it is too late, that they bee upon us,) and then ther is no mercie, therefore if you love or respect me, as yo[u]r Child release me from this bondage, and save my life, now you may save me, or let me bee slayne, with Infi-delle, aske this man [who delivers this letter], he knoweth that all is true and Just that I say here; if you do redeeme me the Companie must send for me to my Mr Harrod for so is this M[aster's] name.

Apr[il] the 2 day
Yo[u]r loveing sonne
Richard Ffrethorne

Moreover, on the third day of Aprill wee heard that after theis Rogues had got-ten the Pinnace, and had taken all the furnitures as peeces, swords, armour, Coats of male,[10] Powder, shot and all the thinges that they had to trade withall, they killed the Captaine, and Cut of his head, and rowing with the taile of the boat foremost they set up a pole and put the Captaines head upon it, and so rowed home, then the Devill set them on againe, so that they furnished about 200 Canoes with above 1000 Indians, and came and thought to have taken the shipp, but shee was too quicke for them wch thing was very much talked of, for they alwayes feared a ship, but now the Rogues growe verie bold, and can use peeces, some of them, as well or better than an Englishman, ffor an Indian did shoote with Mr Charles my M[aster's] Kindsman at a marke of white paper, and hee hit it at the first, but Mr Charles Could not hit it, But see the Envie of theis slaves, for when they Could not take the ship then o[u]r men saw them threaten Accomack that is the next Plantac[i]on and nowe ther is no Way but starveing ffor the Governour told us and Sir George, that except the [ship] Seaflower come in or that wee can fall foule of theis Rogues and get some Corne from them, above halfe the land will surelie be starved, for they had no Crop last yeare by reason of theis Rogues, so that wee have no Corne but as ships do relieve us, nor wee shall hardlie have anie Crop this yeare, and Wee are as like to perish first as anie Plantac[i]on, for wee have but two Hogs-heads [barrels] of meale left to serve us this two Monethes, if the Seaflower doe stay so long before shee come in, and that meale is but 3 Weeks bread for us, at a loafe for 4 about the bignes [size] of a pennie loafe in England, that is but a halfepenny loafe a day for a man: is it not straunge to me thinke you? but What will it bee when wee shall goe a moneth or two and never see a bit of bread. as my M[aster] doth

---

[7]**redeemed out of Egipt**: In the book of Exodus in the Old Testament, God helped Moses lead the Israelites out of slavery through the wilderness of Egypt.

[8]**vale in Christo**: Latin for "Strength in Christ"; a farewell.

[9]**Pinnace**: A small boat.

[10]**Coats of male**: Flexible armor made of small, linked chains.

say Wee must doe, and he said hee is not able to keepe us all, then wee shalbe turned up to the land and eate barks of trees, or moulds of the Ground therefore with weeping teares I beg of you to helpe me. O that you did see may [my] daylie and hourelie sighes, grones, and teares, and thumpes that I afford mine owne brest, and rue and Curse the time of my birth with holy Job.[11] I thought no head had been able to hold so much water as hath and doth dailie flow from mine eyes.

But this is Certaine I never felt the want of ffather and mother till now, but now deare ffrends full well I knowe and rue it although it were too late before I knew it.

I pray you talke with this honest man [who delivers this letter] he will tell you more then now in my hast I can set downe.

Yo[u]r loveing Sonne
Richard Ffrethorne
Virginia 3d April 1623

QUESTIONS FOR READING AND DISCUSSION

1. According to Frethorne, what were the causes of his "daylie and hourelie sighes, grones, and teares"?
2. Frethorne begged his father to "redeem" him and "save my life." What did he mean? What could his father do? Did Frethorne seem to think his father will be able to help him? Why do you think he entreats his father "not to forget me"?
3. To what extent were Frethorne's miseries the result of his status as an indentured servant? To what extent were they the result of being an English colonist? How did Frethorne describe his relations with his master and other English colonists?
4. Frethorne referred to Indians as "Rogues" and "slaves." How did his letter portray relations between the Indians and colonists? What part did corn and weapons play in their encounters?
5. In the light of Frethorne's experiences, why do you think indentured servants continued to come to Virginia?

DOCUMENT 3–2

Opechancanough's 1622 Uprising in Virginia

Fifteen years after the settlement of Jamestown in 1607, the coastal Algonquian leader Opechancanough — brother of Powhatan, the chief who first encountered the English settlers — organized a surprise attack against the Virginia colonists. The following account of the attack, written in 1622 by Edward Waterhouse, summarized for members of the London-based Virginia Company the colonists' understanding of what happened and what should be done about it. Waterhouse's declaration expressed the colonists' sense of betrayal and outrage coupled with justifications for unrestrained hostility toward Native Americans and explanations of how hostility would benefit the colonists and the Virginia Company. To decipher seventeenth-century words that are spelled differently today, try reading passages aloud.

---

[11]**holy Job**: In the book of Job in the Old Testament, God tests Job's faith by delivering him into the hands of Satan. Job is seen as a symbol of human suffering.

Edward Waterhouse
Declaration, 1622

A DECLARATION of the state of the Colony and Affaires in VIRGINIA. With a Relation of the barbarous Massacre in the time of peace and League, treacherously executed upon *the English by the native Infidels,* 22 *March last.* . . .

[T]hat all men may see the unpartiall ingenuity of this Discourse, we freely confesse, that the Countrey is not so good, as the *Natives* are bad, whose barbarous Savagenesse needs more cultivation then the ground it selfe, being more overspread with incivilitie and treachery, then that with Bryers. For the land being tilled and used well by us, deceived not our expectation, but rather exceeded it farre, being so thankfull as to returne an hundred for one. But the *Savages* though never Nation used so kindly upon so small desert, have in stead of that *Harvest* which our paines merited, returned nothing but Bryers and thornes, pricking even to death many of their Benefactors. . . .

[Last November, 1621] the Country [was] setled in a peace (as all men there thought) sure and unviolable, not onely because it was solemnly ratified and sworne, and at the request of the Native King stamped in Brasse, and fixed to one of his Oakes of note, but as being advantagious to both parts; to the Savages as the weaker, under which they were safely sheltred and defended; to us, as being the easiest way then thought to pursue and advance our projects of buildings, plantings, and effecting their conversion by peaceable and fayre meanes. And such was the conceit of firme peace and amitie, as that there was seldome or never a sword worne, and a Peece[1] seldomer, except for a Deere or Fowle. By which assurance of securitie, the Plantations of particular Adventurers and Planters were placed scatteringly and straglingly as a choyce veyne of rich ground invited them, and the further from neighbors held the better. The houses generally set open to the Savages, who were alwaies friendly entertained at the tables of the English, and commonly lodged in their bed-chambers. The old planters (as they thought now come to reape the benefit of their long travels) placed with wonderfull content upon their private dividents, and the planting of particular Hundreds and Colonies pursued with an hopefull alacrity, all our projects . . . in a faire way, and their familarity with the Natives, seeming to open a faire gate for their conversion to Christianitie.

The Country being in this estate, an occasion was ministred of sending to *Opachankano* the King of these Savages, about the middle of *March* last, what time the Messenger returned backe with these words from him, That he held the peace concluded so firme, as the Skie should sooner fall then it dissolve: yea, such was the treacherous dissimulation of that people who then had contrived our destruction, that even two dayes before the Massacre, some of our men were guided thorow the woods by them in safety. . . .

[O]n the Friday morning (the fatal day) the 22 *of March,* as also in the evening, as in other dayes before, they came unarmed into our houses, without Bowes or arrowes, or other weapons, with Deere, Turkies, Fish, Furres, and other provisions, to sell, and trucke with us, for glasse, beades, and other trifles: yea in some

---

From Susan Myra Kingsbury, ed., *The Records of the Virginia Company of London,* vol. 3 (Washington DC: U.S. Government Printing Office, 1906–1935), 541–64.

[1]**Peece:** Firearm.

places, sate downe at Breakfast with our people at their tables, whom immediately with their owne tooles and weapons, eyther laid downe, or standing in their houses, they basely and barbarously murthered, not sparing eyther age or sexe, man, woman or childe; so sodaine [sudden] in their cruell execution, that few or none discerned the weapon or blow that brought them to destruction. In which manner they also slew many of our people then at their severall workes and husbandries in the fields, and without their houses, some in planting Corne and Tobacco, some in gardening, some in making Bricke, building, sawing, and other kindes of husbandry, they well knowing in what places and quarters each of our men were, in regard of their daily familiarity, and resort to us for trading and other negotiations, which the more willingly was by us continued and cherished for the desire we had of effecting that great master-peece of workes, their conversion. And by this meanes that fatall Friday morning, there fell under the bloudy and barbarous hands of that perfidious and inhumane people, contrary to all lawes of God and men, of Nature and Nations, three hundred forty seven men, women, and children, most by their owne weapons; and not being content with taking away life alone, they fell after againe upon the dead, making as well as they could, a fresh murder, defacing, dragging, and mangling the dead carkasses into many pieces, and carying some parts away in derision, with base and bruitish triumph. . . .

[T]he slaughter had beene universall, if God had not put it into the heart of an Indian belonging to one *Perry*, to disclose it, who living in the house of one *Pace*, was urged by another Indian his Brother (who came the night before and lay with him) to kill *Pace*, (so commanded by their King as he declared) as hee would kill *Perry*: telling further that by such an houre in the morning a number would come from divers places to finish the Execution, who failed not at the time: *Perries* Indian rose out of his bed and reveales it to *Pace*, that used him as a Sonne: And thus the rest of the Colony that had warning given them, by this meanes was saved. Such was (God bee thanked for it) the good fruit of an Infidell converted to Christianity; for though three hundred and more of ours died by many of these Pagan Infidels, yet thousands of ours were saved by the means of one of them alone which was made a Christian. . . .

Pace upon this discovery, securing his house, before day rowed over the River to *James-City* (in that place neere three miles in bredth) and gave notice thereof to the Governor, by which meanes they were prevented there, and at such other Plantations as was possible for a timely intelligence to be given; for where they saw us standing upon our Guard, at the sight of a Peece they all ranne away. In other places that could have no notice, some Peeces with munition (the use whereof they know not) were there carried away, and some few Cattell also were destroyed by them. And as Fame divulgeth (not without probable grounds) their King hath since caused the most part of the Gunpowder by him surprized, to bee sowne, to draw therefrom the like increase, as of his Maize or Corne, in Harvest next. And that it is since discovered, that the last Summer *Opachankano* practised with a King of the Eastern shore (no well-willer of his) to furnish him with store of poison (naturally growing in his country) for our destruction, which he absolutely refused, though he sent him great store of Beades, and other presents to winne him thereunto: which he, with five or six of his great men, offered to be ready to justifie against him. That the true cause of this surprize was most by the instigation of the Devill, (enemy to their salvation) and the dayly feare that possest them, that in time we by our growing continually upon them, would dispossesse them of this Country, as they had beene formerly of the West Indies by the Spaniard; produced this bloody act. That never griefe and shame possessed any people more then themselves, to be thus butchered by so naked and cowardly a people, who dare not stand the presentment of a staffe in manner of a Peece, nor an uncharged Peece in the hands of a woman, from which they flye as so many Hares; much faster then from their tormenting Devill, whom they worship for feare, though they acknowledge they love him not. . . .

[T]his must needs bee for the good of the Plantation after, and the losse of this blood to make the body more healthfull, as by these reasons may be manifest.

First, Because betraying of innocency never rests unpunished. . . .

Secondly, Because our hands which before were tied with gentlenesse and faire usage, are now set at liberty by the treacherous violence of the Savages, not untying the Knot, but cutting it: So that we, who hitherto have had possession of no more ground then their waste, and our purchase at a valuable consideration to their owne contentment, gained; may now by right of Warre, and law of Nations, invade the Country, and destroy them who sought to destroy us: whereby wee shall enjoy their cultivated places, turning the laborious Mattocke into the victorious Sword (wherein there is more both ease, benefit, and glory) and possessing the fruits of others labours. Now their cleared grounds in all their villages (which are situate in the fruitfullest places of the land) shall be inhabited by us, whereas heretofore the grubbing of woods was the greatest labour.

Thirdly, Because those commodities which the Indians enjoyed as much or rather more than we, shall now also be entirely possessed by us. The Deere and other beasts will be in safety, and infinitly increase, which heretofore not onely in the generall huntings of the King (whereat foure or five hundred Deere were usually slaine) but by each particular Indian were destroied at all times of the yeare, without any difference of Male, Damme, or Young. The like may be said of our owne Swine and Goats, whereof they have used to kill eight in tenne more than the English have done. There will be also a great increase of wild Turkies, and other waighty Fowle, for the Indians never put difference of destroying the Hen, but kill them whether in season or not, whether in breeding time, or sitting on their egges, or having new hatched, it is all one to them: whereby, as also by the orderly using of their fishing Weares, no knowne Country in the world will so plentifully abound in victuall.

Fourthly, Because the way of conquering them is much more easie then of civilizing them by faire meanes, for they are a rude, barbarous, and naked people, scattered in small companies, which are helps to Victorie, but hinderances to Civilitie: Besides that, a conquest may be of many, and at once; but civility is in particular, and slow, the effect of long time, and great industry. Moreover, victorie of them may bee gained many waies; by force, by surprize, by famine in burning their Corne, by destroying and burning their Boats, Canoes, and Houses, by breaking their fishing Weares, by assailing them in their huntings, whereby they get the greatest part of their sustenance in Winter, by pursuing and chasing them with our horses, and blood-Hounds to draw after them, and Mastives to teare them, which take this naked, tanned, deformed Savages, for no other then wild beasts, and are so fierce and fell upon them, that they feare them worse then their old Devill which they worship, supposing them to be a new and worse kinde of Devils then their owne. By these and sundry other wayes, as by driving them (when they flye) upon their enemies, who are round about them, and by animating and abetting their enemies against them, may their ruine or subjection be soone effected. . . .

Fifthly, Because the *Indians*, who before were used as friends, may now most justly be compelled to servitude and drudgery, and supply the roome of men that labour, whereby even the meanest of the Plantation may imploy themselves more entirely in their Arts and Occupations, which are more generous, whilest Savages performe their inferiour workes of digging in mynes, and the like. . . .

Sixtly, This will for ever hereafter make us more [cautious] and circumspect, as never to bee deceived more by any other treacheries, but will serve for a great instruction to all posteritie there, to teach them that *Trust is the mother of Deceipt*, and . . . Hee that trusts not is not deceived: and make them know that kindnesses are misspent upon rude natures, so long as they continue rude; as also, that Savages and Pagans are above all other for matter of Justice ever to be suspected. Thus upon this Anvile shall wee now beate out to our selves an armour of proofe, which shall for ever after defend us from barbarous Incursions, and from greater dangers that otherwise might happen. . . .

To conclude then, seeing that *Virginia* is most abundantly fruitfull, and that this Massacre must rather be beneficiall to the Plantation then impaire it, let all men take courage, and put to their helping hands, since now the time is most seasonable and advantagious for the reaping of those benefits which the Plantation hath long promised: and for their owne good let them doe it speedily, that so by taking the prioritie of time, they may have also the prioritie of place, in choosing the best Seats of the Country, which now by vanquishing of the Indians, is like to offer a more ample and faire choice of fruitfull habitations, then hitherto our gentlenesse and faire comportment to the Savages could attaine unto. Wherein no doubt but all the favour that may be, shall be shewed to Adventurers and Planters. . . .

QUESTIONS FOR READING AND DISCUSSION

1. Why did the colonists feel betrayed by Opechancanough's attack?
2. How did Opechancanough prepare for the assault? How did the Virginians survive the attack?
3. According to the Declaration, how did the attack affect the colonists' attitudes about the Indians and about themselves?
4. Why did Waterhouse believe "conquest" was better than "civility"? Why did he think the "Massacre must . . . be beneficial to the Plantation"?
5. Consider the words Waterhouse used to describe Indians. In what ways did his language reveal his views of Indians and their resistance to "cultivation"?
6. How might the Declaration have been different if Opechacanough had written it?

DOCUMENT 3–3

Sex and Race Relations

Whites and blacks, men and women often worked side by side in the seventeenth-century Chesapeake. Sometimes whites were free and blacks were slaves. Sometimes both whites and blacks were servants who looked forward to their freedom. Sometimes blacks were free, and sometimes they were not even black, but racially mixed mulattos. The court inquiry excerpted here provides conflicting testimony about the behavior of a white woman and slave men in Virginia in August 1681. The testimony reveals the potentially explosive mixture of sexual and racial expectations and stereotypes in the small communities of the southern colonies.

Testimony from Virginia Court Records, 1681

The examination of Katherine Watkins, the wife of Henry Watkins of Henrico County in Virginia had and taken this 13 of September 1681 before us William Byrd and John Farrar two of his Majesties justices of the County aforesaid as followeth. . . .

The said Katherine aforesaid on her Oath and examination deposeth, That on fryday being in the Month of August aboute five weeks since, the said Katherine mett with John Long (a Mulatto belonging to Capt. Thomas Cocke) at or neare the pyney slash [pine woods] betweene the aforesaid Cockes and Henry Watkins house, and at the same tyme and place, the said John threw the said Katherine downe (He starting from behinde a tree) and stopped her Mouth with a hand-kerchief, and tooke up the said Katherines Coates [petticoats] and putt his yard [penis] into her and ravished her; Upon which she the said Katherine Cryed out (as she deposeth) and afterwards (being rescued by another Negroe of the said Cockes named jack White) she departed home, and the said John departed to his Masters likewise, or that way; after which abuse she the said Katherine declares that her husband inclinable to the quakers,[1] and therefore would not prosecute, and she being sicke and her Children likewise, she therefore did not make her complaint before she went to Lt. Col. Farrars (which was yesterday, Morning) and this day in the Morning she went to William Randolphs' and found him not at home, But at night met with the gentlemen justices aforesaid at the house of the aforesaid Cocke in Henrico County in Virginia aforesaid before whom she hath made this complaint upon oath. . . .

The deposition of John Aust aged 32 yeares or thereabouts Deposeth, That on fryday being the twelvth of August or thereabouts he came to the house of Mr. Thomas Cocke, and soe went into his Orchard where his servants were a cutting downe weeds, whoe asked the deponent to stay and drinke, soe the deponent stayed and dranke syder with them, and jacke a Mulatto of the said Thomas Cocke went in to draw syder, and he stay'd something long whereupon the deponent followed him, and coming to the doore where the syder was, heard Katherine the wife of Henry Watkins say (Lord) jacke what makes thee refraine our house that you come not oftner, for come when thou wilt thou shalt be as well come as any of My owne Children, and soe she tooke him about the necke and Kissed him, and jacke went out and drawed Syder, and she said jack wilt thou not drinke to me, who sayd yes if you will goe out where our Cupp is, and a little after she came out, where the said Thomas Cockes Negroes were a drinking and there dranke cupp for cupp with them (as others there did) and as she sett Negroe dirke passing by her she tooke up the taile of his shirt (saying) Dirke thou wilt have a good long thing, and soe did several tymes as he past by her; after this she went into the roome where the syder was and then came out againe, and between the two houses she mett Mulatto jacke a going to draw more syder and putt her hand on his codpiece,[2] at which he smil'd, and went on his way and drew syder and she

---

From Warren Billings, ed., *The Old Dominion in the Seventeenth Century: A Documentary History of Virginia, 1606–1689* (Chapel Hill: University of North Carolina Press, 1975), 161–63.

[1]**quakers:** That is, a Quaker believer who did not resort to court prosecution.

[2]**codpiece:** The crotch covering in men's trousers.

came againe into the company but stay'd not long but went out to drinking with two of the said Thomas Cockes Negroes by the garden pale, And a while after she tooke Mingoe one of the said Cocke's Negroes about the Necke and fling on the bedd and Kissed him and putt her hand into his Codpiece, Awhile after Mulatto jacke went into the Fish roome and she followed him, but what they did there this deponent knoweth not for it being near night this deponent left her and the Negroes together, (He thinking her to be much in drinke) and soe this deponent went home about one houre by sunn. . . .

The Deposition of William Harding aged about 35 yeares, Deposeth, That he came to the house of Mr. Thomas Cocke to speake with his brother, where he see Katherine the wife of Henry Watkins, and soe spoke to one there and sayd, that the said Henry Watkins wife had been a drinking; And that this deponent see the said Katherine Watkins turne up the taile of Negroe Dirks shirt, and said that he would have a good pricke, whereupon this deponent sayd is that the trick of a quaker, who made him answer, that what hast thou to say to quakers,[3] It being acted on fryday the 12 of August or thereabouts and further saith not. . . .

The Deposition of Mary Winter aged about 22 years. Deposeth, That Mr. Thomas Cocks Negroes and others being in company with them a drinking of syder, Then came in Katherine Watkins the wife of Henry Watkins and went to drinking with them, and tooke Mulatto jack by the hand in the outward roome and ledd him into the inward roome doore and then thrust him in before her and told him she loved him for his Fathers sake for his Father was a very hansome young Man, and afterwards the said Mulattoe went out from her, and then she fetched him into the roome againe and hugged and kist him. And further saith not. . . .

The Deposition of Lambert Tye aged about 26 yeares. Deposeth That being at Worke at Mr. Thomas Cocks on fryday being the twelvth of August or thereabouts, and coming into the house with William Hobson and the rest of Mr. Thomas Cocks servants and others in Company with them to drinke syder, and being a drinking then comes in Katherine Watkins the wife of Henry Watkins having a very high Colour in her face whereupon this deponent asked Humphrey then servant to the said Thomas Cocke; what made his Countrywoman have such a high Colour; whereupon he made this answear; That the [said] Katherine was at Old Humphrey's a drinking and he gave her a Cupp or two that had turned her braines, and soe being a drinking with their company she went into the Chimney (as this deponent thinketh) to light her pipe, and soe made a posture with her body as if she would have gone to danceing, and then afterwards coming into their company againe, she told Mulatto jack, that she loved him for his father's sake, And then having left the Company and she together a drinking, This deponent went home to his owne house, and afterwards coming from home towards the house of the said Thomas Cocke, he mett with the said Katherine Watkins about halfe an houre by sun in the pathway homewards neare to this deponents house. And further saith not. . . .

---

[3]See note 1.

Humphrey Smith aged 26 yeares, deposeth, That he heard John Aust say (about September last past) what Matter is it what I swore to and likewise the deponent saw Katherine's Mouth (the wife of Henry Watkins) torne and her lipps swell'd, And the handkerchief that she said the Mulatto Stopt her Mouth with very much bloody And the deponent heard the Mulatto confess that he had beene to aske the said Watkins wife forgiveness three tymes, and likewise the Mulatto sayd that Henry Watkins (the last tyme he went) bidd him keepe off his plantation or else he would shoote him and further saith not.

QUESTIONS FOR READING AND DISCUSSION

1. How does Katherine Watkins's testimony differ from that of other witnesses? To what extent does the testimony portray Watkins as the victim or the perpetrator?

2. Who were Katherine Watkins's neighbors, and what did they think of her and her husband? Did they all agree? To what extent did they consider her behavior unusual?

3. What does the testimony suggest about day-to-day encounters between free people, servants, and slaves? Does the testimony indicate that witnesses were especially concerned that John (or Jack) Long was a "mulatto"? Why did slaves give no testimony?

4. In the end, what did the witnesses seem to believe was at stake in this episode? What kinds of disorder—social, sexual, racial, familial—occurred, according to the testimony? What expectations about order did the witnesses reveal?

DOCUMENT 3–4

Bacon's Rebellion

In 1676, Nathaniel Bacon led a group of planters, tenants, and servants in battles against Indians along the Virginia frontier. Bacon had arrived in Virginia only two years earlier and carved out a farm on the frontier. Bacon's status as a member of a prominent English family gained him recognition from Virginia's governor, Sir William Berkeley. When Bacon began his private war against Indians, Berkeley—who hoped to keep peace along the frontier—declared the upstart a rebel. Beneath the dispute about Indian policy smouldered hostility between frontier planters and tidewater gentry, between struggling farmers and privileged grandees. That hostility flared into a full-scale rebellion that convulsed Virginia until it was finally suppressed by government authorities in 1677, after Bacon's death and much destruction of life and property. In the following declaration published in 1676, Bacon detailed his view of the prevailing order in Virginia. Bacon's declaration disclosed the simmering antagonisms engendered by the inequities among whites, both free people and servants, in the seventeenth-century southern colonies.

Nathaniel Bacon

Declaration, 1676

If vertue be a sin, if Piety be giult, all the Principles of morality goodness and justice be perverted, Wee must confesse That those who are now called Rebells may be in danger of those high imputations, Those loud and severall Bulls[1] would affright Innocents and render the defence of our Brethren and the enquiry into our sad and heavy oppressions, Treason. But if there bee as sure there is, a just God to appeal too, if Religion and justice be a sanctuary here, If to plead the cause of the oppressed, If sincerely to aime at his Majesties Honour and the Publick good without any reservation or by Interest, If to stand in the Gap after soe much blood of our dear Brethren bought and sold, If after the losse of a great part of his Majesties Colony deserted and dispeopled, freely with our lives and estates to indeavor to save the remaynders bee Treason God Almighty judge and lett guilty dye, But since wee cannot in our hearts find one single spott of Rebellion or Treason or that wee have in any manner aimed at subverting the setled Government or attempting of the Person of any either magistrate or private man not with standing the severall Reproaches and Threats of some who for sinister ends were disaffected to us and censured our inocent and honest designes, and since all people in all places where wee have yet bin can attest our civill quiet peaseable behaviour farre different from that of Rebellion and tumultuous persons let Trueth be bold and all the world know the real Foundations of pretended giult, Wee appeale to the Country itselfe what and of what nature their Oppressions have bin or by what Caball[2] and mistery the designes of many of those whom wee call great men have bin transacted and caryed on, but let us trace these men in Authority and Favour to whose hands the dispensation of the Countries wealth has been commited; let us observe the sudden Rise of their Estates composed with the Quality in which They first entered this Country Or the Reputation they have held here amongst wise and discerning men, And lett us see wither their extractions and Education have not bin vile, And by what pretence of learning and vertue they could soe soon into Imployments of so great Trust and consequence, let us consider their sudden advancement and let us also consider wither any Publick work for our safety and defence or for the Advancement and propagation of Trade, liberall Arts or sciences is here Extant in any [way] adaquate to our vast chardg, now let us compare these things togit[her] and see what spounges have suckt up the Publique Treasure and wither it hath not bin privately contrived away by unworthy Favourites and juggling Parasites whose tottering Fortunes have bin repaired and supported at the Publique chardg, now if it be so Judg what greater giult can bee then to offer to pry into these and to unriddle the misterious wiles of a powerfull Cabal let all people Judge what can be of more dangerous Import then to suspect the soe long Safe proceedings of Some of our Grandees and wither People may with safety open their Eyes in soe nice a Concerne.

Another main article of our Giult is our open and manifest aversion of all, not onely the Foreign but the protected and Darling Indians, this wee are informed is Rebellion of a deep dye For that both the Governour and Councell are by Colonell Coales Assertion bound to defend the Queen and Appamatocks[3] with their blood

---

From Warren Billings, ed., *The Old Dominion in the Seventeenth Century: A Documentary History of Virginia, 1606–1689* (Chapel Hill: University of North Carolina Press, 1975), 277–79.

[1]A reference to the Virginia governor's declaration (or *bull*) that Bacon and his supporters were rebels.

[2]**Caball**: Secret plot.

[3]**Appamatocks**: An Indian tribe.

Now whereas we doe declare and can prove that they have bin for these Many years enemies to the King and Country, Robbers and Theeves and Invaders of his Majesties' Right and our Interest and Estates, but yet have by persons in Authority bin defended and protected even against His Majesties loyall Subjects and that in soe high a Nature that even the Complaints and oaths of his Majesties Most loyall Subjects in a lawfull Manner proffered by them against those barborous Outlawes have bin by the right honourable Governour rejected and the Delinquents from his presence dismissed not only with pardon and indemnitye but with all incouragement and favour, Their Fire Arms soe destructfull to us and by our lawes prohibited, Commanded to be restored them, and open Declaration before Witness made That they must have Ammunition although directly contrary to our law, Now what greater giult can be then to oppose and indeavour the destruction of these Honest quiet neighbours of ours.

Another main article of our Giult is our Design not only to ruine and extirpate all Indians in Generall but all Manner of Trade and Commerce with them, judge who can be innocent that strike at this tender Eye of Interest; Since the Right honourable the Governour hath bin pleased by his Commission to warrant this trade who dare oppose it, or opposing it can be innocent, Although Plantations be deserted, the blood of our dear Brethren Spilt, on all Sides our complaints, continually Murder upon Murder renewed upon us, who may or dare think of the generall Subversion of all Mannor of Trade and Commerce with our enemies who can or dare impeach any of [word missing] Traders at the Heades of the Rivers if contrary to the wholesome provision made by lawes for the countries safety, they dare continue their illegall practises and dare asperse the right honourable Governours wisdome and justice soe highly to pretend to have his warrant to break that law which himself made, who dare say That these Men at the Heads of the Rivers buy and sell our blood, and doe still notwithstanding the late Act made to the contrary,[4] admit Indians painted and continue to Commerce, although these things can be proved yet who dare bee soe guilty as to doe it.

Another Article of our Guilt is To Assert all those neighbour Indians as well as others to be outlawed, wholly unqualifyed for the benefitt and Protection of the law, For that the law does reciprocally protect and punish, and that all people offending must either in person or Estate make equivalent satisfaction or Restitution according to the manner and merit of the Offences Debts or Trespasses; Now since the Indians cannot according to the tenure and forme of any law to us known be prosecuted, Seised or Complained against, Their Persons being difficulty distinguished or known, Their many nations languages, and their subterfuges such as makes them incapeable to make us Restitution or satisfaction would it not be very giulty to say They have bin unjustly defended and protected these many years.

If it should be said that the very foundation of all these disasters the Grant of the Beaver trade to the Right Honourable Governour[5] was illegall and not granteable by any power here present as being a monopoly, were not this to deserve the name of Rebell and Traytor.

Judge therefore all wise and unprejudiced men who may or can faithfully or truely with an honest heart attempt the country's good, their vindication and

---

[4]Recent legislation prohibited trade with Indians who wore paint, a sign of unreliability, according to Bacon and many other Virginians.

[5]By monopolizing the trade in beaver skins, the governor reaped handsome profits for himself.

libertie without the aspersion of Traitor and Rebell, since as soe doing they must of necessity gall[6] such tender and dear concernes, But to manifest Sincerity and loyalty to the World, and how much wee abhorre those bitter names, may all the world know that we doe unanimously desire to represent our sad and heavy grievances to his most sacred Majesty as our Refuge and Sanctuary, where wee doe well know that all our Causes will be impartially heard and Equall justice administred to all men.

QUESTIONS FOR READING AND DISCUSSION

1. According to Bacon, what were the real foundations of the trouble in Virginia? How did he propose "to unriddle the misterious wiles of a powerfull Cabal"?

2. What was Bacon's plan for "the protected and Darling Indians"? Why did he favor such a plan, and why did others oppose it?

3. What did Bacon's statement suggest about the distribution and exercise of political power in the seventeenth-century Chesapeake? What changes in political power did he seek? What principles did he believe should govern colonial society?

4. How might Bacon's arguments have been answered by his opponents, both in the colonial government and among the Indians?

DOCUMENT 3–5

Pedro Naranjo Describes Pueblo Revolt

In 1675, during a prolonged drought and numerous attacks by Comanche raiders, Spanish officials in New Mexico tried to eliminate the traditional religious practices of Pueblo people. They arrested almost fifty Pueblo spiritual leaders and executed several. Among those arrested was Popé, who, after his release by the Spaniards, organized a large-scale revolt against the Spaniards in the summer of 1680. The Pueblo uprising killed more than half the priests in New Mexico and nearly four hundred other Spaniards. In the passage excerpted below, Pedro Naranjo, one of the Pueblo religious leaders captured by the Spanish, testified about why the revolt occurred and how it changed life among the Pueblo people. Naranjo's testimony reveals the powerful opposition to Christianity and Spanish rule rooted in the Pueblo people's ancient beliefs and lifestyle.

Declaration of Pedro Naranjo of the Queres Nation, December 19, 1681

For the prosecution of the judicial proceedings of this case[,] his lordship [a Spanish official] caused to appear before him an Indian prisoner named Pedro Naranjo, a native of the pueblo of San Felipe, of the Queres nation, who was captured in the [Spaniards'] advance and attack upon the pueblo of La Isleta.

---

[6]**gall**: Cause bitterness or rancor.

From Charles Wilson Hackett, *Revolt of the Pueblo Indians of New Mexico and Otermín's Attempted Reconquest, 1680–1682* (Albuquerque: University of New Mexico, 1942), 2: 245–49. English translation by Charmion Clair Shelby.

He makes himself understood very well in the Castilian [Spanish] language and speaks his mother tongue and the Tegua. He took the oath in due legal form in the name of God, our Lord, and a sign of the cross, under charge of which he promised to tell the truth concerning what he knows and as he might be questioned, and having understood the seriousness of the oath and so signified through the interpreters. . . .

Asked [by the Spanish interrogators] whether he knows the reason or motives which the Indians of this kingdom had for rebelling, forsaking the law of God and obedience to his Majesty, and committing such grave and atrocious crimes, and who were the leaders and principal movers, and by whom and how it was ordered; and why they burned the images, temples, crosses, rosaries, and things of divine worship, committing such atrocities as killing priests, Spaniards, women, and children, and the rest that he might know touching the question, he [Pedro Naranjo] said that . . . [since 1675 the Pueblo Indians] have planned to rebel on various occasions through conspiracies of the Indian sorcerers [spiritual leaders], and that although in some pueblos the messages were accepted, in other parts they would not agree to it; and that it is true that . . . [in 1675] seven or eight Indians were hanged for this same cause, whereupon the unrest subsided. Some time thereafter they [the conspirators] sent from the pueblo of Los Taos through the pueblos of the . . . [region] two deerskins with some pictures on them signifying conspiracy after their manner, in order to convoke the people to a new rebellion, and the said deerskins passed to the province of Moqui [near Taos], where they refused to accept them. The pact which they had been forming ceased for the time being, but they always kept in their hearts the desire to carry it out, so as to live as they are living to-day.

Finally, in the past years, at the summons of an Indian named Popé who is said to have communication with the devil, it happened that in an estufa [kiva; house of worship] of the pueblo of Los Taos there appeared to the said Popé three figures of Indians who never came out of the estufa. They gave the said Popé to understand that they were going underground to the lake of Copala. He saw these figures emit fire from all the extremities of their bodies, and that one of them was called Caudi, another Tilini, and the other Tleume; and these three beings spoke to the said Popé, who was in hiding from the [Spanish] . . . , who wished to punish him as a sorcerer. They [Caudi, Tilini, and Tleume] told him to make a cord of maguey [cactus] fiber and tie some knots in it which would signify the number of days that they must wait before the rebellion. He [Pedro Naranjo] said that the cord was passed through all the pueblos of the kingdom so that the ones which agreed to it [the rebellion] might untie one knot in sign of obedience, and by the other knots they would know the days which were lacking; and this was to be done on pain of death to those who refused to agree to it. As a sign of agreement and notice of having concurred in the treason and perfidy they were to send up smoke signals to that effect in each one of the pueblos singly.

The said cord was taken from pueblo to pueblo by the swiftest youths under the penalty of death if they revealed the secret. Everything being thus arranged, two days before the time set for . . . [the revolt's] execution, because his lordship had learned of it and had imprisoned two Indian accomplices from the pueblo of Tesuque, it was carried out prematurely that night, because it seemed to them that they were now discovered; and they killed religious [priests], Spaniards, women, and children. This being done, it was proclaimed in all the pueblos that everyone in common should obey the commands of their father whom they did not know, which would be given through El Caydi or El Popé. This was heard by Alonso Catití, who came to the pueblo of this declarant [Pedro Naranjo] to say that everyone must unite to go to the villa to kill the governor and the Spaniards who had remained with him, and that he who did not obey would, on their return, be beheaded; and in fear of this they agreed to it.

Finally the señor governor and those who were with him escaped from the siege, and later this declarant [Naranjo] saw that as soon as the Spaniards had left the kingdom an order came from the said Indian, Popé, in which he commanded all the Indians to break the lands and enlarge their cultivated fields, saying that now they were as they had been in ancient times, free from the labor they had performed for the religious and the Spaniards, who could not now be alive. He said that this is the legitimate cause and the reason they had for rebelling, because they had always desired to live as they had when they came out of the lake of Copala. Thus he replies to the question.

Asked [by the Spanish interrogators] for what reason they so blindly burned the images, temples, crosses, and other things of divine worship, he stated that the said Indian, Popé, came down in person, and with him . . . [other leaders] from the pueblo of Los Taos, and other captains and leaders and many people who were . . . [following him], and he ordered in all the pueblos through which he passed that they instantly break up and burn the images of the holy Christ, the Virgin Mary and the other saints, the crosses, and everything pertaining to Christianity, and that they burn the temples, break up the bells, and separate from the wives whom God had given them in marriage and take those whom they desired. In order to take away their baptismal names, the water, and the holy oils, they were to plunge into the rivers and wash themselves with amole, which is a root native to the country, washing even their clothing, with the understanding that there would thus be taken from them the character of the holy sacraments. They did this, and also many other things which he does not recall, given to understand that this mandate had come from the Caudi and the other two who emitted fire from their extremities in the said estufa of Taos, and that they [the Pueblo people] thereby returned to the state of their antiquity, as when they came from the lake of Copala; that this was the better life and the one they desired, because the God of the Spaniards was worth nothing and theirs was very strong, the Spaniard's God being rotten wood. These things were observed and obeyed by all except some who, moved by the zeal of Christians, opposed it, and such persons the said Popé caused to be killed immediately. He saw to it that they at once erected and rebuilt their houses of idolatry which they call estufas, and made very ugly masks in imitation of the devil in order to dance the dance of the cacina [kachina, in which the dancers represent various deities]; and he said likewise that the devil had given them to understand that living thus in accordance with the law of their ancestors, they would harvest a great deal of maize, many beans, a great abundance of cotton, calabashes [squash], and very large watermelons and cantaloupes; and that they could erect their houses and enjoy abundant health and leisure. As he has said, the people were very much pleased, living at their ease in this life of their antiquity, which was the chief cause of their falling into such laxity. Following what has already been stated, in order to terrorize . . . [the Pueblo people] further and cause them to observe the diabolical commands, there came to them a pronouncement from the three demons already described, and from El Popé, to the effect that he who might still keep in his heart a regard for the [Spanish] priests, the governor, and the Spaniards would be known from his unclean face and clothes, and would be punished. And he stated that the said four persons stopped at nothing to have their commands obeyed. . . .

Asked what arrangements and plans they [the Pueblo revolt's leaders] had made for the contingency of the Spaniards' return, [Pedro Naranjo] . . . said that what he knows concerning the question is that they were always saying they would have to fight to the death, for they do not wish to live in any other way than they are living at present; and the demons in the estufa of Taos had given them to understand that as soon as the Spaniards began to move toward this kingdom they would warn them so that they might unite, and none of them would be caught.

He having been questioned further and repeatedly touching the case, he said that he has nothing more to say except that [the Spaniards] . . . should be always on the alert, because the . . . Indians were continually planning to follow the Spaniards and fight with them by night, in order to drive off the horses and catch them afoot, although they might have to follow them for many leagues. What he [Naranjo] has said is the truth, and what happened, on the word of a Christian who confesses his guilt. He said that he has come to the pueblos through fear to lead in idolatrous dances, in which he greatly fears in his heart that he may have offended God, and that now having been absolved and returned to the fold of the church, he has spoken the truth in everything he has been asked. His declaration being read to him, he affirmed and ratified all of it. He declared himself to be eighty years of age, and he signed it with his lordship and the interpreters and assisting witnesses.

QUESTIONS FOR READING AND DISCUSSION

1. According to Pedro Naranjo, why did the Pueblo revolt occur? How did Pueblo people organize the revolt?
2. What was the significance of Popé's "communication with the devil"? Who were Caudi, Tilini, and Tleume? What meanings did they have for Popé and his followers? For the Spaniards?
3. In what ways did the Pueblo people return "to the state of their antiquity" after the revolt? How did that way of life contrast with their experience under the Spaniards' rule?
4. In general, what does Naranjo's testimony suggest about attitudes toward Christianity among the Pueblo people? Why did the followers of Popé believe that "the God of the Spaniards was worth nothing and theirs was very strong, the Spaniards' God being rotten wood"? Did the Pueblo people agree about Christianity, according to Naranjo?
5. How did Naranjo's status as both a captive of the Spaniards and a Pueblo spiritual leader influence his testimony? Can you spot specific words in his testimony that reveal his awareness of the conflicting perspectives of the Spaniards and the followers of Popé?

COMPARATIVE QUESTIONS

1. What do these documents reveal about attitudes toward Native Americans among English and Spanish colonists? What do the documents reveal about Native American attitudes toward English and Spanish colonists?

2. How did the production of tobacco influence the experiences of the individuals described by these documents? How did experiences differ according to social rank, gender, race, age, religion, and ethnicity?

3. Opechancanough's uprising, Bacon's rebellion, and the Pueblo revolt reveal fundamental conflicts over land rights and religion that arose in the southern colonies during the seventeenth century. To what extent did the three events display similar (or contrasting) conflicts?

4. Each of the documents provides evidence of important concepts of order and disorder. To what extent do the documents suggest broad agreement among free white colonists about the fundamental patterns of order and sources of potential disorder? To what extent did Indians, slaves, and servants share those notions?

4 The Northern Colonies in the Seventeenth Century

1601–1700

Religion made an indelible impression on the New England and Middle colonies in the seventeenth century. Puritans in New England built churches and towns, distributed land, raised families, passed laws, and rendered verdicts. In all of their activities, Puritans aspired to live according to their views of God's law. Although many New Englanders were not church members, those who were governed society both in principle and in practice.

The Quakers who founded Pennsylvania also sought to establish a civil order in their colony that was grounded in their own religious principles, but one that allowed colonists more freedom in the way they chose to worship God. White colonists recognized, however, that most Native Americans did not adhere to any form of Christianity, providing a durable reminder of the limited scope of religious orthodoxy. In addition, the colonists' behavior often conflicted with their religious ideals. The following documents exhibit the Puritans' and Quakers' high standards, illustrate some of the difficulties they had in disciplining themselves and others to live up to those aspirations, and depict the contrasting perspectives of Native Americans.

DOCUMENT 4–1

The Arbella *Sermon*

John Winthrop, Puritan leader of the great migration to New England and first governor of the Massachusetts Bay Colony, delivered perhaps the most famous sermon in American history in 1630 while crossing the Atlantic with his fellow Puritans aboard the Arbella. *Although Winthrop was not a minister, Puritan doctrines suffused his sermon. He put into words the Puritans' understanding of their migration to New England—the goals they hoped to achieve and the responsibilities they assumed. The sermon, the source of the following selection, bore the title "A Model of Christian Charity."*

John Winthrop
A Model of Christian Charity, 1630

A Model Hereof

God Almighty in his most holy and wise providence hath so disposed of the condition of mankind, as in all times some must be rich, some poor, some high and eminent in power and dignity, others mean and in subjection.

The Reason Hereof

First, to hold conformity with the rest of his works, being delighted to show forth the glory of his wisdom in the variety and difference of the creatures; and the glory of his power, in ordering all these differences for the preservation and good of the whole; and the glory of his greatness, that as it is the glory of princes to have many officers, so this great king will have many stewards, counting himself more honored in dispensing his gifts to man by man, than if he did it by his own immediate hands.

Secondly, that he might have the more occasion to manifest the work of his spirit: first upon the wicked in moderating and restraining them, so that the rich and mighty should not eat up the poor, nor the poor and despised rise up against their superiors and shake off their yoke; secondly in the regenerate, in exercising his graces in them, as in the great ones, their love, mercy, gentleness, temperance, etc.; in the poor and inferior sort, their faith, patience, obedience, etc.

Thirdly, that every man might have need of other, and from hence they might be all knit more nearly together in the bonds of brotherly affection. From hence it appears plainly that no man is made more honorable than another or more wealthy, etc., out of any particular and singular respect to himself, but for the glory of his creator and the common good of the creature, man. . . . All men being thus (by divine providence) ranked into two sorts, rich and poor, under the first are comprehended all such as are able to live comfortably by their own means duly improved; and all others are poor according to the former distribution.

There are two rules whereby we are to walk one towards another: justice and mercy. . . .

There is likewise a double law by which we are regulated in our conversation one towards another in both the former respects: the law of nature and the law of grace, or the moral law or the law of the gospel. . . . By the first of these laws man as he was enabled so withal [is] commanded to love his neighbor as himself. Upon this ground stands all the precepts of the moral law, which concerns our dealings with men. To apply this to the works of mercy, this law requires two things. First, that every man afford his help to another in every want or distress. Secondly, that he performed this out of the same affection which makes him careful of his own goods, according to that of our Savior. Matthew: "Whatsoever ye would that men should do to you." . . .

This law of the gospel propounds . . . [that] there is a time when a Christian must sell all and give to the poor, as they did in the Apostles' times. There is a time also when a Christian (though they give not all yet) must give beyond their ability. . . . Likewise community of perils calls for extraordinary liberality, and so doth community in some special service for the church. Lastly, when there is no other

---

From Alan Heimert and Andrew Delbanco, eds., *The Puritans in America: A Narrative Anthology* (Cambridge, MA: Harvard University Press, 1985), 82–92.

means whereby our Christian brother may be relieved in his distress, we must help him beyond our ability, rather than tempt God in putting him upon help by miraculous or extraordinary means. . . .

Having already set forth the practice of mercy according to the rule of God's law, it will be useful to lay open the grounds of it also, . . . and that is the affection from which this exercise of mercy must arise. The Apostle tells us that this love is the fulfilling of the law. . . . The way to draw men to works of mercy is not by force of argument from the goodness or necessity of the work; for though this course may enforce a rational mind to some present act of mercy, as is frequent in experience, yet it cannot work such a habit in a soul, as shall make it prompt upon all occasions to produce the same effect, but by framing these affections of love in the heart which will as natively bring forth the other, as any cause doth produce effect.

The definition which the scripture gives us of love is this: "Love is the bond of perfection." First, it is a bond or ligament. Secondly, it makes the work perfect. There is no body but consists of parts and that which knits these parts together gives the body its perfection, because it makes each part so contiguous to others as thereby they do mutually participate with each other, both in strength and infirmity, in pleasure and pain. To instance in the most perfect of all bodies: Christ and his church make one body. The several parts of this body, considered apart before they were united, were as disproportionate and as much disordering as so many contrary qualities or elements, but when Christ comes and by his spirit and love knits all these parts to himself and each to other, it is become the most perfect and best proportioned body in the world. . . .

The next consideration is how this love comes to be wrought. Adam in his first estate was a perfect model of mankind in all their generations, and in him this love was perfected in regard of habit. But Adam rent himself from his creator, rent all his posterity also one from another; whence it comes that every man is born with this principle in him, to love and seek himself only, and thus a man continueth till Christ comes and takes possession of the soul and infuseth another principle, love to God and our brother. And this latter having continual supply from Christ, as the head and root by which he is united, gets the predomining[1] in the soul, so by little and little expels the former. . . . [T]his love is the fruit of the new birth, and none can have it but the new creature. Now when this quality is thus formed in the souls of men, it works like the spirit upon the dry bones. . . . It gathers together the scattered bones, or perfect old man Adam, and knits them into one body again in Christ, whereby a man is become again a living soul.

The third consideration is concerning the exercise of this love. . . . We must take in our way that maxim of philosophy . . . , like will to like. . . . This is the cause why the Lord loves the creature, so far as it hath any of his image in it; he loves his elect because they are like himself, he beholds them in his beloved son. So a mother loves her child, because she thoroughly conceives a resemblance of herself in it. Thus it is between the members of Christ. Each discerns, by the work of the spirit, his own image and resemblance in another, and therefore cannot but love him as he loves himself. . . .

So is it in all the labor of love among Christians. The party loving, reaps love again . . . , which the soul covets more than all the wealth in the world. Thirdly,

---

[1]**predomining**: Becomes predominant.

nothing yields more pleasure and content to the soul than when it finds that which it may love fervently, for to love and live beloved is the soul's paradise, both here and in heaven. In the state of wedlock there be many comforts to bear out the troubles of that condition; but let such as have tried the most, say if there be any sweetness in that condition comparable to the exercise of mutual love. . . .

It rests now to make some application of this discourse. . . . Herein are four things to be propounded: first, the persons; secondly, the work; thirdly, the end; fourthly, the means.

First for the persons. We are a company professing ourselves fellow members of Christ, in which respect only though we were absent from each other many miles, and had our imployments as far distant, yet we ought to account ourselves knit together by this bond of love, and live in the exercise of it, if we would have comfort of our being in Christ. . . .

Secondly for the work we have in hand. It is by a mutual consent, through a special overvaluing providence and a more than an ordinary approbation of the churches of Christ, to seek out a place of cohabitation and consortship under a due form of government both civil and ecclesiastical. In such cases as this, the care of the public must oversway all private respects, by which not only conscience but mere civil policy doth bind us. For it is a true rule that particular estates cannot subsist in the ruin of the public.

Thirdly, the end is to improve our lives to do more service to the Lord; the comfort and encrease of the body of Christ whereof we are members; that ourselves and posterity may be the better preserved from the common corruptions of this evil world, to serve the Lord and work out our salvation under the power and purity of his holy ordinances.

Fourthly, for the means whereby this must be effected. They are twofold, a conformity with the work and end we aim at. These we see are extraordinary, therefore we must not content ourselves with usual ordinary means. Whatsoever we did or ought to have done when we lived in England, the same must we do, and more also, where we go. That which the most in their churches maintain as a truth in profession only, we must bring into familiar and constant practice, as in this duty of love. We must love brotherly without dissimulation; we must love one another with a pure heart fervently. We must bear one another's burthens. We must not look only on our own things, but also on the things of our brethren, neither must we think that the Lord will bear with such failings at our hands as he doth from those among whom we have lived; and that for three reasons:

First, in regard of the more near bond of marriage between him and us, wherein he hath taken us to be his after a most strict and peculiar manner, which will make him the more jealous of our love and obedience. So he tells the people of Israel, "You only have I known of all the families of the earth, therefore will I punish you for your transgressions." Secondly, because the Lord will be sanctified in them that come near him. We know that there were many that corrupted the service of the Lord, some setting up altars before his own, others offering both strange fire and strange sacrifices also. . . . Thirdly, when God gives a special commission he looks to have it strictly observed in every article. . . .

Thus stands the cause between God and us. We are entered into covenant with him for this work. We have taken out a commission, the Lord hath given us leave to draw our own articles. We have professed to enterprise these actions, upon these and those ends, we have hereupon besought him of favor and blessing.

Now if the Lord shall please to hear us, and bring us in peace to the place we desire, then hath he ratified this covenant and sealed our commission, [and] will expect a strict performance of the articles contained in it. But if we shall neglect the observation of these articles which are the ends we have propounded and, dissembling with our God, shall fall to embrace this present world and prosecute our carnal intentions, seeking great things for ourselves and our posterity, the Lord will surely break out in wrath against us, be revenged of such a perjured people, and make us know the price of the breach of such a covenant.

Now the only way to avoid this shipwreck, and to provide for our posterity, is to follow the counsel of Micah, to do justly, to love mercy, to walk humbly with our God. For this end, we must be knit together in this work as one man. We must entertain each other in brotherly affection, we must be willing to abridge ourselves of our superfluities, for the supply of others' necessities. We must uphold a familiar commerce together in all meekness, gentleness, patience, and liberality. We must delight in each other, make others' conditions our own, rejoice together, mourn together, labor and suffer together, always having before our eyes our commission and community in the work, our community as members of the same body. So shall we keep the unity of the spirit in the bond of peace. The Lord will be our God, and delight to dwell among us as his own people, and will command a blessing upon us in all our ways, so that we shall see much more of his wisdom, power, goodness, and truth, than formerly we have been acquainted with. We shall find that the God of Israel is among us, when ten of us shall be able to resist a thousand of our enemies; when he shall make us a praise and glory that men shall say of succeeding plantations, "the Lord make it like that of New England." For we must consider that we shall be as a city upon a hill. The eyes of all people are upon us, so that if we shall deal falsely with our God in this work we have undertaken, and so cause him to withdraw his present help from us, we shall be made a story and a by-word through the world. We shall open the mouths of enemies to speak evil of the ways of God, and all professors for God's sake. We shall shame the faces of many of God's worthy servants, and cause their prayers to be turned into curses upon us till we be consumed out of the good land whither we are agoing.

And to shut up this discourse with that exhortation of Moses, that faithful servant of the Lord, in his last farewell to Israel, Deuteronomy 30: Beloved, there is now set before us life and good, death and evil, in that we are commanded this day to love the Lord our God, and to love one another, to walk in his ways and to keep his commandments and his ordinance and his laws, and the articles of our covenant with him, that we may live and be multiplied, and that the Lord our God may bless us in the land whither we go to possess it. But if our hearts shall turn away, so that we will not obey, but shall be seduced, and worship other gods, our pleasures and profits, and serve them; it is propounded unto us this day, we shall surely perish out of the good land whither we pass over this vast sea to possess it.

Therefore let us choose life, that we and our seed may live by obeying his voice and cleaving to him, for he is our life and our prosperity.

QUESTIONS FOR READING AND DISCUSSION

1. What goals did Winthrop set for the migrants to New England? How did Puritan faith shape those goals? What was the significance of the "covenant" between God and Puritans?

2. Why, according to Winthrop, was migration to New England important? What was at stake for the migrants, for the new colony, for England, and for Christianity? What did he mean that New England "shall be as a city upon a hill"?

3. Did Winthrop envision a society dedicated to human equality or inequality? How should people demonstrate that "Love is the bond of perfection"?

4. How were Puritans different from other people, according to Winthrop? How did he think they should manifest their distinctive responsibilities? How did he think they should act toward people who were not Puritans or Christians?

DOCUMENT 4–2

Observations of New England Indians

Puritan minister Roger Williams arrived in Boston in 1631 and preached there, in Salem, and in Plymouth before being banished from Massachusetts in 1635 and taking up residence in what would become Providence, Rhode Island. In both Plymouth and Providence, Williams spent considerable time among Indians. While sailing back to England in 1643, he wrote a dictionary of New England Indian words, including numerous observations—excerpted here—of Indian customs and beliefs. An unusually perceptive observer, Williams noted Native American traits that caught his eye, revealing his Puritan viewpoint as well as the intricacies of the encounters between Indians and English colonists. Most colonists were far less willing than Williams to try to learn Indians' languages or to understand their cultures.

Roger Williams
A Key into the Language of America, 1643

The Natives are of two sorts, (as the English are.) Some more Rude and Clownish, who are not so apt to Salute, but upon *Salutation* resalute lovingly. Others, and the generall, are *sober* and *grave*, and yet chearfull in a meane, and as ready to begin a Salutation as to Resalute, which yet the English generally begin, out of desire to Civilize them. . . . There is a savour of *civility* and *courtesie* even amongst these wild Americans, both amongst *themselves* and towards *strangers*. . . .

Whomsoever commeth in when they are eating, they offer them to eat of that which they have, though but little enough prepar'd for themselves. If any provision of *fish* or *flesh* come in, they make their neighbours partakers with them.

If any stranger come in, they presently give him to eate of what they have; many a time, and at all times of the night (as I have fallen in travell upon their houses) when nothing hath been ready, have themselves and their wives, risen to prepare me some refreshing. . . . It is a strange *truth*, that a man shall generally finde more free entertainment and refreshing amongst these *Barbarians*, then amongst thousands that call themselves *Christians*. . . .

From Roger Williams, *A Key into the Language of America* (London: Gregory Dexter, 1643), eds. John J. Teunissen and Evelyn J. Hinz (Detroit: Wayne State University Press, 1973).

Having no Letter nor Arts, 'tis admirable how quick they are in casting [tallying] up great numbers, with the helpe of graines of Corne, instead of *Europes* pens or counters. . . .

Their *affections*, especially to their children, are very strong; so that I have knowne a *Father* take so grievously the losse of his *childe*, that hee hath cut and stob'd himselfe with *griefe* and *rage*.

This extreme *affection*, together with want of *learning*, makes ther children sawcie, bold, and undutifull.

I once came into a *house*, and requested some *water* to drinke; the *father* bid his sonne (of some 8. yeeres of age) to fetch some *water*: the *boy* refused, and would not stir; I told the *father*, that I would correct my *child*, if he should so disobey me, &c. Upon this the *father* took up a sticke, the *boy* another, and flew at his *father*: upon my perswasion, the poore *father* made him smart a little, throw down his stick, and run for *water*, and the *father* confessed the benefit of *correction*, and the evill of their too indugent *affections*. . . .

They are as full of businesse, and as impatient of hinderance (in their kind) as any Merchant in *Europe*. . . .

Whence they call *English-men* Chauquaquock, that is, *Knive-men*, stone formerly being to them in stead of *Knives*, *Awle-blades*, *Hatchets* and *Howes*. . . .

It is almost incredible what burthens the poore women carry of *Corne*, of *Fish*, of *Beanes*, of *Mats*, and a childe besides. . . .

Yet some cut their haire round, and some as low and as short as the sober *English*; yet I never saw any so to forget nature it selfe in such excessive length and monstrous fashion, as to the shame of the *English* Nation, I now (with griefe) see my Country-men in *England* are degenerated into. . . .

Mowêsu, & Sukêsu, [their words for] *Blacke*, or *swarfish*. . . . Hence they call a *Blackamore* (themselves are tawnie, by the Sunne and their annoyntings, yet they are borne white:)

Suckáutacone, [their word for] *A cole blacke man*. For, *Sucki* is black, and *Waûtacone*, one that weares clothes, whence *English*, *Dutch*, *French*, *Scotch*, they call *Wautaconâuog*, or *Coatmen*. . . .

Nature knowes no difference between *Europe* and *Americans* in blood, birth, bodies, &c. God having of one blood made all mankind . . . and all by nature being children of wrath. . . .

Their desire of, and delight in newes, is great, as the *Athenians*, and all men, more or lesse; a stranger that can relate newes in their owne language, they will stile him *Manittóo*, a God. . . .

Their manner is upon any tidings to sit round, double or treble, or more, as their numbers be; I have seene neer a thousand in a round, where *English* could not well neere halfe so many have sitten: Every man hath his pipe of their *Tobacco*, and a depe silence they make, and attention give to him that speaketh; and many of them will deliver themselves, either in a relation of news, or in a consultation, with very emphaticall speech and great action, commonly an houre, and sometimes two houres together. . . .

As one answered me when I had discoursed about many points of God, of the creation, of the soule, of the danger of it, and the saving of it, he assented; but when I spake of the rising againe of the body, he cryed out, I shall never believe this. . . .

Canounicus, the old high *Sachim* of the *Nariganset Bay* (a wise and peacable Prince) once in a solemne Oration to my selfe, in a solemne assembly . . . said, I have never suffered any wrong to be offered to the *English* since they landed; nor never will: he often repeated this . . . if the *Englishman* speake true, if hee meane truly, then shall I goe to my grave in peace, and hope that the *English* and my posteritie shall live in love and peace together. I replied, that he had no cause (as I hoped) to question *Englishmans* . . . faithfulnesse, he having had long experience of their friendlinesse and trustinesse. He tooke a sticke, and broke it into ten pieces, and related ten instances (laying downe a sticke to every instance) which gave him cause thus to feare and say; I satisfied him in some presently, and presented the rest to the Governours of the *English*, who, I hope, will be far from giving just cause to have *Barbarians* to question their . . . faithfulnesse. . . .

This question they oft put to me: Why come the *Englishmen* hither? and measuring others by themselves; they say, It is because you want *firing*[1] for they, having burnt up the *wood* in one place, (wanting draughts[2] to bring *wood* to them) they are faine [willing] to follow the *wood*; and so to remove to a fresh new place for the *woods* sake. . . .

I have heard of many *English* lost, and have oft been lost my selfe, and my selfe and others have often been found, and succoured by the *Indians*. . . .

They are joyfull in meeting of any in travell, and will strike fire either with stones or sticks, to take Tobacco, and discourse a little together. . . .

The *Indians* having abundance of these sorts of Foule [ducks] upon their waters, take great pains to kill any of them with their Bow and Arrowes; and are marvellous desirous of our *English* Guns, powder, and shot (though they are wisely and generally denied by the *English*) yet with those which they get from the *French*, and some others (*Dutch* and *English*) they kill abundance of Fowle, being naturally excellent marks-men; and also more hardened to endure the weather, and wading, lying, and creeping on the ground, &c.

I once saw an exercise of training of the *English*, when all the *English* had mist the mark set up to shoot at, an *Indian* with his owne Peece (desiring leave to shoot) onely hit it. . . .

The *Natives* are very exact and punctuall in the bounds of their Lands, belonging to this or that Prince or People, (even to a River, Brooke &c.) And I have knowne them make bargaine and sale amongst themselves for a small piece, or quanitity of Ground: notwithstanding a sinfull opinion amongst many that Christians have right to *Heathens* Lands. . . .

The Women set or plant, weede, and hill, and gather and barne [store] all the corne, and Fruites of the field: Yet sometimes the man himselfe, (either out of love to his Wife, or care for his Children, or being an old man) will help the Woman which (by the custome of the Countrey) they are not bound to.

When a field is to be broken up, they have a very loving sociable speedy way to dispatch it: All the neighbours men and Women forty, fifty, a hundred &c, joyne, and come in to help freely.

With friendly joyning they breake up their fields, build their Forts, hunt the Woods, stop and kill fish in the Rivers, it being true with them as in all the World in the Affaires of Earth or Heaven: By concord little things grow great, by discord the greatest come to nothing. . . .

They have a two-fold nakednesse:

First ordinary and constant, when although they have a Beasts skin, or an English mantle on, yet that covers ordinarily but their hinder parts and all the

---

[1]**want *firing***: Lack firewood.
[2]**draughts**: Sleds or conveyances.

foreparts from top to toe, (except their secret parts, covered with a little Apron, after the patterne of their and our first Parents) I say all else open and naked.

Their male children goe starke naked, and have no Apron untill they come to ten or twelve yeeres of age; their Female they, in a modest blush cover with a little Apron of an hand breadth from their very birth.

Their second nakednesse is when their men often abroad, and both men and women within doores, leave off their beasts skin, or English cloth, and so (excepting their little Apron) are wholly naked; yet but few of the women but will keepe their skin or cloth (though loose) neare to them ready to gather it up about them.

Custome hath used their minds and bodies to it, and in such a freedom from any wantonesse, that I have never seen that wantonesses amongst them, as, (with griefe) I have heard of in *Europe*. . . .

Our English clothes are so strange unto them, and their bodies inured so to indure the weather, that when (upon gift &c.) some of them have had *English* cloathes, yet in a showre of raine, I have seen them rather expose their skins to the wet then their cloaths, and therefore pull them off, and keep them drie. . . .

While they are amongst the *English* they keep on the *English* apparell, but pull of all, as soone as they come againe into their owne Houses, and Company. . . . He that questions whether God made the World, the Indians will teach him. I must acknowledge I have received in my converse with them many Confirmations of those two great points. . . .

1. That God is.

2. That hee is a rewarder of all them that diligently seek him.

They will generally confesse that God made all: but then in speciall, although they deny not that *English-mans* God made *English* Men, and the Heavens and Earth there! yet their Gods made them, and the Heaven and Earth where they dwell. . . .

But herein is their Misery.

First they branch their God-head into many Gods.

Secondly, attribute it to Creatures. . . .

Even as the Papists[3] have their He and Shee Saint Protectors as St. *George*, St. *Patrick*, St. *Denis*, Virgin *Mary*, &c. . . .

I confesse to have most of these their customes by their owne Relation, for after once being in their Houses and beholding what their Worship was, I durst never bee an eye witnesse, Spectatour, or looker on, least I should have been partaker of Sathans Inventions and Worships. . . .

After I had (as farre as my language would reach) discoursed (upon a time) before the chiefe *Sachim* or *Prince* of the Countrey, with his *Archpriests*, and many others in a full Assembly; and being night, wearied with travell and discourse, I lay downe to rest; and before I slept, I heard this passage:

A[n] . . . Indian (who had heard our discourse) told the *Sachim*. . . . that soules went [not] up to Heaven, or downe to Hell; For, saith he, Our fathers have told us, that our soules goe to the *Southwest*.

The *Sachim* answered, But how doe you know your selfe, that your soules goe to the *Southwest*; did you ever see a soule goe thither?

The Native replyed; when did he (naming my selfe) see a soule goe to Heaven or Hell?

---

[3]**Papists**: Roman Catholics.

The *Sachim* agine replied: He hath books and writings, and one which God himselfe made, concerning mens soules, and therefore may well know more then wee that have none, but take all upon trust from our forefathers. . . .

I could never discerne that excesse of scandalous sins amongst them, which *Europe* aboundeth with. Drunkennesse and gluttony, generally they know not what sinnes they be; and although they have not so much to restraine them (both in respect of knowledge of God and Lawes of Men) as the *English* have, yet a man shall never heare of such crimes amongst them of robberies, murthers, adulteries, &c as amongst the *English*. . . .

The *Indians* bring downe all their sorts of Furs, which they take in the Countrey, both to the *Indians* and to the *English* for this *Indian Money*:[4] this Money the *English, French*, and *Dutch*, trade to the Indians, six hundred miles in severall parts (North and South from *New-England*) for their Furres, and whatsoever they stand in need of from them: as Corne, Venison, &c. . . .

This one fathom of this their stringed money, now worth of the English but five shillings (sometimes more) some few yeeres since was worth nine, and sometimes ten shillings *per* Fathome: the fall is occasioned by the fall of Beaver in *England*: the Natives are very impatient, when for English commodities they pay so much more of their money, and not understanding the cause of it; and many say the English cheat and deceive them, though I have laboured to make them understand the reason of it. . . .

Who ever deale or trade with them, had need of Wisedom, Patience, and Faithfulnesse in dealing: for they frequently say . . . you lye . . . you deceive me. . . .

O the infinite wisedome of the most holy wise *God*, who hath so advanced *Europe*, above *America*, that there is not a sorry *Howe, Hatchet, Knife*, nor a rag of cloth in all *America*, but what comes over the dreadfull *Atlantick* Ocean from *Europe*: and yet that *Europe* be not proud, nor *America* discouraged. What treasures are hid in some parts of *America*, and in our *New-English* parts, how have foule hands (in smoakie houses) the first handling of those Furres which are after worne upon the hands of Queens and heads of Princes?

QUESTIONS FOR READING AND DISCUSSION

1. What made Indians "barbarians," according to Williams? What standard of comparison did he use, and why?

2. How did Williams think Indians compared to the English? Did Williams believe English colonists mistreated Indians?

3. According to Williams, what did Indians think about English settlers? What did their word for a "cole blacke man" reveal about their notion of racial differences? What did the overheard conversation about the destination of souls reveal about Indian assessments of colonists?

4. In what ways did Williams's religious ideas influence his observations? What did he mean by saying that the source of the Indians' "misery" was that "they branch their God-head into many Gods. . . . [and] attribute it to Creatures . . . even as the Papists have their He and Shee Saint Protectors"?

5. If Indians had written observations of Puritans like Williams, what might they have noticed?

---

[4]***Indian Money***: Wampum, a string of beads made from whelk or quahog shells.

DOCUMENT 4–3

Wampanoag Grievances at the Outset of King Philip's War

In 1675, John Easton, the deputy governor of Rhode Island, met with the Wampanoag leader Metacom, whom the English colonists called King Philip, in an attempt to avoid full-scale war between the colonists and the Indians. Easton, a Quaker whose religious beliefs had caused his family to be expelled from Massachusetts, explained the Indians' complaints against the colonists in a private letter to the governor of New York, excerpted below. Easton's letter, which was not published until 1858, offers a rare and relatively dispassionate account of the Indians' perspectives on the growth and development of the New England colonies during the seventeenth century, and of the circumstances that precipitated war.

John Easton
A Relation of the Indian War, 1675

A true relation of what I know and of reports, and my understanding concerning the beginning and progress of the war now between the English and the Indians. . . .

For 40 years . . . reports and jealousies of war had been so very frequent that we did not think that now a war was breaking forth; but about a week before it did we had cause to think it would. Then to endeavor to prevent it, we sent a man to [King] Philip to say that if he would come to . . . [meet with us] we would come . . . to speak with him. . . . Philip called his council and agreed to come to us; he came himself unarmed and about 40 of his men armed. Then 5 of us went over; three were magistrates. We sat very friendly together. We told him our business was to endeavor that they might not receive or do wrong. They said that was well—they had done no wrong, the English wronged them. We said we knew the English said the Indians wronged them and the Indians said the English wronged them, but our desire was the quarrel might rightly be decided in the best way, and not as dogs decided their quarrels. The Indians owned that fighting was the worst way; then they propounded how right might take place, we said by arbitration. They said all English agreed against them, and so by arbitration they had had much wrong, many miles square of land so taken from them; for English would have English arbitrators, and once they [the Indians] were persuaded to give in their arms, that thereby jealousy might be removed, and the English having their arms would not deliver them as they had promised, until they consented to pay a 100 pounds [currency], and now they had not so much land or money, that they were as good to be killed as to leave all their livelihood. . . .

We . . . said to them when in war against the English[,] blood was spilt that engaged all Englishmen, for we were to be all under one king. We knew what their complaints would be, and in our colony [Rhode Island] had removed some of them [their complaints] in sending for Indian rulers . . . [when] the crime con-

---

From John Easton, "A Relation of the Indian War" in *Narratives of the Indian Wars, 1675–1699*, ed. Charles Henry Linoln (New York: Charles Scribner's Sons, 1913), 2–13. Ed. Paul Royster, 2006.

cerned Indians' lives, which they very lovingly accepted, and agreed with us to their execution, and said so they were able to satisfy their subjects when they knew an Indian suffered duly, but [they] said in whatever was only between their Indians and not in townships that we had purchased, they would not have us prosecute [Indians], and that they had a great fear lest any of their Indians should be called or forced to be Christian Indians. They said that such were in everything more mischievous, only dissemblers [pretenders], and that then the English made them [Christian Indians] not subject to their own [Indian] kings, and by their lying to wrong their kings. We knew it to be true, and we promising them that however in government to Indians all should be alike and that we knew it was our king's will it should be so. . . .

But Philip charged it to be dishonesty in us to put off the hearing of their complaints; and therefore we consented to hear them. They said they had been the first in doing good to the English, and the English the first in doing wrong; they said when the English first came, their king's father was as a great man and the English as a little child. He constrained other Indians from wronging the English and gave them corn and showed them how to plant and was free to do them any good and had let them have a 100 times more land than now the king [of the Indians] had for his own people. But their king's brother, when he was king, came miserably to die by being forced into [the English colonists'] court and, as they judged, poisoned. And another grievance was if 20 of their honest Indians testified that a Englishman had done them wrong, it was as nothing; and if but one of their worst Indians testified against any Indian or their king when it pleased the English, that was sufficient. Another grievance was when their kings sold land the English would say it [the land sold] was more than they [the Indian kings] agreed to and a writing must be proof against all them, and some of their kings had done wrong to sell so much that he left his people none, and some being given to drunkenness, the English made them drunk and then cheated them in bargains, but now their [Indian] kings were forewarned not to part with land for nothing in comparison to the value thereof. Now whomever the English had once owned [recognized] for [the Indians'] king or queen, they [the English] would later disinherit, and make another king that would give or sell them [the English] their [the Indians'] land, that now they had no hopes left to keep any land. Another grievance was that the English cattle and horses still increased so that when they removed 30 miles from where the English had anything to do, they could not keep their corn from being spoiled, they never being used to fence, and thought that when the English bought land of them that they [the English] would have kept their cattle upon their own land. Another grievance was that the English were so eager to sell the Indians liquors that most of the Indians spent all in drunkenness and then ravened upon [plundered] the sober Indians and, they did believe, often did hurt the English cattle, and their [Indian] kings could not prevent it. We knew beforehand that these were their grand complaints, but then we only endeavored to persuade them that all complaints might be righted without war, . . . that they should lay down their arms, for the English were too strong for them. They said, then the English should do to them as they [the Indians] did when they were too strong for the English. . . .

In this time some Indians fell to pilfering some houses that the English had left, and an old man and a lad going to one of those houses did see 3 Indians run out thereof. The old man bid the young man shoot, so he did, and an Indian fell down but got away again. It is reported that then some Indians came to the garrison and asked why they shot the Indian. They [the English] asked whether he was dead. The Indians said yea. An English lad said it was no matter. The men endeavored to inform them it was but an idle lad's words, but the Indians in haste went away and did not harken to them. The next day the lad that shot the Indian and his father and five more English were killed; so the war began with Philip. . . .

After the English army, without our consent or informing us, came into our colony [Rhode Island], they brought the Narragansett Indians to articles of agreement with them. Philip being fled, about 150 Indians came in to a Plymouth garrison voluntarily. The Plymouth authorities sold all but about six of them for slaves, to be carried out of the country. It is true the Indians generally are very barbarous people, but in this war I have not heard of their tormenting any; but that the English army caught an old Indian and tormented him. He was well known to have been for a long time a very decrepit and harmless Indian. . . .

The English were jealous that there was a general plot of all Indians against the English, and the Indians were in like manner jealous of the English. I think it was general that they were unwilling to be wronged and that the Indians do judge the English to be partial against them. . . .

I having often informed the Indians that English men would not begin a war otherwise, it was brutish so to do. I am sorry that the Indians have cause to think me deceitful, for the English thus began the war with the Narragansetts after we had sent off our Island many Indians and informed them, if they kept by the watersides and did not meddle, that the English would do them no harm; although it was also not safe for us to let them live here. The army first took all those prisoners, then fell upon the Indian houses, burned them, and killed some men. The war began without proclamation; and some of our people did not know the English had begun mischief to the Indians, and being confident and having cause to be so, believed that the Indians would not hurt them before the English began. So they did not keep their garrison exactly. But the Indians, having received that mischief, came unexpectedly upon them and destroyed 145 of them beside other great loss. But the English army commanders . . . sold the Indians that they had taken . . . for slaves, except for one old man that was carried off our Island upon his son's back. He was so decrepit he could not go, and when the army took them, his son upon his back carried him to the garrison. Some [English colonists] would have had him devoured by dogs, but the tenderness of some of them prevailed to cut off his head. And afterwards they came suddenly upon the Indians where the Indians had prepared to defend themselves, and so received and did much mischief. And for about six weeks since, the time has been spent by both parties to recruit; and now the English army is out to seek after the Indians, but it is most likely that those most able to do mischief will escape, and the women and children and impotent may be destroyed; and so the most able will have the less encumbrance to doing mischief.

But I am confident it would be best for English and Indians that a peace were made upon honest terms for each to have a due propriety and to enjoy it without oppression or usurpation by one to the other. But the English dare not trust the Indians' promises; neither the Indians to the English's promises; and each has great cause therefore. . . . It has always been a principle in our Colony that there should be but one supreme authority for Englishmen both in our native country and wherever English have jurisdiction; and so we know that no English should begin a war and not first offer for the king to be umpire, and not persecute those that will not conform to their worship, even if their worship be what is not owned by the king. . . .

I am persuaded that New England's priests are so blinded by the spirit of persecution and anxious to have their hire [salaries] and to have more room to be mere hirelings, that they have been the cause that the law of nations and the law of arms have been violated in this war, and that the war would not have been started if there had not been a hireling who, for his management of what he calls the gospel, to have it spread by violence, and to have his gain from his quarters paid for; and if any magistrates are unwilling to act as their pack horses, they will be trumpeting for innovation or war.

QUESTIONS FOR READING AND DISCUSSION

1. According to Easton, what "grand complaints" did Philip and his supporters express? Did Easton believe these grievances were justified?

2. What did Easton mean by saying that the conflicts between the Indians and the English colonists should not be settled "as dogs decided their quarrels"? How should they be decided, according to Easton and to the Indians?

3. What did the Indians mean by saying that "the English should do to them as they [the Indians] did when they were too strong for the English"?

4. Easton wrote that "the Indians generally are very barbarous people." Did he consider all Indians barbarous? Did he think the English colonists were barbarous?

5. Easton concluded that "the English dare not trust the Indians' promises; neither the Indians to the English's promises; and each has great cause therefore." To what extent did he believe "the spirit of persecution" and greed of "New England's priests" contributed to this mutual mistrust?

DOCUMENT 4–4

A Provincial Government Enacts Legislation

In December 1682 William Penn, the proprietor of Pennsylvania, assembled the colony's first legislature, which enacted seventy-one specific laws for the colony, excerpted here. They indicate the most important concerns of Penn and the legislators as they contemplated the kind of society they sought to build and govern. The laws illustrate Pennsylvania's distinctive relationship between religion and government, between sacred and secular authority, and between the proprietor and the colonists.

The Laws of Pennsylvania, 1682

Whereas the Glory of Almighty God and the Good of Mankind is the Reason and End of Government and therefore Government in it selfe is a Venerable ordinance of God and for as much as it is principally desired and intended by the Proprietary and Governor [William Penn] and the Freemen of the Province of Pennsilvania and Territorys thereunto Belonging to Make and Establish Such

---

From "The Great Law Or the Body of Laws of the Province of Pennsilvania and territorys thereunto Belonging past at an Assemble at Chester alias Upland the 7th day of the 10th Month December 1682," Record Group 26, Records of the Department of State, Pennsylvania State Archives.

Laws as shall best preserve true Christian and Civill Liberty in Opposition to all UnChristian Licentious and Unjust Practices whereby God may have his Due Caesar his Due and the People their Due from Tyranny and Oppression on the One Side of Insolency & Licentiousness on the Other So that the best and firmist Foundation may be Laid for the Present and future happiness . . . Be it therefore Enacted. . . .

Chapter 1 Almighty God being only Lord of Conscience Father of Lights & Spirits and the Author as well as Object of all divine Knowledge Faith and Worship who only can Enlighten the Mind and perswade and Convince the Understanding of People in Due Reverance to his Soveraingty over the Souls of Mankind it is Enacted . . . that no Person now or at Any time hereafter Liveing in this Province who Shall Confess and acknowledge one Almighty God to be the Creatour Upholder and Ruler of the World and that professeth him or herselfe Obliged in Conscience to Live Peaceably and Justly under the Civill Government shall in any case be Molested or Prejudiced for his or her Conscientious Perswasion or Practice nor shall he or she at any time be Compelled to frequent or Maintaine any Religious Worshipp place or Ministry whatever Contrary to his or her mind but shall freely and fully Enjoy his or her Christian Liberty without any Interuption or reflection and if any Person shall abuse or deride any Other for his or her Diferant Perswasion and Practice in Matters of Religion Such shall be Lookt upon as a disturber of the Peace and be punished accordingly But to the End that Looseness Irreligion & Ath[e]ism may not creep in under pretence of Conscience in this Province Be it further Enacted . . . that according to the Example of the Primitive Christians and for the Ease of the Creation Every first day of the Week called the Lords day People Shall Abstaine from their Usuall and Common Toyle & Labour that Wheather Masters Parents Children or Servants they may the Better dispose themselves to read the Scriptures of truth at home or frequent such Meetings of Religious Worship abroad as may best Sute their Respective Perswasions.

Chapter 2 . . . all Officers & Persons Commissionated and Imployed in the Service of the Government of this Province and all Members and Deputys Elected to Serve in Assembly thereof and all that have Right to Elect such deputies shall be Such as profess and Declare they Believe in Jesus Christ to be the Son of God the Savior of the World and that are not Convicted of ill fame or Unsober and Dishonest Conversation and that are of One and Twenty Years of age at Least.

Chapter 3 . . . that whosoever shall Swear in their Conversation by the Name of God or Christ or Jesus being Legally Convicted thereof shall pay for Every Such offence five Shillings or Suffer five days Imprisonment in the house of Correction at hard Labour to the behoof of the Publike and be fed with bread and Water only during that time. . . .

Chapter 6 . . . whosoever Shall in their Conversation at any time curse himselfe or an Other or any thing belonging to himselfe or any other and is Legally Convicted thereof Shall pay for Every Such offence five Shillings or Suffer five days Imprisonment as aforesaid. . . .

Chapter 9 . . . whosoever defileth the Marriage bed by Lying with an other Woman or Man then [than] their own wife or husband being Legally Convicted thereof Shall for the first offence be publikely Whipt and Suffer one Whole years Imprisonment in the house of Correction at hard Labour to the behoofe of the Publick and Longer if the Chief Magistrate See meet and both he and the Woman shall be Liable to a bill of Divorsement if required by the greived husband or Wife within the Said terme of One whole Year after Conviction and for the Second offence imprisonment in Manner aforesaid during Life and if the Party with whom the husband or Wife shall defile their bedds be unmarried for the first offence they shall Suffer half a years Imprisonment in the Manner aforesaid and for the Second offence Imprisonment for Life. . . .

Chapter 11 . . . if any Person shall be Legally Convicted of the Unnaturall Sin of Sodomy or Joyning with beasts such persons shall be whipt and forfeit one third part of his or her Estate and worke Six months in the house o[f] Correction at hard Labour and for the Second offence Imprisonment as aforesaid during Life.

Chapter 12 . . . whosoever shall be Legally Convicted of a Rape or Ravishment that is forsing A Maid Widdow or Wife shall forfeit one third of his Estate to the Parent of the Said Maid and for want of a Parent to the Said Maid and if a Widdow to the Said Widdow and if a Wife to the husband and the Said party be Whipt and Suffer a Years Imprisonment in the house of Correction at hard Labour and for the Second offence Imprisonment in manner aforesaid during Life.

Chapter 13 . . . whosoever shall be Convicted of Uncleanness or the Commission of fornication that is if any Single Man shall defile a Single Woman they Shall Suffer three Months Imprisonment in the house of Correction at hard Labour and after the Expiration of the Said terme Shall take one an Other in Marriage & Live as Man and Wife together but if the Man be Married he shall forfeit one third of his Estate and both be Imprisoned as aforesaid and be it Enacted by the Authority aforesaid that Whoso Ever Shall be Convicted of Speaking an Unclean Word shall for Every Such offence pay one Shilling or Sit in the Stocks two houres. . . .

Chapter 15 . . . Every Person disordering and abusing himselfe with drinke unto drunkenness being Legally Convicted thereof shall for the first time pay five Shillings or Worke five dayes in the house of Correction at hard Labour and be fed only with bread and water and for the Second offence and Ever after tenn Shillings or ten days Labour. . . .

Chapter 17 . . . if any Person shall drinke healths which may provoke people to unnecessary and Excessive drinking being Legally convicted thereof shall for Every Such offence forfeit five shillings and whosoever shall pledge the same Shall be Lyable to the Same punishment.

Chapter 18 . . . And whereas divers Persons as English Dutch Sweeds &ct have been wont to Sell to the Indians Rum and Brandy and Such Like Distilled Spirrits though they know the Said Indians are not able to Govern themselves in the use their of but do commonly drinke of it to Such Excess as makes them Sometimes to Destroy one another and Grievously anoy and disquiet the People of this Province and Peradventure those of Neighbouring Governments whereby they make the poore Natives worse and not better for their coming among them which is an heinous offence to God and a Reproach to the Blessed name of Christ and his Holy Religion It is therefore Enacted . . . that no Person within this Province do from henseforth presume to Sell or Exchange any Rum or Brandy or any Other Strong Liquors at any time to any Indian within this Province and if any one shall offend therein the Person Convicted thereof Shall for Every Such offence pay five pounds.

Chapter 19 . . . whosoEver be convicted of Wilfully firing of any Mans house warehouse Outhouse Barnes Stacks or Ricks of corne Vessells or boats in any part of this Province or Territory thereunto Annexed Every such offender shall be Lyable to make Satisfaction double the Vallue and suffer Imprisonment for one year in the house of Correction and bear Such Corporall punishment as shall be

Inflicted by the Court of Justice of that County where the party offending hath Committed the fact. . . .

Chapter 23 . . . if any persons to the Number of three shall meet together with Clubbs Staves or any other hurtful Weapon to the terror of any of the Peaceable People of this Province and Comitt or Designe to Comitt any Violence or Injury upon the person or goods of any of the Said Inhabitants and be Convicted thereof they shall be Reputed and Punisht as Rioters and that act of Terror and Violence or Design of Violence accounted a Riot.

Chapter 24 . . . whosoEver shall assault or Menace a parent and shall be duly proved Guilty thereof shall be Committed to the house of Correction and their [there] remaine at hard Labour during the pleasure of the Said Parent.

Chapter 25 . . . if any Person shall assault or Menace a Magistrate and be Duly convicted thereof he shall be fined according to the Nature of the fact and be Comitted to the house of Correction at hard Labour for One Month after Conviction.

Chapter 26 . . . if any Servant assault or Menace his or her Master or Mistress and be Convicted thereof shall be punisht at the Discretion of Two Justices of the Peace so it be Suteable to the Nature of the offence. . . .

Chapter 28 . . . whosoEver shall challenge an other Person to fight he that Challengeth and he that accepteth the Challenge shall for Every Such offence pay five pounds or Suffer three Months Imprisonment in the house of Correction at hard Labour.

Chapter 29 . . . whosoEver shall introduce into this Province or frequent Such rude and Riotus Sports & practices as Prized or Stage Plays Masks Revells Bulbaits Cock fightings with such Like being convicted thereof shall be reputed and fined as Breakers of the Peace and Suffer at Least tenn days Imprisonment in the house of Correction at hard Labour or forfeit twenty Shillings.

Chapter 30 . . . if any Person be Convicted of Playing at Cards Dice Lotterys or Such Like Enticing Vaine and Evill Sports and Games Such persons shall for Every Such offence pay five shillings or suffer five Days imprisonment at hard Labour in the House of Correction. . . .

Chapter 33 . . . all Scandalous and Malicious reporters Defamers and Spreaders of false News whether against Magistrates or Private Persons being convicted thereof Shall be accordingly Severely punisht as Enemys to the Peace & Concord of the Province. . . .

Chapter 57 . . . there shall be a Registry for all Servants where theire Names time Wages and days of freedom or Payment Shall be Registered.

Chapter 58 . . . Servants Shall not be kept Longer than their time and Such as are Carefull shall Be boath Justly and Kindly Used in their Service and put in fitting Equipage at the Expiration thereof according to Custom and Such as Runaway and Serve not their time when Caught shall serve twice the time he or she was absent and pay the Charges or Serve out the Vallue after their time is Expired and if any Master abuse his Servant on Complaint to the next Justices of the Peace he shall take Care to redress the Said Grieveance. . . .

Chapter 67 And to the End that it may be knowne who those are that in this Province and territorys thereunto belonging have Right of freemen to Chuse or to be Chosen and with the Proprietary and Governor make and Enact Laws that Every Inhabitant of the said Province and Territorys thereunto Annexed that is or Shall be a purchase of one hundred Acres of Land and hath seated the Same his Heirs and Assignes and Every person who Shall have paid his passage and taken up his fifty Acres of Land and Seated the Same and every inhabitant Artificer or Other Resident in the Said Province that payeth Scott and Lott [a tax] to the Government Shall be Deemed and accounted A freeman of this Province and territorie thereof and Such only Shall have Rights of Election or being Elected to any Service in the Government thereof. . . .

Chapter 70 And be it further Enacted by the Authority aforesaid that the Laws of this Province from time to time shall be publisht & Printed that Every Person may have the Knowlege thereof and they shall be one of the books taught in the Schooles of this Province and Territorys thereof. . . .

QUESTIONS FOR READING AND DISCUSSION

1. According to the laws of Pennsylvania, what was the relationship between religion and the government of the colony? To what degree did the laws provide religious freedom? Religious tolerance?

2. What forms of disorder concerned the lawmakers, judging from the laws in this excerpt? How did the laws seek to punish or control disorder?

3. According to the laws, what were the proper relations between men and women, husbands and wives, parents and children, masters and servants, colonists and Indians, and freemen and the government?

4. How did the laws provide that "God may have his Due Caesar his Due and the People their Due from Tyranny and Oppression on the One Side of Insolency & Licentiousness on the Other"?

DOCUMENT 4–5

Words of the Bewitched

New Englanders believed that witches were capable of using their occult powers to cause bad things to happen to people. Usually, they believed, witches were in league with the devil, who used them as his agents to cause havoc. During the seventeenth century, approximately three hundred New Englanders were accused in court of being witches, about four-fifths of them women. The largest and most famous outbreak of witchcraft accusations occurred at Salem in 1692. The prominent Puritan minister Cotton Mather summarized the testimony against some of the accused witches in his book Wonders of the Invisible World *(1692), the source of the following testimony against Bridget Bishop. Bishop was a married, middle-aged woman; both she and her husband were church members. Eight days after her trial, she was executed by hanging.*

Cotton Mather

Testimony against Accused Witch Bridget Bishop, 1692

The trial of Bridget Bishop . . . at the Court of Oyer and Terminer held at Salem, June 2, 1692.

From Cotton Mather, *Wonders of the Invisible World* (1692), in *Witch-Hunting in Seventeenth-Century New England: A Documentary History, 1638–1692*, ed. David D. Hall (Boston: Northeastern University Press, 1991), 296–301.

I. She was indicted for bewitching of several persons in the neighborhood, the indictment being drawn up, according to the form in such cases usual. And pleading, not guilty, there were brought in several persons, who had long undergone many kinds of miseries, which were preternaturally inflicted, and generally ascribed unto a horrible witchcraft. There was little occasion to prove the witchcraft; it being evident and notorious to all beholders. Now to fix the witchcraft on the prisoner at the bar, the first thing used was, the testimony of the bewitched; whereof, several testified, that the shape of the prisoner did oftentimes very grievously pinch them, choke them, bite them, and afflict them; urging them to write their names in a book, which the said specter called, ours. One of them did further testify, that it was the shape of this prisoner, with another, which one day took her from her [spinning] wheel, and carrying her to the riverside, threatened there to drown her, if she did not sign to the book mentioned: which yet she refused. Others of them did also testify, that the said shape, did in her threats, brag to them, that she had been the death of sundry persons, then by her named; that she had ridden a man, then likewise named. Another testified, the apparition of ghosts unto the specter of Bishop, crying out, you murdered us! About the truth whereof, there was in the matter of fact, but too much suspicion.

II. It was testified, that at the examination of the prisoner, before the magistrates, the bewitched were extremely tortured. If she did but cast her eyes on them, they were presently struck down; and this in such a manner as there could be no collusion in the business. But upon the touch of her hand upon them, when they lay in their swoons, they would immediately revive; and not upon the touch of anyone's else. Moreover, upon some special actions of her body, as the shaking of her head, or the turning of her eyes, they presently and painfully fell into the like postures. . . .

IV. One Deliverance Hobbs, who had confessed her being a witch, was now tormented by the specters, for her confession. And she now testified, that this Bishop, tempted her to sign the book again, and to deny what she had confessed. She affirmed, that it was the shape of this prisoner, which whipped her with iron rods, to compel her thereunto. And she affirmed, that this Bishop was at a general meeting of the witches, in a field at Salem Village and there partook of a diabolical sacrament, in bread and wine then administered!

V. To render it further unquestionable, that the prisoner at the bar, was the person truly charged in this witchcraft, there were produced many evidences of other witchcrafts, by her perpetrated. For instance, John Cook testified, that about five or six years ago, one morning, about sunrise, he was in his chamber, assaulted by the shape of this prisoner: which looked on him, grinned at him, and very much hurt him, with a blow on the side of the head: and that on the same day, about noon, the same shape walked in the room where he was, and an apple strangely flew out of his hand, into the lap of his mother, six or eight foot from him.

VI. Samuel Gray, testified, that about fourteen years ago, he waked on a night, and saw the room where he lay, full of light; and that he then saw plainly a woman between the cradle, and the bedside, which looked upon him. He rose, and it vanished; though he found the doors all fast. Looking out at the entry door, he saw the same woman, in the same garb again; and said, In God's name, what do you come for? He went to bed, and had the same woman again assaulting him. The child in the cradle gave a great screech, and the woman disappeared. It was long before the child could be quieted; and though it were a very likely thriving child, yet from this time it pined away, and after divers months died in a sad condition. He knew not Bishop, nor her name but when he saw her after this, he knew by her countenance, and apparel, and all circumstances, that it was the apparition of this Bishop, which had thus troubled him.

VII. John Bly and his wife, testified, that he bought a sow of Edward Bishop, the husband of the prisoner; and was to pay the price agreed, unto another person. This prisoner being angry that she was thus hindered from fingering the money, quarrelled with Bly. Soon after which the sow, was taken with strange fits; jumping, leaping, and knocking her head against the fence, she seemed blind and deaf, and would neither eat nor be sucked. Whereupon a neighbor said, she believed the creature was over-looked; and sundry other circumstances concurred, which made the deponents believe that Bishop had bewitched it. . . .

IX. Samuel Shattuck testified, that in the year 1680, this Bridget Bishop, often came to his house upon such frivolous and foolish errands, that they suspected she came indeed with a purpose of mischief. Presently whereupon his eldest child, which was of as promising health and sense, as any child of its age, began to droop exceedingly; and the oftener that Bishop came to the house, the worse grew the child. As the child would be standing at the door, he would be thrown and bruised against the stones, by an invisible hand, and in like sort knock his face against the sides of the house, and bruise it after a miserable manner. Afterwards this Bishop would bring him things to dye, whereof he could not imagine any use; and when she paid him a piece of money, the purse and money were unaccountably conveyed out of a locked box, and never seen more. The child was immediately hereupon taken with terrible fits, whereof his friends thought he would have died: indeed he did almost nothing but cry and sleep for several months together: and at length his understanding was utterly taken away. . . .

XI. William Stacy testified, that receiving money of this Bishop, for work done by him, he was gone but a matter of three rods from her, and looking for his money, found it unaccountably gone from him. Some time after, Bishop asked him whether his father would grind her grist for her? He demanded why? She replied, Because folks count me a witch. He answered, No question, but he will grind it for you. Being then gone about six rods from her, with a small load in his cart, suddenly the off-wheel slumped and sunk down into a hole upon plain ground, so that the deponent, was forced to get help for the recovering of the wheel. But stepping back to look for the hole which might give him this disaster, there was none at all to be found. . . .

XII. To crown all, John Bly, and William Bly, testified, that being employed by Bridget Bishop, to help take down the cellar wall, of the old house, wherein she formerly lived, they did in holes of the said old wall, find several poppets, made up of rags, and hog's bristles, with headless pins in them, the points being outward. Whereof she could now give no account unto the court, that was reasonable or tolerable.

XIII. One thing that made against the prisoner was, her being evidently convicted of gross lying, in the court, several times, while she was making her plea. But besides this, a jury of women, found a preternatural teat upon her body; but upon a second search, within three or four hours, there was no such thing to be seen. There was also an account of other people whom this woman had afflicted. And there might have been many more, if they had been, inquired for. But there was no need of them.

QUESTIONS FOR READING AND DISCUSSION

1. What made Bishop's witchcraft "evident and notorious to all beholders"? Much of the testimony recalled events that had occurred many years earlier; why had her witchcraft only become "evident and notorious to all beholders" in 1692?

2. In what ways did Bishop act like a witch, according to her accusers? Why did her accusers believe she—rather than an accident or chance—had caused their misfortunes?

3. In what ways did Bishop's gender contribute to the accusations against her? Why were "poppets, made up of rags, and hog's bristles, with headless pins in them" and "a preternatural teat upon her body" considered evidence against her?

4. Judging from the testimony against Bishop, what would protect a person from being accused of witchcraft?

5. What does the testimony reveal about how seventeenth-century New Englanders interpreted unexplained events?

COMPARATIVE QUESTIONS

1. How did the ideals of the *Arbella* sermon differ, if at all, from those expressed by the laws of Pennsylvania? To what extent did the ideals of the *Arbella* sermon influence the grievances expressed by the Wampanoags and the testimony against Bridget Bishop?

2. How did the forms of order and disorder that Williams observed among Indians compare with the Wampanoags' grievances? How did they compare with the ideals in the *Arbella* sermon and the laws of Pennsylvania?

3. What was the significance of religious tolerance (or intolerance) in the events described by these documents? To what extent do the documents offer evidence of important beliefs, attitudes, and behavior that were not specifically religious?

4. Judging from the documents in this chapter, to what extent did settlers succeed in creating a new England in the northern colonies during the seventeenth century? Do these documents illustrate successes, failures, or both? How and why? Were the successes or failures the result of Puritanism or in spite of it?

5 | Colonial America in the Eighteenth Century
1701–1770

Eighteenth-century colonists lived in a world of change. Older certainties of faith eroded. New patterns of commerce spread. Choices abounded. Where to live? What faith to profess? What kind of work to do? What goods to buy and sell? These and other choices made many colonists think about changing themselves through education, training, discipline, introspection, or religious conversion, among other ways. For slaves, choices were far fewer than for free colonists, a reality many slaves understood all too well since they had suffered enslavement as free people in Africa. The documents that follow illustrate the different choices available to slaves, immigrants, and native-born free white colonists. The choices they made helped create the changes they all experienced.

DOCUMENT 5–1

Elizabeth Ashbridge Becomes an Indentured Servant in New York

Like tens of thousands of other young people in England during the eighteenth century, Elizabeth Ashbridge fell upon hard times and decided to emigrate to the colonies. Ashbridge became an active Quaker and a few years before her death in 1755 wrote an autobiography that circulated widely in handwritten form among Quakers before it was published in the early nineteenth century. In the excerpt below, Ashbridge described the circumstances of her early life in England and her experiences as an indentured servant in New York. Ashbridge portrayed her early life as a prelude of despair and sorrow that she contrasted—in a portion of her autobiography not reprinted here—with her spiritual awakening and enlightenment once she became a Quaker. As you read, keep in mind that Ashbridge was looking back on her early life from the perspective of a deeply religious adult woman.

Some Account of the Early Part of the Life of Elizabeth Ashbridge, Who Died in . . . 1755 (1807)

My life having been attended with many uncommon occurrences, some of which I through disobedience brought upon myself, and other I believe were for my Good, I therefore thought proper to make some remarks on the Dealings of Divine Goodness to me, . . . and most earnestly I desire that whosoever reads the following lines, may take warning, and shun the Evils that I have thro' the Deceitfulness of Satan been drawn into.

To begin with my beginning. I was born in Middlewich in Cheshire in the year 1713 of Honest Parents. . . . My Father was a Man that bore a good Character, but not so Strictly Religious as my Mother, who was a pattern of Virtue to me. . . . Soon after my birth, my Father took to the sea & followed his Profession [surgeon] on board a ship, in many long voyages, till I arrived to the Age of twelve years & then left off; so my Education lay mostly on my Mother, in which she discharged her duty by endeavoring to instill in me, in my tender Age, the principles of virtue. . . .

From my Infancy till fourteen years of age I was as innocent as most Children, about which time my Sorrows began, and have continued for the most part of my life ever since; by giving way to a foolish passion, in Setting my affections on a young man who Courted me without my Parents' Consent; till I consented, and with sorrow of Heart may say, I suffered myself to be carried off in the night . . . and was married. . . .

I was soon smote with remorse, for thus leaving my parents, whose right it was to have disposed of me to their contents, or at least to have been consulted in the Affair. I was soon Chastised for my disobedience—Divine Providence let me see my error. In five months I was stripped of the Darling of my Soul, and left a young & disconsolate Widow. I had then no home to fly to. My Husband was poor, and had nothing but his Trade, which was a Stocking Weaver, & my Father was so displeased, he would do nothing for me. . . .

My Father still keeping me at such a distance that I thought myself quite shut out of his Affections, I therefore Concluded since my Absence was so Agreeable, he should have it; and getting acquainted with a Gentlewoman that then lately came from Pensilvania (& was going back again) where I had an Uncle, my Mother's Brother, I soon agreed with her for my passage & being ignorant of the Nature of an Indenture soon became bound, tho' in a private manner, (for fear I should be found out) tho' this was repugnant to law. As soon as this was over, She invited me to go & see the Vessel I was to go in, to which I readily consented, not Knowing what would follow, & when I came on board, I found a Young Woman I afterward understood was of a very good Family and had been deluded away by this creature. I was extremely pleased to think that I should have such an agreeable Companion & while we were in discourse, our Kidnapper left us & went on shore, & when I wanted to go, was not permitted. . . .

From Elizabeth Ashbridge, *Some Account of the Early Part of the Life of Elizabeth Ashbridge, Who Died, in the Truth's Service, at the House of Robert Lucky, in the County of Carlow, Ireland, the 16th of 5th Month, 1755. Written by Herself* (Philadelphia: Benjamin Kite, 1807).

In Nine Weeks from the time I left Ireland we arrived at New York, . . . on the 15th of the 7 mo 1732 & then those to whom I had been Instrumental under Providence to save Life, proved Treacherous to me: I was a Stranger in a Strange Land. The Captain got an Indenture wrote & Demanded of me to Sign it, withal Threatning a Gaol [jail] if I refused it; I told him I could find means to Satisfy him [funds to pay him] for my Passage without becoming bound [as a servant]: they then told me I might take my Choice Either to Sign that, or have that I had signed in Ireland in force against me (by this time I had learned the Character of the afforesaid Woman, that she was a Vile Creature, & feared that if ever I was in her Power she would use me Ill on her Brother's Account). I therefore in a fright Signed that, & tho' there was no Magistrate present, I being Ignorant in such Cases, it Did well enough to Make me a Servant four Years.

In two Weeks time I was Sold, & Were it Possible to Convey in Characters a sense of the Sufferings of my Servitude, it would make the most strong heart pity the Misfortunes of a young creature as I was, who had a Tender Education; for tho' my Father had no great Estate, yet he lived well. I had been used to Little but my School, but now it had been better for me if I had been brought up to more hardship. For a While at first I was Pretty well used, but in a Little time the Scale turned. Occasioned by a Difference that happened between my Master & me, wherein I was Innocent: from that time he set himself against me and was Inhuman. He would not suffer [allow] me to have Clothes to be Decent in, having to go barefoot in his Service in the Snowey Weather & the Meanest drudgery, wherein I Suffered the Utmost Hardship that my Body was able to Bear, which, with the afforesaid Troubles, had like to have been my Ruin to all Eternity had not Almighty God in Mercy interposed. . . .

To one Woman (& no other) I had Discovered the Nature of the Difference which Two years before had happened between My master & Me; by her means he heard of it, & tho' he knew it was True yet he sent for the Town Whipper to Correct me. I was Called In; he never asked me Whether I had told any such thing but ordered me to strip; at which my heart was ready to burst; for I could as freely have given up my Life as Suffer such Ignominy. I then said if there be a God, be graciously Pleased to Look down on one of the most unhappy Creatures & plead my Cause for thou knows what I have said is the truth; and were it not for a principle more noble than he was Capable of I would have told it before his wife. I then fixed my Eyes on the Barbarous man, & in a flood of Tears said: "Sir, if you would have no Pity on me, yet for my Father's Sake spare me from this Shame (for before this time had heard of my Father &C. several ways) & if you think I deserve such punishment, do it your Self." He then took a turn over the Room & bid the Whipper go about his business, and I came off without a blow, which I thought something Remarkable, but now I began to think my Credit was gone (for they said many things of me which I blessed God were not True) & here I suffer so much Cruelty I cannot bear it.

The Enemy [i.e., Satan] Immediately Came in & put me in a way how to be rid of it all & tempted me to End my Miserable Life: I joyn'd with it & for that Purpose went into the garret to hang my Self. Now it was I was convinced there was a God, for as my feet Entered the Place Horrour seized to that degree, I trembled much, and as I stood like the one in Amaze, it seemed as tho' I heard a Voice say, "there is a Hell beyond the grave;" at which I was greatly astonished, & now Convinced that there was an almighty Power, to whom I then Prayed, saying, "God be merciful & Enable me to bear what thou in thy Providence shall bring or

Suffer to Come upon me for my Disobedience." I then went Down again but Let none know what I had been about. Soon after this I had a Dream, & tho' some make a ridicule of Dreams, yet this seemed a significant one to me & therefore shall mention it. I thought somebody knocked at the Door, by which when I had opened it there stood a Grave woman, holding in her right hand an oil lamp burning, who with a Solid Countenance fixed her Eyes upon me & said "I am sent to tell thee that If thou'l return to the Lord thy God, who hath Created thee, he will have mercy on thee, & thy Lamp shall not be put out in obscure darkness"; upon which the Light flamed from the Lamp in an extraordinary Manner, & She left me and I awoke.

But alas! I did not give up nor Comply with the heavenly Vision, as I think I may Call it, for after this I had like to have been caught in another Snare, which if I had would Probably have been my Ruin, from which I was also preserved. I was Counted a fine Singer & Dancer, in which I took great Delight, and once falling in with some of the Play house company then at New York, they took a Great fancy to me, as they said, & Perswaded me to become an Actress amongst them, & they would find means to get me from my cruel Servitude, & I should Live Like a Lady. The Proposal took with me & I used no small Pains to Qualify my Self for it Reading their Play Books, even when I should have Slept, yet was put to the Demur [hesitated] when I came to Consider what my Father would say who had forgiven my Disobedience in marrying and earnestly desiring to see me again had sent for me home, but my proud heart would not Consent to return in so mean a Condition; therefore I chose Bondage rather.

So when I had Served near three years, I bought off the remainder of my Time [indenture contract] & then took to my Needle [became a seamstress], by which I could maintain my Self handsomely: but, alas, I was not Sufficiently Punished; I had got released from one cruel Servitude & then not Contented got into another, and this for Life. A few months after, I married a young man that fell in Love with me for my Dancing, a Poor Motive for a man to Choose a Wife, or a Woman a Husband. But for my Part I fell in Love with nothing I saw in him and it seems unaccountable that I who had refused several, both in this Country & Ireland, at Last married a man I had no Value for.

In a few Days after we were Married he took me from [New] York. Being a Schoolmaster he had hired in the Country to keep school; he led me to New England and there settled in . . . Rhode Island. . . . With regard to Religion he was much like my Self, without any, and . . . I now saw my Self ruined . . . being joined to a man I had no Love for & . . . then I began to think what a Couple we were, like two joining hands and going to destruction, & there upon Concluded if I was not forsaken of heaven to alter my Course of Life.

Questions for Reading and Discussion

1. How did Ashbridge's relations with her parents and her husbands influence her life? Why did she disobey her parents' "right to have disposed of me to their contents"?
2. Why and how did Ashbridge become an indentured servant? How did the "Kidnapper" and ship captain influence her?
3. Ashbridge observed that when she arrived in New York she "was a Stranger in a Strange Land." What experiences illustrate what she termed "the Sufferings of my Servitude"?

4. Why did Ashbridge not "Comply with the heavenly Vision" revealed to her? What were the consequences?

5. To what extent do you think Ashbridge's religion as an adult woman shaped her account of her early life? How do you think her views when she was a young woman "without any" religion might have differed from those expressed in her autobiography?

DOCUMENT 5–2

Poor Richard's Advice

In 1732, Benjamin Franklin began to publish Poor Richard's Almanac, *a calendar packed with astronomical observations, miscellaneous information, and pithy advice about almost everything, all of it written by Franklin under the pseudonym of Richard Saunders. Widely read, the almanac became highly profitable for Franklin, and he continued to publish it every year until 1757. For the last issue, Franklin composed a synthesis of Poor Richard's wisdom in the form of a speech given by an old man. The speech, which follows, describes the temptations faced by eighteenth-century colonists and how they should resist them. The popularity of the almanac suggests that the old man's views were shared by many other colonists.*

Benjamin Franklin

Father Abraham's Speech from Poor Richard's Almanac, 1757

Courteous Reader,

I have heard that nothing gives an Author so great Pleasure, as to find his Works respectfully quoted by other learned Authors. This Pleasure I have seldom enjoyed. . . . I concluded at length, that the People were the best judges of my Merit; for they buy my Works; and besides, in my Rambles, where I am not personally known, I have frequently heard one or other of my Adages repeated, with, *as Poor Richard* says, at the End on't; this gave me some Satisfaction, as it showed not only that my Instructions were regarded, but discovered likewise some Respect for my Authority; and I own, that to encourage the Practice of remembering and repeating those wise Sentences, I have sometimes *quoted myself* with great Gravity.

Judge then how much I must have been gratified by an Incident I am going to relate to you. I stopt my Horse lately where a great Number of People were collected at a Vendue[1] of Merchant Goods. The Hour of Sale not being come, they were conversing on the Badness of the Times, and one of the Company call'd to a plain clean old Man, with white Locks, *Pray, Father Abraham, what think you of the Times? Won't these heavy Taxes quite ruin the Country? How shall we be ever able to pay them? What would you advise us to?* —Father Abraham stood up, and reply'd,

---

From *Poor Richard's Almanac*, in Benjamin Franklin, *Writings*, ed. J. A. Leo Lemay (New York: Library of America, 1987), 1294–1303.

[1]**Vendue**: A public auction.

If you'd have my Advice, I'll give it you in short, for a *Word to the Wise is enough,* and *many Words won't fill a Bushel, as Poor Richard* says. They join'd in desiring him to speak his Mind, and gathering round him, he proceeded as follows;

"Friends," says he, "and Neighbours, the Taxes are indeed very heavy, and if those laid on by the Government were the only Ones we had to pay, we might more easily discharge them; but we have many others, and much more grievous to some of us. We are taxed twice as much by our *Idleness,* three times as much by our *Pride,* and four times as much by our *Folly,* and from these Taxes the Commissioners cannot ease or deliver us by allowing an Abatement. However let us hearken to good Advice, and something may be done for us; *God helps them that help themselves, as Poor Richard* says. . . .

It would be thought a hard Government that should tax its People one tenth Part of their *Time,* to be employed in its Service. But *Idleness* taxes many of us much more, if we reckon all that is spent in absolute *Sloth,* or doing of nothing, with that which is spent in idle Employments or Amusements, that amount to nothing. *Sloth,* by bringing on Diseases, absolutely shortens Life. *Sloth, like Rust, consumes faster than Labour wears, while the used Key is always bright, as Poor Richard* says.—How much more than is necessary do we spend in Sleep! forgetting that *The sleeping Fox catches no Poultry,* and that *there will be sleeping enough in the Grave, as Poor Richard* says. If Time be of all Things the most precious, *wasting Time* must be, as *Poor Richard* says, *the greatest Prodigality,* since, as he elsewhere tells us, *Lost Time is never found again.* . . . Let us then up and be doing, and doing to the Purpose; so by Diligence shall we do more with less Perplexity. *Sloth makes all Things difficult, but Industry all easy, as Poor Richard* says; and *He that riseth late, must trot all Day, and shall scarce overtake his Business at Night.* While *Laziness travels so slowly, that Poverty soon overtakes him,* as we read in *Poor Richard,* who adds, *Drive thy Business, let not that drive thee;* and *Early to Bed, and early to rise, makes a Man healthy, wealthy and wise.*

So what signifies *wishing* and *hoping* for better Times. We may make these Times better if we bestir ourselves. *Industry need not wish, as Poor Richard* says, and *He that lives upon Hope will die fasting. There are no Gains, without Pains.* . . . And, as *Poor Richard* likewise observes, *He that hath a Trade hath an Estate,* and *He that hath a Calling hath an Office of Profit and Honour;* but then the *Trade* must be worked at, and the *Calling* well followed, or neither the *Estate,* nor the *Office,* will enable us to pay our Taxes.—If we are industrious we shall never starve; for, as *Poor Richard* says, *At the working Man's House Hunger looks in, but dares not enter.* Nor will the Bailiff or the Constable enter, for *Industry pays Debts, while Despair encreaseth them,* says *Poor Richard.*—What though you have found no Treasure, nor has any rich Relation left you a Legacy, *Diligence is the Mother of Good-luck, as Poor Richard* says, and *God gives all Things to Industry.* Then *plough deep, while Sluggards sleep, and you shall have Corn to sell and to keep,* says *Poor Dick.* Work while it is called To-day, for you know not how much you may be hindered To-morrow which makes *Poor Richard* say, *One To-day is worth two Tomorrows;* and farther, *Have you somewhat to do To-morrow, do it To-day.* If you were a Servant, would you not be ashamed that a good Master should catch you idle? Are you then your own Master, *be ashamed to catch yourself idle, as Poor Dick* says. . . .

Methinks I hear some of you say, *Must a Man afford himself no Leisure?* I will tell thee, my Friend, what *Poor Richard* says, *Employ thy Time well if thou meanest to gain Leisure;* and, *since thou art not sure of a Minute, throw not away an Hour.* Leisure is Time for doing something useful; this Leisure the diligent Man will obtain, but the lazy Man never. . . .

But with our Industry, we must likewise be *steady, settled and careful*, and oversee our own Affairs *with our own Eyes*, and not trust too much to others; for, as *Poor Richard* says,

> *I never saw an oft removed Tree,*
> *Nor yet an oft removed Family,*
> *That throve so well as those that settled be.*

And again, *Three Removes is as bad as a Fire*; and again, *Keep thy Shop, and thy Shop will keep thee*; and again, *If you would have your Business done, go; If not, send.* . . . And again, *The Eye of a Master will do more Work than both his Hands*; and again, *Want of Care does us more Damage than Want of Knowledge*; and again, *Not to oversee Workmen, is to leave them your Purse open.* Trusting too much to others Care is the Ruin of many; for, as the *Almanack* says, *In the Affairs of this World, men are saved, not by Faith, but by the Want of it.* . . . And farther, *If you would have a faithful Servant, and one that you like, serve yourself.* . . .

So much for Industry, my Friends, and Attention to one's own Business; but to these we must add *Frugality*, if we would make our *Industry* more certainly successful. A Man may, if he knows not how to save as he gets, *keep his Nose all his Life to the Grindstone*, and die not worth a *Groat*[2] at last. *A fat Kitchen makes a lean Will*, as Poor Richard says; and,

> *Many Estates are spent in the Getting,*
> *Since Women for Tea forsook Spinning and Knitting,*
> *And Men for Punch forsook Hewing and Splitting.*

If you would be wealthy, says he, in another Almanack, *think of Saving as well as of Getting: The* Indies *have not made* Spain *rich, because her* Outgoes *are greater than her* Incomes. Away then with your expensive Follies, and you will not have so much Cause to complain of hard Times, heavy Taxes, and chargeable Families. . . . And farther, *What maintains one Vice, would bring up two Children.* You may think perhaps, That a *little* Tea, or a *little* Punch now and then, Diet a *little* more costly, Clothes a *little* finer, and a *little* Entertainment now and then, can be no great Matter; but remember what *Poor Richard* says, *Many a Little makes a Mickle*;[3] and farther, *Beware of little Expences; a small Leak will sink a great Ship*; and again, . . . *Fools make Feasts, and wise Men eat them.*

Here you are all got together at this Vendue of *Fineries* and *Knicknacks*. You call them Goods, but if you do not take Care, they will prove Evils to some of you. You expect they will be sold *cheap*, and perhaps they may for less than they cost; but if you have no Occasion for them, they must be dear to you. Remember what *Poor Richard* says, *Buy what thou hast no Need of, and ere long thou shalt sell thy Necessaries.* . . . Many a one, for the Sake of Finery on the Back, have gone with a hungry Belly, and half starved their Families; *Silks and Sattins, Scarlet and Velvets*, as Poor

---

[2]**Groat**: An English coin.
[3]**Mickle**: A large amount.

Richard says, *put out the Kitchen Fire*. These are not the *Necessaries* of Life; they can scarcely be called the *Conveniencies*, and yet only because they look pretty, how many *want* to *have* them. The *artificial* Wants of Mankind thus become more numerous than the *natural*. . . . By these, and other Extravagancies, the Genteel are reduced to Poverty, and forced to borrow of those whom they formerly despised, but who through *Industry* and *Frugality* have maintained their Standing; in which Case it appears plainly, that a *Ploughman on his Legs is higher than a Gentleman on his Knees*, as *Poor Richard* says. . . . *If you would know the Value of money, go and try to borrow some*; for, *he that goes a borrowing goes a sorrowing*; and indeed so does he that lends to such People, when he goes to get it in again. *Poor Dick* farther advises, and says, *Fond Pride of Dress, is sure a very Curse*. . . . When you have bought one fine Thing you must buy ten more, that your Appearance may be all of a Piece; but *Poor Dick* says, *'Tis easier to suppress the first Desire, than to satisfy all that follow it*. And 'tis as truly Folly for the Poor to ape the Rich, as for the Frog to swell, in order to equal the Ox.

> *Great Estates may venture more,*
> *But little Boats should keep near Shore.*

'Tis however a Folly soon punished; for . . . *Pride breakfasted with Plenty, dined with Poverty and supped with Infamy*. And after all, of what Use is this *Pride of Appearance*, for which so much is risked, so much is suffered? It cannot promote Health, or ease Pain; it makes no Increase of Merit in the Person, it creates Envy, it hastens Misfortune. . . . But what Madness must it be to *run in Debt* for these Superfluities! We are offered, by the Terms of this Vendue, *Six Months Credit*; and that perhaps has induced some of us to attend it, because we cannot spare the ready Money, and hope now to be fine without it. But, ah, think what you do when you run in Debt; *You give to another Power over your Liberty*. If you cannot pay at the Time, you will be ashamed to see your Creditor; you will be in Fear when you speak to him; you will make poor pitiful sneaking Excuses, and by Degrees come to lose your Veracity, and sink into base downright lying; for, as *Poor Richard* says . . . *Lying rides upon Debt's Back*. Whereas a freeborn Englishman ought not to be ashamed or afraid to see or speak to any Man living. But Poverty often deprives a Man of all Spirit and Virtue: *'Tis hard for an empty Bag to stand upright*, as *Poor Richard* truly says. What would you think of that Prince, or that Government, who should issue an Edict forbidding you to dress like a Gentleman or a Gentlewoman, on Pain of Imprisonment or Servitude? Would you not say, that you are free, have a Right to dress as you please, and that such an Edict would be a Breach of your Privileges, and such a Government tyrannical? And yet you are about to put yourself under that Tyranny when you run in Debt for such Dress! Your Creditor has Authority at his Pleasure to deprive you of your Liberty, by confining you in Gaol [jail] for Life, or to sell you for a Servant, if you should not be able to pay him! When you have got your Bargain, you may, perhaps, think little of Payment; but *Creditors, Poor Richard* tells us, *have better Memories than Debtors*. . . . *The Borrower is a Slave to the Lender, and the Debtor to the Creditor*, disdain the Chain, preserve your Freedom; and maintain your Independency: Be *industrious* and *free*; be *frugal* and *free*. . . .

This Doctrine, my Friends, is *Reason* and *Wisdom*; but after all, do not depend too much upon your own *Industry*, and *Frugality*, and *Prudence*, though excellent Things, for they may all be blasted without the Blessing of Heaven; and therefore ask that Blessing humbly, and be not uncharitable to those that at present seem to want it, but comfort and help them. Remember *Job* suffered, and was afterwards prosperous.

And now to conclude, . . . remember this, *They that won't be counselled, can't be helped*, as *Poor Richard* says: And farther, *That if you will not hear Reason, she'll surely rap your Knuckles."*

Thus the old Gentleman ended his Harangue. The People heard it, and approved the Doctrine, and immediately practised the contrary, just as if it had been a common Sermon; for the Vendue opened, and they began to buy extravagantly, notwithstanding all his Cautions, and their own Fear of Taxes. . . .

I am, as ever,
Thine to serve thee,
Richard Saunders.

July 7, 1757

QUESTIONS FOR READING AND DISCUSSION

1. According to Father Abraham, what temptations were likely to lead his contemporaries astray, and how could they be resisted?
2. In what ways were idleness, pride, and folly taxes? How would industry, frugality, and reason avoid or minimize such taxes?
3. According to Father Abraham, what were the goals of disciplined behavior? Did people who did not discipline their behavior appropriately have different goals? What, for example, did they think about time, consumption, and debt?
4. After the speech, the people who heard it began "to buy extravagantly." What does their behavior suggest about the old man's wisdom? To what extent did Father Abraham's advice partake of the ethos of individualism, and to what extent did it criticize that ethos?
5. Many of Father Abraham's maxims are still repeated today. Why? Do you think they are more or less important today than they were in the eighteenth century? Why?

DOCUMENT 5–3

An Anglican Criticizes New Light Baptists and Presbyterians in the South Carolina Backcountry

After decades as a prosperous merchant and planter in South Carolina, Charles Woodmason—a pious Anglican—was ordained by the Church of England to be an itinerant minister to backcountry settlers. Woodmason traveled throughout the frontier regions of the Carolinas, preaching to colonists who had migrated south from Pennsylvania and Virginia. Woodmason's journal and sermons—one of which is excerpted below—provide a rare glimpse of backcountry life among German and Scots-Irish immigrants as well as native-born settlers who were professed Presbyterians, Baptists, Lutherans, Quakers, and many other variants of Protestant conviction. Woodmason's sermon lambastes New Light religion, revealing as much about backcountry life and his own Anglican perspectives as about the consequences of what historians have termed the Great Awakening, which accounted for the growing influence of New Light Christianity in the middle decades of the eighteenth century.

Charles Woodmason

Sermon on the Baptists and the Presbyterians, ca. 1768

But surely, if Persons have received more and better [religious] Edification by resorting to the Schism Shop [of New Light Protestant sects such as the Baptists and Presbyterians], then . . . certainly it will display it Self in their Lives and Manners. . . . Because I hear so much Talk about *Conversion*, certainly there must be some very Great Reformation of Morals among You. . . .

You doubtless will allow, That keeping Holy the Lords day, is a positive Command of God, and enjoin'd by the Laws of this Land. . . . But . . . as my Station leads me to travel over most parts of this Country, and ofttimes on Sundays, as well as other Days, I do aver [assert], that there is little or no Reformation of Manners . . . save in some few Environs of a Meeting House . . . For the same riding the Woods, Shooting Cattle Hunting—driving Waggons, Hogs Horses—Travelling to and fro—Fishing—Fowling—Trapping—Taverning, Swimming and Bathing, and various Field and Domestic Matters, are carried on, and followed up as usual. . . . [T]he Sabbath is not so regularly observ'd, as when You us'd . . . to resort to [the Anglican] Church: But since quitting of the [Anglican] Church, the Sabbath is but seldom oberv'd—for we see none resort to any Place of Worship, but when some Itinerant Babler, or Vagrant Ignorant Bellweather[1] comes to a Meeting House and then the Silly Herd run in Droves to listen to what none can comprehend and this for greater Edification. If therefore staying at Home, Sleeping and Lounging privately tipling [drinking] and wantoning, be hallowing the Lords Day, I will acknowledge that in this Sense it is *highly* sanctified—tho' I think it would more rationally and more religiously be so, would People resort to their proper [Anglican] Churches to hear the Word of God solemnly read, and their Duty explain'd to them in a sober, sensible, and judicious Manner.

There is one Circumstance . . . [that] not only occasions the Non-observance of the Sabbath but is an Evil in it Self, and scandalous to the Country—and that is—The transacting of all Public Business on Saturdays. Thus We see Magistrates have their Sittings [courts]—Militia Officers their Musters—Merchants their Vendues [auctions]—Planters their Sales, all on Saturdays: Is there any Shooting, Dancing, Revelling, Drinking Matches carrying on? It is all begun on Saturday, and . . . all these Meetings and Transactions are executed at Taverns . . . So that at these Rendezvous there is more Company of a Saturday, than in the Church on Sunday: And these Assemblies are not only carried on under Eye of the Magistrates, but even by them—Most of them being Store or Tavern Keepers. Thus Vice and Wickedness is countenanc'd by those whose Duty it is to suppress it—but their Interest to promote it. And yet several of these Magistrates are Heads of these New [Baptist and Presbyterian] Congregations; Consequently, all this . . . tends to all Kinds of Debauchery: For of those who may quit the Tavern and return home, they are so heavy, sleepy drunk and stupid, as to be unable, utterly unfit to

---

From Charles Woodmason, Sermon Book III, 465–96, ca. 1768, in *The Carolina Backcountry on the Eve of the Revolution: The Journal and Other Writings of Charles Woodmason, Anglican Itinerant*, ed. Richard J. Hooker (Chapel Hill: University of North Carolina Press, 1953), 95–108.

[1]**Bellweather**: A castrated ram with a bell hung around its neck, used to lead a flock of sheep.

attend Public Worship on Sunday. Herefrom they stay at home to sleep off their Dose, and thereby confine their families likewise. . . .

But let us go on, and examine if in the General Corruption of Manners these New Lights have made any reform in the Vice of Drunkenness? Truly . . . [t]here is not one Hogshead [barrel] of Liquor less consum'd since their visiting us, or any Tavern shut up—So far from it, that there has been Great Increase of Both. Go to any Common Muster or Vendue, Will you not see the same Fighting, Brawling, Gouging, Quarreling as ever? And this too among the Holy ones of our New Israel? Are Riots, Frolics, Races, Games, Cards, Dice, Dances, less frequent now than formerly? Are fewer persons to be seen in Taverns? or reeling or drunk on the Roads. . . .

We will further enquire, if Lasciviousness, or Wantoness, Adultery or Fornication [are] less common than formerly, before the Arrival of these *Holy* Persons? Are there fewer Bastards born? Are more Girls with their Virginity about them, Married, than were heretofore? The Parish Register will prove the Contrary: There are rather more Bastards, more Mullatoes born than before. Nor out of 100 Young Women that I marry in a Year have I seen . . . Six but what are with Child. . . . And as for Adulteries, the present State of most Persons around 9/10 of whom now labour under a filthy Distemper[2] (as is well known to all) . . . shews that the Saints however outwardly precise and Reserved are not one Whit more Chaste than formerly, and possibly are more privately Vicious.

And nothing more leads to this Than what they call their Love Feasts and Kiss of Charity. To which Feasts, celebrated at Night, much Liquor is privately carried. . . . All this indeed contributes to multiply subjects for the King in this frontier Country, and . . . gives great Occasion to the Enemies of Virtue, to triumph, for Religion to be scandalized and brought into Contempt . . . [and] Confusion— Anarchy and ev'ry Evil Work will be the Consequence of such Lewdness and Immorality.

But certainly these Reformers have put some Stop to the many Thefts and Depradations so openly committed of late Years? . . . Magistrates and Courts of Justice . . . are ready to declare, that since the Appearance of these New Lights, more Enormities of all Kinds have been committed—More Robberies Thefts, Murders, Plunderings, Burglaries and Villanies of ev'ry Kind, than ever before. And the Reason . . . is, That most of these Preaching fellows were most notorious Theives, Jockeys, Gamblers, and what not in the Northern Provinces, and since their Reception and Success here have drawn Crowds of their old Acquaintances after them; So that the Country never was so full as at present of Gamesters, Prostitutes, Filchers, Racers, Fidlers, and all the refuse of Mankind. . . . In short, they have filled the Country with Idle and Vagrant Persons, who live by their Criminalities. For it is a Maxim with these Vermin of Religion, That a Person must first be a Sinner e're He can be a Saint. . . .

For only draw a Comparison between them and Us. . . . [Consider] our Solemn, Grave, and Serious Sett Forms,[3] or their Wild Extempore Jargon, nauseaus to any Chaste or refin'd Ear. There are so many Absurdities committed by them, as wou'd shock one of our *Cherokee* Savages; And was a Sensible Turk or Indian to view some of their Extravagancies it would quickly determine them against

---

[2]**Distemper**: Venereal disease.
[3]**Sett Forms**: Church services.

Christianity. Had any such been in their Assembly . . . last Sunday when they communicated, the Honest Heathens would have imagin'd themselves rather amidst a Gang of frantic Lunatics broke out of Bedlam, rather than among a Society of religious Christians. . . . Here, one Fellow mounted on a Bench with the Bread, and bawling, *See the Body of Christ* . . . One on his knees in a Posture of Prayer—Others singing—some howling—These Ranting—Those Crying—Others dancing, Skipping, Laughing and rejoycing. Here two or 3 Women falling on their Backs, kicking up their Heels, exposing their Nakedness to all Bystanders and others sitting Pensive, in deep Melancholy lost in Abstraction, like Statues, quite insensible. . . . [They declare that] their Souls had taken flight to Heav'n, and they knew nothing of what they said or did. . . .

But another vile Matter . . . Is, what they call their *Experiences*; It seems, that before a Person be dipp'd [baptized], He must give an Account of his Secret Calls, Conviction, Conversion, Repentance. . . . To see . . . a Sett of Mongrels under Pretext of Religion, Sit, and hear for Hours together a String of Vile, cook'd up, Silly and Senseless Lyes, What they . . . are Sensible has not the least foundation in Truth or Reason. . . .

Then again to see them Divide and Sub divide, Split into Parties—Rail at and excommunicate one another . . . And a Gang of them getting together and gabbling . . . on Abstruse Theological Question[s] . . . To hear Ignorant Wretches, who can not write—Who never read ten Pages in any Book, and can hardly read the Alphabett discussing such Knotty Points for the Edification of their Auditors, is . . . farcical . . . [and] excels any Exhibition of Folly that has ever yet appear'd in the World. . . .

[B]eyond all This to greive the Hearts and Minds of serious Christians . . . is their Mode of Baptism, to which Lascivious Persons of both Sexes resort, as to a Public Bath. I know not whether it would not be less offensive to Modesty for them to strip wholly into Buff at once, than to be dipp'd with those very thin Linen Drawers they are equipp'd in—Which when wet, so closely adheres to the Limbs, as exposes the Nudities equally as if [not clothed] at All. . . .

I saw lately practis'd at Marriage of one of their Notable She Saints around whom ([after] the [baptism] Ceremony ended) they marched in Circles singing Hymns . . . with a vast Parade of Prayer Thanks givings and Religious Foppery; Which had such marvellous Effect on the virtuous Devotee as to cause her to bring a Child in five Months after, as a Proof that their Prayers for her being fruitful was answer'd.

This Devotee was highly celebrated for her extraordinary Illuminations, Visions, and Communications. It is the same [woman] who in her Experience told a long Story of an Angel coming to visit her in the Night thro' the Roof of her Cabbin—In flames of Fire too! It was very true that she was visited in the Night, and that the Apparition did jump down upon her Bed thro' the Shingles by an opening she had made for the Purpose—and that it came to her all on Fire. Yes! But it was the Fire of Lust; And this Angel was no other than her Ghostly Teacher, to whom she communicated a Revelation that it was ordain'd He should caress Her; and He Good Man, was not disobedient to this Heav'nly Call—He afterward had a Revelation That it was the Will of God [that another] Man was to take her to Wife Which the Poor unthinking Booby did, in Conformity to the Divine Will express'd by his prophet—Little dreaming that He was to Father the Prophet's Bastard. All this (and much more) the Woman has confess'd to Me. But You see hereby that Revelations now a days, are not strictly to be depended On. . . .

Some of our qualmish[4] Neighbours whose Consciences keep them in perpetual Disquiet cannot bear the Thought (without Shuddering and Sweating) of Bowing at the Name of *Jesus*. But their *tender* Consciences will never upbraid them or fly in their faces, for bowing down upon a Strumpet, and committing fornication.

Others, will not admit of the Cross in Baptism but their Consciences have not the least Objection to the Stealing of my Horse, or killing my Cattle and Hogs, and saying a Long Grace over their Flesh when cook'd up to their Table.

Again, Others have Scruples of Conscience in respect to use of the Ring in Marriages but have not the least Scruple of running away with other Mens Wives—Of committing adultery . . . or of turning away this Wife, and taking another [or] having 2 or 3 Wives or Concubines at the same Time.

Others more Reighteous over much than these, and whose Consciences rise up in Judgment against them for receiving Holy Commandment [communion] Kneeling, feel no Scruples at not paying of their Just Debts, and cheating and overreaching whomsoever they can deceive under the Mask of Piety. . . .

Some others Consciencies are very nice in respect to Hats—Buttons—Lace, and Ornaments of Dress—Their Consciences would condemn them as Great Sinners in having more than Ten Buttons on their Coat. But they feel no Remorse in drinking Ten Bottle of Wine or Ale, and getting as drunk as Beasts. . . .

So Conscientious are Others that sooner than come over the Threshold of that [church] Door to hear the Word of God read or preached by a Man drest in a White Garment,[5] That they will swim in the River, Bathe in the Creeks, Men and Women publickly together Stark naked in the Stream on Sundays, without any Qualms of Conscience for such Indecent and Immodest Practices.

QUESTIONS FOR READING AND DISCUSSION

1. What "Great Reformation of Morals" did converts to New Light Baptist and Presbyterian churches exhibit, according to Woodmason? Did Woodmason claim that New Light religion made no difference in the lives of converts, or did he believe that New Light religion made converts' lives and society worse?

2. How do you think New Light converts might have responded to Woodmason's sermon? What might they have said to his statement that "it is a Maxim with these Vermin of Religion, That a Person must first be a Sinner e're he can be a Saint"? Do you think they would have defended the practices he ridiculed? Would they have interpreted the social and personal consequences of religion differently?

3. According to Woodmason, how did New Light religion compare to Anglican worship services? From the perspective of members of the congregation, how did New Light services compare with Woodmason's view that in Anglican churches they would have "their Duty explain'd to them in a sober, sensible, and judicious Manner"?

4. Why did Woodmason believe so many backcountry people were attracted by New Light religion? Using the evidence in his sermon, why do you believe they were attracted? Is it possible to decipher what Woodmason and the New Lights considered authentic religious experiences?

---

[4]**qualmish**: Overly scrupulous, squeamish.
[5]**White Garment**: Robe worn by an Anglican minister.

DOCUMENT 5–4

Advertisements for Runaway Slaves

African slaves came to the British North American colonies in unprecedented numbers during the eighteenth century. Because most eighteenth-century slaves could neither read nor write, few documents survive that record their point of view. Advertisements for runaway slaves provide an imperfect but revealing glimpse of specific slaves who defied their masters and mistresses by absconding. Published in local South Carolina and Virginia newspapers, the following advertisements described runaways in sufficient detail for them to be recognized and, masters hoped, recaptured. In addition to listing the characteristics of individual runaways, the advertisements also suggested the conditions of servitude among the many slaves who did not run away.

South Carolina Gazette *and* Virginia Gazette, 1737–1745

South Carolina Gazette, October 29–November 5, 1737

Run away a short squat Negro man, named Stephen, was Patroon [operator] of a large Wood Boat, also a lusty strong Angola Negro, flat Nose, and much mark'd with the small Pox, is branded on the Shoulder AD. Whoever takes up these Negroes and carries them to Gaol, or my Plantation in Goose Creek, shall receive 10 £ for the first and 5 £ for the other.

Alexander Vander Dussen.

South Carolina Gazette, February 2–9, 1738

Run away from Tho: Wright, about two Years since, a Negro Man named Trampuse, branded on the right Shoulder TW in one, he could not speak English when he went away. If any Person gives any Intelligence of him so that he may be apprehended or discover'd shall receive upon Demand 50£ reward. Also run away in August last, a Negro Man named Paul, who had been one Year in my Plantation near Silk-Hope, he spoke little or no English. Whoever brings him to said Plantation, or can give any Intelligence of him, shall have 10 £ paid upon Demand. Also run away in November last, a Negro Man named Charles, he speaks pretty good English, is an elderly Fellow, is branded TW in one, on the right Shoulder, and has had a large Cut on the Small of his Back, he is supposed to be harboured by the Negroes of Silk-Hope Plantation. Whosoever apprehends him and brings him to my Plantation near Silk-Hope, shall have 5 £. Also run away in January last, from my Plantation near Silk-Hope, two new Negro Men, they speak but little English, they are branded on the right Shoulder TW in one, one of them is named Will, the other Summer. If any Person brings them to said Plantation, shall receive 40 s. reward for each.

Thomas Wright.

South Carolina Gazette, March 9–16, 1738

RUN AWAY from Ferdinando Dart in April last, a Negro Man, named Norcott, he could not speak English when he went away, & in October last, 3 Negro

From *South Carolina Gazette* and *Virginia Gazette*, 1737–1745.

Men, Sambo, Boswine, & Peter; Boswine branded on his Back D. And the 12th Instant, two Negro man, Adam & Strafford, both speak English, stought, able Fellows. Whoever carries them to my Plantation at Pon-Pon, or brings them to me in Charles-Town, shall have 40 s. for each of the two last, and 10 £ for each of the 4 first, from

John Dart.

South Carolina Gazette, March 23–30, 1738

Run away from Benjamin Godin's Plantation, about 3 Weeks since, 3 Angola Negro Men, named Harry, Cyrus and Chatham, they have been in the Country three Years, and speak little English, they are branded BG on the right or left Breast, and are suppos'd to be gone towards Winyaw, Harry having before (about a Year ago) run away and been taken up in that Part of the Country. Also run away a Mustee[1] Negro Man, named Sam, he is a short thick well made Fellow, and a Gambia Negro Man, named Ned, he speaks English, and is a lusty, tall Fallow, branded as aforesaid. Whoever shall apprehend the said Negroes or any of them, shall receive 10 £ per Head, from

Benj. Godin.

South Carolina Gazette, September 21, 1738

Run away from my Plantation at Goose-Creek, the 10th of Sept. a Negro Boy, named Hector, about 14 Years old, he had on when he went away, a Negro Cloth Jacket dyed Yellow, branded with a Blotch on each Breast, and upon his left Buttock JR. Whosoever brings the said Boy to me at my Plantation, or to Gaol in Charles-Town shall be paid by me the Sum of 40 s. as Witness my Hand,

Ja: Rockford.

South Carolina Gazette, February 1, 1739

Run away from Rebeccah Massey in Charlestown, about 10 Weeks past, a Mustee young Wench, named Ruth, is suppos'd to be gone towards Ponpon or Dorchester; she speaks good English, born in the said Town, and brought up here in a Family; she is of a middle Stature, and her upper fore Teeth are a little rotten. Whoever takes her up, gives her 50 good Lashes, and delivers her to me, shall have 10 £ reward.

Rebeccah Massey.
Robert Chesley.

Virginia Gazette, October 19–26, 1739

RAN away from the Subscriber, living at Capt. Anthony Thornton's Quarter, in Caroline County, a Negro Man; he is a middle-siz'd Fellow, has Three Marks down each Temple, and can't speak a word of English: He had on when he went away, an old Checkt Shirt, and an old pair of Oznabrig[2] Trowsers. Whoever will apprehend the said Slave, so that I may have him again, shall have a Pistole Reward, besides what the Law allows—

John Pearce.

---

[1]**Mustee**: A person of mixed racial ancestry.
[2]**Oznabrig**: Osnaburg was a coarse fabric.

Virginia Gazette, October 26–November 2, 1739

RAN away on the 30th of September last, from the Subscriber, living in Hanover County, Two Negros, viz. A Negro Man, nam'd Roger, born at Angola, a pretty tall, well-set Fellow, about 30 Years Old: He had on, when he went away, a new Oznabrig shirt, and an old Cotton Wastecoat, a Pair of Virginia Cloth Breeches, striped Black and White, and a Pair of Country-made Shoes. The other, a thick square Woman, named Moll, about 18 Years old, Virginia born; is Wife to the above-nam'd Roger, and is very big with Child. She had on, an old Oznabrig Shift, an old cotton Wastecoat and Petticoat. They both speak tolerable good English. Whoever will bring the said Negroes to me, at my House, in Hanover county, shall have a Pistole Reward for each of them, besides what the Law allows.

John Shelton.

Virginia Gazette, May 2–9, 1745

RAN away, on the 17th of April last, from the Subscriber in Caroline County, a lusty, tawney Negro Man, nam'd Will; he is hollow-chested, stoops in the Shoulders a little, and is about 30 Years old. Also a small Mulatto Man, nam'd Peter, aged about 21 Years; well known by the Gentlemen in the Country, for keeping of Horses. He always has a great Quid of Tobacco in his Mouth. He had with him a Pair of Pumps, a Check Shirt, a brown double breasted Coat, and a Felt Hat. Whoever takes up and convoys them, or either of them, to my House in the County aforesaid, shall have a Pistole Reward, for each.

Henry Armistead.

N.B. I desire each Constable to give them 20 Lashes.

And whoever will apprehend the said Servant and Slave, and bring them to me, in St. Mary's County, on Potowmack, or to Major John Waughop, in Northumberland County, Virginia, on Potowmack River, shall have 6 pistoles Reward, and reasonable Charges, paid by Major Waughop, aforesaid, or by me.

Virginia Gazette, May 9–16, 1745
North Carolina, April 24, 1745

RAN away, on the 18th Instant, from the Plantation of the late Col. William Wilson, deceas'd, Two Slaves belonging to the Subscriber, the one a tall Yellow Fellow, named Emanuel, about 6 Feet high, six or seven and Twenty Years of Age; hath a Scar on the outside of his left Thigh, which was cut with an Ax; he had on when he went away, a blue Jacket, an Ozenbrig Shirt and Trousers, and a Worsted[3] Cap; he speaks pretty good English, and calls himself a Portugueze; is by Trade a Cooper, and took with him some Cooper's Tools. The other is a short, thick, well-set Fellow, stoops forward pretty much as he walks; does not speak so plain as the other; had on when he went away an Ozenbrig Pair of Trousers and Shirt, a white Negro Cotton Jacket, and took with him an Axe: They went away in a small Cannoe, and were seen at Capt. Pearson's, on Nuse River, the 18th Inst. and 'tis believ'd are gone towards Virginia. Whoever takes up the said Negros, and brings them to my House on Trent River, North-Carolina, or secures them so that I may have them again, shall have Four Pistoles Reward for each, paid by

Mary Wilson.

---

[3]**Worsted**: Textile made with twisted yarn.

Virginia Gazette, May 9–16, 1745

RAN away from the Subscriber's Quarter, on the Robinson River, in Orange County, the following Negro's, viz. Sambo, a small, thin visaged Fellow, about 30 Years of Age, speaks English so as to be understood; had on, when he went away, a Hat, an Oznabrig Shirt, a dark colour'd Coat, with a small Cape to it, lin'd with velvet, and is too long for him, Cotton Jacket and Breaches, a Pair of Yarn stockings, London Fall Shoes and Buckles. Aaron, a tall Fellow, much Pock-fretten, about 35 Years of Age, can't speak English; he took with him a Hat, an Oznabrig Shirt, Cotton Jacket and Breaches, a Pair of Plaid Hose, and Shoes. Berwick, a tall, smooth-faced Fellow, about 20 Years of Age, can't speak English; he took with him a Hat, an Oznabrig Shirt, a fearnothing Coat, Cotton Jacket and Breaches, a Pair of Plaid Hose, and Shoes. They are all new Negro's, and went together; they have not been above 8 Months in the Country. Whoever takes up, and convoys the said Negro's to the aforesaid Quarter, or me, at Fredericksburg, shall have Twenty Shillings Reward for each, besides what the Law allows, and reasonable Charges.

William Hunter.

Virginia Gazette, October 3–10, 1745

RAN away from the Subscriber, living in Hanover, two new Negro Men, imported from Gambia, in the Brig. Ranger, and sold at Newcastle the 5th of September last; they understand no English, and are near 6 Feet high, each; one of them is nam'd Jack, a right Black, with a Scar over the Right Eye-brow; the other a yellow Fellow, with 3 small Strokes on each Side of his Face, like this Mark ( ). They had on, each, a knap'd new Cotton Jacket and Breeches, without either Buttons or Button-holes, a new Oznabrig Shirt, and new Felt Hats. They stole a fine Damask Table-Cloth, 10 qrs. square, 5 Yards and a Half of fine Scot Linen, 3 Yards and a Half of Scots 3 qr. Check, a white Holland Shirt, and a Silk Handkerchief. Whoever takes up the said Negroes, and Goods, and brings them to me, or to Mr. Robert Brown, Merchant, in Newcastle, shall be rewarded, as the law allows.

Margaret Arbuthnott.

QUESTIONS FOR READING AND DISCUSSION

1. How did the advertisers describe Africans? What assumptions did they make about how readers of the ads would recognize the runaways? What do those assumptions suggest about the relationships between whites and blacks, free people and slaves, native-born and African-born people?
2. What did the runaways' names suggest about them and their masters? What evidence suggests how masters treated these runaways?
3. Why were some slaves more valuable than others? What clues can you find in the ads to explain the differences in rewards?
4. Do the advertisements contain hints about why the runaways absconded? What might have accounted for the lag of time between running away and the placement of the advertisement?
5. What were the differences between the advertisements in South Carolina and in Virginia? How did those differences suggest contrasts in slavery in the two colonies in the eighteenth century?

DOCUMENT 5–5

A Moravian Missionary Interviews Slaves in the West Indies, 1767–1768

Few Europeans expressed much interest in the views of the millions of African men, women, and children enslaved during the eighteenth century. Christian George Andreas Oldendorp was a rare exception. A Moravian minister, Oldendorp was in his fifties when he traveled from Germany to the West Indies to write a history of Moravian missionary activities there. Oldendorp interviewed numerous slaves in the West Indies and described what he learned from them in a book published in 1777. Oldendorp's narrative, translated from German to English and excerpted below, emphasized the differences among Africans and the contributions of those differences to the slave trade. Had anybody taken the trouble to interview enslaved Africans in North America, the slaves probably would have echoed many of the observations made by the people Oldendorp interviewed.

Christian George Andreas Oldendorp

History of the Evangelical Brethren's Mission on the Caribbean Islands, 1777

The reports about the political and moral conditions of different black nations in Guinea and other African countries . . . have been gathered through interviews with Negroes from approximately thirty nations. I hoped, by means of these interviews with baptized slaves who were known as intelligent and upstanding people, to contribute additional and more reliable information concerning these nations than that which had been known heretofore. Yet the considerable ignorance of these people and their inability to articulately express their ideas has caused my hope to remain very much unfulfilled. . . .

Europeans obtained black slaves from that part of the African coast which lies between . . . the Senegal or Niger River to the foothills of the Black Mountains — a stretch of some 800 German miles. . . . This . . . same area contains many large and small kingdoms and peoples who differ in language, tradition, and custom. The number of these kingdoms is often exaggerated, because of misunderstandings caused by the different names which one nation may be given. . . . Often when a black is asked for the name of his nation, he gives the name of the location of the nation in Guinea. Thus the location can easily be mistaken for the name of a nation. Even these names are pronounced differently by the Negroes. . . .

There [is] . . . just as much variation among this race as exists among the white. . . . The Negroes divide themselves into many peoples, which differ more or less in language, customs, traditions, and religion. They form many individual states almost all of which have a despotic political structure wherein the regent arbitrarily rules over his subjects. . . .

From Christian George Andreas Oldendorp, *History of the Evangelical Brethren's Mission on the Caribbean Islands of St. Thomas, St. Cross, and St. John* (Leipzig, 1777), trans. from German in Soi-Daniel W. Brown, "From the Tongues of Africa: A Partial Translation of Oldendorp's Interviews," *Plantation Society*, II (1983), 37–61.

I obtained a report about the *Kanga* nation from four Negro men and two Negro women. They share borders with the *Mandingo* and *Fula*, but don't understand their language. They do, however, understand the *Mangree* who live deep in the middle of the land. . . . They do business with whites on the ocean, with whom they trade slaves, tiger pelts, and ivory for weapons, powder, lead, iron, corals, and rum. The Negro merchants who do this trade can reason mathematically and read. Iron rings which the *Kanga* forge themselves serve as currency within the tribe. Only the well-off have gold and the gold is not used for money. There are almost constant internal wars. One tribe attacks another solely for the purpose of capturing men to be sold to whites as slaves. . . .

Now I come to the nations of the Goldcoast and from there eastward into the inland, the area in which most of the slaves brought to the West Indies originate. The most powerful nation on this coast is the *Amina*. I sought information on the *Amina* nation from five intelligent Negroes. One of them, a rich merchant and slave catcher in Guinea, knew more than usual because of his journeys. Another was the king's brother and the third had been in command of a 3,000-man army belonging to a relative who was a vassal of the king. The remaining two were of the common folk. . . .

The nation is under a king, who governs the different provinces of his realm by vassal-kings. . . . Their territory is very large and has many villages. Their neighbors fear them because of their power. They war almost constantly against the *Sante, Akkran, Beremang, Assein, Kiseru, Atti, Okkan,* and *Adansi* for the sole purpose of kidnapping. They have rifles while their enemies generally use bow and arrows. In addition, civil wars are often caused by the many royal heirs and heirs of vassal-kings who make the succession of government disputable for one another. There is much gold in the territory, but no iron, therefore iron is very valuable. Their money consists of gold pieces and partly of a type of ocean mussel they call *Bujis* or *Cowris*. . . . They trade gold, ivory and slaves with the Europeans for iron, weapons, etc. . . . The *Amina*, like many other African nations, hold slaves as servants, who, in their opinion, are not treated as harshly as the West Indian slaves. . . .

The *Sokko* or *Asokko*, of which I spoke to three Negroes, border the *Amina* on one side and *Uwong* on the other. They take from six to seven weeks to reach the seacoast from their country. Their king, who has many lesser kings or governors under him, is always called *Mansa*. They have to fight a continuous defensive war against the *Amina* and other nations which invade their states for the purpose of kidnapping. Nevertheless, they inflict the same injustice upon their neighbors that they find abominable in the *Amina*, only they don't kidnap any of their own people. They trade with the Whites and also have regular small shops. They use coral and mussels among themselves instead of small coins. They lack neither gold nor iron in their country, nor artisans to work the metals. . . . I understand from the narration of one of the three *Sokko* Negroes who lived far from the other two, that a part of this nation is Islamic, and also some have employed the worship habits of Christians. They call God, Allah, and worship him in houses set aside for that purpose, and the priests who are in charge use a book during the worship service. They hold their morning and evening prayers very punctually. They get up before the sunrise and observe a deep silence until they have washed themselves. As soon as the sun appears, the father of the house kneels down with his family on a mat and leads the prayer with his face toward the sun. The evening prayer is done similarly after having washed their faces, hands, and feet. They have been introduced to baptism, as well as circumcision. The latter is performed on every slave, because, as they say, he otherwise could not be intelligent or speak. . . .

The *Kalabari* live apparently on the river *Kalabar*. It is also possible that they are sold for the most part on this river, and received their name for that reason. The five Negroes from this nation to whom I spoke were cheerful and hearty. They told me they had lived very far from the sea, and that a large stream flows through their land. . . . The *Ibo*, a very populous people, are their neighbors and friends who share the same language with them. Among their other neighbors they also named the *Apur* and the *Bibi* or *Bivi*. They claim that the latter were cannibals. Therefore they were very afraid of being captured by them. I have seen one of these *Bibi* myself, who recently was brought from Guinea to St. Thomas. His upper and lower teeth were filed to points like a saw; he had a fearsome countenance and was very strong. The land of the *Karabari* has gold, however, they use sea mussels instead of coins. Their king is called *Delemango*, which means a great man. Insults cause civil wars to break out frequently among chiefs or governors, whom he places over different provinces of his kingdom. The wars are put to an end by him, only when it appears that they are going too far with it. Their weapons consist of flintlocks, sabers, spears and poisoned arrows. They sell their prisoners of war who then are passed from one master to another so that one often has had 50 or more masters before he is sold to the Europeans on the coast. . . .

A *Loango* Negro called the highest regent of his nation *Aressan Congo*. Two kings, *Maluango* and *Macongo*, are his vassals, between whom war broke out because the latter refused to continue to give the former a young woman as yearly tribute. They have firearms, bow and arrows as weapons. The *Loango* land is rich in gold. The king's throne is made from this precious metal and the women wear golden arm and leg bands. . . . It is known that the English, Dutch and French get many slaves from this coast. . . .

The Negroes from the *Congo* nation who came to the West Indies have, for the most part, a recognition of the true God and of Jesus Christ, and are more intelligent and cultured than other blacks. This is due to the influence of the Portuguese, who, from their arrival on this coast [of Africa], made an effort to enlighten and better this unknowledgeable people. They achieved that intention with those who lived near them; those who lived far from them deep in the inland had a religion that was a combination of Christian ceremonies and heathen superstition. . . .

As I discussed [different crimes and punishments] . . . with the Negroes, an *Amina* who had been a merchant gave the answer that in Guinea one did not know much about sins, for everyone considered that which he did to be right. The Whites had a conscience indeed, but the Negroes had no self-reproach about anything. Also when they were punished for a crime, they did not seek the guilt in themselves. On the contrary, they blame all evil on the devil. Whereas a Negro is very forgiving toward himself, he tends to punish others harshly when they have committed some wrongdoing against him. Certain actions that negatively affect life, goods, or rights are consistently considered to be crimes and punishable. . . .

The *Amina* merchant who was a slave in St. Thomas would give his debtors a grace period of three months in Guinea. If the payment was not made within that period, he would have the members of the debtor's family caught, if he could, especially the children, and paid himself by selling them to the Europeans. Many a debtor gives his wife or his daughter—of his own accord—in payment of a debt. The Negro believes he has as much right over them as over any other type of his possessions. Surely for this reason it must not be as strange for the Negro when he is sold, as for the European who was raised under different customs. Kidnapping is generally frequent among the Negroes not only to gain retribution but, like every other theft, for unjustified reasons as well. Since the European pays so well for this product, almost no Negro is safe from being sold into slavery by the first one who can overpower him. Because the regents themselves commit this injustice publicly, and invade each other's lands solely for this purpose, kidnapping has a privileged status among injustices. Furthermore, since one nation exercises its right to revenge on the other, enduring wars come about, which increase the misery in these nations to a point which complete anarchy would not exceed. . . .

The Negro nations are as unknowledgeable as they are superstitious. The first case is due more to lack of teaching than to the lack of ability. A slave that has just been traded from Guinea to the West Indies is apparently as dumb as a child. But there is no lack of examples of such who with time, especially after they are enlightened through the teaching of Jesus Christ, have achieved a healthy mind and great physical dexterity. Even in Guinea there are different nations in which the art of reading and writing are not completely unknown. In addition to the *Fula*, . . . many *Mandinga* not only can read and write, but can do math and have a knack for business. Also many crafts are done among them, and spinning, sewing, and weaving are arts that they know.

QUESTIONS FOR READING AND DISCUSSION

1. Oldendorp stressed the differences among Africans. In what ways were those differences important to the Africans? To Europeans?

2. What might have motivated the "baptized slaves" Oldendorp interviewed "who were known as intelligent and upstanding people"? How might their motives have shaped what they told Oldendorp?

3. "Kidnapping is generally frequent among the Negroes," Oldendorp declared. How was kidnapping related to slavery in Africa and to the transatlantic trade in African slaves? According to Oldendorp, how did Africans become enslaved? How did the slaves Oldendorp interviewed probably account for their own enslavement?

4. Do you think the observation of the *Amina* merchant who told Oldendorp that, "in Guinea one did not know much about sins, for every one considered that which he did to be right," sheds any light on slavery? Why or why not? Was the merchant opposed to slavery? Were the other Africans Oldendorp interviewed? Was Oldendorp? Why or why not?

5. How did Oldendorp account for the differences between Africans and Europeans? Did he believe such differences were innate or permanent? Do you think Oldendorp's narrative was shaped in important ways by his Christian faith? If so, how? If not, why not?

COMPARATIVE QUESTIONS

1. How did the choices made by Ashbridge, New Light converts, and the slaves compare with those recommended by Father Abraham? What basic values guided the behavior of each?

2. What role does religion play in the documents in this chapter? What forms of faith are exhibited in the documents?

3. In what ways do the documents reflect the significance of individualism in the eighteenth-century colonies? What freedoms and constraints did individuals experience? In what ways were individuals forced to conform to values imposed by the greater society?

4. According to the documents, how did relations among people from different racial groups compare with those among people in the same racial group? To what extent do the documents suggest contrasts or similarities between racial relationships in the northern and southern colonies?

5. The documents illustrate many of the ways that commerce influenced the eighteenth-century colonies. To what extent did commerce introduce change and novelty in the lives of eighteenth-century residents of British North America? In what ways did commerce create conditions of stability and order? To what extent did it foster turmoil and disorder?

6

The British Empire and the Colonial Crisis

1754–1775

British policies toward the colonies had the effect of making legally constituted authority seem unjust and illegitimate to many colonists. In such
circumstances, many colonists concluded that it was necessary to point
out injustices and petition for their redress while others resolved to take justice
into their own hands. When existing structures of authority began to crumble,
colonists loyal to the British found themselves judged by crowds who did not
share their notions of justice while British officials debated how to respond to the
disorder. Native Americans maneuvered to take advantage of the colonial crisis as
best they could. The following documents disclose the ideas that animated rebellious colonists and some of the ways they and some Native Americans acted on
those ideas.

DOCUMENT 6–1

Mary Jemison Is Captured by Seneca Indians during the Seven Years' War

*During the Seven Years' War, French soldiers and their Seneca Indian allies captured
Mary Jemison and her family on their frontier farm in southern Pennsylvania. Jemison,
who was about fifteen years old at the time, was eventually adopted by the Seneca and lived
for decades among the Indians. When she was about eighty years old, she told her story
to minister James E. Seaver, who published it. In the excerpt below, Jemison describes her
capture by the French and Seneca, her experiences as an adopted Seneca, and the negotiations on the eve of the American Revolution between the Indians, the colonists, and the
British. Jemison's narrative highlights the terrors of frontier warfare, the satisfactions of
peace, and the unsteady balance of alliances among the Indians, the French, the colonists,
and the British.*

James E. Seaver

A Narrative of the Life of Mrs. Mary Jemison, 1824

Resolved to leave the land of their nativity [Jemison's parents left] . . . Ireland . . . [and] set sail for this country, in the year 1742 or 3 on board the ship Mary William, bound to Philadelphia. . . .

The intestine divisions, civil wars, and ecclesiastical rigidity and domination that prevailed those days, were the causes of their leaving their mother country. . . .

Excepting my birth, nothing remarkable occurred to my parents on their passage, and they were safely landed at Philadelphia. My father being fond of rural life, and having been bred to agricultural pursuits, soon left the city, and removed his family to the then frontier settlements of Pennsylvania, to a tract of excellent land. . . . At that place he cleared a large farm, and for seven or eight years enjoyed the fruits of his industry. Peace attended their labors; and they had nothing to alarm them. . . .

In the spring of 1752, and through the succeeding seasons, the stories of Indian barbarities inflicted upon the whites in those days, frequently excited in my parents the most serious alarm for our safety.

The next year the storm gathered faster; many murders were committed; and many captives were exposed to meet death in its most frightful form. . . .

In 1754, an army for the protection of the settlers, and to drive back the French and Indians, was raised from the militia of the colonial governments, and placed (secondarily) under the command of Col. George Washington. . . . The French and Indians, after the surrender of Fort Necessity by Col. Washington, . . . grew more and more terrible. The death of the whites, and plundering and burning their property, was apparently their only object. . . .

The return of a new-year's day [after the beginning of the Seven Years' War] found us unmolested. . . . I got home with the horse very early in the morning, where I found a man that lived in our neighborhood, and his sister-in-law who had three children. . . . Immediately after I got home, the man took the horse to go to his house after a bag of grain, and took his gun in his hand for the purpose of killing game. . . . Our family, as usual, was busily employed about their common business. Father was . . . at the side of the house; mother was making preparations for breakfast;—my two oldest brothers were at work near the barn; and the little ones, with myself, and the woman and her three children, were in the house.

Breakfast was not yet ready, when we were alarmed by the discharge of a number of guns, that seemed to be near. Mother and the woman . . . almost fainted at the report, and every one trembled with fear. On opening the door, the man and horse lay dead near the house, having just been shot by the Indians. . . . They first secured my father, and then rushed into the house, and without the least resistance made prisoners of my mother, . . . [the rest of Jemison's family except two of her brothers, who escaped], the woman and her three children, and myself, and then commenced plundering. . . .

The party that took us consisted of six Indians and four Frenchmen, who . . . took what they considered most valuable; consisting principally of bread, meal and meat. Having taken as much provision as they could carry, they set out

From James E. Seaver, *A Narrative of the Life of Mrs. Mary Jemison* (Canandaigua, NY: J. D. Bemis, 1824).

with their prisoners in great haste, for fear of detection, and soon entered the woods. . . .

[A few days later], an . . . Indian took the little boy and myself by the hand, to lead us off from the company, when my mother exclaimed, "Don't cry Mary—don't cry my child. God will bless you! Farewell—farewell!"

The Indian led us some distance into the bushes, or woods, and there lay down with us to spend the night. . . . but our friends were left behind. It is impossible for any one to form a correct idea of what my feelings were at the sight of those savages, whom I supposed had murdered my parents and brothers, sister, and friends. . . . But what could I do? A poor little defenceless girl; without the power or means of escaping; without a home to go to, even if I could be liberated; without a knowledge of the direction or distance to my former place of residence; and without a living friend to whom to fly for protection. . . .

My suspicions as to the fate of my parents proved too true; for soon after I left them they were killed and scalped, together with [three of Jemison's siblings], and the woman and her two children, and mangled in the most shocking manner. . . .

After a hard day's march we encamped in a thicket, where the Indians made a shelter of boughs, and then built a good fire to warm and dry our benumbed limbs and clothing. . . . Here we were again fed as before. When the Indians had finished their supper they took from their baggage a number of scalps and went about preparing them for the market . . . by straining them over small hoops . . . and then drying and scraping them by the fire. . . . Those scalps I knew at the time must have been taken from our family by the color of the hair. My mother's hair was red; and I could easily distinguish my father's and the children's from each other. . . .

When we set off [down the Ohio river], an Indian in the forward canoe took the scalps of my former friends, strung them on a pole that he placed upon his shoulder, and in that manner carried them, standing in the stern of the canoe, directly before us [in a following canoe] as we sailed down the river. . . .

It was my happy lot to be accepted for adoption; and at the time of the ceremony I was received by the two squaws . . . and I was ever considered and treated by them as a real sister, the same as though I had been born of their mother. . . .

[Four years later] I had then been with the Indians four summers and four winters, and had become so far accustomed to their mode of living, habits and dispositions, that my anxiety to get away, to be set at liberty, and leave them, had almost subsided. With them was my home; my [Indian] family was there, and there I had many friends to whom I was warmly attached in consideration of the favors, affection and friendship with which they had uniformly treated me, from the time of my adoption. Our labor was not severe; and that of one year was exactly similar, in almost every respect, to that of the others, without that endless variety that is to be observed in the common labor of the white people. Notwithstanding the Indian women have all the fuel and bread to procure, and the cooking to perform, their task is probably not harder than that of white women, who have those articles provided for them; and their cares certainly are not half as numerous, nor as great. In the summer season, we planted, tended and harvested our corn, and generally had all our children with us; but had no master to oversee or drive us, so that we could work as leisurely as we pleased. . . .

Notwithstanding all that has been said against the Indians, in consequence of their cruelties to their enemies—cruelties that I have witnessed, and had abundant proof of—it is a fact that they are naturally kind, tender and peaceable

towards their friends, and strictly honest; and that those cruelties have been practised, only upon their enemies, according to their idea of justice. . . .

After the conclusion of the French war, our tribe had nothing to trouble it till
the commencement of the Revolution. For twelve or fifteen years the use of the
implements of war was not known. . . . No people can live more happy than the
Indians did in times of peace, before the introduction of spirituous liquors amongst
them. Their lives were a continual round of pleasures. Their wants were few,
and easily satisfied; and their cares were only for to-day; the bounds of their
calculations for future comfort not extending to the incalculable uncertainties of
to-morrow. . . . The moral character of the Indians was . . . uncontaminated. Their
fidelity was perfect . . . ; they were strictly honest; they despised deception and
falsehood; and chastity was held in high veneration, and a violation of it was
considered sacrilege. They were temperate in their desires, moderate in their passions, and candid and honorable in the expression of their sentiments on every
subject of importance.

Thus, at peace amongst themselves, and with the neighboring whites, . . . our
Indians lived quietly and peaceably at home, till a little before the breaking out of
the revolutionary war, when they were sent for, together with the Chiefs and
members of the Six Nations generally, by the people of the States, to . . . ascertain . . . who they should esteem and treat as enemies, and who as friends, in the
great war which was then upon the point of breaking out between them and the
King of England.

Our Indians obeyed the call, and . . . a treaty made, in which the Six Nations
solemnly agreed that if a war should eventually break out, they would not take
up arms on either side; but that they would observe a strict neutrality. With that
the people of the states were satisfied, as they had not asked their assistance, nor
did not wish it. . . .

About a year passed off, and we, as usual, were enjoying ourselves in the
employments of peaceable times, when a messenger arrived from the British
Commissioners, requesting . . . a council of the Six Nations . . . to engage their
assistance in subduing the rebels, the people of the states, who had risen up
against the good King, their master, and were about to rob him of a great part of
his possessions and wealth, and added that they [the British] would amply reward
them [the Indians] for all their services.

The Chiefs . . . informed the [British] Commissioners of the nature and extent
of the treaty which they had entered into with the people of the states, the year
before, and that they should not violate it by taking up the hatchet against them.

The Commissioners continued their entreaties without success, till they addressed their [the Indians'] avarice, by telling our people that the people of the
states were few in number, and easily subdued; and that on the account of their
disobedience to the King, they justly merited all the punishment that it was
possible for white men and Indians to inflict upon them; and added, that the King
was rich and powerful, both in money and subjects: That his rum was as plenty
as the water in lake Ontario: that his men were as numerous as the sands upon the
lake shore: — and that the Indians, if they would assist in the war, and persevere
in their friendship to the King, till it was closed, should never want for money or
goods. Upon this the Chiefs concluded a treaty with the British Commissioners,
in which they agreed to take up arms against the rebels, and continue in the
service of his Majesty. . . .

As soon as the treaty was finished, the Commissioners made a present to each
Indian of a suit of clothes, a brass kettle, a gun and tomahawk, a scalping knife,

a quantity of powder and lead, a piece of gold, and promised a bounty on every scalp that should be brought in. Thus richly clad and equipped, they returned home . . . full of the fire of war, and anxious to encounter their enemies. . . . Hired to commit depredations upon the whites, who had given them no offence, they waited impatiently to commence their labor, till sometime in the spring of 1776, when a convenient opportunity offered for them to make an attack. . . .

QUESTIONS FOR READING AND DISCUSSION

1. How did what Jemison termed "Indian barbarities" and the colonists' responses to them shape her life?
2. Why did Jemison become "accustomed to" the Senecas' "mode of living, habits, and disposition"? How did life for women among the Seneca compare to that among white settlers, according to Jemison?
3. Why did Jemison believe the Seneca were "naturally kind, tender and peaceable towards their friends, and strictly honest"? To what extent would other white colonists have been likely to agree?
4. Why did the "Chiefs" agree to "take up arms against the rebels, and continue in the service of his Majesty"?
5. Jemison dictated her memoir long after the American Revolution when she was quite elderly. To what extent do you think her account of her life among the Seneca might have been influenced by her age and the successful conclusion of the Revolution?

DOCUMENT 6–2

An Oration on the Second Anniversary of the Boston Massacre

For many years after 1770, Bostonians commemorated the Boston Massacre with an address by a leading patriot. This oration by Joseph Warren on March 5, 1772, attacked British policies and reminded colonists of their duties to themselves and their ancestors. Warren, a Boston physician and political activist, later served as a militia officer and was killed at Bunker Hill. His Boston Massacre oration, excerpted here, illustrates the arguments that made sense to many colonists and the passion with which they defended their beliefs.

Joseph Warren

Boston Massacre Oration, March 5, 1772

Let us now allow ourselves a few moments to examine the late Acts of the British Parliament for taxing America. Let us with candour judge whether they are constitutionally binding upon us; if they are, in the name of justice let us submit to them, without one murmuring word.

First, I would ask whether the members of the British House of Commons are the democracy of this province? If they are, they are either the people of this

From Hezekiah Niles, ed., *Centennial Offering: Republication of the Principles and Acts of the Revolution in America* (New York: A. S. Barres, 1876), 753–59.

province, or are elected by the people of this province to represent them, and have therefore a constitutional right to originate a bill for taxing them; it is most certain they are neither; and therefore nothing done by them can be said to be done by the democratic branch of our constitution. I would next ask, whether the lords, who compose the aristocratic branch of the legislature, are peers of America? I never heard it was ... so much as pretended, and if they are not, certainly no act of theirs can be said to be the act of the aristocratic branch of our constitution. . . . I do not conceive it to be of the least importance to us by whom our property is taken away, so long as it is taken without our consent; and I am very much at a loss to know by what figure of rhetoric, the inhabitants of this province can be called free subjects, when they are obliged to obey implicitly, such laws as are made for them by men three thousand miles off, whom they know not, and whom they never empowered to act for them, or how they can be said to have property, when a body of men, over whom they have not the least control, and who are not in any way accountable to them, shall oblige them to deliver up any part, or the whole of their substance without even asking their consent; and yet whoever pretends that the late Acts of the British Parliament for taxing America ought to be deemed binding upon us, must admit at once that we are absolute slaves, and have no property of our own; or else that we may be freemen, and at the same time under a necessity of obeying the arbitrary commands of those over whom we have no control or influence, and that we may have property of our own which is entirely at the disposal of another. Such gross absurdities, I believe, will not be relished in this enlightened age: and it can be no matter of wonder that the people quickly perceived, and seriously complained of the inroads which these Acts must unavoidably make upon their liberty, and of the hazard to which their whole property is by them exposed; for, if they may be taxed without their consent, even in the smallest trifle, they may also, without their consent, be deprived of everything they possess, although never so valuable, never so dear. . . . [A]s it was soon found that this taxation could not be supported by reason and argument, it seemed necessary that one act of oppression should be enforced by another, and therefore, contrary to our just rights as possessing, or at least having a just title to possess, all the liberties and immunities of British subjects, a standing army was established among us in time of peace; and evidently for the purpose of . . . enforcement of obedience to acts which, upon fair examination, appeared to be unjust and unconstitutional. . . .

That this was the avowed design of stationing an armed force in this town is sufficiently known; and we, my fellow citizens, have seen, we have felt the tragical effects! *The fatal fifth of March, 1770, can never be forgotten.* The horrors of *that dreadful night* are but too deeply impressed on our hearts. Language is too feeble to paint the emotion of our souls, when our streets were stained with the blood of our brethren — when our ears were wounded by the groans of the dying, and our eyes were tormented with the sight of the mangled bodies of the dead.

When our alarmed imagination presented to our view our houses wrapped in flames, our children subjected to the barbarous caprice of the raging soldiery, our beauteous virgins exposed to all the insolence of unbridled passion, our virtuous wives, endeared to us by every tender tie, falling a sacrifice to worse than brutal violence, and perhaps like the famed Lucretia[1] distracted with anguish and

---

[1]**Lucretia**: A virtuous woman of ancient Rome whose suicide, after her rape by the son of King Tarquinius Superbus, led to the expulsion of the Tarquin line of kings and the establishment of the Roman republic.

despair, ending their wretched lives by their own fair hands. When we beheld the authors of our distress parading in our streets, or drawn up in a regular *battalia*, as though in a hostile city, our hearts beat to arms; we snatched our weapons, almost resolved by one decisive stroke to avenge the death of our slaughtered brethren, and to secure from future danger all that we held most dear: but propitious heaven forbade the bloody carnage and saved the threatened victims of our too keen resentment, not by their discipline, not by their regular array, no, it was royal George's livery that proved their shield—it was that which turned the pointed engines of destruction from their breasts. The thoughts of vengeance were soon buried in our inbred affection to Great Britain, and calm reason dictated a method of removing the troops more mild than an immediate resource to the sword. With united efforts you urged the immediate departure of the troops from the town—you urged it, with a resolution which ensured success—you obtained your wishes, and the removal of the troops was effected without one drop of their blood being shed by the inhabitants. . . .

I do not know one single advantage which can arise to the British nation from our being enslaved. I know not of any gains which can be wrung from us by oppression which they may not obtain from us by our own consent in the smooth channel of commerce. We wish the wealth and prosperity of Britain; we contribute largely to both. . . . The amazing increase of riches to Britain, the great rise of the value of her lands, the flourishing state of her navy, are striking proofs of the advantages derived to her from her commerce with the colonies; and it is our earnest desire that she may still continue to enjoy the same emoluments, until her streets are paved with *American gold*; only, let us have the pleasure of calling it our own whilst it is in our own hands; but this it seems is too great a favour. We are to be governed by the *absolute command of others; our property is to be taken away without our consent*. If we complain, our complaints are treated with contempt; if we assert our rights, that assertion is deemed insolence; if we humbly offer to submit the matter to the impartial decision of reason, the *sword* is judged the most proper argument to silence our murmurs! But this cannot long be the case. Surely the British nation will not suffer the reputation of their justice and their honour to be thus sported away by a capricious ministry; no, they will in a short time open their eyes to their true interest. They nourish in their own breasts a noble love of liberty; they hold her dear, and they know that all who have once possessed her charms had rather die than suffer her to be torn from their embraces. They are also sensible that Britain is so deeply interested in the prosperity of the colonies that she must eventually feel every wound given to their freedom; they cannot be ignorant that more dependence may be placed on the affections of a brother than on the forced service of a slave; they must approve your efforts for the preservation of your rights; from a sympathy of soul they must pray for your success. And I doubt not but they will, ere long, exert themselves effectually, to redress your grievances. . . .

You have, my friends and countrymen, frustrated the designs of your enemies by your unanimity and fortitude. It was your union and determined spirit which expelled those troops who polluted your streets with innocent blood. You have appointed this anniversary as a standard memorial of the *bloody consequences of placing an armed force in a populous city*, and of your deliverance from the dangers which then seemed to hang over your heads; and I am confident that you never will betray the least want of spirit when called upon to guard your freedom. None but they who set a just value upon the blessings of liberty are worthy to enjoy her. Your illustrious fathers were her zealous votaries. When the blasting frowns of tyranny drove her from public view they clasped her in their arms, they cherished her in their generous bosoms, they brought her safe over the rough ocean and fixed her seat in this then dreary wilderness; they nursed her infant age with the most tender care; for her sake they patiently bore the severest hardships; for her support they underwent the most rugged toils, in her defence they boldly encountered the most alarming dangers; neither the ravenous beasts that ranged the woods for prey, nor the more furious savages of the wilderness could damp ardour! . . . God prospered their valour, they preserved her brilliancy unsullied; they enjoyed her whilst they lived, and dying, bequeathed the dear inheritance to your care. And as they left you this glorious legacy, they have undoubtedly transmitted to you some portion of their noble spirit, to inspire you with virtue to merit her, and courage to preserve her. You surely cannot, with such examples before your eyes, as every page of the history of this country affords, suffer your liberties to be ravished from you by lawless force, or cajoled away by flattery and fraud.

The voice of your fathers' blood cries to you from the ground, *my sons scorn to be slaves!* In vain we met the frowns of tyrants. In vain we crossed the boisterous ocean, found a new world and prepared it for the happy residence of liberty. In vain we toiled. In vain we fought. We bled in vain, if you, our offspring, want valour to repel the assaults of her invaders! Stain not the glory of your worthy ancestors, but like them resolve never to part with your birthright; be wise in your deliberations, and determined in your exertions for the preservation of your liberties. Follow not the dictates of passion, but enlist yourselves under the sacred banner of reason; use every method in your power to secure your rights; at least prevent the curses of posterity from being heaped upon your memories.

If you, with united zeal and fortitude, oppose the torrent of oppression; if you feel the true fire of patriotism burning in your breasts; if you, from your souls, despise the most gaudy dress that slavery can wear; if you really prefer the lonely cottage (whilst blest with liberty) to gilded palaces surrounded with the ensigns of slavery, you may have the fullest assurance that tyranny, with her whole accursed train, will hide their hideous heads in confusion, shame, and despair. If you perform your part, you must have the strongest confidence that the same Almighty Being who protected your pious and venerable forefathers — who enabled them to turn a barren wilderness into a fruitful field, who so often made bare his arm for their salvation, will still be mindful of you, their offspring.

May this Almighty Being graciously preside in all our councils. May he direct us to such measures as he himself shall approve, and be pleased to bless. May we ever be a people favoured of God. May our land be a land of liberty, the seat of virtue, the asylum of the oppressed, a name and a praise in the whole earth, until the last shock of time shall bury the empires of the world in one common undistinguished ruin!

QUESTIONS FOR READING AND DISCUSSION

1. According to Joseph Warren, why were the taxes imposed on the colonies unjust? What did he believe would happen if the colonies submitted to the taxes? How were the colonists threatened with becoming "absolute slaves"?

2. Why was an army stationed in Boston? What dangers did citizens face from such an army?

3. Did Warren believe British policy would change? What did he mean by asserting that the British "cannot be ignorant that more dependence may be placed

on the affections of a brother than on the forced service of a slave"? In what ways might British soldiers have criticized Warren's arguments?

4. How should the colonists' history guide them? How did their ancestors preserve liberty?

5. Why do you think Warren feminized the concept of liberty? How would his audience have been likely to respond to his descriptions of liberty?

DOCUMENT 6–3

A Boston Shoemaker Recalls British Arrogance and the Boston Tea Party

The high-handed arrogance of many British officials rankled many colonists. British assertions of supremacy in face-to-face encounters with colonists seemed to parallel parliamentary assertions of power over the colonies. George R. T. Hewes, a shoemaker in Boston during the 1770s, refused to back down to a haughty customs official and participated in the Boston Tea Party. Many years later, when Hewes was more than ninety years old, he recalled those events in an interview published in 1834. Hewes's narrative illustrates the contagious assertion of colonial rights among many Bostonians in the 1770s.

George R. T. Hewes

Memoir, 1834

One day . . . as I was returning from dinner, I met a man by the name of John Malcom, who was a custom-house officer, and a small boy, pushing his sled along, before him and just as I was passing the boy, he said to Malcom, what, sir, did you throw my chips into the snow for, yesterday? Upon which Malcom angrily replied, do you speak to me, you rascal; and, as he raised a cane he had in his hand, aiming it at the head of the boy, I spoke to Malcom, and said to him, you are not about to strike that boy with your cudgel, you may kill him; upon my saying that, he was suddenly diverted from the boy, and turning upon me, says, you d——d rascal, do you presume too, to speak to me? I replied to him, I am no rascal, sir, be it known to you; whereupon he struck me across the head with his cane, and knocked me down, and by the blow cut a hole in my hat two inches in length. At this moment, one Captain Godfry came up, and raising me up, asked who had struck me; Malcom, replied the by standers, while he, for fear of the displeasure of the populace, ran to his house, and shut himself up. The people, many of whom were soon collected around me, advised me to go immediately to Doctor Warren, and get him to dress my wound, which I did without delay; and the doctor, after [he] dressed it, observed to me it can be considered no misfortune that I had a thick skull, for had not yours been very strong, said he, it would have been broke; you have come within a hair's breath of losing your life. He then advised me to go to Mr. Quincy, a magistrate, and get a warrant, for the purpose of arresting

From James Hawkes, *A Retrospect of the Boston Tea-Party with a Memoir of George R. T. Hewes* (New York: S. S. Bliss, 1834), 33–43.

Malcom, which I did, and carried it immediately to a constable, by the name of Justine Hale, and delivered it to him, to serve, but when he came to the house where Malcom was locked up, it was surrounded by such a multitude he could not serve it. The people, however, soon broke open the door, and took Malcom into their custody. They then took him to the place where the massacre was committed, and there flogged him with thirty-nine stripes. After which, they besmeared him thoroughly with tar and feathers; they then whipped him through the town, till they arrived at the gallows, on the neck, where they gave him thirty-nine stripes more, and then, after putting one end of a rope about his neck, and throwing the other end over the gallows, told him to remember that he had come within one of being hanged. They then took him back to the house from whence they had taken him, and discharged him from their custody.

The severity of the flogging they had given him, together, with the cold coat of tar with which they had invested him, had such a benumbing effect upon his health, that it required considerable effort to restore his usual circulation. . . . I shall carry to my grave the scar which the wound Malcom gave me left on my head. . . . [Hewes goes on to describe the Boston Tea Party and its aftermath.]

The tea . . . was contained in three ships, laying near each other, at what was called at that time Griffin's wharf, and were surrounded by armed ships of war; the commanders of which had publicly declared, that if the rebels, as they were pleased to style the Bostonians, should not withdraw their opposition to the landing of the tea before . . . the 17th day of December, 1773, they should on that day force it on shore, under the cover of their cannon's mouth. On the day preceding the seventeenth, there was a meeting of the citizens of the county of Suffolk, convened at one of the churches in Boston, for the purpose of consulting on what measures might be considered, expedient to prevent the landing of the tea, or secure the people from the collection of the duty. At that meeting a committee was appointed to wait on Governor Hutchinson, and request him to inform them whether he would take any measures to satisfy the people on the object of the meeting. To the first application of this committee, the governor told them he would give them a definite answer by five o'clock in the afternoon. At the hour appointed, the committee again repaired to the governor's house, and, on inquiry, found he had gone to his country seat at Milton, a distance of about six miles. When the committee returned and informed the meeting of the absence of the governor, there was a confused murmur among the members, and the meeting was immediately dissolved, many of them crying out, Let every man do his duty, and be true to his country; and there was a general huzza[1] for Griffin's wharf. It was now evening, and I immediately dressed myself in the costume of an Indian, equipped with a small hatchet, which I and my associates denominated the tomahawk, with which, and a club, after having painted my face and hands with coal dust in, the shop of a blacksmith, I repaired to Griffin's wharf, where the ships lay that contained the tea. When I first appeared in the street, after being thus disguised, I fell in with many who were dressed, equipped and painted as I was, and who fell in with me, and marched in order to the place of our destination. When we arrived at the wharf, there were three of our number who assumed an authority to direct our operations, to which we readily submitted. They divided us into

---

[1]**huzza**: Shout of exclamation.

three parties, for the purpose of boarding the three ships which contained the tea at the same time. The name of him who commanded the division to which I was assigned, was Leonard Pitt. The names of the other commanders I never knew. We were immediately ordered by the respective commanders to board all the ships at the same time, which we promptly obeyed. The commander of the division to which I belonged, as soon as we were on board the ship, appointed me boat-swain,[2] and ordered me to go to the captain and demand of him the keys to the hatches and a dozen candles. I made the demand accordingly, and the captain promptly replied, and delivered the articles; but requested me at the same time to do no damage to the ship or rigging. We then were ordered by our commander to open the hatches, and take out all the chests of tea and throw them overboard, and we immediately proceeded to execute his orders; first cutting and splitting the chests with our tomahawks, so as thoroughly to expose them to the effects of the water. In about three hours from the time we went on board, we had thus broken and thrown overboard every tea chest to be found in the ship; while those in the other ships were disposing of the tea in the same way, at the same time. We were surrounded by British armed ships, but no attempt was made to resist us. We then quietly retired to our several places of residence, without having any conversation with each other, or taking any measures to discover who were our associates. . . . There appeared to be an understanding that each individual should volunteer his services, keep his own secret, and risk the consequences for himself. No disorder took place during that transaction, and it was observed at that time, that the still-est night ensued that Boston had enjoyed for many months.

During the time we were throwing the tea overboard, there were several attempts made by some of the citizens of Boston and its vicinity, to carry off small quantities of it for their family use. To effect that object, they would watch their opportunity to snatch up a handful from the deck, where it became plentifully scattered, and put it into their pockets. One Captain O'Conner, whom I well knew, came on board for that purpose, and when he supposed he was not noticed, filled his pockets, and also the lining of his coat. But I had detected him, and gave infor-mation to the captain of what he was doing. We were ordered to take him into custody, and just as he was stepping from the vessel I seized him by the skirt of his coat, and in attempting to pull him back, I tore it off; but springing forward, by a rapid effort, he made his escape. He had however to run a gauntlet through the crowd upon the wharf; each one, as he passed, giving him a kick or a stroke.

The next day, we nailed the skirt of his coat, which I had pulled off, to the whipping post in Charlestown, the place of his residence, with a label upon it, commemorative of the occasion which had thus subjected the proprietor to the popular indignation.

Another attempt was made to save a little tea from the ruins of the cargo, by a tall aged man, who wore a large cocked hat and white wig, which was fash-ionable at that time. He had slightly slipped a little into his pocket, but being detected, they seized him, and taking his hat and wig from his head, threw them, together with the tea, of which they had emptied his pockets, into the water. In consideration of his advanced age, he was permitted to escape, with now and then a slight kick.

---

[2]**boatswain**: A ship's petty officer.

The next morning, after we had cleared the ships of the tea, it was discovered that very considerable quantities of it was floating upon the surface of the water; and to prevent the possibility of any of its being saved for use, a number of small boats were manned by sailors and citizens, who rowed them into those parts of the harbour wherever the tea was visible, and by beating it with oars and paddles, so thoroughly drenched it, as to render its entire destruction inevitable. . . . [Hewes goes on to describe the abuses visited on those who continued to sell tea.]

Mrs. Philips, a tory, . . . would import tea and sell to the tories. To witness the public indignation towards her, . . . a great number of young men in Boston, collected one Saturday evening and employed some menials to besmear her house with substances very offensive to the smell. She discovered what they were doing, and called out to them from her window, You rascals you may plaster, but I will sell tea as much as I please; but the condition in which her house was discovered the next morning, gave such publicity to her name and character, that her gains afterwards in the sale of that article, were acquired at the expense of her peace and the public odium.

There was also a man by the name of Theophalus Lilly, who imported and sold tea; and as a token of contempt and derision, some one nailed a sign upon a post in front of his house, with a hand painted upon it, with a finger pointing to his house, and a notice in writing under it "That is an importer of tea."

QUESTIONS FOR READING AND DISCUSSION

1. What precipitated crowd action against the custom-house officer, John Malcom? What assumptions about the colonists were revealed by Malcom's behavior and by his statement, "Do you presume too, to speak to me"?

2. How and why did Hewes and others destroy the tea? Why did they take care "to do no damage to the ship or rigging"?

3. Hewes and the crowd took action against those who tried to take a little tea for themselves. Why? What values did the crowd see itself upholding?

4. How did the attitudes of Malcom compare with those of the Bostonians who imported and sold tea after the Tea Party? Why did Hewes and other members of the crowd believe their actions were more just than those of Malcom and the tea sellers?

DOCUMENT 6–4

Daniel Leonard Argues for Loyalty to the British Empire

One of the wealthiest lawyers in Massachusetts, Daniel Leonard defended the actions of Britain and criticized the rebellious colonists. When his outspoken loyalist views caused supporters of colonial independence to threaten him with violence, Leonard evacuated his home outside Boston and moved into the city, and then to London in 1776. Between December 1774 and April 1775, Leonard wrote seventeen letters, excerpted below, outlining his arguments for loyalty to Britain. Published in a Boston newspaper and in pamphlet form, Leonard's letters documented the colonists' deep social, political, and ideological conflict on the eve of independence.

To the Inhabitants of the Province of Massachusetts-Bay, 1774–1775

December 12, 1774

The press, when open to all parties and influenced by none, is a salutary engine in a free state, perhaps a necessary one to preserve the freedom of that state; but when . . . the press itself becomes an engine of oppression or licentiousness . . . [then it] is as pernicious to society as otherwise it would be beneficial. It is too true to be denied, that ever since the origin of our controversy with Great Britain, the press in this town [Boston], has been much devoted to the partisans of liberty [i.e., of colonial independence]. . . . In short, the changes have been rung so often upon oppression, tyranny and slavery, that whether sleeping or waking, they are continually vibrating in our ears; and it is now high time to ask ourselves, whether we have not been deluded by sound only.

My dear countrymen, let us divest ourselves of prejudice, take a view of our present wretched situation, contrast it with our former happy one, carefully investigate the cause, and industriously seek some means to escape the evils we now feel, and prevent those we have reason to expect. . . .

[P]erhaps many of us are insensible of our true state and real danger. Should you be told, that acts of high treason are flagrant through the country, that a great part of the province is in actual rebellion; would you believe it true? . . . Are not the bands of society cut asunder, and the sanctions, that hold man to man, trampled upon? Can any of us recover a debt, or obtain compensation for an injury, by law? Are not many persons, whom once we respected and revered, driven from their homes and families, and forced to fly to the army for protection, for no other reason but their having accepted commissions under our king? Is not civil government dissolved? . . . [W]hat kind of offence . . . is [it] for a number of men to assemble armed, and forceably to obstruct the course of justice, even to prevent the king's courts from being held at their stated terms; for a body of people to seize upon the king's provincial revenue, I mean monies collected . . . for the support of his [majesty's] government within this province; for a body of men to assemble without being called by authority, and to pass governmental acts; or for a number of people to take the militia out of the hands of the king's representatives; or to form a new militia, or to raise men and appoint officers for a public purpose, without the order or permission of the king or his representative; or for a number of men to take to their arms, and march with a professed design of opposing the king's troops. . . .

We already feel the effects of anarchy: mutual confidence, affection and tranquillity, those sweeteners of human life, are succeeded by distrust, hatred, and wild uproar; the useful arts of agriculture and commerce are neglected for cabalizing [plotting], mobbing this or the other man, because he acts, speaks, or is suspected of thinking different from the prevailing sentiment of the times, in purchasing arms and forming a militia, O height of madness! with a professed design of opposing Great-Britain. I suspect many of us have been induced to join in these measures, or but faintly to oppose them, from an apprehension that Great-Britain

---

From [Daniel Leonard], *Massachusettensis: Or a Series of Letters, Containing a Faithful State of Many Important and Striking Facts, Which Laid the Foundation of the Present Troubles in the Province of the Massachusetts-Bay* (Boston: 1776), 1–37.

would not or could not exert herself sufficiently to subdue America. Let us consider this matter: However closely we may hug ourselves in the opinion that the parliament has no right to tax or legislate for us, the people of England hold the contrary opinion as firmly: they tell us we are a part of the British empire; that every state from the nature of government must have a supreme uncontroulable power coextensive with the empire itself; and that, that power is vested in parliament. . . . If the colonies are not a part of the British empire already, and subject to the supreme authority of the state, Great-Britain will make them so. . . . For what has she protected and defended the colonies against the maritime powers of Europe, from their first British settlement to this day? For what did she purchase New-York of the Dutch? For what was she so lavish of her best blood and treasure in the conquest of Canada, and other territories in America? Was it to raise up a rival state, or to enlarge her own empire? Or, if the consideration of empire was out of the question, what security can she have of our trade, when once she has lost our obedience? . . . [Y]ou are much deceived, if you imagine that Great-Britain will accede to the claims of the colonies: she will as soon conquer New-England as Ireland or Canada, if either of them revolted; and by arms, if the milder influences of government prove ineffectual. . . . [C]an any of you, that think soberly upon the matter, be so deluded as to believe that Great-Britain, who so lately carried her arms with success to every part of the globe, triumphed over the united powers of France and Spain, and whose fleets give law to the ocean, is unable to conquer us? Should the colonies unite in a war with Great-Britain (which by the way is not a supposable case) the colonies south of Pennsylvania would be unable to furnish any men; they have not more than is necessary to govern their numerous slaves, and to defend themselves against the Indians. I will suppose that the northern colonies can furnish as many, and indeed more men than can be used to advantage; but have you arms fit for a campaign? If you have arms, have you military stores, or can you procure them? When this war is proclaimed, all supplies from foreign parts will be cut off. Have you the money to maintain the war? Or had you all those things, some others are still wanting, which are absolutely necessary to encounter regular troops, that is discipline, and that subordination whereby each can command all below him from a general officer to the lowest subaltern; these you neither have nor can have in such a war. . . . [L]et us now turn our eyes to our extensive sea coast, and that we find wholly at the mercy of Great-Britain; our trade, fishery, navigation and maritime towns taken from us, the very day that war is proclaimed. Inconceivably shocking the scene, if we turn our views to the wilderness; our back settlements a prey to our ancient enemy, the Canadians, whose wounds received from us in the late war will bleed afresh at the prospect of revenge, and to the numerous tribes of savages, whose tender mercies are cruelties; thus with the British navy in the front, Canadians and savages in the rear, a regular army in the midst, we must be certain that, when ever the sword of civil war is unsheathed, devastation will pass through our land like a whirlwind, our houses burnt to ashes, our fair possessions laid waste. . . .

I have as yet said nothing of the difference in sentiment among ourselves: upon a superficial view we might imagine, that this province was nearly unanimous [in supporting colonial independence], but the case is far different. A very considerable part of the men of property in this province are at this day firmly attached to the cause of [British] government; bodies of men compelling persons to disavow sentiments, to resign commissions, or to subscribe leagues and covenants, have wrought no change in their sentiments: it has only attached them more closely to government, and caused them to wish more fervently, and to pray more devoutly for its restoration; these and thousands beside, if they fight at all, will fight under the banners of loyalty. . . . And now, in God's name, what is it that has brought us to this brink of destruction? Has not the government of Great-Britain been as mild and equitable in the colonies as in any part of her extensive dominions? Has not she been a nursing mother to us from the days of our infancy to this time? Has she not been indulgent almost to a fault? . . . Will not posterity be amazed, when they are told that the present distraction took its rise from a three-penny duty on tea, and call it a more unaccountable frenzy, and more disgraceful to the annals of America than that of the *witchcraft*.

January 2, 1775
[A] committee of correspondence. . . . is the foulest, subtlest and most venomous serpent, that ever issued from the eggs of sedition. These committees generally consist of the highest whigs.[1] . . . They are commonly appointed at thin-town-meetings. . . . in fact, but a small proportion of the town have had a hand in the matter. . . . [T]hese committees when once established, think themselves amenable to none; they assume a dictatorial stile, and have an opportunity . . . of clandestinely wreaking private revenge on individuals, by traducing their characters, and holding them up as enemies to their country . . . as also of misrepresenting facts and propagating sedition through the country. . . . These committees, as they are not known in law, and can derive no authority from thence, lest they should not get their share of power, sometimes engross it all; they frequently erect themselves into a tribunal, where the same persons are at once legislator, accusers, witnesses, judges and jurors, and the mob the executioners. The accused has no day in court, and the execution of the sentence is the first notice he receives. This is the channel through which liberty matters have been chiefly conducted the summer and fall past. . . . It is chiefly owing to these committees, that so many respectable persons have been abused, and forced to sign recantations and resignations; that so many persons, to avoid such reiterated insults, as are more to be deprecated by a man of sentiment than death itself, have been obliged to quit their houses, families and business, and fly to the army for protection; that husband has been separated from wife, father from son, brother from brother. . . . My countrymen, I beg you to pause and reflect on this conduct: have not these people, that are thus insulted, as good a right to think and act for themselves in matters of the last importance as the whigs? Are they not as closely connected with the interest of their country as the whigs? Do not their former lives and conversations appear to have been regulated by principle, as much as those of the whigs? You must answer, yes. Why then do you suffer them to be cruelly treated for differing in sentiment from you? Is it consistent with the liberty you profess? . . . I do not address myself to whigs or tories,[2] but to the *whole people*. I know you well. You are loyal at heart, friends to good order, and do violence to yourselves in harbouring, one moment, disrespectful sentiments towards Great-Britain, the land of our forefathers' nativity, and sacred repository of their bones: but you have been most insidiously induced to believe, that Great-Britain is rapacious, cruel, and vindictive, and envies us the inheritance purchased by the sweat and blood of our ancestors. Could that thick

---

[1]**whigs**: Supporters of colonial independence.
[2]**tories**: Supporters of the king.

mist that hovers over the land . . . be but once dispelled, that you might see our sovereign . . . and Great-Britain . . . as they really are; long live our gracious king and happiness to Britain, would resound from one end of the province to the other.

QUESTIONS FOR READING AND DISCUSSION

1. What actions by "partisans of liberty" did Leonard consider "treason," "rebellion," and "anarchy"? What consequences did these acts have, according to Leonard?
2. What did Leonard consider "our true state and real danger"? Why did Leonard believe that so many colonists disagreed with his loyalist views? What role did committees of correspondence play, according to Leonard?
3. Who did Leonard consider his "countrymen"? Who were the "men of property" and how did their views compare to Leonard's, according to him?
4. What differences distinguished the British empire from the single "province" of Massachusetts or the colonies in North America? To what extent did Great Britain and the colonies share a common interest, according to Leonard?
5. Why did Leonard believe that "posterity" would consider the colonial independence movement "more disgraceful" than "witchcraft"?

DOCUMENT 6–5

Edmund Burke Urges Reconciliation with the Colonies

Edmund Burke, a leading member of the British Parliament, argued forcefully that attempts to coerce the North American colonies to comply with taxation and other colonial regulations were misguided. Burke pointed out that British self-interest demanded conciliation of the colonies, not coercion, for reasons he explained in his speech to Parliament excerpted below. Burke's speech illustrates the disputes among British leaders about how best to govern the colonies, disputes that involved judgments about the character of the colonies, the British empire, and of liberty.

Speech to Parliament, March 22, 1775

[My] proposition is Peace. . . . It is simple Peace; sought in its natural course, and in its ordinary haunts. It is Peace sought in the Spirit of Peace; and laid in principles purely pacific. I propose, by removing the Ground of the difference, and by restoring the *former unsuspecting confidence of the Colonies in the Mother Country*, to give permanent satisfaction to your people; and . . . to reconcile them to each other in the same act, and by the bond of the very same interest which reconciles them to British Government. . . .

I mean to give peace. Peace implies reconciliation; and, where there has been a material dispute, reconciliation does in a manner always imply concession on

From Edmund Burke, *Select Works of Edmund Burke, and Miscellaneous Writings,* eds. E. J. Payne and Francis Canavan (Indianapolis, IN: Liberty Fund, Inc., 1999).

the one part or on the other. In this state of things I make no difficulty in affirming that the proposal ought to originate from us. . . . Because after all our struggle, whether we will or not, we must govern America, according to that nature, and to those circumstances; and not according to our own imaginations; nor according to abstract ideas of right; by no means according to mere general theories of government. . . .

The first thing that we have to consider . . . is the number of people in the Colonies. . . . I can by no calculation justify myself in placing the number below Two Millions of inhabitants of our own European blood and colour; besides at least 500,000 others, who form no inconsiderable part of the strength and opulence of the whole. . . . Whilst we spend our time in deliberating on the mode of governing Two Millions, we shall find we have Millions more to manage. Your children do not grow faster from infancy to manhood, than they spread from families to communities, and from villages to nations. . . .

But . . . the commerce of your Colonies is out of all proportion beyond the numbers of the people. . . . The export trade to the Colonies consists of three great branches. The African, which, terminating almost wholly in the Colonies, must be put to the account of their commerce; the West Indian; and the North American. All these are so interwoven, that the attempt to separate them, would tear to pieces the contexture of the whole; . . . in effect they are, one trade. From Five Hundred and odd Thousand [pounds sterling in 1704], it has grown to Six Millions [pounds sterling by 1772]. It has increased no less than twelve-fold. This is the state of the Colony trade. . . . The trade with America alone is now within less than 500,000 [pounds sterling] of being equal to what this great commercial nation, England, carried on at the beginning of this century with the whole world! . . . Our general trade has been greatly augmented; . . . of the Six Millions which in the beginning of the century constituted the whole mass of our export commerce, the Colony trade was but one twelfth part; it is now (as a part of Sixteen Millions) considerably more than a third of the whole. . . .

When I contemplate these things; when I know that the Colonies in general owe little or nothing to any care of ours, and that they are not squeezed into this happy form by the constraints of watchful and suspicious government, but that, through a wise and salutary neglect, a generous nature has been suffered to take her own way to perfection; when I reflect upon these effects, when I see how profitable they have been to us, I feel all the pride of power sink, and all presumption in the wisdom of human contrivances melt and die away within me. My rigour relents. I pardon something to the spirit of liberty. . . .

America . . . is an object well worth fighting for. Certainly it is, if fighting a people be the best way of gaining them. . . . But I confess, possibly for want of this knowledge, my opinion is much more in favour of prudent management, than of force; considering force not as an odious, but a feeble instrument, for preserving a people so numerous, so active, so growing, so spirited as this, in a profitable and subordinate connexion with us. . . . Let me add, that I do not choose wholly to break the American spirit; because it is the spirit that has made the country. . . .

In this Character of the Americans, a love of Freedom is the predominating feature which marks and distinguishes the whole: and as an ardent is always a jealous affection, your Colonies become suspicious, restive, and untractable, whenever they see the least attempt to wrest from them by force, or shuffle from them by [chicanery], what they think the only advantage worth living for. This fierce spirit of Liberty is stronger in the English Colonies probably than in any other people of the earth; and this from a great variety of powerful causes. . . .

First, the people of the Colonies are descendants of Englishmen. England, Sir, is a nation, which still I hope respects, and formerly adored, her freedom. The Colonists emigrated from you when this part of your character was most predominant; and they took this bias and direction the moment they parted from your hands. They are therefore not only devoted to Liberty, but to Liberty according to English ideas, and on English principles. Abstract Liberty, like other mere abstractions, is not to be found. Liberty inheres in some sensible object; and every nation has formed to itself some favourite point, which by way of eminence becomes the criterion of their happiness. It happened, you know, Sir, that the great contests for freedom in this country were from the earliest times chiefly upon the question of Taxing. . . . On this point of Taxes the ablest pens, and most eloquent tongues, have been exercised; the greatest spirits have acted and suffered. . . . They took infinite pains to inculcate, as a fundamental principle, that in all monarchies the people must in effect themselves, mediately or immediately, possess the power of granting their own money, or no shadow of liberty can subsist. The Colonies draw from you, as with their life-blood, these ideas and principles. Their love of liberty, as with you, fixed and attached on this specific point of taxing. Liberty might be safe, or might be endangered, in twenty other particulars, without their being much pleased or alarmed. Here they felt its pulse; and as they found that beat, they thought themselves sick or sound. I do not say whether they were right or wrong in applying your general arguments to their own case. . . . The fact is, that they did thus apply those general arguments; and your mode of governing them, whether through [leniency] or indolence, through wisdom or mistake, confirmed them in the imagination, that they, as well as you, had an interest in these common principles.

They were further confirmed in this pleasing error by the form of their provincial legislative assemblies. Their governments are popular in an high degree; some are merely popular; in all, the popular representative is the most weighty; and this share of the people in their ordinary government never fails to inspire them with lofty sentiments, and with a strong aversion from whatever tends to deprive them of their chief importance. . . .

Religion, always a principle of energy, in this new people is no way worn out or impaired; and their mode of professing it is also one main cause of this free spirit. The people are protestants; and of that kind which is the most adverse to all implicit submission of mind and opinion. This is a persuasion not only favourable to liberty, but built upon it. . . . The dissenting interests have sprung up in direct opposition to all the ordinary powers of the world; and could justify that opposition only on a strong claim to natural liberty. Their very existence depended on the powerful and unremitted assertion of that claim. All protestantism, even the most cold and passive, is a sort of dissent. But the religion most prevalent in our Northern Colonies is a refinement on the principle of resistance; it is the dissidence of dissent, and the protestantism of the protestant religion. This religion, under a variety of denominations agreeing in nothing but in the communion of the spirit of liberty, is predominant in most of the Northern provinces; where the Church of England, notwithstanding its legal rights, is in reality no more than a sort of private sect, not composing most probably the tenth of the people. The Colonists left England when this spirit was high, and in the emigrants was the highest of all; and even that stream of foreigners, which has been constantly flowing into these Colonies, has, for the greatest part, been composed of dissenters from the establishments of their several countries, and have brought with them a temper and character far from alien to that of the people with whom they mixed. . . .

In the Southern Colonies the Church of England forms a large body, and has a regular establishment. . . . There is, however, a circumstance attending these Colonies, which, in my opinion, fully counterbalances this difference, and makes the spirit of liberty still more high and haughty than in those to the North-ward. It is, that in Virginia and the Carolinas they have a vast multitude of slaves. Where this is the case in any part of the world, those who are free, are by far the most proud and jealous of their freedom. Freedom is to them not only an enjoyment, but a kind of rank and privilege. Not seeing there, that freedom, as in countries where it is a common blessing, and as broad and general as the air, may be united with much abject toil, with great misery, with all the exterior of servitude, liberty looks, amongst them, like something that is more noble and liberal. I do not mean, Sir, to commend the superior morality of this sentiment, which has at least as much pride as virtue in it; but I cannot alter the nature of man. The fact is so; and these people of the Southern Colonies are much more strongly, and with an higher and more stubborn spirit, attached to liberty, than those to the North-ward. Such . . . will be all masters of slaves, who are not slaves themselves. In such a people, the haughtiness of domination combines with the spirit of freedom, fortifies it, and renders it invincible. . . .

Another circumstance in our Colonies . . . contributes no mean part towards the growth and effect of this untractable spirit. I mean their education. In no country perhaps in the world is the law so general a study. The profession itself is numerous and powerful; and in most provinces it takes the lead. The greater number of the Deputies sent to the Congress were Lawyers. But all who read, (and most do read,) endeavour to obtain some smattering in that science. I have been told by an eminent Bookseller, that in no branch of his business, after tracts of popular devotion, were so many books as those on the Law exported to the Plantations. The Colonists have now fallen into the way of printing them for their own use. . . . In other countries, the people, more simple, and of a less mercurial cast, judge of an ill principle in government only by an actual grievance; here they anticipate the evil, and judge of the pressure of the grievance by the badness of the principle. They augur misgovernment at a distance; and snuff the approach of tyranny in every tainted breeze.

The last cause of this disobedient spirit in the Colonies is hardly less powerful than the rest, as it is not merely moral, but laid deep in the natural constitution of things. Three thousand miles of ocean lie between you and them. No contrivance can prevent the effect of this distance in weakening government. Seas roll, and months pass, between the order and the execution; and the want of a speedy explanation of a single point is enough to defeat a whole system. You have, indeed, winged ministers of vengeance, who carry your bolts in their pounces to the remotest verge of the sea. But there a power steps in, that limits the arrogance of raging passions and furious elements, and says, *So far shalt thou go, and no farther.* Who are you, that you should fret and rage, and bite the chains of Nature? . . .

Then, Sir, from these six capital sources; of Descent; of Form of Government; of Religion in the Northern Provinces; of Manners in the Southern; of Education; of the Remoteness of Situation from the First Mover of Government; from all these causes a fierce Spirit of Liberty has grown up. It has grown with the growth of the people in your Colonies, and increased with the increase of their wealth; a Spirit, that unhappily meeting with an exercise of Power in England, which, however lawful, is not reconcileable to any ideas of Liberty, much less with theirs, has kindled this flame that is ready to consume us.

QUESTIONS FOR READING AND DISCUSSION

1. According to Burke, why was it wise for the British government to conciliate the American colonies?

2. What were the results of what Burke termed "salutary neglect"? Was neglect salutary for both the British and the Americans?

3. Why, according to Burke, was the colonists' "Spirit of Liberty" important for the British government to consider? How and why did Americans' spirit of liberty arise?

4. What arguments might other British officials have used to criticize Burke's proposal? What might American colonial leaders have said about Burke's views?

COMPARATIVE QUESTIONS

1. How did Joseph Warren's arguments about colonial grievances compare with those expressed by Daniel Leonard, George Hewes, and Edmund Burke? How might Warren and Hewes have responded to Leonard's and Burke's arguments?

2. How might Warren, Hewes, and Burke have interpreted the rebellious activities Leonard criticized? How would they have viewed the Iroquois Confederacy's treaty with the British?

3. Fundamental assumptions about law, liberty, government, and society divided colonists. To what extent do the documents in this chapter reveal those divisions? To what extent, if at all, did patriots and loyalists share common assumptions about such basic matters?

4. Do the documents in this chapter suggest that colonists were unified in rebellion? What were the most important sources of unity and of conflict? Do these documents provide evidence of a distinctive American identity among colonists?

5. Judging from the documents in this chapter, why did so many colonists decide to support open and active rebellion against British rule? Why did other colonists decide instead to continue to ally with the British? How did their views compare to those of the Iroquois Confederacy recalled by Mary Jemison?

7

The War for America
1775–1783

The Declaration of Independence made crystal clear the momentous stakes of the conflict between the colonies and Great Britain. An independence that seemed impossible, if not unimaginable, to many Americans in 1775 was boldly asserted in 1776 and, after much bloodshed, successfully defended by 1783. Ideas about monarchy and popular government that most British officials and many of their colonial allies, including Native Americans, considered subversive began to seem sensible to many Americans. Independence became a means to move from promising ideas to practical achievements, but only if the American army could defeat the British and defend independence. The shifting fortunes of war often caused many colonists to confront painful decisions that required balancing loyalty and self-interest. Enslaved African Americans frequently sought a different form of independence by fleeing from the rebellious colonists and seeking their freedom among the British. The following documents illustrate ideas and experiences that made revolution seem reasonable to many Americans—whites and blacks—despite its great risks and sometimes bleak realities.

DOCUMENT 7–1

Thomas Paine Makes the Case for Independence

By the end of 1775, colonial minutemen had faced royal troops in battle, but the debate about what the colonists should do next continued to rage. Tories believed that the rebellious upstarts should be suppressed. Lukewarm Tories and hesitant patriots still hoped that some basis could be found for reconciliation. Militant rebels believed the time for independence had arrived. Thomas Paine made the case for independence in his compelling pamphlet, Common Sense, *published in January 1776. Paine's arguments, excerpted here, rang true to many leading colonists. Yes, they agreed, revolution was now common sense.*

Common Sense, January 1776

There is something exceedingly ridiculous in the composition of monarchy; it first excludes a man from the means of information, yet empowers him to act in cases where the highest judgment is required. The state of a king shuts him from the world, yet the business of a king requires him to know it thoroughly; wherefore the different parts, unnaturally opposing and destroying each other, prove the whole character to be absurd and useless. . . .

Mankind being originally equals in the order of creation, the equality could only be destroyed by some subsequent circumstance. . . .

But there is . . . [a] distinction for which no truly natural or religious reason can be assigned, and that is, the distinction of men into KINGS and SUBJECTS. Male and female are the distinctions of nature, good and bad the distinctions of heaven; but how a race of men came into the world so exalted above the rest, and distinguished like some new species, is worth inquiring into, and whether they are the means of happiness or of misery to mankind. . . .

As the exalting one man so greatly above the rest cannot be justified on the equal rights of nature, so neither can it be defended on the authority of scripture. . . .

That the Almighty hath . . . entered his protest against monarchial government is true, or the scripture is false. . . . For monarchy in every instance is the Popery of government.

To the evil of monarchy we have added that of hereditary succession. . . . For all men being originally equals, no *one by birth* could have a right to set up his own family in perpetual preference to all others for ever. . . . One of the strongest natural proofs of the folly of hereditary right in kings, is, that nature disapproves it, otherwise she would not so frequently turn it into ridicule by giving mankind an *ass for a lion.* . . .

[C]ould we take off the dark covering of antiquity, and trace [the present lineage of kings] to their first rise, . . . we should find the first of them nothing better than the principal ruffian of some restless gang, whose savage manners or pre-eminence in subtlety obtained him the title of chief among plunderers. . . .

But it is not so much the absurdity as the evil of hereditary succession which concerns mankind. Did it ensure a race of good and wise men it would have the seal of divine authority, but as it opens a door to the *foolish*, the *wicked*, and the *improper*, it hath in it the nature of oppression. Men who look upon themselves born to reign, and others to obey, soon grow insolent; selected from the rest of mankind their minds are early poisoned by importance; and the world they act in differs so materially from the world at large, that they have but little opportunity of knowing its true interests, and when they succeed to the government are frequently the most ignorant and unfit of any throughout the dominions. . . .

In England a k—— hath little more to do than to make war and give away places; which in plain terms, is to impoverish the nation and set it together by the ears. A pretty business indeed for a man to be allowed eight hundred thousand sterling a year for, and worshipped into the bargain! Of more worth is one honest man to society, and in the sight of God, than all the crowned ruffians that ever lived. . . .

From Thomas Paine, *Common Sense* (1776).

THOUGHTS ON THE PRESENT STATE
OF AMERICAN AFFAIRS

In the following pages I offer nothing more than simple facts, plain arguments, and common sense. . . .

Volumes have been written on the subject of the struggle between England and America. Men of all ranks have embarked in the controversy, from different motives, and with various designs; but all have been ineffectual, and the period of debate is closed. Arms, as the last resource, decide the contest; the appeal was the choice of the king, and the continent hath accepted the challenge. . . .

The sun never shined on a cause of greater worth. 'Tis not the affair of a city, a country, a province, or a kingdom, but of a continent—of at least one eighth part of the habitable globe. 'Tis not the concern of a day, a year, or an age; posterity are virtually involved in the contest, and will be more or less affected, even to the end of time, by the proceedings now. Now is the seed time of continental union, faith and honour. . . .

I have heard it asserted by some, that as America hath flourished under her former connection with Great Britain, that the same connection is necessary towards her future happiness, and will always have the same effect. Nothing can be more fallacious than this kind of argument. . . . I answer roundly, that America would have flourished as much, and probably much more, had no European power had any thing to do with her. The commerce by which she hath enriched herself are the necessaries of life, and will always have a market while eating is the custom of Europe. . . .

Alas, we have been long led away by ancient prejudices, and made large sacrifices to superstition. We have boasted the protection of Great Britain, without considering, that her motive was *interest* not attachment; that she did not protect us from our enemies on our account, but from *her enemies* on *her own account.* . . .

But Britain is the parent country, say some. Then the more shame upon her conduct. Even brutes do not devour their young, nor savages make war upon their families. . . . Europe, and not England, is the parent country of America. This new world hath been the asylum for the persecuted lovers of civil and religious liberty from *every part* of Europe. Hither have they fled, not from the tender embraces of the mother, but from the cruelty of the monster; and it is so far true of England, that the same tyranny which drove the first emigrants from home, pursues their descendants still. . . .

I challenge the warmest advocate for reconciliation, to shew, a single advantage that this continent can reap, by being connected with Great Britain. I repeat the challenge, not a single advantage is derived. Our corn will fetch its price in any market in Europe, and our imported goods must be paid for buy them where we will.

But the injuries and disadvantages we sustain by that connection, are without number; and our duty to mankind at large, as well as to ourselves, instruct us to renounce the alliance: Because, any submission to, or dependence on Great Britain, tends directly to involve this continent in European wars and quarrels; and sets us at variance with nations, who would otherwise seek our friendship, and against whom, we have neither anger nor complaint. As Europe is our market for trade, we ought to form no partial connection with any part of it. It is the true interest of America to steer clear of European contentions, which she never can do, while by her dependence on Britain, she is made the make-weight in the scale of British politics.

Europe is too thickly planted with kingdoms to be long at peace, and whenever a war breaks out between England and any foreign power, the trade of America goes to ruin, *because of her connection with Britain.* . . . Every thing that is right or natural pleads for separation. The blood of the slain, the weeping voice of nature cries, 'TIS TIME TO PART. Even the distance at which the Almighty hath placed England and America, is a strong and natural proof, that the authority of the one, over the other, was never the design of Heaven. . . .

Men of passive tempers look somewhat lightly over the offences of Britain, and, still hoping for the best, are apt to call out, *"Come we shall be friends again for all this."* . . . But if you say, you can still pass the violations over, then I ask, Hath your house been burnt? Hath your property been destroyed before your face? Are your wife and children destitute of a bed to lie on, or bread to live on? Have you lost a parent or a child by their hands, and yourself the ruined and wretched survivor? If you have not, then are you not a judge of those who have. But if you have, and can still shake hands with the murderers, then are you unworthy the name of husband, father, friend, or lover, and whatever may be your rank or title in life, you have the heart of a coward, and the spirit of a sycophant. . . .

I mean not to exhibit horror for the purpose of provoking revenge, but to awaken us from fatal and unmanly slumbers, that we may pursue determinately some fixed object. It is not in the power of Britain or of Europe to conquer America, if she did not conquer herself by *delay and timidity.* . . .

It is repugnant to reason, to the universal order of things, to all examples from the former ages, to suppose, that this continent can longer remain subject to any external power. . . . Reconciliation is and was a fallacious dream. Nature hath deserted the connection, and Art cannot supply her place. . . .

Small islands not capable of protecting themselves, are the proper objects for kingdoms to take under their care; but there is something very absurd, in supposing a continent to be perpetually governed by an island. In no instance hath nature made the satellite larger than its primary planet, and as England and America, with respect to each other, reverses the common order of nature, it is evident they belong to different systems: England to Europe, America to itself. . . .

But the most powerful of all arguments, is, that nothing but independence, i.e.[,] a continental form of government, can keep the peace of the continent and preserve it inviolate from civil wars. . . .

If there is any true cause of fear respecting independence, it is because no plan is yet laid down. Men do not see their way out, Wherefore, as an opening into that business, I offer the following hints. . . .

LET the assemblies be annual, with a President only. The representation more equal. Their business wholly domestic, and subject to the authority of a Continental Congress.

Let each colony be divided into six, eight, or ten, convenient districts, each district to send a proper number of delegates to Congress. . . .

[L]et a CONTINENTAL CONFERENCE be held. . . . [L]et their business be to frame a CONTINENTAL CHARTER, or Charter of the United Colonies; (answering to what is called the Magna Charta of England) fixing the number and manner of choosing members of Congress, members of Assembly, with their date of sitting, and drawing the line of business and jurisdiction between them: (Always remembering, that our strength is continental, not provincial:) Securing freedom and property to all men, and above all things the free exercise of religion, according to the dictates of conscience; with such other matter as is necessary for a charter to contain. . . .

But where says some is the King of America? I'll tell you Friend, he reigns above, and doth not make havoc of mankind like the Royal—of Britain. Yet that we may not appear to be defective even in earthly honours, let a day be solemnly set apart for proclaiming the charter; let it be brought forth placed on the divine law, the word of God; let a crown be placed thereon, by which the world may know, that so far as we approve of monarchy, that in America THE LAW IS KING. For as in absolute governments the King is law, so in free countries the law *ought* to be King; and there ought to be no other. But lest any ill use should afterwards arise, let the crown at the conclusion of the ceremony be demolished, and scattered among the people whose right it is.

A government of our own is our natural right: And when a man seriously reflects on the precariousness of human affairs, he will become convinced, that it is infinitely wiser and safer, to form a constitution of our own in a cool deliberate manner, while we have it in our power, than to trust such an interesting event to time and chance. . . . Ye that oppose independence now, ye know not what ye do; ye are opening a door to eternal tyranny, by keeping vacant the seat of government. There are thousands and tens of thousands, who would think it glorious to expel from the continent, that barbarous and hellish power, which hath stirred up the Indians and Negroes to destroy us; the cruelty hath a double guilt, it is dealing brutally by us, and treacherously by them. . . .

O ye that love mankind! Ye that dare oppose, not only the tyranny, but the tyrant, stand forth! Every spot of the old world is over-run with oppression. Freedom hath been hunted round the globe. Asia, and Africa, have long expelled her— Europe regards her like a stranger, and England hath given her warning to depart. O! receive the fugitive, and prepare in time an asylum for mankind.

QUESTIONS FOR READING AND DISCUSSION

1. How did Paine use concepts of equality, reason, and nature to criticize the legitimacy of monarchical government and British control of the colonies?
2. What arguments did Paine give for independence? How were his observations about monarchy connected to his reasons for independence? Why did he propose that law should be "King of America"?
3. Why did he believe that attempts at reconciliation were "a fallacious dream"?
4. Independence, according to Paine, would "expel from the continent, that barbarous and hellish power, which hath stirred up the Indians and Negroes to destroy us" and would create "an asylum for mankind." In what sense would an independent America be an asylum, and for whom?

DOCUMENT 7–2

Letters of John and Abigail Adams

While the Second Continental Congress deliberated in Philadelphia on the colonial crisis, Massachusetts delegate John Adams maintained a correspondence with his wife, Abigail, who remained at home. A leader in the independence movement, Adams exchanged news, ideas, and concerns with his wife. The following selections from the Adams's correspondence illustrates the determination tempered by anxiety that accompanied the fateful passage of the Declaration of Independence.

Correspondence, 1776
John Adams to Abigail Adams

[Philadelphia,] February 18, 1776

My dearest Friend

I sent you from New York a Pamphlet intitled Common Sense, written in Vindication of Doctrines which there is Reason to expect that the further Encroachments of Tyranny and Depredations of Oppression, will soon make the common Faith: unless the cunning Ministry, by proposing Negociations and Terms of Reconciliation, should divert the present Current from its Channell.

Reconciliation if practicable and Peace if attainable, you very well know would be as agreable to my Inclinations and as advantageous to my Interest, as to any Man's. But I see no Prospect, no Probability, no Possibility. And I cannot but despise the Understanding, which sincerely expects an honourable Peace, for its Credulity, and detest the hypocritical Heart, which pretends to expect it, when in Truth it does not. The News Papers here are full of free Speculations, the Tendency of which you will easily discover. The Writers reason from Topicks which have been long in Contemplation, and fully understood by the People at large in New England, but have been attended to in the southern Colonies only by Gentlemen of free Spirits and liberal Minds, who are very few. I shall endeavour to inclose to you as many of the Papers and Pamphlets as I can, as long as I stay here.

The Events of War are uncertain: We cannot insure Success, but We can deserve it.

Write me as often as you can—tell me all the News.

Abigail Adams to John Adams

[Braintree, Mass.,] Saturday Evening March 2 [1776]

. . . I heartily wish every Tory was Extirpated [from] America, they are continually by secret means undermineing and injuring our cause.

I am charmed with the Sentiments of Common Sense; and wonder how an honest Heart, one who wishes the welfare of their country, and the happiness of posterity can hesitate one moment at adopting them; I want to know how those Sentiments are received in Congress? I dare say their would be no difficulty in procuring a vote and instructions from all the Assemblies in New England for independancy. I most sincerely wish that now in the Lucky Minuet it might be done.

I have been kept in a continual state of anxiety and expectation ever since you left me. It has been said to morrow and to morrow for this month, but when the dreadfull to morrow will be I know not—but hark! the House this instant shakes with the roar of Cannon.—I have been to the door and find tis a cannonade from our Army, orders I find are come for all the remaining Militia to repair to the Lines a monday night by twelve o clock. No Sleep for me to Night; and if I cannot who

---

From L. H. Butterfield, ed., *Adams Family Correspondence*, vols. 1 and 2 (Cambridge, MA: Harvard University Press, 1963), 193–202.

have no guilt upon my Soul with regard to this Cause, how shall the misirible wretches who have been the procurers of this Dreadfull Scene and those who are to be the actors, lie down with the load of Guilt upon their Souls.

Sunday Eve March 3

I went to Bed after 12 but got no rest, the Cannon continued firing and my Heart Beat pace with them all night. We have had a pretty quiet day, but what to morrow will bring forth God only knows.

Monday Evening

Tolerable quiet to day. The Militia have all musterd with 3 days provision and are all marched by 8 o clock this afternoon tho their notice was no longer than 8 o clock Saturday, and now we have scarcly a Man but our regular guards . . . and the Militia from the more remote towns are call'd in as Sea coast Guards. Can you form to yourself an Idea of our Sensations.

I have just returned from P[enn']s Hill where I have been sitting to hear the amazing roar of cannon and from whence I could see every shell which was thrown. The sound I think is one of the Grandest in Nature and is of the true Species of the Sublime. Tis now an incessant Roar. But O the fatal Ideas which are connected with the sound. How many of our dear country men must fall?

Tuesday Morning

I went to bed about 12 and rose again a little after one. I could no more sleep than if I had been in the ingagement. The ratling of the windows, the jar of the house and the continual roar of 24 pounders, the Bursting of shells give us such Ideas, and realize a scene to us of which we could scarcly form any conception. About Six this morning, there was quiet; I rejoiced in a few hours calm. I hear we got possession of Dorchester Hill Last Night. 4000 thousand men upon it to day — lost but one Man. The Ships are all drawn round the Town.

Sunday Eve March 10

I had scarcly finished these lines when my Ears were again assaulted with the roar of Cannon. I could not write any further. My Hand and heart will tremble, at this domestick fury, and firce civil Strife, which cumber all our parts. Tho,

Blood and destruction are so much in use
And Dreadfull objects so familiar,

Yet is not pitty chok'd, nor my Heart grown Callous. I feel for the unhappy wretches who know not where to fly for safety. I feel still more for my Bleading Country men who are hazarding their lives and their Limbs. — A most Terible and incessant Cannonade from half after 8 till Six this morning. I hear we lost four men kill'd and some wounded in attempting to take the Hill nearest the Town call'd Nook Hill. . . .

I have not got all the perticuliars I wish I had but, as I have an opportunity of sending this I shall endeavour to be more perticuliar in my next. . . .

If we have [no] Reinforcements here, I believe we shall be driven from the sea coast, but in what so ever state I am I will endeavour to be therewith content.

Man wants but Little here below
Nor wants that Little long.

You will excuse this very incorrect Letter. You see in what purtubation it has been written and how many times I have left of. Adieu pray write me every opportunity.

John Adams to Abigail Adams

[Philadelphia,] March 19, 1776

. . . [M]y worthy fellow Citizens may be easy about me. I never can forsake what I take to be their Interests. My own have never been considered by me, in Competition with theirs. My Ease, my domestic Happiness, my rural Pleasures, my Little Property, my personal Liberty, my Reputation, my Life, have little Weight and ever had, in my own Estimation, in Comparison of the great Object of my Country. I can say of it with great Sincerity, as Horace says of Virtue—to America only and her Friends a Friend.

You ask, what is thought of Common sense. Sensible Men think there are some Whims, some Sophisms, some artfull Addresses to superstitious Notions, some keen attempts upon the Passions, in this Pamphlet. But all agree there is a great deal of good sense, delivered in a clear, simple, concise and nervous Style.

His Sentiments of the Abilities of America, and of the Difficulty of a Reconciliation with G[reat].B[ritain]. are generally approved. But his Notions, and Plans of Continental Government are not much applauded. Indeed this Writer has a better Hand at pulling down than building.

It has been very generally propagated through the Continent that I wrote this Pamphlet. But altho I could not have written any Thing in so manly and striking a style, I flatter myself I should have made a more respectable Figure as an Architect, if I had undertaken such a Work. This Writer seems to have very inadequate Ideas of what is proper and necessary to be done, in order to form Constitutions for single Colonies, as well as a great Model of Union for the whole.

Your Distresses which you have painted in such lively Colours, I feel in every Line as I read. I dare not write all that I think upon this Occasion. . . .

Abigail Adams to John Adams

Braintree, March 31, 1776

I wish you would ever write me a Letter half as long as I write you; and tell me if you may where your Fleet are gone? What sort of Defence Virginia can make against our common Enemy? Whether it is so situated as to make an able Defence? Are not the Gentery Lords and the common people vassals, are they not like the uncivilized Natives Brittain represents us to be? I hope their Riffel Men who have shewen themselves very savage and even Blood thirsty; are not a specimen of the Generality of the people.

I am willing to allow the Colony great merrit for having produced a Washington but they have been shamefully duped by a Dunmore. I have sometimes been ready to think that the passion for Liberty cannot be Eaquelly Strong in the Breasts of those who have been accustomed to deprive their fellow Creatures of theirs. Of this I am certain that it is not founded upon that generous and christian principal of doing to others as we would that others should do unto us. . . .

I feel very differently at the approach of spring to what I did a month ago. We knew not then whether we could plant or sow with safety, whether when we had toild we could reap the fruits of our own industery, whether we could rest in our own Cottages, or whether we should not be driven from the sea coasts to seek shelter in the wilderness, but now we feel as if we might sit under our own vine and eat the good of the land.

Tho we felicitate ourselves, we sympathize with those who are trembling least the Lot of Boston should be theirs. But they cannot be in similar circumstances unless pusilanimity and cowardise should take possession of them. They have time and warning given them to see the Evil and shun it. — I long to hear that you have declared an independancy — and by the way in the new Code of Laws which I suppose it will be necessary for you to make I desire you would Remember the Ladies, and be more generous and favourable to them than your ancestors. Do not put such unlimited power into the hands of the Husbands. Remember all Men would be tyrants if they could. If perticuliar care and attention is not paid to the Laidies we are determined to foment a Rebelion, and will not hold ourselves bound by any Laws in which we have no voice, or Representation.

That your Sex are Naturally Tyrannical is a Truth so thoroughly established as to admit of no dispute, but such of you as wish to be happy willingly give up the harsh title of Master for the more tender and endearing one of Friend. Why then, not put it out of the power of the vicious and the Lawless to use us with cruelty and indignity with impunity. Men of Sense in all Ages abhor those customs which treat us only as the vassals of your Sex. Regard us then as Beings placed by providence under your protection and in immitation of the Supreem Being make use of that power only for our happiness.

Your ever faithful friend.

John Adams to Abigail Adams

[Philadelphia], April 14, 1776

You justly complain of my short Letters, but the critical State of Things and the Multiplicity of Avocations must plead my Excuse. — ask what Sort of Defence Virginia can make. I believe they will make an able Defence. Their Militia and minute Men have been some time employed in training them selves, and they have Nine Battallions of regulars as they call them, maintained among them, under good Officers, at the Continental Expence. They have set up a Number of Manufactories of Fire Arms, which are busily employed. They are tolerably supplied with Powder, and are successfull and assiduous, in making Salt Petre. Their neighbouring Sister or rather Daughter Colony of North Carolina, which is a warlike Colony, and has several Battallions at the Continental Expence, as well as a pretty good Militia, are ready to assist them, and they are in very good Spirits, and seem determined to make a brave Resistance. — The Gentry are very rich, and the common People very poor. This Inequality of Property, gives an Aristocratical Turn to all their Proceedings, and occasions a strong Aversion in their Patricians, to Common Sense. But the Spirit of these Barons, is coming down, and it must submit.

As to Declarations of Independency, be patient. Read our Privateering Laws, and our Commercial Laws. What signifies a Word.

As to your extraordinary Code of Laws, I cannot but laugh. We have been told that our Struggle has loosened the bands of Government every where. That Children and Apprentices were disobedient—that schools and Colledges were grown turbulent—that Indians slighted their Guardians and Negroes grew insolent to their Masters. But your Letter was the first Intimation that another Tribe more numerous and powerfull than all the rest were grown discontented. — This is rather too coarse a Compliment but you are so saucy, I wont blot it out.

Depend upon it, We know better than to repeal our Masculine systems. Altho they are in full Force, you know they are little more than Theory. We dare not exert our Power in its full Latitude. We are obliged to go fair, and softly, and in Practice you know We are the subjects. We have only the Name of Masters, and rather than give up this, which would compleatly subject Us to the Despotism of the Peticoat, I hope General Washington, and all our brave Heroes would fight. I am sure every good Politician would plot, as long as he would against Despotism, Empire, Monarchy, Aristocracy, Oligarchy, or Ochlocracy. — A fine Story indeed. I begin to think the Ministry as deep as they are wicked. After stirring up Tories, Landjobbers, Trimmers, Bigots, Canadians, Indians, Negroes, Hanoverians, Hessians, Russians, Irish Roman Catholicks, Scotch Renegadoes, at last they have stimulated the ladies to demand new Priviledges and threaten to rebell.

John Adams to Abigail Adams

[Philadelphia], May 17, 1776

. . . When I consider the great Events which are passed, and those greater which are rapidly advancing, and that I may have been instrumental of touching some Springs, and turning some small Wheels, which have had and will have such Effects, I feel an Awe upon my Mind, which is not easily described.

G[reat] B[ritain] has at last driven America, to the last Step, a compleat Seperation from her, a total absolute Independence, not only of her Parliament but of her Crown, for such is the Amount of the Resolve of the 15th.

Confederation among ourselves, or Alliances with foreign Nations are not necessary, to a perfect Seperation from Britain. That is effected by extinguishing all Authority, under the Crown, Parliament and Nation as the Resolution for instituting Governments, has done, to all Intents and Purposes. Confederation will be necessary for our internal Concord, and Alliances may be so for our external Defense.

I have Reasons to believe that no Colony, which shall assume a Government under the People, will give it up. There is something very unnatural and odious in a Government 1000 Leagues off. An whole Government of our own Choice, managed by Persons whom We love, revere, and can confide in, has charms in it for which Men will fight. Two young Gentlemen from South Carolina, now in this City, who were in Charlestown when their new Constitution was promulgated, and when their new Governor and Council and Assembly walked out in Procession, attended by the Guards, Company of Cadetts, Light Horse &c., told me, that they were beheld by the People with Transports and Tears of Joy. The People gazed at them, with a Kind of Rapture. They both told me, that the Reflection that these were Gentlemen whom they all loved, esteemed and revered, Gentlemen of their own Choice, whom they could trust, and whom they could displace if any of them should behave amiss, affected them so that they could not help crying.

They say their People will never give up this Government. . . .

John Adams to Abigail Adams

Philadelphia, July 3, 1776

. . . Yesterday the greatest Question was decided, which ever was debated in America, and a greater perhaps, never was or will be decided among Men. A Resolution was passed without one dissenting Colony "that these united Colonies, are, and of right ought to be free and independent States, and as such, they have, and of Right ought to have full Power to make War, conclude Peace, establish Commerce, and to do all the other Acts and Things, which other States may rightfully do." You will see in a few days a Declaration setting forth the Causes, which have impell'd Us to this mighty Revolution, and the Reasons which will justify it, in the Sight of God and Man. A Plan of Confederation will be taken up in a few days.

When I look back to the Year 1761, and recollect the Argument concerning Writs of Assistance, in the Superiour Court which I have hitherto considered as the Commencement of the Controversy, between Great Britain and America, and run through the whole Period from that Time to this, and recollect the series of political Events, the Chain of Causes and Effects, I am surprized at the Suddenness, as well as Greatness of this Revolution. Britain has been fill'd with Folly, and America with Wisdom, at least this is my Judgment. — Time must determine. It is the Will of Heaven, that the two Countries should be sundered forever. It may be the Will of Heaven that America shall suffer Calamities still more wasting and Distresses yet more dreadfull. If this is to be the Case, it will have this good Effect, at least: it will inspire Us with many Virtues, which We have not, and correct many Errors, Follies, and Vices, which threaten to disturb, dishonour, and destroy Us. The furnace of Affliction produces Refinement, in States as well as Individuals. And the new Governments we are assuming, in every Part, will require a Purification from our Vices, and an Augmentation of our Virtues or they will be no Blessings. The People will have unbounded Power. And the People are extreamly addicted to Corruption and Venality, as well as the Great. — I am not without Apprehensions from this Quarter. But I must submit all my Hopes and Fears, to an overruling Providence, in which, unfashionable as the Faith may be, I firmly believe.

John Adams to Abigail Adams

Philadelphia, July 3d, 1776

. . . [T]he Delay of this Declaration [of Independence] to this Time, has many great Advantages attending it. — The Hopes of Reconciliation, which were fondly entertained by Multitudes of honest and well meaning tho weak and mistaken People, have been gradually and at last totally extinguished. Time has been given for the whole People, maturely to consider the great Question of Independence and to ripen their Judgments, dissipate their Fears, and allure their Hopes, by discussing it in News Papers and Pamphletts, by debating it, in Assemblies, Conventions, Committees of Safety and Inspection, in Town and County Meetings, as well as in private Conversations, so that the whole People in every Colony of the 13, have now adopted it, as their own Act. — This will cement the Union, and avoid those Heats and perhaps Convulsions which might have been occasioned, by such a Declaration Six Months ago.

But the Day is past. The Second Day of July 1776, will be the most memorable Epocha, in the History of America. — I am apt to believe that it will be celebrated, by succeeding Generations, as the great anniversary Festival. It ought to be commemorated, as the Day of Deliverance by solemn Acts of Devotion to God Almighty. It ought to be solemnized with Pomp and Parade, with Shews, Games, Sports, Guns, Bells, Bonfires and Illuminations from one End of this Continent to the other from this Time forward forever more.

You will think me transported with Enthusiasm but I am not. — I am well aware of the Toil and Blood and Treasure, that it will cost Us to maintain this Declaration, and support and defend these States. — Yet through all the Gloom I can see the Rays of ravishing Light and Glory. I can see that the End is more than worth all the Means. And that Posterity will tryumph in that Days Transaction, even altho We should rue it, which I trust in God We shall not.

QUESTIONS FOR READING AND DISCUSSION

1. What did John and Abigail Adams think of Thomas Paine's *Common Sense*? How did they believe it had influenced others? Did their ideas deviate from Paine's in important ways?

2. What did Abigail recommend the new government do in order to "Remember the Ladies"? How did John respond to her suggestions? What did their exchange suggest about the scope and limits of equality among leading supporters of the Revolution?

3. How did the Adamses view southern colonists? What did Abigail mean by asking, "Are not the Gentery Lords and the common people vassals"? How did John respond to her inquiry?

4. Why did John believe that independence would be permanent? What did he anticipate the consequences of independence to be?

DOCUMENT 7–3

J. Hector St. John de Crevecoeur Describes the Distresses of a Frontier Farmer during the Revolution

The bloody fighting between British and Continental soldiers rippled throughout American society as ordinary citizens took sides and often singled out neighbors they considered their political enemies for intimidation, persecution, and violence. J. Hector St. John de Crevecoeur, who lived on the New York frontier with his family, described the terror he confronted in trying to negotiate the dangerous political landscape of the American Revolution. The selection below from his book, Letters From an American Farmer, *published in 1782 after he fled to London, highlights the dilemma of many ordinary colonists who had to balance their desires to protect their families and their livelihoods against the dangers of committing to one side or the other. Crevecoeur illustrates the deep uncertainty among many colonists about how their personal interests aligned with the revolutionary struggle.*

Distresses of a Frontier Man, 1782

I wish for a change of place; the hour is come at last, that I must fly from my house and abandon my farm! But what course shall I steer, inclosed as I am? . . .

Once happiness was our portion; now it is gone from us, and I am afraid not to be enjoyed again by the present generation! Whichever way I look, nothing but the most frightful precipices present themselves to my view, in which hundreds of my friends and acquaintances have already perished. . . . Never was a situation so singularly terrible as mine, in every possible respect, as a member of an extensive society [the British empire], as a citizen of an inferior division of the same society [the colony of New York], as a husband, as a father, as a man who exquisitely feels for the miseries of others as well as for his own! But alas! so much is everything now subverted among us, that . . . tired with feeling for the miseries of others, every one feels now for himself alone. . . .

You know the position of our settlement; I need not therefore describe it. To the west it is inclosed by a chain of mountains . . . ; to the east, the country is as yet but thinly inhabited; we are almost insulated, and the houses are at a considerable distance from each other. From the mountains we have but too much reason to expect our dreadful enemy [Indian allies of the British]; the wilderness is a harbour where it is impossible to find them. It is a door through which they can enter our country whenever they please; and, as they seem determined to destroy the whole chain of frontiers, our fate cannot be far distant: from Lake Champlain, almost all has been conflagrated [burned] one after another. What renders these incursions still more terrible is, that they most commonly take place in the dead of the night; we never go to our fields but we are seized with an involuntary fear. . . . We never sit down either to dinner or supper, but the least noise immediately

From J. Hector St. John de Crevecoeur, "Distresses of a Frontier Man," in *Letters From an American Farmer* (London: T. Davies, 1782).

spreads a general alarm and prevents us from enjoying the comfort of our meals. . . . [S]ometimes I start awake, as if the great hour of danger was come; at other times the howling of our dogs seems to announce the arrival of the enemy: we leap out of bed and run to arms; my poor wife with panting bosom and silent tears, takes leave of me, as if we were to see each other no more; she snatches the youngest children from their beds, who, suddenly awakened, increase by their innocent questions the horror of the dreadful moment. She tries to hide them in the cellar, as if our cellar was inaccessible to the fire. I place all my servants at the windows, and myself at the door, where I am determined to perish. Fear industriously increases every sound; we all listen; each communicates to the other his ideas and conjectures. We remain thus sometimes for whole hours, our hearts and our minds racked by the most anxious suspense. . . .

As a member of a large society [the British empire] which extends to many parts of the world, my connection with it is too distant to be as strong as that which binds me to the inferior division in the midst of which I live. I am told that the great nation, of which we are a part, is just, wise, and free, beyond any other on earth, within its own insular boundaries; but not always so to its distant conquests: I shall not repeat all I have heard, because I cannot believe half of it. As a citizen of a smaller society, I find that any kind of opposition to its now prevailing sentiments, immediately begets hatred: how easily do men pass from loving, to hating and cursing one another! I am a lover of peace, what must I do? I am divided between the respect I feel for the ancient connection, and the fear of innovations, with the consequence of which I am not well acquainted; as they are embraced by my own countrymen. I am conscious that I was happy before this unfortunate Revolution. I feel that I am no longer so; therefore I regret the change. This is the only mode of reasoning adapted to persons in my situation. If I attach myself to the Mother Country, which is 3000 miles from me, I become what is called an enemy to my own region; if I follow the rest of my countrymen, I become opposed to our ancient masters: both extremes appear equally dangerous to a person of so little weight and consequence as I am, whose energy and example are of no avail. As to the argument on which the dispute is founded, I know little about it. Much has been said and written on both sides, but who has a judgment capacious and clear enough to decide? . . .

The innocent class are always the victim of the few; they are in all countries and at all time . . . ; they clamour, and must toil, and bleed, and are always sure of meeting with oppression and rebuke. It is for the sake of the great leaders on both sides, that so much blood must be spilt; that of the people is counted as nothing. Great events are not achieved for us, though it is by us that they are principally accomplished; by the arms, the sweat, the lives of the people. . . . After all, most men reason from passions; and shall such an ignorant individual as I am decide, and say this side is right, that side is wrong? Sentiment and feeling are the only guides I know. Alas, how should I unravel an argument, in which reason herself hath given way to brutality and bloodshed! What then must I do? . . . Shall I discard all my ancient principles, shall I renounce that name, that nation which I held once so respectable? I feel the powerful attraction; the sentiments they inspired grew with my earliest knowledge, and were grafted upon the first rudiments of my education. On the other hand, shall I arm myself against that country where I first drew breath, against the play-mates of my youth, my bosom friends, my acquaintance?—the idea makes me shudder! Must I be called a parricide, a traitor, a villain, lose the esteem of all those whom I love, to preserve my own; be shunned like a rattlesnake, or be pointed at like a bear? I have neither heroism nor magnanimity enough to make so great a sacrifice. Here I am tied, I am fastened by numerous strings, nor do I repine at the pressure they cause; ignorant as I am, I can pervade the utmost extent of the calamities which have already overtaken our poor afflicted country. I can see the great and accumulated ruin yet extending itself as far as the theatre of war has reached; I hear the groans of thousands of families now ruined and desolated by our aggressors. I cannot count the multitude of orphans this war has made; nor ascertain the immensity of blood we have lost. Some have asked, whether it was a crime to resist; to repel some parts of this evil. Others have asserted, that a resistance so general makes pardon unattainable, and repentance useless: and dividing the crime among so many, renders it imperceptible. What one party calls meritorious, the other denominates flagitious [wicked, immoral]. These opinions vary, contract, or expand, like the events of the war on which they are founded. What can an insignificant man do in the midst of these jarring contradictory parties, equally hostile to persons situated as I am? And after all who will be the really guilty?—Those most certainly who fail of success. Our fate, the fate of thousands, is then necessarily involved in the dark wheel of fortune. . . . [H]e who governs himself according to what he calls his principles, may be punished either by one party or the other, for those very principles. He who proceeds without principle, as chance, timidity, or self-preservation directs, will not perhaps fare better; but he will be less blamed. What are we in the great scale of events, we poor defenceless frontier inhabitants? . . .

Self-preservation, therefore, the rule of nature, seems to be the best rule of conduct; what good can we do by vain resistance, by useless efforts? The cool, the distant spectator, placed in safety, may arraign me for ingratitude, . . . but let him come and reside with us one single month, let him pass with us through all the successive hours of necessary toil, terror, and affright, let him watch with us, his musket in his hand, through tedious, sleepless nights, his imagination furrowed by the keen chisel of every passion; let his wife and his children become exposed to the most dreadful hazards of death; let the existence of his property depend on a single spark, blown by the breath of an enemy; . . . let his alarmed imagination predict to him the night, the dreadful night when it may be his turn to perish, as so many have perished before. Observe then, whether the man will not get the better of the citizen, whether his political maxims will not vanish! Yes, he will cease to glow so warmly with the glory of the metropolis; all his wishes will be turned toward the preservation of his family! Oh, were he situated where I am, were his house perpetually filled, as mine is, with miserable victims just escaped from the flames and the scalping knife, telling of barbarities and murders that make human nature tremble; his situation would suspend every political reflection, and expel every abstract idea. . . .

Must I then, in order to be called a faithful subject, coolly, and philosophically say, it is necessary for the good of Britain, that my children's brains should be dashed against the walls of the house in which they were reared; that my wife should be stabbed and scalped before my face; that I should be either murdered or captivated; or that for greater expedition we should all be locked up and burnt to ashes as . . . [one] family . . . was? . . . Shall I wait to be punished with death, or else to be stripped of all food and raiment, reduced to despair without redress and without hope. . . . No, it is impossible! . . . Even those great personages who are so far elevated above the common ranks of men, those, I mean, who wield and direct so many thunders; those who have let loose against us these demons of war, could they be transported here, and metamorphosed into simple planters [farmers] as we are, they would, from being the arbiters of human destiny, sink into miserable victims; they would feel and exclaim as we do, and be as much at a loss what line of conduct to prosecute. Do you well comprehend the difficulties of our situation? If we stay we are sure to perish at one time or another; no vigilance on our part can save us; if we retire, we know not where to go; every house is filled with refugees as wretched as ourselves; and if we remove we become beggars. . . . If we take up arms to defend ourselves, we are denominated rebels; should we not be rebels against nature, could we be shamefully passive? Shall we then, like martyrs, glory in an allegiance, now become useless, and voluntarily expose ourselves to a species of desolation which, though it ruin us entirely, yet enriches not our ancient masters. By this inflexible and sullen attachment, we shall be despised by our countrymen, and destroyed by our ancient friends.

QUESTIONS FOR READING AND DISCUSSION

1. How did Crevecoeur contrast the "large society" of the British empire with the "smaller society" he inhabits on the frontier of New York? What were his connections to each?

2. Why, according to Crevecoeur, were "the innocent class . . . always the victims of the few"? Who did he believe belonged to "the innocent class" in the American Revolution? Who were "the few" who victimized them and why?

3. Crevecoeur declared that "self-preservation . . . seems to be the best rule of conduct." How did that rule contrast with the perspective of "the cool, the distant spectator" during the Revolution? To what extent were the dangers of the Revolution responsible for Crevecoeur's emphasis on self-preservation?

4. According to Crevecoeur, how did the Revolution confront Americans with what he termed "the difficulties of our situation"? What choices did ordinary citizens confront?

DOCUMENT 7–4

Boston King Seeks Freedom by Running Away to the British Army

Boston King, an enslaved African American who worked as a carpenter in Charleston, South Carolina, ran away from his master and sought freedom among the British army. In his memoir, excerpted below, King recounts his experiences in slavery and freedom, offering a rare glimpse of the experiences of roughly 100,000 slaves who fled to the British during the American Revolution. By the time King published his memoir he had become a Methodist minister and moved to Sierra Leone in Africa. King's narrative illustrates the challenges of both slavery and freedom as well as the resourcefulness of slaves who, like King, sought to achieve their own form of independence in the turmoil of the Revolution.

Memoir, 1798

When 16 years old, I was bound apprentice to a trade. After being in the shop about two years, I had the charge of my master's tools, which being very good, were often used by the men, if I happened to be out of the way: When this was the case, or any of them were lost, or misplaced, my master beat me severely, striking me upon my head, or any other part without mercy. One time in the holy-days, my master and the men being from home, and the care of the house devolving upon me and the younger apprentices, the house was broke open, and robbed of many valuable articles, thro' the negligence of the apprentice who had then the charge of it. When I came home in the evening, and saw what had happened, my consternation was inconceivable, as all that we had in the world could not make good the loss. The week following, when the master came to town, I was beat in the most unmerciful manner, so that I was not able to do any thing for a fortnight. About eight months after, we were employed in building a store-house, and nails were very dear at that time, it being in the American war, so that the work-men had their nails weighed out to them; on this account they made the younger apprentices watch the nails while they were at dinner. It being my lot one day to take care of them, which I did till an apprentice returned to his work, and then I went to dine. In the mean time he took away all the nails belonging to one of the journeymen, and he being of very violent temper, accused me to the master with stealing of them. For this offense I was beat and tortured most cruelly, and was laid up three weeks before I was able to do any work. My proprietor, hearing of the bad usage I received, came to town, and severely reprimanded my master for beating me in such a manner, threatening him, that if he ever heard the like again, he would take me away and put me to another master to finish my time, and make him pay for it. This had a good effect and he behaved much better to me, the two succeeding years, and I began to acquire a proper knowledge of my trade. My master being apprehensive that Charles-Town was in danger on account of the war, removed into the country, about 38 miles off. Here we built a large house for Mr. Waters, during which time the English took Charles-Town. Having obtained leave one day to see my parents, who had lived about 12 miles off, and it being late before I could go, I was obliged to borrow one of Mr. Waters's horses; but a servant of my master's, took the horse from me to go a little journey, and stayed two or three days longer than he ought. This involved me in the greatest per-plexity, and I expected the severest punishment, because the gentleman to who the horse belonged was a very bad man, and knew not how [to] shew mercy. To escape his cruelty, I determined to go Charles-Town, and throw myself into the hands of the English. They received me readily, and I began to feel the happiness, liberty, of which I knew nothing before, altho' I was grieved at first, to be obliged to leave my friends, and [to be] among strangers. In this situation I was seized with the small-pox and suffered great hardships; for all the Blacks affected with that disease, were ordered to be carried a mile from the camp, lest the soldiers should be infected, and disabled from marching. This was a grievous circum-stance to me and many others. We lay sometimes a whole day without any thing to eat or drink; but Providence sent a man, who belonged to the York volunteers whom I was acquainted with, to my relief. He brought me such things as I stood in need of; and by the blessing of the Lord I began to recover. . . .

Being recovered, I marched with the army . . . to a place about 35 miles off, where we stayed two months: at the expiration of which, a express came to

From Boston King, "Memoirs of the Life of Boston King, A Black Preacher," *The Methodist Magazine* 21 (March 1798), 106–10; and 21 (April 1798), 15.

the Colonel to decamp in fifteen minutes. When these orders arrived I was at a distance from the camp, catching some fish for the captain that I waited upon; upon returning to the camp, to my great astonishment, I found all the English were gone, and had left only a few militia. I felt my mind greatly alarmed, but Captain Lewes, who commanded the militia, said, "You need not be uneasy, for you will see your regiment before 7 o'clock tonight." This satisfied me for the present, and in two hours we set off. As we were on the march, the Captain asked, "How will you like me to be your master?" I answered that I was Captain Grey's servant. "Yes," said he; "but I expect they are all taken prisoners before now; and I have been long enough in the English service, and am determined to leave them." These words roused my indignation, and I spoke some sharp things to him. But he calmly replied, "If you do not behave well, I will put you in irons, and give you a dozen stripes every morning." I now perceived that my case was desperate, and that I had nothing to trust to, but to wait the first opportunity for making my escape. . . .

   I . . . resolved to go to the English army. After traveling 24 miles, I came to a farmer's house, where I tarried all night, and was well used. Early in the morning I continued my journey till I came to the ferry, and . . . being arrived at the headquarters, I informed my Captain that Mr. Lewes had deserted. . . . Three weeks after, our Light-horse[1] went to the Island and burnt his house; they likewise brought back forty of the horses. . . . I tarried with Captain Grey about a year, and then left him. . . . Soon after I went to Charles-Town, and entered on board a man of war. As we were going to Chesepeak bay . . . [we then] . . . sailed for New-York, where I went on shore. Here I endeavoured to follow my trade, but for want of tools was obliged to relinquish it, and enter into service. But the wages were so low that I was not able to keep myself in clothes, so that I was under the necessity of leaving my master and going to another. I stayed with him four months, but he never paid me, and I was obliged to leave him also, and work about the town until I was married. A year after I was taken very ill, but the Lord raised me up again in about five weeks. I then went out in a pilotboat. We were at sea eight days, and had only provisions for five, so that we were in danger of starving. On the 9th day we were taken by an American whale-boat. I went on board them with a cheerful countenance, and asked for bread and water, and made very free with them. They carried me to Brunswick, and used me well. Notwithstanding which, my mind was fairly distressed at the thought of being again reduced to slavery [by the Americans], and separated from my wife and family; and at the same time it was exceeding difficult to escape from my bondage, because the river at Amboy [New York] was above a mile over, and likewise another to cross at Staten-Island. I called to remembrance the many great deliverances the Lord had wrought for me, and besought him to save me this once, and I would serve him all the days of my life. . . . I was thankful that I was not confined in a jail, and my master used me as well as I could expect; and indeed the slaves about Baltimore, Philadelphia, and New-York, have as good victuals as many of the English; for they have meat once a day, and milk for breakfast and supper; and what is better than all, many of the masters send their slaves to school at night, that they may learn to read the Scriptures. This is a privilege indeed. But alas, all these enjoyments could not satisfy me without liberty! Sometimes I thought, if it was the will of God that I should be a

---

[1]**Light-horse**: A cavalry unit.

slave, I was ready to resign myself to his will; but at other times I could not find the least desire to content myself in slavery. . . .

Being permitted to walk about when my work was done, I used to go to the ferry, and observed, that when it was low water the people waded across the river; tho' at the same time I saw there were guards posted at the place to prevent the escape of prisoners and slaves. As I was at prayer on Sunday evening, I thought the Lord heard me, and would mercifully deliver me. Therefore putting my confidence in him, about one o'clock in the morning I went down to the river side, and found the guards were either asleep or in the tavern. I instantly entered into the river [and crossed it]. . . . When I had got a little distance from the shore, I fell down upon my knees, and thanked God for the deliverance. I traveled till about five in the morning, and then concealed myself till seven o'clock at night, when I proceeded forward, thro' bushes and marshes, near the road, for fear of being discovered. When I came to the river, opposite Staten-Island, I found a boat . . . and cutting the rope, got safe over [the river]. . . .

When I arrived at [British-occupied] New-York, my friends rejoiced to see me once more restored to liberty, and joined me in praising the Lord for his mercy and goodness. But notwithstanding this great deliverance, and the promises I had made to serve God, yet my good resolutions soon vanished away like the morning dew: The love of this world extinguished my good desires, and stole away my heart from God, so that I rested in a mere form of religion for near three years. About which time, the horrors and devastation of war happily terminated and peace was restored between America and Great Britain, which diffused universal joy among all parties; except us, who had escaped from slavery and taken refuge in the English army; for a report prevailed at New-York, that all the slaves, in number 2000, were to be delivered up to their masters altho' some of them had been three or four years among the English. This dreadful rumour filled us all with inexpressible anguish and terror, especially when we saw our old masters coming from Virginia, North-Carolina, and other parts, and seizing upon their slaves in the streets of New-York, or even dragging them out of their beds. Many of the slaves had very cruel masters, so that the thoughts of returning home with them embittered life to us. For some days we lost our appetite for food, and sleep departed from our eyes. The English had compassion upon us in the day of distress, and issued out a Proclamation: . . . That all slaves should be free, who had taken refuge in the British lines, and claimed the sanction and privileges of the Proclamations respecting the security and protection of Negroes. In consequence of this, each of us received a certificate from the commanding officer at New-York, which dispelled all our fears, and filled us with joy and gratitude. Soon after, ships were fitted out, and furnished with every necessary for conveying us to Nova Scotia. We arrived [there] . . . in the month of August, where we all safely landed. Every family had a lot of land, and we exerted all our strength in order to build comfortable huts before the cold weather set in.

QUESTIONS FOR READING AND DISCUSSION

1. According to King, what were the differences between slavery and freedom? Did he believe he had a choice about being a slave? When? Why or why not?

2. When King escaped to the British, how did his life change? How did the British behave toward him? Why did the end of the war diffuse "universal joy among all parties; except us, who had escaped from slavery"?

3. What hardships did King experience as a free man? To what did he attribute his ability to overcome these hardships?

4. To what extent did the British show "compassion" to King and other former slaves? Did King and the British share the same motives and goals? Why or why not?

DOCUMENT 7–5

Joseph Brant Appeals to British Allies to Keep Promises

In the American Revolution, many Indians allied with the British against the rebellious colonists. In 1776, Joseph Brant, a Mohawk leader, accompanied British colonial officials on a trip to England, where he met the king and queen and delivered an address to the secretary of state, Lord Germain, whom Brant called by the Iroquois name Gorah. Brant asked the British to fulfill the promises that had been made to the Mohawks and other Indians. In the context of the accelerating American Revolution, Brant's address represented an attempt to remind the British that it was in their interest to court Mohawk allies. In 1783, under the Treaty of Paris that ended the Revolution, Britain surrendered to the newly independent states all of the territory east of the Mississippi, from Florida to the Great Lakes, without consulting its Indian allies. Brant wrote the governor of Quebec an impassioned letter asking if it was true that the British had signed the treaty without considering the claims of their loyal Indian allies. Brant's appeals document Indians' difficulty in getting European allies to live up to promises made when Indian allies were important but then neglected when Europeans found it expedient to do so.

Address to British Secretary of State Lord Germain, 1776

Brother Gorah:

We have cross'd the great Lake and come to this kingdom with our Superintendant Col. Johnson[1] from our Confederacy the Six Nations and their Allies, that we might see our Father the Great King, and joyn in informing him, his Councillors and wise men, of the good intentions of the Indians our bretheren, and of their attachment to His Majesty and his Government.

Brother: The Disturbances in America give great trouble to all our Nations, as many strange stories have been told to us by the people in that country. The Six Nations who alwayes loved the King, sent a number of their Chiefs and Warriors with their Superintendant to Canada last summer, where they engaged their allies to joyn with them in the defence of that country, and when it was invaded by the New England people, they alone defeated them.

From E. B. O'Callaghan, ed., *Documents Relative to the Colonial History of the State of New York*, 15 vols. (Albany: Weed, Parsons, 1853–87), 8:670–71; Public Record Office, C.O. 42/44, 133–35, reprinted in Charles M. Johnson, ed., *Valley of the Six Nations* (Toronto: Champlain Society, 1964), 38–41.

[1]**Col. Johnson**: Sir William Johnson, an official in the British Indian department who died in 1774.

Brother: In that engagement we had several of our best Warriors killed and wounded, and the Indians think it very hard they should have been so deceived by the White people in that country, the enemy returning in great numbers, and no White people supporting the Indians, they were oblidged to retire to their vilages and sit still. We now Brother hope to see these bad children chastised, and that we may be enabled to tell the Indians, who have always been faithfull and ready to assist the King, what His Majesty intends.

Brother: The Mohocks our particular Nation, have on all occasions shewn their zeal and loyalty to the Great King; yet they have been very badly treated by his people in that country, the City of Albany laying an unjust claim to the lands on which our lower Castle is built, as one Klock and others do to those of Conijoharrie our Upper Viliage. We have been often assured by our late great friend Sr William Johnson who never deceived us, and we know he was told so that the King and wise men here would do us justice; but this notwithstanding all our applications has never been done, and it makes us very uneasie. We also feel for the distress in which our Bretheren on the Susquehanna are likely to be involved by a mistake made in the Boundary we setled in 1768. This also our Superintendant has laid before the King, and we beg it may be remembered. And also concerning Religion and the want of Ministers of the Church of England, he knows the designs of those bad people and informs us he has laid the same before the King. We have only therefore to request that his Majesty will attend to this matter: it troubles our Nation & they cannot sleep easie in their beds. Indeed it is very hard when we have let the Kings subjects have so much of our lands for so little value, they should want to cheat us in this manner of the small spots we have left for our women and children to live on. We are tired out in making complaints & getting no redress. We therefore hope that the Assurances now given us by the Superintendant may take place, and that he may have it in his power to procure us justice.

Brother: We shall truly report all that we hear from you, to the Six Nations at our return. We are well informed there has been many Indians in this Country who came without any authority, from their own, and gave much trouble. We desire Brother to tell you this is not our case. We are warriors known to all the Nations, and are now here by approbation of many of them, whose sentiments we speak.

Brother: We hope these things will be considered and that the King or his great men will give us such an answer as will make our hearts light and glad before we go, and strengthen our hands, so that we may joyn our Superintendant Col. Johnson in giving satisfaction to all our Nations, when we report to them, on our return; for which purpose we hope soon to be accomodated with a passage.

Dictated by the Indians and taken down by

Jo[nathan] Chew. Sec[retar]y

Message to Governor of Quebec, Frederick Haldimand, 1783

Brother Asharekowa and Representatives of the King, the sachems [chiefs] and War Chieftains of the Six United Nations of Indians and their Allies have heard that the King, their Father, has made peace with his children the Bostonians. The Indians distinguish by Bostonians, the Americans in Rebellion, as it first began in Boston, and when they heard of it, they found that they were forgot and no mention made of them in said Peace, wherefore they have now sent me to inform themselves before you of the real truth, whether it is so or not, that they are not partakers of that Peace with the King and the Bostonians.

Brother, listen with great attention to our words, we were greatly alarmed and cast down when we heard that news, and it occasions great discontent and surprise with our People; wherefore tell us the real truth from your heart and we beg that the King will be put in mind by you and recollect what we have been when his people first saw us, and what we have since done for him and his subjects.

Brother, we, the Mohawks, were the first Indian Nation that took you by the hand like friends and brothers, and invited you to live amongst us, treating you with kindness upon your debarkation in small parties. The Oneidas, our neighbors, were equally well disposed towards you and as a mark of our sincerity and love towards you we fastened your ship to a great mountain at Onondaga, the Center of our Confederacy, the rest of the Five Nations approving of it. We were then a great people, conquering all Indian Nations round about us, and you in a manner but a handfull, after which you increased by degrees and we continued your friends and allies, joining you from time to time against your enemies, sacrificing numbers of our people and leaving their bones scattered in your enemies country. At last we assisted you in conquering all Canada, and then again, for joining you so firmly and faithfully, you renewed your assurances of protecting and defending ourselves, lands and possessions against any encroachment whatsoever, procuring for us the enjoyment of fair and plentiful trade of your people, and sat contented under the shade of the Tree of Peace, tasting the favour and friendship of a great Nation bound to us by Treaty, and able to protect us against all the world.

Brother, you have books and records of our mutual Treaties and Engagements, which will confirm the truth of what I have been telling, and as we are unacquainted with the art of writing, we keep it fresh in our memory by Belts of Wampum deposited in our Council House at Onondaga. We have also received an Ornament for the Head, i.e. a crown, from her late Majesty, Queen Ann, as a token of her mutual and unalterable friendship and alliance with us and our Confederacy. Wherefore, we on our side have maintained an uninterrupted attachment towards you, in confidence and expectation of a Reciprocity, and to establish a Perpetual Friendship and Alliance between us, of which we can give you several instances, to wit, when a few years after the Conquest of Canada, your people in this country thought themselves confined on account of their numbers with regard to a Scarcity of Land, we were applied to for giving up some of ours, and fix a Line or mark between them and Us. We considered upon it, and relinquished a great Territory to the King for the use of his Subjects, for a Trifling consideration, merely as a Confirmation of said Act, and as a proof of our sincere Regard towards them. This happened so late as the year 1768 at Fort Stanwix, and was gratefully Accepted and Ratified by the different Governors and Great men of the respective Colonies on the Sea Side, in presence of our Late Worthy Friend and Superintendent, Sir William Johnson, when we expected a Permanent, Brotherly love and Amity, would be the Consequence, but in vain. The insatiable thirst for Power and the next Object of dissatisfaction to the King's Subjects on the Sea Coast, and they to blind our Eyes, Sent Priests from New England amongst us, whom we took for Messengers of Peace, but we were Surprisingly undeceived when we found soon after, that they came to sow the Seeds of discord among our People, in order to alienate our ancient attachments and Alliance from the King our Father, and join them in Rebellion against him, and when they stood up against him, they first endeavored to ensnare us, the Mohawks, and the Indians of the Six Nations living on the Susquehanna River, and the Oneidas, by which division they imagined the remainder of the Confederacy would soon follow, but to not the Least effect.

About this Sad Period we lost our Greatest Friend, Sir William Johnson, notwithstanding we were unalterably determined to stick to our Ancient Treaties with the Crown of England and when the Rebels attempted to insult the Families and Descendents of our late Superintendent, on whom the management of our affairs devolved, we stuck to them and Protected them as much as in our Power, conducting them to Canada with a determined Resolution inviolably to adhere to our Alliance at the Risque of our Lives Families and Property, the rest of the Six Nations finding the Firmness and Steadiness of us, the Mohawks . . . , followed our Example and espoused the King's cause to this Present Instant.

It is as I tell you, Brother, and would be too tedious to repeat on this Pressing Occasion the many Proofs of Fidelity we have given the King our Father.

Wherefore Brother, I am now Sent in behalf of all the King's Indian Allies to receive a decisive answer from you, and to know whether they are included in the Treaty with the Americans, as faithful Allies should be or not, and whether those Lands which the Great Being above has pointed out for Our Ancestors, and their descendants, and Placed them there from the beginning and where the Bones of our forefathers are laid, is secure to them, or whether the Blood of their Grand Children is to be mingled with their Bones, thro' the means of Our Allies for whom we have often so freely Bled.

QUESTIONS FOR READING AND DISCUSSION

1. What was Brant's message to the British in his statement that "The Disturbances in America give great trouble to all our Nations"? What promises had the British made to the Mohawks? Why had the promises not been kept?

2. Why had the Mohawks "shewn their zeal and loyalty to the Great King"? Did Brant consider the Indians and the British equal partners? How had the Mohawks helped the British, according to Brant?

3. Who were the "Bostonians," and why did Brant think they were important? What were the consequences of the colonists' "insatiable thirst for Power"?

4. Brant affirmed that the British "have books and records of our mutual Treaties and Engagements, which will confirm the truth of what I have been telling, and as we are unacquainted with the art of writing, we keep it fresh in our memory by Belts of Wampum deposited in our Council House." To what extent did these contrasting traditions of communication and record keeping influence Brant's negotiations and their outcomes?

COMPARATIVE QUESTIONS

1. How might Thomas Paine and Abigail and John Adams have responded to the dilemmas of ordinary citizens described by J. Hector St. John de Crevecoeur?

2. To what extent did Boston King and Joseph Brant disagree with ideas expressed by Paine and the Adamses? How might Paine and the Adamses have responded to King's and Brant's alliance with the British?

3. To what extent did the revolutionary experiences documented in this chapter support the ideals of a government of laws advanced in *Common Sense*? To what extent did those experiences provide evidence of a commitment to equality? To self-interest?

4. Judging from the documents in this chapter, what were the perceived achievements and limitations of independence? How did they compare to the promises and aspirations of Paine and the Adamses?

8 Building a Republic
1775–1789

After the Revolution, Americans sought to realize some of the gains they hoped that independence would bring. Individuals and groups debated proposals for religious, social, and governmental reforms, as well as for new forms of government. These often bitter debates reflected the conflicting aspirations of Americans and their differing views of the Revolution's achievements and limitations.

DOCUMENT 8–1
Richard Allen Founds the First African Methodist Church

After the Revolution, the religious diversity that had long characterized America increased when Richard Allen, a black Methodist preacher, founded the first African Methodist church in Philadelphia. In this selection from his memoir published shortly after his death in 1831, Allen chronicled his journey from his awakening of faith when he was a slave to his achievement of freedom, his years as an itinerant minister, and his devotion to Methodist preaching among African Americans. Allen's narrative demonstrates the powerful religious impulses that coursed through the nation in the early republic, impulses that often expressed racial solidarity but that sometimes bridged the divisions between blacks and whites.

Life, Experience, and Gospel Labours, 1833

I was born in the year of our Lord 1760, on February 14th, a slave to Benjamin Chew, of Philadelphia. My mother and father and four children of us were sold into Delaware State, near Dover, and I was a child and lived with him [my new

---

From Richard Allen, *The Life, Experience, and Gospel Labours of the Rt. Rev. Richard Allen. To Which Is Annexed the Rise and Progress of the African Methodist Episcopal Church in the United States of America* (Philadelphia: Martin & Boden, 1833).

---

master] until I was upwards of twenty years of age, during which time I was awakened and brought to see myself poor, wretched and undone, and without the mercy of God must be lost. . . . My soul was filled. . . . Now my confidence was strengthened that the Lord, for Christ's sake, had heard my prayers, and pardoned all my sins. I was constrained to go from house to house, exhorting my old companions, and telling to all around what a dear Saviour I had found. I joined the Methodist society, and met in class at Benjamin Wells's, in the forest, Delaware State. John Gray was the class-leader. I met in his class for several years.

My master was an unconverted man, and all the family; but he was what the world called a good master. He was more like a father to his slaves than any thing else. He was a very tender, humane man. My mother and father lived with him for many years. He was brought into difficulty, not being able to pay for us; and mother having several children after he had bought us, he sold my mother and three children. My mother sought the Lord and found favour with him, and became a very pious woman. There were three children of us remained with our old master. My oldest brother embraced religion, and my sister. Our neighbours, seeing that our master indulged us with the privilege of attending meeting once in two weeks, said that Stokeley's negroes would soon ruin him; and so my brother and myself held a council together that we would attend more faithfully to our master's business, so that it should not be said that religion made us worse servants, we would work night and day to get our crops forward, so that they should be disappointed. . . . We always continued to keep our crops more forward than our neighbours; and we would attend public preaching once in two weeks, and class meeting once a week. At length our master said he was convinced that religion made slaves better and not worse, and often boasted of his slaves for their honesty and industry. Some time after . . . my master believed . . . that he could not be satisfied to hold slaves, believing it to be wrong. And after that he proposed to me and my brother buying our times, to pay him sixty pounds gold and silver, or two thousand dollars continental money, which we complied with in the year 17–.

We left our master's house, and I may truly say it was like leaving our father's house; for he was a kind, affectionate, and tender-hearted master, and told us to make his house our home when we were out of a place or sick. . . .

I had it often impressed upon my mind that I should one day enjoy my freedom; for slavery is a bitter pill, notwithstanding we had a good master. But when we would think that our day's work was never done, we often thought that after our master's death we were liable to be sold to the highest bidder, as he was much in debt; and thus my troubles were increased. . . . But I have had reason to bless my dear Lord that a door was opened unexpectedly for me to buy my time, and enjoy my liberty. When I left my master's house I knew not what to do, not being used to hard work, what business I should follow to pay my master and get my living. I went to cutting of cord wood. . . . After I was done cutting, I was employed in a brick-yard . . . at fifty dollars a month, continental money. After I was done with the brick-yard I went to days' work, but . . . while my hands were employed to earn my bread, my heart was devoted to my dear Redeemer. . . . I was after this employed in driving a wagon in time of the continental war, in drawing salt from . . . Sussex county, in Delaware. I had my regular stops and preaching places on the road. . . .

After peace was proclaimed I then travelled extensively, striving to preach the Gospel. . . .

February, 1786, I came to Philadelphia. . . . I preached at different places in the city. My labour was much blessed. I soon saw a large field open in seeking and instructing my African brethren, who had been a long forgotten people and few of them attended public worship. . . . I frequently preached twice a day, at 5 o'clock in the morning and in the evening, and it was not uncommon for me to preach from four to five times a day. I established prayer meetings; I raised a society in 1786 of forty-two members. I saw the necessity of erecting a place of worship for the coloured people. I proposed it to the most respectable people of colour in this city; but here I met with opposition. I had but three coloured brethren that united with me in erecting a place of worship—the Rev. Absalom Jones, William White, and Dorus Ginnings. . . . The Rev Mr. W [a white man] . . . was much opposed to an African church, and used very degrading and insulting language to us, to try and prevent us from going on. . . . We established prayer meetings and meetings of exhortation, and the Lord blessed our endeavours, and many souls were awakened; but the elder[1] soon forbid us holding any such meetings; but we viewed the forlorn state of our coloured brethren, and that they were destitute of a place of worship. . . .

A number of us usually attended St. George's Church in Fourth street; and when the coloured people began to get numerous in attending the church, they moved us from the seats we usually sat on, and placed us around the wall, and on Sabbath morning we went to church and the sexton stood at the door, and told us to go in the gallery. He told us to go, and we would see where to sit. We expected to take the seats over the ones we formerly occupied below, not knowing any better. We took those seats. Meeting had begun, and they were nearly done singing, and just as we got to the seats, the elder said, "let us pray." We had not been long upon our knees before I heard considerable scuffling and low talking. I raised my head up and saw one of the trustees, H—— M——, having hold of the Rev. Absalom Jones, pulling him up off of his knees, and saying, "You must get up—you must not kneel here." Mr. Jones replied, "wait until prayer is over." Mr. H—— M—— said "no, you must get up now, or I will call for aid and force you away." Mr. Jones said, "wait until prayer is over, and I will get up and trouble you no more." With that he beckoned to one of the other trustees, Mr. L—— S—— to come to his assistance. He came, and went to William White to pull him up. By this time prayer was over, and we all went out of the church in a body, and they were no more plagued with us in the church. This raised a great excitement and inquiry among the citizens, in so much that I believe they were ashamed of their conduct.

But my dear Lord was with us, and we were filled with fresh vigour to get a house erected to worship God in. Seeing our forlorn and distressed situation, many of the hearts of our citizens were moved to urge us forward; notwithstanding we had subscribed largely towards finishing St. George's Church, in building the gallery and laying new floors, and just as the house was made comfortable, we were turned out from enjoying the comforts of worshiping therein. We then hired a store room, and held worship by ourselves. Here we were pursued with threats of being disowned, and read publicly out of meeting if we did continue worship in the place we had hired; but we believed the Lord would be our friend. We got subscription papers out to raise money to build the house of the Lord. By

---

[1]**elder**: A respected, senior member of the congregation.

this time we had waited on Dr. [Benjamin] Rush and Mr. Robert Ralston, and told them of our distressing situation. . . . They pitied our situation, and subscribed largely towards the church, and were very friendly towards us, and advised us how to go on. . . . They were the two first gentlemen who espoused the cause of the oppressed, and aided us in building the house of the Lord for the poor Africans to worship in. Here was the beginning and rise of the first African church in America. . . .

We bore much persecution from many of the Methodist connexion; but we have reason to be thankful to Almighty God, who was our deliverer. The day was appointed to go and dig the cellar. . . . Having by this time two or three teams of my own—as I was the first proposer of the African church, I put the first spade in the ground to dig a cellar for the same. This was the first African church or meeting house that was erected in the United States of America. We intended it for the African preaching house or church. . . . We were in favour of being attached to the Methodist connexion; for I was confident that there was no religious sect or denomination would suit the capacity of the coloured people as well as the Methodist; for the plain and simple gospel suits best for any people, for the unlearned can understand, and the learned are sure to understand; and the reason that the Methodist is so successful in the awakening and conversion of the coloured people, the plain doctrine and having a good discipline. But in many cases the [white Methodist] preachers would act to please their own fancy, without discipline, till some of them became such tyrants, and more especially to the coloured people. They would turn them out of society, giving them no trial, for the smallest offence, perhaps only hearsay. They would frequently, in meeting the class, impeach some of the members of whom they had heard an ill report, and turn them out, saying, "I have heard thus and thus of you, and you are no more a member of society"—without witnesses on either side. This has been frequently done, notwithstanding in the first rise and progress in Delaware State, and elsewhere, the coloured people were their greatest support; for there were but few of us free; but the slaves would toil in their little patches many a night until midnight to raise their little truck and sell to get something to support them more than what their masters gave them, but we used often to divide our little support among the white preachers of the Gospel. This was once a quarter. It was in the time of the old revolutionary war between Great Britain and the United States. The Methodists were the first people that brought glad tidings to the coloured people. I feel thankful that ever I heard a Methodist preach. We are beholden to the Methodists, under God, for the light of the Gospel we enjoy; for all other denominations preached so high-flown that we were not able to comprehend their doctrine. Sure am I that reading sermons will never prove so beneficial to the coloured people as spiritual or extempore preaching.

QUESTIONS FOR READING AND DISCUSSION

1. In what ways did Richard Allen's religious faith influence his life as a slave? Did his experiences in slavery also influence his religion? If so, how and why?
2. To what extent did Allen's African descent influence his experiences as a preacher? Who attended his preachings and how did they respond?
3. What significance did he ascribe to the "first African church" that he founded? Why did he start the church? Why did some white people oppose his efforts while others supported him?

4. Why, according to Allen, did "no religious sect or denomination . . . suit the capacity of the coloured people as well as the Methodist"?

5. Do you think the achievement of American independence in 1783 influenced Allen and his work?

DOCUMENT 8–2

Thomas Jefferson on Slavery and Race

Slavery seemed to many Americans to be inconsistent with the principles of the Revolution. Northern states, where few slaves lived, took the lead in outlawing slavery, but no southern states abolished slavery. In Notes on the State of Virginia, *written in 1782, Thomas Jefferson explained some of the most important reasons why emancipation never received serious consideration in southern legislatures. Jefferson's explanation, excerpted here, discloses racial views that were widespread among white Americans, North and South.*

Notes on the State of Virginia, 1782

Many of the laws which were in force during the monarchy being relative merely to that form of government, or inculcating principles inconsistent with republicanism, the first assembly which met after the establishment of the commonwealth appointed a committee to revise the whole code, to reduce it into proper form and volume, and report it to the assembly. . . .

The following . . . [is one of] the most remarkable alterations proposed:

To emancipate all slaves born after passing the act. The bill reported by the revisors does not itself contain this proposition; but an amendment containing it was prepared, to be offered to the legislature whenever the bill should be taken up, and further directing, that they should continue with their parents to a certain age, then be brought up, at the public expence, to tillage, arts or sciences, according to their geniuses, till the females should be eighteen, and the males twenty-one years of age, when they should be colonized to such place as the circumstances of the time should render most proper, sending them out with arms, implements of household and of the handicraft arts, feeds, pairs of the useful domestic animals, &c. to declare them a free and independent people, and extend to them our alliance and protection, till they have acquired strength; and to send vessels at the same time to other parts of the world for an equal number of white inhabitants; to induce whom to migrate hither, proper encouragements were to be proposed. It will probably be asked, Why not retain and incorporate the blacks into the state, and thus save the expence of supplying by importation of white settlers, the vacancies they will leave? Deep rooted prejudices entertained by the whites; ten thousand recollections, by the blacks, of the injuries they have sustained; new provocations; the real distinctions which nature has made; and many other circumstances, will divide us into parties, and produce convulsions, which will probably never end but in the extermination of the one or the other race. — To these objections, which are political, may be added others, which are physical and

From Thomas Jefferson, *Notes on the State of Virginia* (1782).

moral. The first difference which strikes us is that of colour. Whether the black of the negro resides in the reticular membrane between the skin and scarf-skin, or in the scarf-skin itself; whether it proceeds from the colour of the blood, the colour of the bile, or from that of some other secretion, the difference is fixed in nature, and is as real as if its seat and cause were better known to us. And is this difference of no importance? Is it not the foundation of a greater or less share of beauty in the two races? Are not the fine mixtures of red and white, the expressions of every passion by greater or less suffusions of colour in the one, preferable to that eternal monotony, which reigns in the countenances, that immoveable veil of black which covers all the emotions of the other race? Add to these, flowing hair, a more elegant symmetry of form, their own judgment in favour of the whites, declared by their preference of them, as uniformly as is the preference of the Oranootan [orangutan] for the black women over those of his own species. The circumstance of superior beauty, is thought worthy of attention in the propagation of our horses, dogs, and other domestic animals; why not in that of man? Besides those of colour, figure, and hair, there are other physical distinctions proving a difference of race. They have less hair on the face and body. They secrete less by the kidnies, and more by the glands of the skin, which gives them a very strong and disagreeable odour. This greater degree of transpiration renders them more tolerant of heat, and less so of cold than the whites. . . . They seem to require less sleep. A black after hard labour through the day, will be induced by the slightest amusements to sit up till midnight, or later though knowing he must be out with the first dawn of the morning. They are at least as brave, and more adventuresome. But this may perhaps proceed from a want of forethought, which prevents their seeing a danger till it be present. When present, they do not go through it with more coolness or steadiness than the whites. They are more ardent after their female: but love seems with them to be more an eager desire, than a tender delicate mixture of sentiment and sensation. Their griefs are transient. Those numberless afflictions, which render it doubtful whether heaven has given life to us in mercy or in wrath, are less felt, and sooner forgotten with them. In general, their existence appears to participate more of sensation than reflection. To this must be ascribed their disposition to sleep when abstracted from their diversions, and unemployed in labour. An animal whose body is at rest, and, who does not reflect, must be disposed to sleep of course. Comparing them by their faculties of memory, reason, and imagination, it appears to me that in memory they are equal to the whites; in reason much inferior, as I think one could scarcely be found capable of tracing and comprehending the investigations of Euclid; and that in imagination they are dull, tasteless, and anomalous. It would be unfair to follow them to Africa for this investigation. We will consider them here, on the same stage with the whites, and where the facts are not apocryphal on which a judgement is to be formed. It will be right to make great allowances for the difference of condition, of education, of conversation, of the sphere in which they move. Many millions of them have been brought to, and born in America. Most of them indeed have been confined to tillage, to their own homes, and their own society: yet many have been so situated, that they might have availed themselves of the conversation of their masters; many have been brought up to the handicraft arts, and from that circumstance have always been associated with the whites. Some have been liberally educated, and all have lived in countries where the arts and sciences are cultivated to a considerable degree, and have had before their eyes samples of the best works from abroad. The Indians, with no advantages of this kind, will often carve figures on their pipes not destitute of design and merit. They will crayon out an animal, a plant, or a country, so as to prove the existence of a germ in their minds which only wants cultivation. They astonish you with strokes of the most sublime oratory; such as prove their reason and sentiment strong, their imagination glowing and elevated. But never yet could I find that a black had uttered a thought above the level of plain narration; never see even an elementary trait of painting or sculpture. In music they are more generally gifted than the whites with accurate ears for tune and time, and they have been found capable of imagining a small catch.[1] Whether they will be equal to the composition of a more extensive run of melody, or of complicated harmony, is yet to be proved. Misery is often the parent of the most affecting touches in poetry.—Among the blacks is misery enough, God knows, but no poetry. . . . Their love is ardent, but it kindles the senses only, not the imagination. Religion indeed has produced a Phyllis Whately;[2] but it could not produce a poet. The compositions published under her name are below the dignity of criticism. . . . The improvement of the blacks in body and mind, in the first instance of their mixture with the whites, has been observed by every one, and proves that their inferiority is not the effect merely of their condition of life. . . .

It is not their condition then, but nature, which has produced the distinction.—Whether further observation will or will not verify the conjecture, that nature has been less bountiful to them in the endowments of the head, I believe that in those of the heart she will be found to have done them justice. That disposition to theft with which they have been branded, must be ascribed to their situation, and not to any depravity of the moral sense. The man, in whose favour no laws of property exist, probably feels himself less bound to respect those made in favour of others. When arguing for ourselves, we lay it down as a fundamental, that laws, to be just, must give a reciprocation of right: that, without this, they are mere arbitrary rules of conduct, founded in force, and not in conscience: and it is a problem which I give to the master to solve, whether the religious precepts against the violation of property were not framed for him as well as his slave? And whether the slave may not as justifiably take a little from one, who has taken all from him, as he may slay one would slay him? That a change in the relations in which a man is placed should change his ideas of moral right and wrong, is neither new, nor peculiar to the colour of the blacks. . . .

Notwithstanding these considerations which must weaken their respect for the laws of property, we find among them numerous instances of the most rigid integrity, and as many as among their better instructed masters, of benevolence, gratitude, and unshaken fidelity.—The opinion, that they are inferior in the faculties of reason and imagination, must be hazarded with great diffidence. To justify a general conclusion, requires many observations. . . . [L]et me add too, as a circumstance of great tenderness, where our conclusion would degrade a whole race of men from the rank in the scale of beings which their Creator may perhaps have given them. To our reproach it must be said, that though for a century and a half we have had under our eyes the races of black and of red men, they have never yet been viewed by us as subjects of natural history. I advance it therefore as a

---

[1] **small catch**: A short piece of music.

[2] **Phyllis Whately**: Jefferson refers here to Phillis Wheatley (1753?–1784), an African-born poet generally considered the first well-known black writer in America.

suspicion only, that the blacks, whether originally a distinct race, or made distinct by time and circumstances, are inferior to the whites in the endowments both of body and mind. It is not against experience to suppose, that different species of the same genus, or varieties of the same species, may possess different qualifications. Will not a lover of natural history then, one who views the gradations in all the races of animals with the eye of philosophy, excuse an effort to keep those in the department of man as distinct as nature has formed them? This unfortunate difference of colour, and perhaps of faculty, is a powerful obstacle to the emancipation of these people. . . .

There must doubtless be an unhappy influence on the manners of our people produced by the existence of slavery among us. The whole commerce between master and slave is a perpetual exercise of the most boisterous passions, the most unremitting despotism on the one part, and degrading submissions on the other. Our children see this, and learn to imitate it; for man is an imitative animal. This quality is the germ of all education in him. From his cradle to his grave he is learning to do what he sees others do. If a parent could find no motive either in his philanthropy or his self-love, for restraining the intemperance of passion towards his slave, it would always be a sufficient one that his child is present. But generally it is not sufficient. The parent storms, the child looks on, catches the lineaments of wrath, puts on the same airs in the circle of smaller slaves, gives a loose to his worst of passions, and thus nursed, educated, and daily exercised in tyranny, cannot but be stamped by it with odious peculiarities. The man must be a prodigy who can retain his manners and morals undepraved by such circumstances. And with what execration should the statesman be loaded, who permitting one half the citizens thus to trample on the rights of the other, transforms those into despots, and these into enemies, destroys the morals of the one part, and the amor patriae[3] of the other. For if a slave can have a country in this world, it must be any other in preference to that in which he is born to live and labour for another: in which he must lock up the faculties of his nature, contribute as far as depends on his individual endeavours to the evanishment of the human race, or entail his own miserable condition on the endless generations proceeding from him. With the morals of the people, their industry also is destroyed. For in a warm climate, no man will labour for himself who can make another labour for him. This is so true, that of the proprietors of slaves a very small proportion indeed are ever seen to labour. And can the liberties of a nation be thought secure when we have removed their only firm basis, a conviction in the minds of the people that these liberties are of the gift of God? That they are not to be violated but with his wrath? Indeed I tremble for my country when I reflect that God is just: that his justice cannot sleep for ever: that considering numbers, nature and natural means only, a revolution of the wheel of fortune, an exchange of situation is among possible events: that it may become probable by supernatural interference! The almighty has no attribute which can take side with us in such a contest. . . . I think a change already perceptible, since the origin of the present revolution. The spirit of the master is abating, that of the slave rising from the dust, his condition mollifying, the way I hope preparing, under the auspices of heaven, for a total emancipation, and that this is disposed, in the order of events, to be with the consent of the masters, rather than by their extirpation.

---

[3]**amor patriae**: Love of country.

QUESTIONS FOR READING AND DISCUSSION

1. What were the terms of the emancipation proposal considered by Virginia legislators? Why did the proposal call for colonization?

2. According to Jefferson, what were the differences between the races? Why did he conclude that "It is not their [blacks'] condition, then, but nature, which has produced the distinction"? Did Jefferson believe that blacks were inferior?

3. How did slavery influence masters and other whites? Did slavery have effects on them that Jefferson failed to mention? How did slavery influence slaves, according to Jefferson?

4. Did Jefferson believe that slavery was wrong? Why did he say, "I tremble for my country when I reflect that God is just"? How did he fear slavery would end? How did his hopes for the end of slavery differ from his fears?

5. Reading between the lines of Jefferson's *Notes,* can you detect whether he seemed to believe that his views of slavery and race were typical or unusual as compared with those of other white Americans of the era?

DOCUMENT 8–3

Benjamin Rush Proposes a Proper Education for a Republic

Prominent Philadelphia physician Benjamin Rush believed education should be reformed to nurture good citizens for the new republic. A fervent supporter of the American Revolution and signer of the Declaration of Independence, Rush advocated educational principles and practices that he believed would perpetuate the Revolution's republican achievements. In an essay published in 1786, excerpted below, Rush described the attributes of an ideal republican education and disclosed his convictions about the interdependence of religion, liberty, learning, and government.

Of the Mode of Education Proper in a Republic, 1786

The business of education has acquired a new complexion by the independence of our country. The form of government we have assumed, has created a new class of duties to every American. It becomes us, therefore, . . . in laying the foundations for nurseries of wise and good men, to adapt our modes of teaching to the peculiar form of our government.

The first remark that I shall make upon this subject is, that an education in our own [country], is to be preferred to an education in a foreign country. The principle of patriotism stands in need of the reinforcement of prejudice. And it is well known that our strongest prejudices in favour of our country are formed in the first one and twenty years of our lives. . . .

From Benjamin Rush, "Of the Mode of Education Proper in a Republic," in *A Plan for the Establishment of Public Schools and the Diffusion of Knowledge in Pennsylvania* (Philadelphia: Thomas Dobson, 1786).

I conceive the education of our youth in this country to be peculiarly necessary in Pennsylvania, while our citizens are composed of the natives of so many different kingdoms in Europe. Our schools of learning, by producing one general, and uniform system of education, will render the mass of the people more homogeneous, and thereby fit them more easily for uniform and peaceable government. . . .

I beg leave to remark, that the only foundation for a useful education in a republic is to be laid in Religion. Without this there can be no virtue, and without virtue there can be no liberty, and liberty is the object and life of all republican governments.

Such is my veneration for every religion that reveals the attributes of the Deity, or a future state of rewards and punishments, that I had rather see the opinions of Confucius or Mahomed inculcated upon our youth, than see them grow up wholly devoid of a system of religious principles. But the religion I mean to recommend in this place, is that of the New Testament.

It is foreign to my purpose to hint at the arguments which establish the truth of the Christian revelation. My only business is to declare, that all its doctrines and precepts are calculated to promote the happiness of society, and the safety and well being of civil government. A Christian cannot fail of being a republican. The history of the creation of man, and of the relation [of] our species to each other by birth, which is recorded in the Old Testament, is the best refutation that can be given to the divine right of kings, and the strongest argument that can be used in favor of the original and natural equality of all mankind. A Christian, I say again, cannot fail of being a republican, for every precept of the Gospel inculcates those degrees of humility, self-denial, and brotherly kindness, which are directly opposed to the pride of monarchy and the pageantry of a court. A Christian cannot fail of being useful to the republic, for his religion teacheth him, that no man "liveth to himself." And lastly, a Christian cannot fail of being wholly inoffensive, for his religion teacheth him, in all things to do [to] others what he would wish, in like circumstances, they should do to him. . . .

Next to the duty which young men owe to their Creator, I wish to see a regard to their country, inculcated upon them. . . . Our country includes family, friends, and property, and should be preferred to them all. Let our pupil be taught that he does not belong to himself, but that he is public property. Let him be taught to love his family, but let him be taught, at the same time, that he must forsake, and even forget them, when the welfare of his country requires it. He must watch for the state, as if its liberties depended upon his vigilance alone, but he must do this in such a manner as not to defraud his creditors, or neglect his family. He must love private life, but he must decline no station, however public or responsible it may be, when called to it by the suffrages of his fellow citizens. He must love popularity, but he must despise it when set in competition with the dictates of his judgement, or the real interest of his country. He must love character, and have a due sense of injuries, but he must be taught to appeal only to the laws of the state, to defend the one, and punish the other. He must love family honour, but must be taught that neither the rank nor antiquity of his ancestors, can command respect, without personal merit. He must avoid neutrality in all questions that divide the state, but he must shun the rage, and acrimony of party spirit. He must be taught to love his fellow creatures in every part of the world, but he must cherish with a more intense and peculiar affection, the citizens of Pennsylvania and of the United States. I do not wish to see our youth educated with a single prejudice against any nation our country; but we impose a task upon human nature, repugnant alike to reason, revelation, and the ordinary dimensions of the human heart, when we require him to embrace, with equal affection, the whole family of mankind. He must be taught to amass wealth, but it must be only to encrease his power of contributing to the wants and demands of the state. He must be indulged occasionally in amusements, but he must be taught that study and business should be his principal pursuits in life. Above all he must love life, and endeavour to acquire as many of its conveniences as possible by industry and economy, but he must be taught that this life "is not his own," when the safety of his country requires it. . . .

While we inculcate these republican duties upon our pupil, we must not neglect, at the same time, to inspire him with republican principles. He must be taught that there can be no durable liberty but in a republic, and that government, like all other sciences, is of a progressive nature. The chains which have bound this science in Europe are happily unloosed in America. Here it is open to investigation and improvement. . . . I conceive, that it is possible to combine power in such a way as not only to encrease the happiness, but to promote the duration of republican forms of government far beyond the terms limited for them by history, or the common opinions of mankind.

To assist in rendering religious, moral, and political instructions more effectual upon the minds of our youth, it will be necessary to subject their bodies to physical discipline. To obviate [prevent] the inconveniences of their studious and sedentary mode of life, they should live upon a temperate diet, consisting chiefly of broths, milk, and vegetables. . . . They should avoid tasting Spirituous liquors. They should also be accustomed occasionally to work with their hands, in the intervals of Study, and in the busy seasons of the year in the country. Moderate sleep, silence, occasional solitude and cleanliness, should be inculcated upon them, and the utmost advantage should be taken of a proper direction of those great principles in human conduct,—sensibility, habit, imitations, and association. . . .

From the observations that have been made it is plain, that I consider it is possible to convert men into republican machines. This must be done, if we expect them to perform their parts properly, in the great machine of the government of the state. That republic is sophisticated with monarchy or aristocracy that does not revolve upon the wills of the people, and these must be fitted to each other by means of education before they can be made to produce regularity and unison in government. . . .

Too much pains cannot be taken to teach our youth to read and write our American language with propriety and elegance. . . . The advantages of a perfect knowledge of our language to young men intended for the professions of law, physic, or divinity are too obvious to be mentioned, but in a state which boasts of the first commercial city in America, I wish to see it cultivated by young men, who are intended for the compting house [bank or merchant bookkeeper] for many such, I hope, will be educated in our colleges. . . .

Connected with the study of language is the study of Eloquence. . . . It is the first accomplishment in a republic, and often sets the whole machine of government in motion. Let our youth, therefore, be instructed in this art. We do not extol it too highly when we attribute as much to the power of eloquence as to the sword, in bringing about American revolution.

With the usual arts and sciences that are taught in our American colleges, I wish to see a regular course of lectures given upon History and Chronology. The science of government, whether it [is] related to constitutions or laws, can only be advanced by a careful selection of facts, and these are to be found chiefly in history. Above all, let our youth be instructed in the history of the ancient republics, and the progress of liberty and tyranny in the different states of Europe. I wish likewise to see the numerous facts that relate to the origin and present state of commerce, together with the nature and principles of Money, reduced to such a system, as to be intelligible and agreeable to a young man. If we consider the commerce of our metropolis [Philadelphia] only as the avenue of the wealth of the state, the study of it merits a place in a young man's education; but, I consider commerce in a much higher light when I recommend the study of it in republican seminaries. I view it as the best security against the influence of hereditary monopolies of land, and, therefore, the surest protection against aristocracy. I consider its effects as next to those of religion in humanizing mankind, and, lastly, I view it as the means of uniting the different nations of the world together by the ties of mutual wants and obligations. . . .

Again, let your youth be instructed in all the means of promoting national prosperity and independence, whether they relate to improvements in agriculture, manufactures, or inland navigation. Let him be instructed further in the general principles of legislation, whether they relate to revenue, or to the preservation of life, liberty, or property. . . .

I beg pardon for having delayed so long to say any thing of the separate and peculiar mode of education proper for women in a republic. I am sensible that they must concur in all our plans of education for young men, or no laws will ever render them effectual. To qualify our women for this purpose, they should not only be instructed in the usual branches of female education, but they should be taught the principles of liberty and government; and the obligations of patriotism should be inculcated upon them. The opinions and conduct of men are often regulated by the women in the most arduous enterprises of life; and their approbation is frequently the principal reward of the hero's dangers, and the patriot's toils. Besides, the first impressions upon the minds of children are generally derived from the women. Of how much consequence, therefore, is it in a republic, that they should think justly upon the great subjects of liberty and government! . . .

From the combined and reciprocal influence of religion, liberty, and learning upon the morals, manners, and knowledge of individuals, of these, upon government, and of government, upon individuals, it is impossible to measure the degrees of happiness and perfection to which mankind may be raised.

QUESTIONS FOR READING AND DISCUSSION

1. According to Rush, how did education make it "possible to convert men into republican machines"? Why was that desirable?
2. Why did he believe that "A Christian cannot fail of being a republican"? How might Christians who lived in monarchies respond to Rush's arguments?
3. Why should a student be taught that "he does not belong to himself, but that he is public property"?
4. According to Rush, why was the study of commerce so important?
5. How, if at all, did Rush's views of the "separate and peculiar mode of education proper for women in a republic" differ from his views of the education of men?

DOCUMENT 8–4

Making the Case for the Constitution

In the debate on the ratification of the Constitution, Americans argued about how to create a government that defended the achievements of the Revolution without sacrificing its principles. The debate reflected disagreements about the Revolution's achievements and aims. In Federalist Number 10, *James Madison explained that the distinctive perils posed by the republican governments instituted during the Revolution were remedied by the proposed federal Constitution. Madison's analysis illustrates the viewpoint of the Constitution's Federalist advocates about the problems and possibilities of American politics.*

James Madison
Federalist Number 10, 1787

Among the numerous advantages promised by a well constructed Union, none deserves to be more accurately developed, than its tendency to break and control the violence of faction. The friend of popular governments, never finds himself so much alarmed for their character and fate, as when he contemplates their propensity to this dangerous vice. He will not fail, therefore, to set a due value on any plan which, without violating the principles to which he is attached, provides a proper cure for it. The instability, injustice, and confusion introduced into the public councils, have, in truth, been the mortal diseases under which popular governments have everywhere perished; as they continue to be the favorite and fruitful topics from which the adversaries to liberty derive their most precious declamations. The valuable improvements made by the American Constitutions on the popular models, both ancient and modern, cannot certainly be too much admired; but it would be an unwarrantable partiality, to contend that they have as effectually obviated the danger on this side, as was wished and expected. Complaints are everywhere heard from our most considerate and virtuous citizens, equally the friends of public and private faith, and of public and personal liberty, that our governments are too unstable; that the public good is disregarded in the conflicts of rival parties; and that measures are too often decided, not according to the rules of justice, and the rights of the minor party, but by the superior force of an interested and overbearing majority. However anxiously we may wish that these complaints had no foundation, the evidence of known facts will not permit us to deny that they are in some degree true. It will be found, indeed, on a candid review of our situation, that some of the distresses under which we labor, have been erroneously charged on the operations of our governments: but it will be found, at the same time, that other causes will not alone account for many of our heaviest misfortunes; and, particularly, for that prevailing and increasing distrust of public engagements, and alarm for private rights, which were echoed from one end of the continent to the other. These must be chiefly, if not wholly, effects of the unsteadiness and injustice, with which a factious spirit has tainted our public administration.

From E. H. Scott, ed., *The Federalist and Other Constitutional Papers*, vol. 1 (Chicago: Scott, Foresman, 1894), 569–74.

By a faction, I understand a number of citizens, whether amounting to a majority or minority of the whole, who are united and actuated by some common impulse of passion, or of interest, adverse to the rights of other citizens, or to the permanent and aggregate interests of the community.

There are two methods of curing the mischiefs of faction: The one by removing its causes; the other by controlling its effects.

There are again two methods of removing the causes of faction: The one by destroying the liberty which is essential to its existence; the other, by giving to every citizen the same opinions, the same passions, and the same interests.

It could never be more truly said, than of the first remedy, that it is worse than the disease. Liberty is to faction, what air is to fire, an aliment, without which it instantly expires. But it could not be a less folly to abolish liberty, which is essential to political life, because it nourishes faction, than it would be to wish the annihilation of air, which is essential to animal life, because it imparts to fire its destructive agency.

The second expedient is as impracticable, as the first would be unwise. As long as the reason of man continues fallible, and he is at liberty to exercise it, different opinions will be formed. As long as the connection subsists between his reason and his self-love, his opinions and his passions will have a reciprocal influence on each other; and the former will be the objects to which the latter will attach themselves. The diversity in the faculties of men, from which the rights of property originate, is not less an insuperable obstacle to an uniformity of interests. The protection of these faculties, is the first object of government. From the protection of different and unequal faculties of acquiring property, the possession of different degrees and kinds of property immediately results: and from the influence of these on the sentiments and views of the respective proprietors, ensues a division of the society into different interests and parties.

The latent causes of faction are thus sown in the nature of man; and we see them everywhere brought into different degrees of activity, according to the different circumstances of civil society. A zeal for different opinions concerning religion, concerning government, and many other points, as well of speculation as of practice; an attachment to different leaders, ambitiously contending for preeminence and power; or to persons of other descriptions, whose fortunes have been interesting to the human passions, have, in turn, divided mankind into parties, inflamed them with mutual animosity, and rendered them much more disposed to vex and oppress each other, than to co-operate for their common good. So strong is this propensity of mankind, to fall into mutual animosities, that where no substantial occasion presents itself, the most frivolous and fanciful distinctions have been sufficient to kindle their unfriendly passions, and excite their most violent conflicts. But the most common and durable source of factions, has been the various and unequal distribution of property. — Those who hold and those who are without property, have ever formed distinct interests in society. Those who are creditors, and those who are debtors, fall under a like discrimination. A landed interest, a manufacturing interest, a mercantile interest, a monied interest, with many lesser interests, grow up of necessity in civilized nations, and divide them into different classes, actuated by different sentiments and views. The regulation of these various and interfering interests, forms the principal task of modern legislation, and involves the spirit of party and faction in the necessary and ordinary operations of government.

No man is allowed to be a judge in his own cause; because his interest would certainly bias his judgment, and, not improbably, corrupt his integrity. With equal, nay, with greater reason, a body of men are unfit to be both judges and parties, at the same time; yet, what are many of the most important acts of legislation but so many judicial determinations, not indeed concerning the rights of single persons, but concerning the rights of large bodies of citizens? And what are the different classes of legislators, but advocates and parties to the causes which they determine? Is a law proposed concerning private debts? It is a question to which the creditors are parties on the one side, and the debtors on the other. Justice ought to hold the balance between them. Yet the parties are, and must be, themselves the judges; and the most numerous party, or, in other words, the most powerful faction, must be expected to prevail. Shall domestic manufactures be encouraged, and in what degree, by restrictions on foreign manufactures? are questions which would be differently decided by the landed and the manufacturing classes; and probably by neither with a sole regard to justice and the public good. The apportionment of taxes, on the various descriptions of property, is an act which seems to require the most exact impartiality; yet there is, perhaps, no legislative act in which greater opportunity and temptation are given to a predominant party, to trample on the rules of justice. Every shilling with which they overburden the inferior number, is a shilling saved to their own pockets.

It is in vain to say, that enlightened statesmen will be able to adjust these clashing interests, and render them all subservient to the public good. Enlightened statesmen will not always be at the helm: nor, in many cases, can such an adjustment be made at all, without taking into view indirect and remote considerations, which will rarely prevail over the immediate interest which one party may find in disregarding the rights of another, or the good of the whole.

The inference to which we are brought is, that the causes of faction cannot be removed; and that relief is only to be sought in the means of controlling its effects.

If a faction consists of less than a majority, relief is supplied by the republican principle, which enables the majority to defeat its sinister views, by regular vote. It may clog the administration, it may convulse the society; but it will be unable to execute and mask its violence under the forms of the Constitution. When a majority is included in a faction, the form of popular government, on the other hand, enables it to sacrifice to its ruling passion or interest, both the public good and the rights of other citizens. To secure the public good and private rights against the danger of such a faction, and at the same time to preserve the spirit and the form of popular government, is then the great object to which our inquiries are directed. . . .

By what means is this object attainable? Evidently by one of two only. Either the existence of the same passion or interest in a majority, at the same time, must be prevented; or the majority, having such co-existent passion or interest, must be rendered, by their number and local situation, unable to concert and carry into effect schemes of oppression. If the impulse and the opportunity be suffered to coincide, we well know, that neither moral nor religious motives can be relied on as an adequate control. . . .

From this view of the subject, it may be concluded that a pure democracy, by which I mean a society consisting of a small number of citizens, who assemble and administer the government in person, can admit of no cure for the mischiefs of faction. A common passion or interest will, in almost every case, be felt by a majority of the whole; a communication and concert, results from the form of government itself; and there is nothing to check the inducements to sacrifice the weaker party, or an obnoxious individual. Hence it is, that such democracies have ever been spectacles of turbulence and contention; have ever been found incompatible with personal security, or the rights of property; and have, in general, been as short in their lives, as they have been violent in their deaths. Theoretic politicians, who have patronized this species of government, have erroneously supposed, that by reducing mankind to a perfect equality in their political rights, they would, at the same time, be perfectly equalized and assimilated in their possessions, their opinions, and their passions.

A republic, by which I mean a government in which the scheme of representation takes place, opens a different prospect, and promises the cure for which we are seeking. Let us examine the points in which it varies from pure democracy, and we shall comprehend both the nature of the cure, and the efficacy which it must derive from the union.

The two great points of difference, between a democracy and a republic, are, first, the delegation of the government, in the latter, to a small number of citizens elected by the rest; secondly, the greater number of citizens, and greater sphere of country, over which the latter may be extended.

The effect of the first difference is, on the one hand, to refine and enlarge the public views, by passing them through the medium of a chosen body of citizens, whose wisdom may best discern the true interest of their country, and whose patriotism and love of justice will be least likely to sacrifice it to temporary or partial considerations. Under such a regulation, it may well happen, that the public voice, pronounced by the representatives of the people, will be more consonant to the public good, than if pronounced by the people themselves, convened for the purpose. On the other hand, the effect may be inverted. Men of factious tempers, of local prejudices, or of sinister designs, may by intrigue, by corruption, or by other means, first obtain the suffrages and then betray the interest of the people. The question repeating is whether small or extensive republics are most favorable for the election of proper guardians of the public weal; and it is clearly decided in favor of the latter by two obvious considerations.

In the first place, it is to be remarked, that however small the republic may be, the representatives must be raised to a certain number, in order to guard against the cabals of a few; and that however large it may be, they must be limited to a certain number, in order to guard against the confusion of a multitude. Hence the number of representatives in the two cases not being in proportion to that of the constituents and being proportionably greatest in the small republic, it follows, that if the proportion of fit characters be not less in the large than in the small republic, the former will present a greater option, and consequently a greater probability of a fit choice.

In the next place, as each representative will be chosen by a greater number of citizens in the large than in the small republic, it will be more difficult for unworthy candidates to practice with success the vicious arts, by which elections are too often carried; and the suffrages of the people being more free, will be more likely to centre in men who possess the most attractive merit, and the most diffusive and established characters.

It must be confessed, that in this, as in most other cases, there is a mean, on both sides of which inconveniences will be found to lie. By enlarging too much the number of electors, you render the representative too little acquainted with all their local circumstances and lesser interests; as by reducing it too much, you render him unduly attached to these, and too little fit to comprehend and pursue great and national objects. The Federal Constitution forms, in this respect, a happy combination; the great and aggregate interest being referred to the National—the local and particular, to the State Legislatures.

The other point of difference is, the greater number of citizens and extent of territory, which may be brought within the compass of republican, than of democratic government; and it is this circumstance principally which renders factious combinations less to be dreaded in the former, than in the latter. The smaller the society, the fewer probably will be the distinct parties and interests composing it; the fewer the distinct parties and interests, the more frequently will a majority be found of the same party; and the smaller the number of individuals composing a majority, and the smaller the compass within which they are placed, the more easily will they concert and execute their plans of oppression. Extend the sphere, and you take in a greater variety of parties and interest; you make it less probable that a majority of the whole will have a common motive to invade the rights of other citizens; or if such a common motive exists, it will be more difficult for all who feel it to discover their own strength, and to act in unison with each other. . . .

Hence it clearly appears, that the same advantage, which a republic has over a democracy, in controlling the effects of faction, is enjoyed by a large over a small republic—is enjoyed by the Union over the States composing it. Does this advantage consist in the substitution of representatives, whose enlightened views and virtuous sentiments render them superior to local prejudices, and to schemes of injustice? It will not be denied, that the representation of the Union will be most likely to possess these requisite endowments. Does it consist in the greater security afforded by a greater variety of parties, against the event of any one party being able to outnumber and oppress the rest? In an equal degree does the increased variety of parties, comprised within the Union, increase this security? Does it, in fine, consist in the greater obstacles opposed to the concert and accomplishment of the secret wishes of an unjust and interested majority? Here, again, the extent of the Union gives it the most palpable advantage.

The influence of factious leaders may kindle a flame within their particular States, but will be unable to spread a general conflagration through the other States. A religious sect may degenerate into a political faction in a part of the Confederacy; but the variety of sects dispersed over the entire face of it must secure the national councils against any danger from that source. A rage for paper money, for an abolition of debts, for an equal division of property, or for any other improper or wicked project, will be less apt to pervade the whole body of the Union, than a particular member of it; in the same proportion as such a malady is more likely to taint a particular county or district, than an entire State.

In the extent and proper structure of the Union, therefore, we behold a republican remedy for the diseases most incident to a republican government. And according to the degree of pleasure and pride we feel in being republicans, ought to be our zeal in cherishing the spirit, and supporting the character of, Federalists.

QUESTIONS FOR READING AND DISCUSSION

1. According to Madison, what was a faction? What caused factions? Why did he believe factions to be undesirable?

2. What did he suggest to eliminate the causes of factions? How might the effects of factions be controlled?

3. Why was Madison concerned about "an interested and overbearing majority"? What made a majority dangerous? How would the new Constitution provide checks on majorities?

4. How did a republic differ from a democracy? Which was preferable, according to Madison, and why? Why was a large republic better than a small one?

5. How would the Constitution provide "a republican remedy for the diseases most incident to republican government"? Did Madison believe the Constitution was necessary or simply desirable? Why?

6. To whom might Madison's arguments have the most appeal? What audiences did he appear to be addressing?

DOCUMENT 8–5

Mercy Otis Warren Opposes the Constitution

Opponents of the new Constitution criticized its provisions and its framers, often charging them with subverting the achievements of the American Revolution. The debate in Massachusetts about ratification of the Constitution prompted Mercy Otis Warren, a member of a distinguished family of revolutionary leaders who traced their origins back to the Mayflower, *to publish her* Observations on the New Constitution *in 1788 under the pseudonym, "a Columbian Patriot." A brilliant and exceptionally well-educated woman who had been anonymously publishing plays, poems, and essays for fifteen years, Warren argued that the Constitution's framers sought to undermine liberties that Americans had only recently defended from British encroachment. Like other Antifederalists, Warren examined specific constitutional provisions to discern Federalists' assumptions about popular government. Her* Observations *disclose Antifederalists' deep suspicion of the Constitution, its supporters, and their secret deliberations and hasty plan for ratification.*

Observations on the New Constitution, 1788

Animated with the firmest zeal for the interest of this country, the peace and union of the American States, and the freedom and happiness of a people who have made the most costly sacrifices in the cause of liberty,—who have braved the power of Britain, weathered the convulsions of war, and waded thro' the blood of friends and foes to establish their independence and to support the freedom of the human mind. . . . obliges every one to remonstrate against the strides of ambition, and a wanton lust of domination, and to resist the first approaches of tyranny, which at this day threaten to sweep away the rights for which the brave sons of America have fought with an heroism scarcely paralleled even in ancient republicks. . . . On these shores freedom has planted her standard, [dyed] in the purple tide that flowed from the veins of her martyred heroes; and here every uncorrupted American yet hopes to see it supported by the vigour, the justice, the

From Mercy Otis Warren, *Observations on the New Constitution, and on the Federal and State Conventions, by a Columbian Patriot* (Boston, 1788).

wisdom and unanimity of the people, in spite of the deep-laid plots, the secret intrigues, or the bold effrontery of those interested and avaricious adventurers for place, who intoxicated with the ideas of distinction and preferment, have prostrated every worthy principle beneath the shrine of ambition. Yet these are the men who tell us republicanism is dwindled into theory—that we are incapable of enjoying our liberties—and that we must have a master. . . . [The] Constitution, which, by the undefined meaning of some parts, and the ambiguities of expression in others, is dangerously adapted to the purposes of an immediate *aristocratic tyranny*; that from the difficulty, if not impracticability of its operation, must soon terminate in the most *uncontrouled despotism.* . . .

And it is with inexpressible anxiety, that many of the best friends to the Union of the States—to the peaceable and equal participation of the rights of nature, and to the glory and dignity of this country, behold the insidious arts, and the strenuous efforts of the partisans of arbitrary power, by their vague definitions of the best established truths, endeavoring to envelope the mind in darkness the concomitant of slavery, and to lock the strong chains of domestic despotism on a country, which by the most glorious and successful struggles is but newly emancipated from the sceptre of foreign dominion. . . .

I will not expatiate long on a Republican *form* of government, founded on the principles of monarchy—a democratick branch with the *features* of aristocracy—and the extravagance of nobility pervading the minds of many of the candidates for office. . . . Some gentlemen with laboured zeal, have spent much time in urging the necessity of government, from the embarrassments of trade—the want of respectability abroad and confidence in the public engagements at home:—These are obvious truths which no one denies; and there are few who do not unite in the general wish for the restoration of public faith, the revival of commerce, arts, agriculture, and industry, under a lenient, peaceable and energetick government: But the most sagacious advocates for the party have not by fair discussion, and rational argumentation, evinced the necessity of adopting this many-headed monster . . . nor have its friends the courage to denominate it a Monarchy, an Aristocracy, or an Oligarchy, and the favoured bantling[1] must have passed through the short period of its existence without a name, had not Mr. [James] *Wilson*,[2] in the fertility of his genius, suggested the happy epithet of a *Federal Republic.* . . .

[1.] It will be allowed by every one that the fundamental principle of a free government, is the equal representation of a free people. . . . And when society has thus deputed a certain number of their equals to take care of their personal rights, and the interest of the whole community, it must be considered that responsibility is the great security of integrity and honour; and that annual election is the basis of responsibility. . . . [T]he best political writers have supported the principles of annual elections with a precision, that cannot be confuted, though they may be darkened, by the sophistical arguments that have been thrown out with design, to undermine all the barriers of freedom.

2. There is no security in the profered system, either for the rights of conscience, or the liberty of the Press: Despotism usually while it is gaining ground, will suffer men to think, say, or write what they please; but when once established,

---

[1]**bantling**: A bratty young child.

[2]**Mr. [James] Wilson**: Pennsylvania leader who helped draft the Constitution and supported ratification.

if it is thought necessary to subserve the purposes of arbitrary power, the most unjust restrictions may take place in the first instance, and an *imprimator*[3] on the Press in the next, may silence the complaints, and forbid the most decent remonstrances of an injured and oppressed people.

3. There are no well defined limits of the Judiciary Powers . . . and as they cannot be comprehended by the clearest capacity, or the most sagacious mind, it would be an Herculean labour to attempt to describe the dangers with which they are replete.

4. The Executive and the Legislative are so dangerously blended as to give just cause of alarm, and every thing relative thereto, is couched in such ambiguous terms—in such vague and indefinite expression, as is a sufficient ground without any other objection, for the reprobation of a system. . . .

5. The abolition of trial by jury in civil causes. . . . [s]hall this inestimable privilege be relinquished in America—either thro' the fear of inquistion for unaccounted thousands of public monies in the hands of some who have been officious in the fabrication of the *consolidated system*, or from the apprehension that some future delinquent possessed of more power than integrity, may be called to a trial by his peers in the hour of investigation?

6. Though it has been said by Mr. *Wilson* and many others, that a Standing-Army is necessary for the dignity and safety of America, yet freedom revolts at the idea, when the . . . Despot, may draw out his dragoons to suppress the murmurs of a few. . . . By the edicts of authority vested in the sovereign power by the proposed constitution, the militia of the country, the bulwark of defence, and the security of national liberty is no longer under the controul of civil authority; but at the rescript of the Monarch, or the aristocracy, they may either be employed to extort the enormous sums that will be necessary to support the civil list—to maintain the regalia of power—and the splendour of the most useless part of the community, or they may be sent into foreign countries for the fulfilment of treaties, stipulated by the President and two thirds of the Senate.

7. Notwithstanding the delusory promise to guarantee a Republican form of government to every State in the Union—If the most discerning eye could discover any meaning at all in the engagement, there are no resources left for the support of internal government, or the liquidation of the debts of the State. Every source of revenue is in the monopoly of Congress. . . .

8. As the new Congress are empowered to determine their own salaries, the requisitions for this purpose may not be very moderate, and the drain for public moneys will probably rise past all calculation. . . .

9. There is no provision for a rotation, nor any thing to prevent the perpetuity of office in the same hands for life; which by a little well timed bribery, will probably be done, to the exclusion of men of the best abilities from their share in the offices of government.—By this neglect we lose the advantages of that check to the overbearing insolence of office, which by rendering him ineligible at certain periods, keeps the mind of man in equilibrio, and teaches him the feelings of the governed, and better qualifies him to govern in his turn.

10. The inhabitants of the United States, are liable to be dragged from the vicinity of their own county, or state, to answer to the litigious or unjust suit of an adversary, on the most distant borders of the Continent; in short the appelate jurisdiction of the Supreme Federal Court, includes an unwarrantable stretch of

---

[3]*imprimator*: Official censor.

power over the liberty, life, and property of the subject, through the wide Continent of America.

11. One Representative to thirty thousand inhabitants is a very inadequate representation; and every man who is not lost to all sense of freedom to his country, must reprobate the idea of Congress altering by law, or on any pretence whatever, interfering with any regulations for the time, places, and manner of choosing our own Representatives.

12. If the sovereignty of America is designed to be elective, the circumscribing the votes to only ten electors in this State [Massachusetts], and the same proportion in all the others, is nearly tantamount to the exclusion of the voice of the people in the choice of their first magistrate. It is vesting the choice solely in an aristocratic junto,[4] who may easily combine in each State to place at the head of the Union the most convenient instrument for despotic sway.

13. A Senate chosen for six years will, in most instances, be an appointment for life, as the influence of such a body over the minds of the people will be coequal to the extensive powers with which they are vested, and they will not only forget, but be forgotten by their constituents—a branch of the Supreme Legislature thus set beyond all responsibility is totally repugnant to every principle of a free government.

14. There is no provision by a bill of rights to guard against the dangerous encroachments of power in too many instances to be named. . . . We are told . . . "that the whole constitution is a declaration of rights"—but mankind must think for themselves, and to many very judicious and discerning characters, the whole constitution with very few exceptions appears to [be a] perversion of the rights of particular states, and of private citizens.—But the gentleman goes on to tell us, "that the primary object is the general government, and that the rights of individuals are only incidentally mentioned, and that there was a clear impropriety in being very particular about them." . . . The rights of individuals ought to be the primary object of all government, and cannot be too securely guarded by the most explicit declarations in their favor. . . .

15. The difficulty, if not impracticability, of exercising the equal and equitable powers of government by a single legislature over an extent of territory that reaches from the Mississippi to the western lakes, and from them to the Atlantic ocean, is an insuperable objection to the adoption of the new system. . . .

16. It is an indisputed fact, that not one legislature in the United States had the most distant idea when they first appointed members for a convention, entirely commercial, or when they afterwards authorised them to consider on some amendments of the Federal union, that they would without any warrant from their constituents, presume on so bold and daring a stride, as ultimately to destroy the state governments, and offer a *consolidated system*. . . .

17. The first appearance of the article which declares the ratification of nine states sufficient for the establishment of the new system, wears the face of dissention, is a subversion of the union of the Confederated States, and tends to the introduction of anarchy and civil convulsions, and may be a means of involving the whole country in blood.

18. The mode in which this constitution is recommended to the people to judge without either the advice of Congress, or the legislatures of the several states, is very reprehensible—it is an attempt to force it upon them before it could be thoroughly understood. . . .

---

[4]**junto**: A self-appointed committee or caucus.

But it is needless to enumerate other instances, in which the proposed constitution appears contradictory to the first principles which ought to govern mankind; and it is equally so to enquire into the motives that induced to so bold a step as the annihilation of the independence and sovereignty of the thirteen distinct states.—They are but too obvious through the whole progress of the business, from the first shutting up the doors of the federal convention and resolving that no member should correspond with gentlemen in the different states on the subject under discussion. . . .

And it is to be feared we shall soon see this country rushing into the extremes of confusion and violence, in consequence of the proceedings of a set of gentlemen, who disregarding the purposes of their appointment, have assumed powers unauthorised by any commission, have unnecessarily rejected the confederation of the United States, and annihilated the sovereignty and independence of the individual governments.

QUESTIONS FOR READING AND DISCUSSION

1. According to Warren, why would the constitution "sweep away" Americans' rights and lead to *"aristocratic tyranny"* or *"uncontrouled despotism"*? Why was the *"Federal Republic"* proposed by the Constitution in reality a "many-headed monster"?

2. In Warren's view, what did the framers of the Constitution perceive as threats? How did they design the Constitution to avoid those threats? In what sense did the Constitution create a *"consolidated system"*?

3. How did Warren disagree with Federalists' diagnosis of threats and their proposals for remedies? What remedies did Warren propose? What constitutional amendments, if any, might have allayed Warren's fears?

4. What assumptions did Warren make about the location and exercise of power?

5. How did Warren's view of the American Revolution influence her critique of the constitution?

COMPARATIVE QUESTIONS

1. How did Richard Allen's experiences compare with Thomas Jefferson's conclusions about the difficulties of emancipation? How might Allen have responded to Jefferson's arguments about slavery and race?

2. How did Jefferson's views about slavery and race compare to James Madison's argument about the dangers of majorities? What minority rights were protected, for example, in Jefferson's and Madison's Virginia?

3. What were the principal differences between Madison's Federalist arguments and Mercy Otis Warren's Antifederalist criticisms? To what extent did Madison and Warren agree? How did their views of human liberty and the limits of government compare to those in Benjamin Rush's proposal for republican education?

4. According to the documents in this chapter, what were the most important qualities for citizens in the new republic? How were those qualities to be created and preserved?

5. What did Allen, Jefferson, Rush, Madison, and Warren see as the most important lessons and legacies of the American Revolution?

9 The New Nation Takes Form
1789–1800

T he newness of the nation in a long-settled society offered many Americans opportunities for a fresh start. Some departed for the promise of a new life in the western vastness beyond the Appalachian Mountains. Many others believed the new opportunities of American life threatened to undermine established institutions, habits, and morals. Divisive disputes arose over just how "new" the new nation should be. Would innovations in government, education, the economy, and politics give shape to recently won liberties, including for women? Or would the innovations undermine liberties, as happened— many believed—in the slave insurrections in the French colony of Saint Domingue (present-day Haiti)? The following documents illustrate both the promises and fears of innovation in the new nation.

DOCUMENT 9–1
Alexander Hamilton on the Economy

No member of George Washington's administration was more important than his brilliant and ambitious secretary of the treasury, Alexander Hamilton. Hamilton had served as Washington's personal secretary and trusted advisor during the Revolution and was a leading proponent of the Constitution and a stronger central government. As secretary of the treasury, Hamilton defined the Federalists' vision of the role of the federal government in the American economy. Encouraging manufacturing was a key feature of that vision, as he explained in his Report on the Subject of Manufactures, *submitted to Congress in 1791. The* Report, *excerpted here, explained how manufacturing strengthened the agrarian United States both at home and in its relations with foreign powers. Hamilton's* Report *disclosed fundamental Federalist assumptions about the powers of both the economy and the government.*

Report on the Subject of Manufactures, 1791

The expediency of encouraging manufactures in the United States, which was not long since deemed very questionable, appears at this time to be pretty generally admitted. The embarrassments which have obstructed the progress of our external trade, have led to serious reflections on the necessity of enlarging the sphere of our domestic commerce. The restrictive regulations, which, in foreign markets, abridge the vent of the increasing surplus of our agricultural produce, serve to beget an earnest desire that a more extensive demand for that surplus may be created at home; and the complete success which has rewarded manufacturing enterprise in some valuable branches . . . justify a hope that the obstacles to the growth of this species of industry are less formidable than they were apprehended to be. . . .

[M]anufacturing establishments not only occasion a positive augmentation of the produce and revenue of the society, but . . . they contribute essentially to rendering them greater than they could possibly be without such establishments. . . .

1. *As to the division of labor*

It has justly been observed, that there is scarcely any thing of greater moment in the economy of a nation than the proper division of labor. The separation of occupations causes each to be carried to a much greater perfection than it could possibly acquire if they were blended. This arises principally from these circumstances:

1st. The greater skill and dexterity naturally resulting from a constant and undivided application to a single object. . . .

2d. The economy of time, by avoiding the loss of it, incident to a frequent transition from one operation to another of a different nature . . . [resulting in] the distractions, hesitations, and reluctances which attend the passage from one kind of business to another.

3d. An extension of the use of machinery. A man occupied on a single object will have it more in his power, and will be more naturally led to exert his imagination, in devising methods to facilitate and abridge labor, than if he were perplexed by a variety of independent and dissimilar operations. Besides this the fabrication of machines, in numerous instances, becoming itself a distinct trade, the artist who follows it has all the advantages which have been enumerated, for improvement in his particular art; and, in both ways, the invention and application of machinery are extended.

And from these causes united, the mere separation of the occupation of the cultivator from that of the artificer, has the effect of augmenting the productive powers of labor, and with them, the total mass of the produce or revenue of a country. In this single view of the subject, therefore, the utility of artificers or manufacturers, towards producing an increase of productive industry, is apparent.

2. *As to an extension of the use of machinery . . .*

The employment of machinery forms an item of great importance in the general mass of national industry. It is an artificial force brought in aid of the natural

---

From Alexander Hamilton, *Report on the Subject of Manufactures* (Philadelphia: Childs and Swaine, 1791).

force of man; and, to all the purposes of labor, is an increase of hands, an accession of strength, unencumbered too by the expense of maintaining the laborer. May it not, therefore, be fairly inferred, that those occupations which give greatest scope to the use of this auxiliary, contribute most to the general stock of industrious effort, and, in consequence, to the general product of industry?

It shall be taken for granted, and the truth of the position referred to observation, that manufacturing pursuits are susceptible, in a greater degree, of the application of machinery, than those of agriculture. If so, all the difference is lost to a community which, instead of manufacturing for itself, procures the fabrics requisite to its supply from other countries. The substitution of foreign for domestic manufactures is a transfer to foreign nations of the advantages accruing from the employment of machinery, in the modes in which it is capable of being employed with most utility and to the greatest extent.

The cotton-mill, invented in England, within the last twenty years, is a signal illustration of the general proposition which has been just advanced. In consequence of it, all the different processes for spinning cotton are performed by means of machines, which are put in motion by water, and attended chiefly by women and children—and by a smaller number of persons, in the whole, than are requisite in the ordinary mode of spinning. And it is an advantage of great moment, that the operations of this mill continue with convenience during the night as well as through the day. The prodigious effect of such a machine is easily conceived. To this invention is to be attributed, essentially, the immense progress which has been so suddenly made in Great Britain, in the various fabrics of cotton.

3. *As to the additional employment of classes of the community not originally engaged in the particular business*

This is not among the least valuable of the means by which manufacturing institutions contribute to augment the general stock of industry and production. In places where those institutions prevail, besides the persons regularly engaged in them, they afford occasional and extra employment to industrious individuals and families, who are willing to devote the leisure resulting from the intermissions of their ordinary pursuits to collateral labors, as a resource for multiplying their acquisitions or their enjoyments. The husbandman [farmer] himself experiences a new source of profit and support from the increased industry of his wife and daughters, invited and stimulated by the demands of the neighboring manufactories.

Besides this advantage of occasional employment to classes having different occupations, there is another. . . . This is the employment of persons who would otherwise be idle, and in many cases a burthen on the community, either from the bias of temper, habit, infirmity of body, or some other cause, indisposing or disqualifying them for the toils of the country. It is worthy of particular remark that, in general, women and children are rendered more useful, and the latter more early useful, by manufacturing establishments, than they would otherwise be. . . .

4. *As to the promoting of emigration from foreign countries*

. . . Manufacturers who, listening to the powerful invitations of a better price for their fabrics or their labor, of greater cheapness of provisions and raw materials, of an exemption from the chief part of the taxes, burthens, and restraints which they endure in the Old World, of greater personal independence and consequence, under the operation of a more equal government, and of what is far more precious than mere religious toleration, a perfect equality of religious privileges, would probably flock from Europe to the United States, to pursue their own trades or professions, if they were once made sensible of the advantages they would enjoy. . . .

If it be true, then, that it is the interest of the United States to open every possible avenue to emigration from abroad, it affords to weighty argument for the encouragement of manufactures. . . .

Here is perceived an important resource, not only for extending the population, and with it the useful and productive labor of the country, but likewise for the prosecution of manufactures, without deducting from the number of hands which might otherwise be drawn to tillage. . . .

5. *As to the furnishing greater scope for the diversity of talents and dispositions, which discriminate men from each other*
    . . . [T]he results of human exertion may be immensely increased by diversifying its objects. When all the different kinds of industry obtain in a community, each individual can find his proper element, and can call into activity the whole vigor of his nature. And the community is benefited by the services of its respective members, in the manner in which each can serve it with most effect.

If there be any thing in a remark often to be met with, namely, that there is, in the genius of the people of this country, a peculiar aptitude for mechanic improvements, it would operate as a forcible reason for giving opportunities to the exercise of that species of talent, by the propagation of manufactures.

6. *As to the affording a more ample and various field for enterprise*
    . . . To cherish and stimulate the activity of the human mind, by multiplying the objects of enterprise, is not among the least considerable of the expedients by which the wealth of a nation may be promoted. Even things in themselves not positively advantageous sometimes become so, by their tendency to provoke exertion. Every new scene which is opened to the busy nature of man to rouse and exert itself, is the addition of a new energy to the general stock of effort.

The spirit of enterprise, useful and prolific as it is, must necessarily be contracted or expanded, in proportion to the simplicity or variety of the occupations and productions which are to be found in a society. It must be less in a nation of mere cultivators, than in a nation of cultivators and merchants; less in a nation of cultivators and merchants, than in a nation of cultivators, artificers, and merchants.

7. *As to the creating . . . a more certain and steady demand for the surplus produce of the soil*
    This . . . is a principal means by which the establishment of manufactures contributes to an augmentation of the produce or revenue of a country, and has an immediate and direct relation to the prosperity of agriculture.

It is evident that the exertions of the husbandman will be steady or fluctuating, vigorous or feeble, in proportion to the steadiness or fluctuation, adequateness or inadequateness, of the markets on which he must depend for the vent of the surplus which may be produced by his labor. . . .

For the purpose of this vent, a domestic market is greatly to be preferred to a foreign one; because it is, in the nature of things, far more to be relied upon. . . .

Considering how fast and how much the progress of new settlements in the United States must increase the surplus produce of the soil, and weighing seriously the tendency of the system which prevails among most of the commercial nations of Europe, . . . there appear strong reasons to regard the foreign demand for that surplus as too uncertain a reliance, and to desire a substitute for it in an extensive domestic market.

To secure such a market there is no other expedient than to promote manufacturing establishments. Manufacturers, who constitute the most numerous class, after the cultivators of land, are for that reason the principal consumers of the surplus of their labor.

This idea of an extensive domestic market for the surplus produce of the soil, is of the first consequence. It is, of all things, that which most effectually conduces to a flourishing state of agriculture. If the effect of manufactories should be to detach a portion of the hands which would otherwise be engaged in tillage, it might possibly cause a smaller quantity of lands to be under cultivation; but, by their tendency to procure a more certain demand for the surplus produce of the soil, they would, at the same time, cause the lands which were in cultivation to be better improved and more productive. And while, by their influence, the condition of each individual farmer would be meliorated, the total mass of agricultural production would probably be increased. . . .

It merits particular observation, that the multiplication of manufactories not only furnishes a market for those articles which have been accustomed to be produced in abundance in a country, but it likewise creates a demand for such as were either unknown or produced in inconsiderable quantities. The bowels as well as the surface of the earth are ransacked for articles which were before neglected. Animals, plants, and minerals acquire a utility and a value which were before unexplored.

QUESTIONS FOR READING AND DISCUSSION

1. In what ways would manufacturing strengthen the United States, according to Hamilton? In his view, how did manufacturing differ from agriculture?

2. In what ways, according to Hamilton, did manufacturing make women and children "more useful"? Why did he think "exertion" was so valuable?

3. How would manufacturing improve the position of the United States in international trade? What was the significance of the "domestic market"? Why would manufacturing stimulate immigration?

4. What assumptions do you think Hamilton was arguing against? What did he believe impeded American manufacturing?

DOCUMENT 9–2

Mary Dewees Moves West to Kentucky

Settlers poured across the Appalachian Mountains into the Ohio Valley to seek a new life in the West. Mary Dewees, her husband, children, and other family members joined the great westward migration in the fall of 1788, leaving home and friends in Philadelphia to settle near Lexington, Kentucky. Mary Dewees kept a journal of the trip, excerpted below, that chronicles the travails and triumphs of westward migration encountered by tens of thousands of other Americans in the new nation.

Journal, 1788–1789

September 27th: 178[8]

Left Philada. about 5 OClock in the afternoon and tore our selves from a number of dear friends that assembled to take a last farewell before we set off for Kentucky, Made our first stage 6 Miles fro[m] the City, being very sick the greatest par[t] of the way. . . .

30th:

. . . much better than I was Lost all the fine prospects the first days Owing to my sickness, which was excessive, being Obliged to be led from the waggon to the bed, and from the bed to the waggon.

[October] 2d:

'Tho but a few days since my friends Concluded I Could not reach Kentucky, will you believe me when I tell you I am setting on the Bank of the Susquehanah, and can take my bit of ham and Biscuit with any of them Returning health has made the face of nature gay, Given beauty to the sun and pleasure to the day. . . .

Oct 5:

. . . proceeded to the Mountain, which we began to climb about 10 O'Clock sometimes riding some times walking; find the roads much better in places than we expected, 'tho in others excessive stony the length which is ten miles renders it very tedious, Oblidgenly favoured with good weather we have halted on the top of the Mountain to refresh ourselves and horses this afternoon decended the west side find it much worse than the east side the road in places for a mile in length so very stony that you can scarce see the earth between. . . .

7th:

Set off for the north mountain which we find so bad we are Obliged to foot it up, and could compair ourselves to nothing but a parcel of goats climbing up some of the Welch Mountains that I have read of. . . . find this the most fatiguing days Journey we have had, the roads so very bad and so very steep that the horses seem ready to fall backwards In many places, you would be surprized to see the Children, Jumping and Skipping. some times quite out of sight some times on horse back some times in the waggon, so you see we have variety, 'tho sometimes would very willingly dispence with some of it — Believe me my dear friends the sight of a log house on these Mountains after a fatiguing days Journey affords more real pleasure that all the magnificent buildings your city contains. . . .

Oct 8th:

Left the foot of the mountain and crosd scrub hill which is very bad. . . . the Children are very hearty and bear fatigue much better than we do, 'tho I think we all do wonderfull, you would be astonished to see the roads we have come some of which seems impassible, Rachael Mostly passes half the day in Spelling and Sally in Singing every house we stop at she enquires if it is not a Kent.y. house and seldom leaves it 'till she informs them she is a Kenty. Lady

---

From Mary Dewees's journal describing her journey from Philadelphia to Lexington, Kentucky, Sept. 27, 1788–Feb. 11, 1789, Library of Congress.

9th:

Crost sidling hill and were the greates[t] part of the day in proforming the Journey the roads being so excessive Steep, sidling and Stony that it seemed impossible to get along. we were obligid to walk the greatest part of the way up 'tho not without company there was five waggons with us all the morning to different parts, this night our difficulties began we were Obliged to put up at a Cabin at the foot of the hill perhaps a dozen logs upon one another, with a few slabs fer a roof and the earth for a floor. & a wooden Chimney Constituted this extrodnary, ordinary the people very Kind but amazing dirty, there was between twenty & thirty of us, all lay on the floor, Except Mrs. Rees the Children and your Maria, who by our dress or adress or perhaps boath were favoured with a bed and I assure you we that thought ourselves to escape being fleaed alive.[1] . . .

11th

Set off for the allagany [Allegheny] Mountain which we began to assend in the afternoon, found it as good as any part of our Jouney we assened in the waggon not with out fear and Trembling, I assure you, we got about Six miles and fell in with a french gentleman and his family going to Pittsburgh we all put up at a little hut on the mountain which was so small that we preffered lodging in our waggon to be crouded with french men & Negroes on an erthen floor. . . .

14th:

. . . we were overtaken by a family who was going our way, which renders it more agreeable travelling than by ourselves I think by this time we may call ourselves Mountain proof. at the close of the day we arrived at a house and thought it prudent to put up for the night, the people are scotch Irish, exceedingly Kind but Surprizingly dirty, we concluded as the Company that was with us made up 18 (besides the family) to lodge in our waggon which we did It rained very hard in the night but we laid pretty Comfortably. . . .

Oct 16

Mr. Dewees and my brother rode about 13 miles to M'Kees ferry to see how the waters are as we are apprehensive they are too low to go down the river the weather still fine —

17th:

Left our little Cabin and proceeded to M'Kees ferry where we staid two days in a little hut not half so good as the little building at the upper end of your garden, and thought our selves happy to meet with so comfartable a dwelling

18th:

Our boat being ready we set off for the river and arrived their at 12 OClock and went on board immediately. . . . at 2 O'Clock we push down the river very slowly, intend Stopping at Fort Pitt, where we expect to meet the waggon with the rest of our Goods. our Beat [Boat] resembling Noahs ark not a little. . . .

---

[1]**fleaed alive**: Eaten by fleas.

19th:

with the assistance of some people that was coming up in a flat [boat] we got off. The water very low, I am much afraid we shall have a tedious passage our boat is 40 foot long our room 16 by 12 with a Comfortable fireplace, our Bed room partioned off with blankets, and far preferable to the Cabbins we met with after we crossd the Mountains, we are clear of flea[s] which I assure you is a great relief fore we were almost devoured when on shore. . . . we are now, Longing for rain as much as we dreaded on the Land for it is impossible to get down untill the water raises. we live entirely Independant, and with that there is a pleasure which Dependants can never be partakers of. we are all very hearty nor have I had the least sign of Sickness Since I came on board. . . .

21st:

We are now laying about a mile from Pittsburgh, and have receiv'd several Invitations to come on shore we have declined all, as the trunks with our cloaths is not come up, and we in our travelling dress, not fit to make our appearance in that gay place. . . .

24

The town all in arms, a report prevailed that a party of Indians within twenty miles coming to attack the Town The drums beating to arms with the militia collecting from every part of the Town has I assure a very disagreeable appearance. . . .

28th:

Mr. Dewees & Mr. Shelby went up to Pitt. am in hopes they will bring some Intelligence of the warriors that went out against the Indians.

29

Still continue at the Island waiting for water, had the pleasure of two ladys Company from the Island, who gave us an Invitation to visit them had a very stormy night and a snow of two or three Inches.

31st.

Still in hopes of the waters raising as we had snow again this Morning and a prospect of rain, this the most tedious part of our Journey as we still continue in one place.

Nov 1:

The weather Clear and cold & no prospect of the water raising am little apprehensive we shall have to winter among the rocks. . . .

4th:

To day the two Mr. Williams came to invite us to their house a mile from this place promising to furnish us with horses and sadles, but we declined accepting their invitation Chusing rather to continue where we are 'till we go down the river.

19th.

. . . proceeded down the Ohio, a very Beatiful river . . . The Country very hilly on boath sides of the river, in places a half a mile wide in other places much narrower, so near we are to the Indian Country and yet think ourselves pretty safe—The wind blowing very hard and being Contrary Obliged us to put on shore 65 Miles below Pittsburgh, the Boat tossing about a good deal occasioned me to feel a little quamish[2] Betsy Rees was so sick she was obliged to go to bed. . . .

Nov. 20

. . . saw another Kentucky Boat and passed by Wheeling a place where a Fort was Kept and attacked last war, Tis pleasently situated on a hill. There was a boat and a good Many people waiting to go down the River—an excessive hard gale of wind Obliged us to put to Shore, after the wind abated, we again put out in the Channal and were Obliged again by a fresh gale to put To Shore on the Indian Coast which caused some disagreeable Sensations, as it is not long since the Indians have done some mischief here abouts, after the wind lulled they thought proper to put out again 'tho it still continued to rain very hard which made it very dark & disagreeable, as it was imposible to discern where the rocks and ripples lay; but not withstanding all the Obstructions we have met with; have gone at the rate of fifty miles in the twenty four hours. . . .

30th

. . . on the first of Decembr. arrived at Lexington, being escarted there by Mr. Gordon and Lady, who came out to B[ry]ans Station to meet us, we were polit[ely] recev'd and welcomed by Mrs. Coburn we all staid at my Brothers 'till the 11th: Decr. when Betsy Rees left us to begin house Keeping, her house not being ready before.

Jany. 1 178[9].

. . . Since I have been here I have been visited by the genteele people in the place and receivd several Invitations both in town & Country, the Society in this place is very agreeable and I flatter my self I shall see many happy days in this Country Lexington is a Clever little Town with a court house and Jail and some pretty good buildings in it Chief[ly] Log my abode I have not seen yet a description of which you shall have [by] and by.

Jan. 29th

I have this day reached south Elk horn, and am much pleased with it tis a snug little Cabbin about 9 mile from Lexington on a pretty ascent surrounded by Sugar trees, a Beatifull pond a little distance from the house, with an excellent spring not far from the Door—I can assure you I have enjoyed more happiness the few days I have been here than I have experienced these four or five years past. I have my little family together and am in full expectations of seeing better days—

Yours &c
MD
Feby. 11th: 178[9]

---

[2]**quamish**: Nauseous.

QUESTIONS FOR READING AND DISCUSSION

1. Why did Mary Dewees record her experiences in her journal? How did her life on the trail west compare to her previous life in Philadelphia? To what extent did she retain ties to Philadelphia?

2. What experiences led Dewees to conclude that she and her family were "Mountain proof"?

3. What did Dewees mean by writing that, "we live entirely Independant, and with that there is a pleasure which Dependants can never be partakers of"? Were she and her family genuinely independent? Why or why not?

4. Upon arriving at her new home, Dewees "enjoyed more happiness . . . than I have experienced these four or five years past." What do you think made her happy? What did her happiness suggest about her previous life in Philadelphia?

DOCUMENT 9–3

Judith Sargent Murray Insists on the Equality of the Sexes

Born in 1751 to a respectable family in Gloucester, Massachusetts, Judith Sargent Murray responded to her disappointment when her father sent her brother to Harvard College by immersing herself in her father's library and educating herself. After marrying at age eighteen, she lived through the turmoil of the American Revolution. Her husband fled to the West Indies in 1786 to avoid prosecution for debts, and died there. Judith soon remarried and settled in Salem, Massachusetts, with her husband and minister, James Murray. She frequently contributed anonymous essays and poems to periodicals, sometimes adopting a female and sometimes a male pseudonym. For her most famous essay, excerpted below, she used the pen name "Constantia." She ridiculed the notion that men were inherently superior to women and championed equality of the sexes. Her writings ultimately brought her to the attention of many famous citizens, including George Washington and John and Abigail Adams.

On the Equality of the Sexes, 1790

Is it upon mature consideration we adopt the idea, that nature is thus partial in her distributions? Is it indeed a fact, that she hath yielded to one half of the human species so unquestionable a mental superiority? I know that to both sexes elevated understandings, and the reverse, are common. But, suffer me to ask, in what the minds of females are so notoriously deficient, or unequal. May not the intellectual powers be ranged under these four heads—imagination, reason, memory and judgment. The province of imagination hath long since been surrendered to us, and we have been crowned and undoubted sovereigns of the

From Judith Sargent Murray, "On the Equality of the Sexes," *The Massachusetts Magazine, or, Monthly Museum Concerning the Literature, History, Politics, Arts, Manners, Amusements of the Age*, Vol. II, 1790, 132–35, 223–26.

regions of fancy. Invention is perhaps the most arduous effort of the mind; this branch of imagination hath been particularly ceded to us, and we have been time out of mind invested with that creative faculty. Observe the variety of fashions (here I bar the contemptuous smile) which distinguish and adorn the female world: how continually are they changing, insomuch that they almost render the wise man's assertion problematical, and we are ready to say, *there is something new under the sun.* . . .

Another instance of our creative powers, is our talent for slander; how ingenious are we at inventive scandal? what a formidable story can we in a moment fabricate merely from the force of a prolifick imagination? how many reputations, in the fertile brain of a female, have been utterly despoiled? how industrious are we at improving a hint? suspicion how easily do we convert into conviction, and conviction, embellished by the power of eloquence, stalks abroad to the surprise and confusion of unsuspecting innocence. Perhaps it will be asked if I furnish these facts as instances of excellency in our sex. Certainly not; but as proofs of a creative faculty, of a lively imagination. Assuredly great activity of mind is thereby discovered, and was this activity properly directed, what beneficial effects would follow. Is the needle and kitchen sufficient to employ the operations of a soul thus organized? I should conceive not, Nay, it is a truth that those very departments leave the intelligent principle vacant, and at liberty for speculation. Are we deficient in reason? we can only reason from what we know, and if an opportunity of acquiring knowledge hath been denied us, the inferiority of our sex cannot fairly be deduced from thence. Memory, I believe, will be allowed us in common. . . .

"But our judgment is not so strong—we do not distinguish so well."—Yet it may be questioned, from what doth this superiority, in this determining faculty of the soul, proceed. May we not trace its source in the difference of education, and continued advantages? Will it be said that the judgment of a male of two years old, is more sage than that of a female's of the same age? I believe the reverse is generally observed to be true. But from that period what partiality! how is the one exalted, and the other depressed, by the contrary modes of education which are adopted! the one is taught to aspire, and the other is early confined and limitted. As their years increase, the sister must be wholly domesticated, while the brother is led by the hand through all the flowery paths of science. Grant that their minds are by nature equal, yet who shall wonder at the *apparent* superiority, if indeed custom becomes *second nature.* . . . At length arrived at womanhood, the uncultivated fair one feels a void, which the employments allotted her are by no means capable of filling. What can she do? to books she may not apply; or if she doth, *to those only of the novel kind,* lest she merit the appellation of a *learned lady*; and what ideas have been affixed to this term, the observation of many can testify. Fashion, scandal, and sometimes what is still more reprehensible, are then called in to her relief; and who can say to what lengths the liberties she takes may proceed. Meantimes she herself is most unhappy; she feels the want of a cultivated mind. Is she single, she in vain seeks to fill up time from sexual employments or amusements. Is she united to a person whose soul nature made equal to her own, education hath set him so far above her, that in those entertainments which are productive of such rational felicity, she is not qualified to accompany him. She experiences a mortifying consciousness of inferiority, which embitters every enjoyment. Doth the person to whom her adverse fate hath consigned her, possess a mind incapable of improvement, she is equally wretched, in being so closely connected with an individual whom she cannot but despise. Now, was she permitted the same instructors as her brother, (with an eye however to their particular departments) for the employment of a rational mind an ample field would be opened. . . . A mind, thus filled, would have little room for the trifles with which our sex are, with too much justice, accused of amusing themselves, and they would thus be rendered fit companions for those, who should one day wear them as their crown. Fashions, in their variety, would then give place to conjectures, which might perhaps conduce to the improvements of the literary world; and there would be no leisure for slander or detraction. Reputation would not then be blasted, but serious speculations would occupy the lively imaginations of the sex. Unnecessary visits would only be indulged by way of relaxation, or to answer the demands of consanguinity and friendship. Females would become discreet, their judgments would be invigorated, and their partners for life being circumspectly chosen, an unhappy Hymen would then be as rare, as is now the reverse.

Will it be urged that those acquirements would supersede our domestick duties. I answer that every requisite in female economy is easily attained; and, with truth I can add, that when once attained, they require no further *mental attention.* Nay, while we are pursuing the needle, or the superintendency of the family, I repeat, that our minds are at full liberty for reflection; that imagination may exert itself in full vigor; and that if a just foundation is early laid, our ideas will then be worthy of rational beings. If we were industrious we might easily find time to arrange them upon paper, or should avocations press too hard for such an indulgence, the hours allotted for conversation would at least become more refined and rational. Should it still be vociferated, "Your domestick employments are sufficient"—I would calmly ask, is it reasonable, that a candidate for immortality, for the joys of heaven, an intelligent being, who is to spend an eternity in contemplating the works of the Deity, should at present be so degraded, as to be allowed no other ideas, than those which are suggested by the mechanism of a pudding, or the sewing the seams of a garment? . . .

Yes, ye lordly, ye haughty sex, our souls are by nature *equal* to yours; the same breath of God animates, enlivens, and invigorates us; and that we are not fallen lower than yourselves, let those witness who have greatly towered above the various discouragements by which they have been so heavily oppressed; and though I am unacquainted with the list of celebrated characters on either side, yet from the observations I have made in the contracted circle in which I have moved, I dare confidently believe, that from the commencement of time to the present day, there hath been as many females, as males, who, by the *mere force of natural powers*, have merited the crown of applause; who, *thus unassisted*, have seized the wreath of fame. . . . But waving this . . . advantage, for *equality only*, we wish to contend. . . .

The exquisite delicacy of the female mind proclaimeth the exactness of its texture, while its nice sense of honour announceth its innate, its native grandeur. And indeed, in one respect, the preeminence seems to be tacitly allowed us; for after an education which limits and confines, and employments and recreations which naturally tend to enervate the body, and debilitate the mind; after we have from early youth been adorned with ribbons, and other gewgaws, dressed out like the ancient victims previous to a sacrifice, being taught by the care of our parents in collecting the most showy materials that the ornamenting our exterior ought to be the principal object of our attention; after, I say, fifteen years thus spent, we are introduced into the world, amid the united adulation of every beholder. Praise is sweet to the soul; we are immediately intoxicated by large draughts of flattery, which being plentifully administered, is to the pride of our hearts, the most acceptable incense. It is expected that with the other sex we should commence immediate war, and that we should triumph over the machinations of the most artful. We must be constantly upon our guard; prudence and discretion must be our characteristiks; and we must rise superiour to, and obtain a complete victory over those who have been long adding to the native strength of their minds, by an unremitted study of men and books, and who have, moreover, conceived from the loose characters which they have seen portrayed in the extensive variety of their reading, a most contemptible opinion of the sex. . . . And if we are allowed an equality of acquirements, let serious studies equally employ our minds, and we will bid our souls arise to equal strengths. We will meet upon even ground, the despot man; we will rush with alacrity to the combat, and, crowned by success, we shall then answer the exalted expectations, which are formed. . . .

[S]ensibility, soft compassion, and gentle commiseration, are inmates in the female bosom. . . . If we meet an equal, a sensible friend, we will reward him with the hand of amity, and through life we will be assiduous to promote his happiness; but from every deep laid scheme, for our ruin, retiring into ourselves, amid the flowery paths of science, we will indulge in all the refined and sentimental pleasures of contemplation: And should it still be urged, that the studies thus insisted upon would interfere with our more peculiar department, I must further reply, that *early hours*, and close application, will do wonders; and to her who is from the first dawn of reason taught to fill up time rationally, both the requisites will be easy. I grant that niggard [selfish or stingy] fortune is too generally unfriendly to the mind; and that much of that valuable treasure, time, is necessarily expended upon the wants of the body; but it should be remembered; that in embarrassed circumstances our companions have as little leisure for literary improvements, as is afforded to us. . . . Nay, we have even more leisure for sedentary pleasures, as our avocations are more retired, much less laborious, and, as hath been observed, by no means require that avidity of attention which is proper to the employments of the other sex. In high life, or, in other words, where the parties are in possession of affluence, the objection respecting time is wholly obviated, and of course falls to the ground; and it may also be repeated, that many of those hours which are at present swallowed up in fashion and scandal, might be redeemed, were we habituated to useful reflections. But in one respect, O ye arbiters of our fate! we confess that the superiority is indubitably yours; you are by nature formed for our protectors; we pretend not to vie with you in bodily strength; upon this point we will never contend for victory. Shield us then, we beseech you, from external evils, and in return we will transact *your* domestick affairs. Yes, *your*, for are you not equally interested in those matters with ourselves?

QUESTIONS FOR READING AND DISCUSSION

1. How did Murray criticize the views of "ye lordly, ye haughty sex"? Why did she emphasize that "our souls are by nature *equal* to yours"?
2. What was Murray's response to conventional views about women's "imagination, reason, memory and judgment"?
3. How did education and child rearing contribute to Murray's observation, "who shall wonder at the apparent superiority [of men], if indeed custom becomes second nature"?
4. To what extent did Murray believe that the "domestick duties" of women were in conflict with their equality?
5. Did Murray's claim that men were "by nature formed for our protectors" compromise her insistence on equality? Why or why not?

DOCUMENT 9–4

A French Sugar Planter Describes the French and Saint Domingue Revolutions

In the midst of revolutionary turmoil in France, slaves in the French colony of Saint Domingue revolted to emancipate themselves from the claims of their masters and the rigors of sugar production. A wealthy, young, white Frenchman, a monarchist from a plantation-owning family, wrote a memoir around 1796, excerpted below, describing his experiences of the horrors of revolution in both France and Saint Domingue. This anonymous author and many other refugees from France and Saint Domingue fled to the United States, where—to many Americans—they personified the terrors of revolutionary uprisings. The slave insurrection in Saint Domingue became a watchword among slaveholders in the United States who feared that American slaves might follow that revolutionary example.

A Sugar Planter of Saint Domingue Experiences Revolution in France and Saint Domingue, 1791

[After leaving Paris in 1791 and arriving in Bordeaux, a merchant] introduced me into the Society of the city, with whom . . . I was very bored, as they were speaking then only about Liberty, Equality, and the Rights of Man, etc. These gentlemen, who owed all their fortune to colonial commerce, graciously said in my presence, knowing me well to be among the proprietors of Saint Domingue, that their most sincere wish was to see the overthrow of that island.

They said to me: "Whereas, my friend,
You have been master long enough,
Your slave in his turn must be.
That is natural. And should steel
Destroy the entire population
Of these colonists, who play the mighty,
Then the Blacks must be the Whites
And there strut in your place." . . .

[Leaving France and sailing to Saint Domingue for refuge from the French Revolution,] I write mournfully:

Farewell France, in past days so beautiful,
Antique abode of Honor;
Today the cruel retreat
Of Crime and Sorrow.
Farewell, people, in the past so tranquil,
Loyal, lovable, and generous;

From Althéa de Puech Parham, trans. and ed., *My Odyssey: Experiences of a Young Refugee from Two Revolutions by a Creole of Saint Domingue* (Baton Rouge, LA: State University Press, 1959).

Today, so vile a rabble,
So wild and meek a herd.
I flee from your criminal principles,
The scourge of our virtues and manners,
From your frightful tortures
And your persecuting tyrants.
Alas! may a just Providence
Soon punish such heinous crimes,
And may I see once again in France
A king, happiness and peace. . . .

The country house of my family [in Saint Domingue] is on a sugar plantation . . . near a pretty little river and in view of the ocean. . . . Wide roads connect
the plantations, which resemble little hamlets, because of the large number of
buildings necessary for the making of sugar and housing of the Negroes. . . .

How often . . . have I been able to recognize the injustice of the written dia-
tribes, that were flooding Europe, against the poor planters of Saint Domingue!
What lies! . . .

During the past months, between the different revolts and insurrections, I
have seen everywhere Negroes who were fat, well cared for, and happy. I have
seen them many times, about a hundred of them occupied with work that twenty
Europeans could achieve in much less time. Their cabins appeared sanitary, com-
modious, and furnished with the necessary utensils for their needs. These cabins
were surrounded by land where they raised pigs and a variety of fowl; they had
me observe their individual gardens, which were perfectly tended and abundantly planted with all the necessary products of our country. . . .

For those who question the discipline under which they live, it is certainly
not more rigorous than that which is observed for soldiers and sailors; and when
one realizes that thirty thousand whites are in the center of six hundred thousand semi-barbaric Africans, one should not hesitate to say that discipline is
necessary. . . .

The day after my arrival, while partaking with my family of the pleasures of
an excellent lunch, a courier arrived to deliver . . . a letter full of the most terri-
fying news. The slaves, enflamed by emissaries sent from France, had burned the
habitations of our neighbors . . . , after assassinating the proprietors without distinction of age or sex.

Already the insurrection was causing devastation on all sides, and they feared
it would soon reach our place of habitation. The report of this terrific catastrophe
was widely spread. The frightened families among our neighbors met together at
our plantation. The men armed to face the storm; the mothers, wives, sisters were
lamenting and gathering in all haste a few precious effects. Desolation and fear
were painted on all faces. The sky seemed on fire. Guns could be heard from afar
and the bells of the plantations were sounding the alarm. The danger increased.
The flames at each moment were approaching and enclosing about us. There was
no time to lose; we fled. The victims who escaped at sword's point came to swell
the number of fugitives, and recounted to us the horrors which they had witnessed. They had seen unbelievable tortures to which they testified. Many women,
young, beautiful, and virtuous, perished beneath the infamous caresses of the
brigands, amongst the cadavers of their fathers and husbands. Bodies, still palpitating, were dragged through roads with atrocious acclamations. Young children

transfixed upon the points of bayonets were the bleeding flags which followed the troop of cannibals. . . .

[I became a soldier and] . . . shouldered my first arms.

We were crushed by this war. One hundred thousand slaves in full revolt and the entire colony of Saint Domingue only defended by two regiments of the regular army. . . .

I pursued a Negro [rebel] whose regalia caused me to judge him to be one of the principal chiefs. As I was about to overtake him, he turned around, took aim, but happily for me, could not make his powder fire as it was too damp. I prepared to cleave his head with my sword, whereupon he fell to his knees, kissed my boots, and told me, with tears in his eyes, that he was my Mother's godson, that he was present at my birth, and carried me in his arms more than once, and beseeched me not to kill him; that he was a good Negro and that he had always loved the Whites. His manner disarmed me; I dismounted from my horse before having him conducted to camp. However, a soft sound made me quickly turn my head, and I saw the miserable hypocrite, who had recharged his gun, aiming point-blank at my head; being troubled at finding himself discovered, prevented him from aiming accurately, and the bullet went past me. I fell upon him, but he was on guard for my attack . . . [W]hen he was about to slash me [I] threw him into some weeds. Even then he had the impudence to maintain that *I had not seen correctly*, and that he loved the son of his godmother too much to try to kill him. When he heard himself convicted by a number of soldiers who had just arrived and had witnessed the incident, he changed his tune and told me in his jargon: "Master, I know that is true. It is the Devil who gets inside of this body of mine. I am a good nigger, but against my will the Devil is too strong." His excuse made me laugh despite my anger, and had I been alone, I would certainly have saved him; but the soldiers seized him and bound him to a tree to be shot. When he saw his fate was sealed, he began to laugh, sing, and joke. At times, however, reviling us in a furious tone, at times jeering at us in mockery. He gave the signal himself and met death without fear or complaint. We found in one of his pockets pamphlets printed in France, filled with commonplaces about the Rights of Man and the Sacred Revolution. . . . On his chest he had a little sack full of hair, herbs, bits of bone, which they call a fetish; with this, they expect to be sheltered from all danger. . . .

But if our slaves were so well treated, why did they revolt? One must ask those composers of phrases who have inundated our country with their incendiary writings; those stupid innovators who brought turmoil to France and killed their King; those Whites of Europe who were found at the head of the insurgents; those idiots who thought that the destruction of commerce would usher in a counter-revolution and who needed an army to sustain their new rights. One must take into account the jealousy, the Machiavellism of a rival nation [Britain]. One must find the reason, at last, in the character of the ignorant populace, principally in the Negroes, like machines which can easier be made to start than to stop! These are the causes which started, accelerated, and prolonged the revolt, and destroyed the most beautiful country upon the earth. . . .

Yesterday I was sitting tranquilly in my tent occupied in cleaning of my firearms, when all of a sudden . . . I saw a glow telling of an immense, encompassing fire. . . . [It was] our plantation. Alas! [The burning] was enough to annihilate the work of long years. The cowardly monsters! . . .

[I]f you could have seen the actual state of this place which, before our arrival, so much care was taken to develop: the sugar refinery, the vats, the furnaces, the vast warehouses, the convenient hospital, the water-mill which was so expensive, all is no more than a specter of walls blackened and crumbled, surrounded by enormous heaps of coals and broken tiles. The cruel ones had not even respected the houses of their brothers; and those homes for the Negroes, solid, safe, shaded by trees, enclosed by gardens, suffered the same fate as the home of the master. . . . [A]nd they did their work with great thoroughness. They demolished the aqueduct which conducted the river water to the great wheel of the mill; and they drained the pond by numerous irrigation trenches, that picturesque lake which carried such coolness to the habitation, and which always furnished such delicious fish. Why such fury in the devastation? Why deprive themselves of that which might have been so useful to them one day? It could not be out of hatred for us personally — we were complete strangers. We had been in France from our earliest years, and then the revolt broke out the day after our return, and so we were never allowed to live among them. . . .

[After fleeing with other victims to a coastal city, the refugees were attacked by rebellious slaves.] These heinous Africans, all stained with blood, were replacing murder with excesses, amidst a [white] population without refuge, without clothes, and without food.

The thousands of unfortunates of different sex and ages were sitting on the ruins of their property crying for the loss of their families and friends. The shore was covered with debris, with weapons, with wounded, with dead and with dying. On one side, a barrier of flames and of swords [in the hands of rebellious slaves]; on the other, the immense expanse of ocean. Over all was misery, want, and suffering! And nowhere was there hope! . . .

[The author got aboard a merchant vessel that set sail for the United States.] I was exhausted with fatigue and in need of food. My clothing, which I had not been able to change for three days, was covered with blood, sweat, and dirt, and was almost entirely in tatters. . . .

I was completely ruined, without home, without money, without clothes; I was going to a country of which I knew not the language, customs, nor habits, and where I had not one person whom I could approach for assistance. I was ignorant of the fate of my family . . . [and] believed them among the number of victims. . . .

After two weeks of hardships, boredom, and privations, we arrived in the waters of the Chesapeake Bay, along the coast of Virginia. What an astounding difference there was between these shores, which the late Spring had recently embellished, and the aspect of those desolate ones which I had just left! . . .

Condemned to a vile estate
Must we go from place to place,
Dragging out our broken existence. . . .
Here then is this country [Saint Domingue], whose possession
Excited jealousy in the stranger's breast.
Alas! It offers now to my pitying heart
Only a picture of endless desolation.
You it is who caused this fearful suffering,
Vain and ignorant Philosophers,

With Humanity upon your lips
But never within your wicked hearts! . . .
You pretend to pity the unhappiness
Of the care-free Negro, who is protected in youth,
Nursed in sickness, and retired in old age;
While from the bosom of luxury and idleness,
You repulse with indignities
The suffering victims who tell you of the misery
Of white men, of Frenchmen, of your brothers!
See now the slave—free but miserable,
Polluted by the blackest crimes,
Cursing your questionable benefits
Which have rendered him wretched and unhappy.

QUESTIONS FOR READING AND DISCUSSION

1. According to the sugar planter of Saint Domingue, why did some people in France believe that he had "been master long enough"? What were the views of the "Vain and ignorant Philosophers" that he found so wrong?

2. Why did the slaves on Saint Domingue revolt, according to the sugar planter? What influence did the French Revolution have on the slaves' uprising? Why did he believe slaves destroyed his plantation since, "It could not be out of hatred for us personally—we were complete strangers"?

3. What were the differences between whites and blacks, according to the sugar planter? Did he believe that all whites had essentially the same views and traits? Did he believe that about all blacks?

4. What significance did the "many women . . . [who] perished beneath the infamous caresses of the brigands" have for the sugar planter? What significance do you think such accounts might have had in the United States?

DOCUMENT 9–5

President George Washington's Parting Advice to the Nation

After serving two terms as president, George Washington announced in 1796 that he would not be a candidate for reelection. In a public farewell address published throughout the nation, Washington advised Americans to resist geographic factionalism, partisan divisions, and foreign entanglements in order to preserve their government and thereby their liberty. Washington's unrivaled eminence as the nation's foremost military and political leader gave authority to his advice. Americans referred to his Farewell Address maxims for decades.

Farewell Address to the People of the United States, 1796

. . . [A] solicitude for your welfare, which cannot end but with my life, and the apprehension of danger, natural to that solicitude, urge me, on an occasion like the present, to offer to your solemn contemplation, and to recommend to your frequent review, some sentiments, which are the result of much reflection, of no inconsiderable observation, and which appear to me all-important to the permanency of your felicity as a People. . . .

Interwoven as is the love of liberty with every ligament of your hearts, no recommendation of mine is necessary to fortify or confirm the attachment.

The unity of Government, which constitutes you one people, is also now dear to you. It is justly so; for it is a main pillar in the edifice of your real independence, the support of your tranquillity at home, your peace abroad; of your safety; of your prosperity; of that very Liberty, which you so highly prize. But as it is easy to foresee, that, from different causes and from different quarters, much pains will be taken, many artifices employed, to weaken in your minds the conviction of this truth; as this is the point in your political fortress against which the batteries of internal and external enemies will be most constantly and actively (though often covertly and insidiously) directed, it is of infinite moment, that you should properly estimate the immense value of your national Union to your collective and individual happiness; that you should cherish a cordial, habitual, and immovable attachment to it; accustoming yourselves to think and speak of it as of the Palladium[1] of your political safety and prosperity; watching for its preservation with jealous anxiety; discountenancing whatever may suggest even a suspicion, that it can in any event be abandoned; and indignantly frowning upon the first dawning of every attempt to alienate any portion of our country from the rest, or to enfeeble the sacred ties which now link together the various parts.

For this you have every inducement of sympathy and interest. Citizens, by birth or choice, of a common country, that country has a right to concentrate your affections. The name of AMERICAN, which belongs to you, in your national capacity, must always exalt the just pride of Patriotism, more than any appellation derived from local discriminations. With slight shades of difference, you have the same religion, manners, habits, and political principles. You have in a common cause fought and triumphed together; the Independence and Liberty you possess are the work of joint counsels, and joint efforts, of common dangers, sufferings, and successes.

But these considerations, however powerfully they address themselves to your sensibility, are greatly outweighed by those, which apply more immediately to your interest. Here every portion of our country finds the most commanding motives for carefully guarding and preserving the Union of the whole.

The *North*, in an unrestrained intercourse with the *South*, protected by the equal laws of a common government, finds, in the productions of the latter, great additional resources of maritime and commercial enterprise and precious materials of manufacturing industry. The *South*, in the same intercourse, benefiting by the agency of the *North*, sees its agriculture grow and its commerce expand. . . . The *East*, in a like intercourse with the *West*, already finds, and in the progressive improvement of interior communications by land and water, will more and more find, a valuable vent for the commodities which it brings from abroad, or manufactures at home. The *West* derives from the *East* supplies requisite to its growth and comfort, and, what is perhaps of still greater consequence, it must of necessity

---

From George Washington, "Farewell Address to the People of the United States," *Claypoole's American Daily Advertiser*, September 19, 1796.

[1]**Palladium**: A statue in ancient Troy that was supposed to protect the safety of the city; in general, a safeguard.

owe the *secure* enjoyment of indispensable *outlets* for its own productions to the weight, influence, and the future maritime strength of the Atlantic side of the Union, directed by an indissoluble community of interest as *one nation*. Any other tenure by which the *West* can hold this essential advantage, whether derived from its own separate strength, or from an apostate and unnatural connexion with any foreign power, must be intrinsically precarious.

While, then, every part of our country thus feels an immediate and particular interest in Union, all the parts combined cannot fail to find in the united mass of means and efforts greater strength, greater resource, proportionably greater security from external danger, a less frequent interruption of their peace by foreign nations; and, what is of inestimable value, they must derive from Union an exemption from those broils and wars between themselves, which so frequently afflict neighbouring countries not tied together by the same governments. . . . Hence, likewise, they will avoid the necessity of those overgrown military establishments, which, under any form of government, are inauspicious to liberty, and which are to be regarded as particularly hostile to Republican Liberty. In this sense it is, that your Union ought to be considered as a main prop of your liberty, and that the love of the one ought to endear to you the preservation of the other. . . .

In contemplating the causes, which may disturb our Union, it occurs as matter of serious concern, that any ground should have been furnished for characterizing parties by *Geographical* discriminations, *Northern* and *Southern, Atlantic* and *Western*; whence designing men may endeavour to excite a belief, that there is a real difference of local interests and views. One of the expedients of party to acquire influence, within particular districts, is to misrepresent the opinions and aims of other districts. You cannot shield yourselves too much against the jealousies and heartburnings, which spring from these misrepresentations; they tend to render alien to each other those, who ought to be bound together by fraternal affection. . . .

To the efficacy and permanency of your Union, a Government for the whole is indispensable. . . . Sensible of this momentous truth, you have improved upon your first essay, by the adoption of a Constitution of Government better calculated than your former for an intimate Union, and for the efficacious management of your common concerns. This Government, the offspring of our own choice, uninfluenced and unawed, adopted upon full investigation and mature deliberation, completely free in its principles, in the distribution of its powers, uniting security with energy, and containing within itself a provision for its own amendment, has a just claim to your confidence and your support. Respect for its authority, compliance with its laws, acquiescence in its measures, are duties enjoined by the fundamental maxims of true Liberty. The basis of our political systems is the right of the people to make and to alter their Constitutions of Government. But the Constitution which at any time exists, till changed by an explicit and authentic act of the whole people, is sacredly obligatory upon all. The very idea of the power and the right of the people to establish Government presupposes the duty of every individual to obey the established Government.

All obstructions to the execution of the Laws, all combinations and associations, under whatever plausible character, with the real design to direct, control, counteract, or awe the regular deliberation and action of the constituted authorities, are destructive of this fundamental principle, and of fatal tendency. They serve to organize factions, to give it an artificial and extraordinary force; to put, in the place of the delegated will of the nation, the will of a party, often a small but artful and enterprising minority of the community. . . .

However combinations or associations of the above description may now and then answer popular ends, they are likely, in the course of time and things, to become potent engines, by which cunning, ambitious, and unprincipled men will be enabled to subvert the power of the people, and to usurp for themselves the reins of government; destroying afterwards the very engines, which have lifted them to unjust dominion.

Towards the preservation of your government, and the permanency of your present happy state, it is requisite, not only that you steadily discountenance irregular oppositions to its acknowledged authority, but also that you resist with care the spirit of innovation upon its principles, however specious the pretexts. One method of assault may be to effect, in the forms of the constitution, alterations, which will impair the energy of the system, and thus to undermine what cannot be directly overthrown. . . .

I have already intimated to you the danger of parties in the state, with particular reference to the founding of them on geographical discriminations. Let me now take a more comprehensive view, and warn you in the most solemn manner against the baneful effects of the spirit of party, generally.

This spirit, unfortunately, is inseparable from our nature, having its root in the strongest passions of the human mind. It exists under different shapes in all governments, more or less stifled, controlled, or repressed; but, in those of the popular form, it is seen in its greatest rankness, and is truly their worst enemy.

The alternate domination of one faction over another, sharpened by the spirit of revenge, natural to party dissension, which in different ages and countries has perpetrated the most horrid enormities, is itself a frightful despotism. But this leads at length to a more formal and permanent despotism. The disorders and miseries, which result, gradually incline the minds of men to seek security and repose in the absolute power of an individual; and sooner or later the chief of some prevailing faction, more able or more fortunate than his competitors, turns this disposition to the purposes of his own elevation, on the ruins of Public Liberty. . . .

There is an opinion, that parties in free countries are useful checks upon the administration of the Government, and serve to keep alive the spirit of Liberty. This within certain limits is probably true; and in Governments of a Monarchical cast, Patriotism may look with indulgence, if not with favor, upon the spirit of party. But in those of the popular character, in Governments purely elective, it is a spirit not to be encouraged. From their natural tendency, it is certain there will always be enough to that spirit for every salutary purpose. And, there being constant danger of excess, the effort ought to be, by force of public opinion, to mitigate and assuage it. A fire not to be quenched, it demands a uniform vigilance to prevent its bursting into a flame, lest, instead of warming, it should consume. . . .

Of all the dispositions and habits, which lead to political prosperity, Religion and Morality are indispensable supports. In vain would that man claim the tribute of Patriotism, who should labor to subvert these great pillars of human happiness, these firmest props of the duties of Men and Citizens. . . .

As a very important source of strength and security, cherish public credit. One method of preserving it is, to use it as sparingly as possible; avoiding occasions of expense by cultivating peace, but remembering also that timely disbursements to prepare for danger frequently prevent much greater disbursements to repel it; avoiding likewise the accumulation of debt, not only by shunning occasions of expense, but to vigorous exertions in time of peace to discharge the debts, which unavoidable wars may have occasioned, not ungenerously throwing upon posterity the burthen, which we ourselves ought to bear. The execution of these maxims belongs to your representatives, but it is necessary that public opinion should cooperate. . . . [I]t is essential that you should practically bear in mind, that towards the payment of debts there must be Revenue; that to have Revenue there must be taxes; that no taxes can be devised, which are not more or less inconvenient and unpleasant. . . .

Observe good faith and justice towards all Nations; cultivate peace and harmony with all. . . . In the execution of such a plan, nothing is more essential, than that permanent, inveterate antipathies against particular Nations, and passionate attachments for others, should be excluded. . . . The Nation, which indulges towards another an habitual hatred, or an habitual fondness, is in some degree a slave. It is a slave to its animosity or to its affection, either of which is sufficient to lead it astray from its duty and its interest. . . .

Against the insidious wiles of foreign influence (I conjure you to believe me, fellow-citizens,) the jealousy of a free people ought to be *constantly* awake; since history and experience prove, that foreign influence is one of the most baneful foes of Republican Government. . . .

The great rule of conduct for us, in regard to foreign nations, is, in extending our commercial relations, to have with them as little *political* connexion as possible. So far as we have already formed engagements, let them be fulfilled with perfect good faith. Here let us stop.

Europe has a set of primary interests, which to us have none, or a very remote relation. Hence she must be engaged in frequent controversies, the causes of which are essentially foreign to our concerns. Hence, therefore, it must be unwise in us to implicate ourselves, by artificial ties, in the ordinary vicissitudes of her politics, or the ordinary combinations and collisions of her friendships or enmities.

Our detached and distant situation invites and enables us to pursue a different course. . . . It is our true policy to steer clear of permanent alliances with any portion of the foreign world. . . .

In offering to you, my countrymen, these counsels of an old and affectionate friend, I . . . may even flatter myself, that they may be productive of some partial benefit, some occasional good; that they may now and then recur to moderate the fury of party spirit, to warn against the mischiefs of foreign intrigue, to guard against the impostures of pretended patriotism.

QUESTIONS FOR READING AND DISCUSSION

1. In what ways, according to Washington, was "unity of Government" the "main pillar" of "independence"? What experiences, ideas, and beliefs did he believe unified Americans? What did he think undermined unity? How did he describe the Constitution as strengthening unity?

2. Why, according to Washington, were parties more dangerous in a republic than in a monarchy? If "the spirit of party" was, as Washington argued, "inseparable from our nature," how could it be controlled or restrained? Was Washington's advice wholly free of party spirit?

3. Why did Washington believe it was so important "to steer clear of permanent alliances"?

4. Would any Americans have been surprised by Washington's advice or opposed to it? If so, why?

COMPARATIVE QUESTIONS

1. How did Judith Sargent Murray's views of education and its significance compare with the sugar planter of Saint Domingue's views about "commonplaces about the Rights of Man and the Sacred Revolution"?

2. Would Hamilton and the sugar planter agree about the division of labor according to class and race in late-eighteenth-century Western society? Did Washington believe that "the right of the people to make and to alter their Constitutions of Government" extended to Murray and the sugar planter's slaves? Explain how Hamilton and Washington might have reconciled the difference between the idea of liberty and how it was put into practice in post-revolutionary America.

3. How did the experiences of Mary Dewees compare with those of the sugar planter from Saint Domingue? How might Dewees have responded to Murray's ideas about equality?

4. To what extent did George Washington and the sugar planter agree about the threats to liberty?

5. Why were Hamilton and Washington optimistic about the future of the nation? To what extent did Murray and Dewees and her family share that optimism?

6. Each of the documents in this chapter envisions liberty as a precious source of power. To what extent did the authors of these documents agree about the uses and abuses of liberty's power? As each author looked toward the future, what threats to liberty did he or she see looming on the horizon, and how did he or she believe these threats might be avoided?

10 Republicans in Power

1800–1824

I n the early republic, Americans continually referred to the ideals of the Revolution to measure the nation's progress, as the following documents illustrate. Signs of unmistakable progress seemed clearest to Jeffersonian Republicans, who claimed to embody the revolutionary legacy. The ideals of the Revolution did not lead simply to virtue and patriotism, however. Many Americans celebrated liberty by engaging in unvirtuous acts of selfishness, irresponsibility, and even crime. Farmers moving to the frontier claimed the right to pursue happiness on lands inhabited for millennia by Indians. Thomas Jefferson and other leaders seldom hesitated to uphold the rights of white citizens at the expense of Native Americans and African Americans. Slaves and free black Americans often embraced the ideals of the Revolution while faulting white Americans for violating them by countless practices of racial discrimination. Some white Americans believed that the inalienable rights inscribed in the Declaration of Independence extended beyond white men, but most did not.

DOCUMENT 10–1

President Thomas Jefferson's Private and Public Indian Policy

Diplomatic relations with Native Americans were among the new nation's most important activities. A growing population and the rush of settlers to frontier farms pushed to the fore issues of access to Indian lands and subordination of tribal authority to the trade, laws, and customs of white Americans. President Thomas Jefferson outlined his strategy for Indian affairs in 1803 in a private letter to the governor of Indiana Territory, William H. Harrison, excerpted here. In public, Jefferson expressed his Indian policy many times when visiting delegations of Native Americans came to Washington, D.C. Jefferson's address to the Mandans—the source of the next selection—illustrates the public face of American policy.

Letter to Governor William H. Harrison, February 27, 1803

You receive from time to time information and instructions as to our Indian affairs. These communications being for the public records, are restrained always to particular objects and occasions; but this letter being unofficial and private, I may with safety give you a more extensive view of our policy respecting the Indians, that you may the better comprehend the parts dealt out to you in detail through the official channel, and observing the system of which they make a part, conduct yourself in unison with it in cases where you are obliged to act without instruction. Our system is to live in perpetual peace with the Indians, to cultivate an affectionate attachment from them, by everything just and liberal which we can do for them within the bounds of reason, and by giving them effectual protection against wrongs from our own people. The decrease of game rendering their subsistence by hunting insufficient, we wish to draw them to agriculture, to spinning and weaving. The latter branches they take up with great readiness, because they fall to the women, who gain by quitting the labors of the field for those which are exercised within doors. When they withdraw themselves to the culture of a small piece of land, they will perceive how useless to them are their extensive forests, and will be willing to pare them off from time to time in exchange for necessaries for their farms and families. To promote this disposition to exchange lands, which they have to spare and we want, for necessaries, which we have to spare and they want, we shall push our trading uses, and be glad to see the good and influential individuals among them run in debt, because we observe that when these debts get beyond what the individuals can pay, they become willing to lop them off by a cession of lands. At our trading houses, too, we mean to sell so low as merely to repay us cost and charges, so as neither to lessen or enlarge our capital. This is what private traders cannot do, for they must gain; they will consequently retire from the competition, and we shall thus get clear of this pest without giving offence or umbrage to the Indians. In this way our settlements will gradually circumscribe and approach the Indians, and they will in time either incorporate with us as citizens of the United States, or remove beyond the Mississippi. The former is certainly the termination of their history most happy for themselves; but, in the whole course of this, it is essential to cultivate their love. As to their fear, we presume that our strength and their weakness is now so visible that they must see we have only to shut our hand to crush them, and that all our liberalities to them proceed from motives of pure humanity only. Should any tribe be fool-hardy enough to take up the hatchet at any time, the seizing the whole country of that tribe, and driving them across the Mississippi, as the only condition of peace, would be an example to others, and a furtherance of our final consolidation.

Combined with these views, and to be prepared against the occupation of Louisiana by a powerful and enterprising people, it is important that, setting less value on interior extension of purchases from the Indians, we bend our whole views to the purchase and settlement of the country on the Mississippi, from its mouth to its northern regions, that we may be able to present as strong a front on our western as on our eastern border, and plant on the Mississippi itself the means

From *The Writings of Thomas Jefferson*, vols. 3 and 4, ed. Henry A. Washington (Washington, DC: Taylor and Maury, 1853–1854).

of its own defence. . . . Of the means, however, of obtaining what we wish, you will be the best judge; and I have given you this view of the system which we suppose will best promote the interests of the Indians and ourselves, and finally consolidate our whole country to one nation only; that you may be enabled the better to adapt your means to the object, for this purpose we have given you a general commission for treating. The crisis is pressing: whatever can now be obtained must be obtained quickly. The occupation of New Orleans, hourly expected, by the French, is already felt like a light breeze by the Indians. You know the sentiments they entertain of that nation; under the hope of their protection they will immediately stiffen against cessions of lands to us. We had better, therefore, do at once what can now be done.

I must repeat that this letter is to be considered as private and friendly, and is not to control any particular instructions which you may receive through official channel. You will also perceive how sacredly it must be kept within your own breast, and especially how improper to be understood by the Indians. For their interests and their tranquillity it is best they should see only the present age of their history.

Address to the Wolf and People of the Mandan Nation, December 30, 1806

My children, the Wolf and people of the Mandan nation:—I take you by the hand of friendship and give you a hearty welcome to the seat of the government of the United States. The journey which you have taken to visit your fathers on this side of our island is a long one, and your having undertaken it is a proof that you desired to become acquainted with us. . . .

My friends and children, we are descended from the old nations which live beyond the great water, but we and our forefathers have been so long here that we seem like you to have grown out of this land. We consider ourselves no longer of the old nations beyond the great water, but as united in one family with our red brethren here. The French, the English, the Spaniards, have now agreed with us to retire from all the country which you and we hold between Canada and Mexico, and never more to return to it. And remember the words I now speak to you, my children, they are never to return again. We are now your fathers; and you shall not lose by the change. As soon as Spain had agreed to withdraw from all the waters of the Missouri and Mississippi, I felt the desire of becoming acquainted with all my red children beyond the Mississippi, and of uniting them with us as we have those on this side of that river, in the bonds of peace and friendship. I wished to learn what we could do to benefit them by furnishing them the necessaries they want in exchange for their furs and peltries. I therefore sent our beloved man, Captain [Meriwether] Lewis, one of my own family, to go up the Missouri river to get acquainted with all the Indian nations in its neighborhood, to take them by the hand, deliver my talks to them, and to inform us in what way we could be useful to them. Your nation received him kindly, you have taken him by the hand and been friendly to him. My children, I thank you for the services you rendered him, and for your attention to his words. He will now tell us where we should establish trading houses to be convenient to you all, and what we must send to them.

My friends and children, I have now an important advice to give you. I have already told you that you and all the red men are my children, and I wish you to live in peace and friendship with one another as brethren of the same family ought to do. How much better is it for neighbors to help than to hurt one another; how much happier must it make them. If you will cease to make war on one another, if you will live in friendship with all mankind, you can employ all your time in providing food and clothing for yourselves and your families. Your men will not be destroyed in war, and your women and children will lie down to sleep in their cabins without fear of being surprised by their enemies and killed or carried away. Your numbers will be increased instead of diminishing, and you will live in plenty and in quiet. My children, I have given this advice to all your red brethren on this side of the Mississippi; they are following it, they are increasing in their numbers, are learning to clothe and provide for their families as we do. Remember then my advice, my children, carry it home to your people, and tell them that from the day that they have become all of the same family, from the day that we became father to them all, we wish, as a true father should do, that we may all live together as one household, and that before they strike one another, they should go to their father and let him endeavor to make up the quarrel.

My children, you are come from the other side of our great island, from where the sun sets, to see your new friends at the sun rising. . . . I very much desire that you should not stop here, but go . . . and visit our great cities . . . and see how many friends and brothers you have here. . . . I wish you, my children, to see all you can, and to tell your people all you see; because I am sure the more they know of us, the more they will be our hearty friends. . . .

My children, I have long desired to see you; I have now opened my heart to you, let my words sink into your hearts and never be forgotten. If ever lying people or bad spirits should raise up clouds between us, call to mind what I have said, and what you have seen yourselves. Be sure there are some lying spirits between us; let us come together as friends and explain to each other what is misrepresented or misunderstood, the clouds will fly away like morning fog, and the sun of friendship appear and shine forever bright and clear between us.

Questions for Reading and Discussion

1. In his private letter to Harrison, what goals did Jefferson state for the nation's policy toward Indians, and how could they be attained? What impediments did Jefferson foresee to carrying out his policy?

2. From the Indians' perspective, why would being drawn into "agriculture, to spinning and weaving" be appealing? How would such a change alter their ways of life? What alternatives did Indians have?

3. What did Jefferson mean by declaring, "For their own interests and their tranquillity it is best they should see only the present age of their history"?

4. In his address to the Mandan people, how did Jefferson's description of the nation's goals differ from that in his letter to Harrison? Why did Jefferson speak so differently to the Mandans and to Harrison?

5. What was implied by Jefferson's referring to the Indians as "my children"? To what extent was Jefferson's plan an assertion of racial and cultural superiority? Did Jefferson overlook alternatives for relations with Indians?

DOCUMENT 10–2

Meriwether Lewis Describes the Shoshone

When President Jefferson arranged the Louisiana Purchase in 1803, he did not know pre-cisely what the nation was buying. He had already arranged for a small expedition, com-manded by Meriwether Lewis and William Clark, both soldiers, to make their way up the Missouri River, from its mouth at St. Louis to its headwaters someplace in the mountains of the uncharted interior, and to search out a route to the Pacific Ocean. Jefferson expected Lewis and Clark to be keen-eyed observers not only of the natural environment but also of the Native Americans they encountered along the way. After almost a year and a half of sailing, rowing, pushing, and pulling their heavily loaded boats upstream, they reached the land of the Shoshone, home of their interpreter Sacajawea, near the Continental Divide in present-day Montana. Lewis and Clark desperately needed horses from the Shoshone in order to cross the Rocky Mountains and make their way to the West Coast. While negotiat-ing for the horses and waiting for them to be rounded up, Lewis noted in his journal—excerpted here—Shoshone traits that caught his eye.

The Journals of the Lewis and Clark Expedition, 1805

Friday August 16th 1805.

. . . [T]he young [Shoshone] man . . . had come to inform us that one of the whitemen had killed a deer. in an instant they all gave their horses the whip and I was taken nearly a mile before I could learn what were the tidings; as I was without [s]tirrups and an Indian behind me the jostling was disagreeable I there-fore reigned up my horse and forbid the indian to whip him who had given him the lash . . . for a mile fearing he should loose a part of the feast. the fellow was so uneasy that he left me the horse dismounted and ran on foot at full speed, I am confident a mile. when they arrived where the deer was which was in view of me they dismounted and ran in tumbling over each other like a parcel of famished dogs each seizing and tearing away a part of the intestens which had been previ-ously thrown out by Drewyer[1] who killed it; the seen was such when I arrived that had I not have had a pretty keen appetite myself I am confident I should not have taisted any part of the venison shortly. each one had a peice of some discription and all eating most ravenously. some were eating the kidnies the melt [spleen] and liver and the blood runing from the corners of their mouths, others were in a simi-lar situation with the paunch and guts but the exuding substance in this case from their lips was of a different discription. one of the last who att[r]acted my attention particularly had been fortunate in his allotment or reather active in the division, he had provided himself with about nine feet of the small guts one end of which he was chewing on while with his hands he was squezzing the contents out at the other. I really did not untill now think that human nature ever presented Itself in a shape so nearly allyed to the brute creation. I viewed these poor starved divils

---

From Gary E. Moulton, ed., *The Journals of the Lewis and Clark Expedition*, vol. 5, July 28–November 1, 1805 (Lincoln: University of Nebraska Press, 1988), 103–59.

[1]**Drewyer**: One of Lewis's men.

with pity and compassion I directed McNeal[2] to skin the deer and reserved a quarter, the ballance I gave the Chief to be divided among his people; they devoured the whole of it nearly without cooking. . . . Drewyer . . . killed a second deer; here nearly the same seene was encored. a fire being kindled we cooked and eat and gave the ballance of the two deer to the Indians who eat the whole of them even to the soft parts of the hoofs. . . .

Monday August 19th 1805.

. . . [F]rom what has (already) been said of the Shoshones it will be readily perceived that they live in a wretched stait of poverty. yet notwithstanding their extreem poverty they are not only cheerfull but even gay, fond of gaudy dress and amusements; like most other Indians they are great egotists and frequently boast of heroic acts which they never performed. they are also fond of games of wrisk. they are frank, communicative, fair in dealing, generous with the little they possess, extreemly honest, and by no means beggarly. each individual is his own sovereign master, and acts from the dictates of his own mind; the authority of the Chief being nothing more than mere admonition supported by the influence which the propiety of his own examplery conduct may have acquired him in the minds of the individuals who compose the band. the title of cheif is not hereditary . . . in fact every man is a chief, but all have not an equal influence on the minds of the other members of the community, and he who happens to enjoy the greatest share of confidence is the principal Chief. The Shoshonees may be estimated at about 100 warriors, and about three times that number of woomen and children. they have more children among them than I expected to have seen among a people who procure subsistence with such difficulty. there are but few very old persons, nor did they appear to treat those with much tenderness or rispect. The man is the sole propryetor of his wives and daughters, and can barter or dispose of either as he thinks proper. a plurality of wives is common among them, but these are not generally sisters as with the Minnetares & Mandans but are purchased of different fathers. The father frequently disposes of his infant daughters in marriage to men who are grown or to men who have sons for whom they think proper to provide wives. the compensation given in such cases usually consists of horses or mules which the father receives at the time of contract and converts to his own uce. the girl remains with her parents untill she is conceived to have obtained the age of puberty which with them is considered to be about the age of 13 or 14 years. the female at this age is surrendered to her sovereign lord and husband agreeably to contract, and with her is frequently restored by the father quite as much as he received in the first instance in payment for his daughter; but this is discretionary with the father. Sah-car-gar-we-ah [Sacajawea] had been thus disposed of before she was taken by the Minnetares, or had arrived to the years of puberty. the husband was yet living and with this band. he was more than double her age and had two other wives. he claimed her as his wife but said that as she had had a child by another man, who was Charbono[3] that he did not want her. They seldom correct their children particularly the boys who soon become masters of their own acts. they give as a reason that it cows and breaks the

---

[2]**McNeal**: Another member of Lewis's party.
[3]**Charbono**: A French trapper who accompanied Lewis.

Sperit of the boy to whip him, and that he never recovers his independence of mind after he is grown. They treat their women but with little rispect, and compel them to perform every species of drudgery. they collect the wild fruits and roots, attend to the horses or assist in that duty cook dreess the skins and make all their apparal, collect wood and make their fires, arrange and form their lodges, and when they travel pack the horses and take charge of all the baggage; in short the man dose little else except attend his horses hunt and fish. the man considers himself degraded if he is compelled to walk any distance, and if he is so unfortunately poor as only to possess two horses he rides the best himself and leavs the woman or women if he has more than one, to transport their baggage and children on the other, and to walk if the horse is unable to carry the additional weight of their persons — the chastity of their women is not held in high estimation, and the husband will for a trifle barter the companion of his bead for a night or longer if he conceives the reward adiquate; tho' they are not so importunate that we should caress their women as the siouxs were and some of their women appear to be held more sacred than in any nation we have seen I have requested the men to give them no cause of jealousy by having connection with their women without their knowledge, which with them strange as it may seem is considered as disgraceful to the husband as clandestine connections of a similar kind are among civilized nations. to prevent this mutual exchange of good officies altogether I know it impossible to effect, particularly on the part of our young men whom some months abstanence have made very polite to those tawney damsels. no evil has yet resulted and I hope will not from these connections. . . . these people are deminutive in stature, thick ankles, crooked legs, thick flat feet and in short but illy formed, at least much more so in general than any nation of Indians I ever saw. their complexion is much that of the Siouxs or darker than the Minnetares mandands or Shawnees. generally both men and women wear their hair in a loos lank flow over the sholders and face. . . . the dress of the men consists of a robe[,] long legings, shirt, tippet and Mockersons, that of the women is also a robe, chemise, and Mockersons; sometimes they make use of short legings. the ornements of both men and women are very similar, and consist of several species of sea shells, blue and white beads, bras and Iron arm bands, plaited cords of the sweet grass, and collars of leather ornamented with the quills of the porcupine dyed of various colours among which I observed the red, yellow, blue, and black. the ear is purforated in the lower part to receive various ornaments but the nose is not, nor is the ear lasserated or disvigored for this purpose as among many nations. the men never mark their skins by birning, cuting, nor puncturing and introducing a colouring matter as many nations do. there women sometimes puncture a small circle on their forehead nose or cheeks and thus introduce a black matter usually soot and grease which leaves an indelible stand tho' this even is by no means common. their arms offensive and defensive consist in the bow and arrows sheild, some lances, and a weapon called by the Cippeways who formerly used it, the pog-gar'-mag-gon.[4] in fishing they employ wairs, gigs, and fishing hooks. the salmon is the principal object of their pursuit. they snair wolves and foxes. I was anxious to learn whether these people had the venerial, and made the enquiry through the intrepreter and his wife; the information was that they sometimes had it but I could not learn their remedy; they most usually die with its effects. this seems a strong proof that these disorders bothe gonaroehah and Louis venerae [syphilis] are native disorders of America. tho' these people have suffered much

---

[4]**pog-gar'-mag-gon**: A weighted war club.

by the small pox which is known to be imported and perhaps those other disorders might have been contracted from other indian tribes who by a round of communication might have obtained from the Europeans since it was introduced into that quarter of the globe. but so much detatched on the other had from all communication with the whites that I think it most probable that those disorders are original with them. . . .

August 21st Wednesday 1805.

. . . Those Indians are mild in their disposition appear Sincere in their friendship, punctial, and decided. kind with what they have, to Spare. They are excessive pore, nothing but horses there Enemies which are noumerous on account of there horses & Defenceless Situation, have Deprived them of tents and all the Small Conveniances of life. . . . The women are held more Sacred among them than any nation we have seen and appear to have an equal Shere in all Conversation, which is not the Case in any othe nation I have Seen. their boeys & Girls are also admited to Speak except in Councils, the women doe all the drugery except fishing and takeing care of the horses, which the men apr. to take upon themselves. . . .

Friday August 23rd 1805.

. . . The metal which we found in possession of these people consited of a few indifferent knives, a few brass kettles some arm bands of iron and brass, a few buttons, woarn as ornaments in their hair, a spear or two of a foot in length and some iron and brass arrow points which they informed me they obtained in exchange for horses from the Crow or Rocky Mountain Indians on the yellowstone River. the bridlebits and stirrips they obtained from the Spaniards, tho' these were but few. many of them made use of flint for knives, and with this instrument, skined the animals they killed, dressed their fish and made their arrows; in short they used it for every purpose to which the knife is applyed. . . .

Saturday August 24th 1805.

. . . [T]hese people have many names in the course of their lives, particularly if they become distinguished characters. for it seems that every important event by which they happen to distinguish themselves intitles them to claim another name which is generally scelected by themselves and confirmed by the nation. those distinguishing acts are the killing and scalping an enemy, the killing a white bear, leading a party to war who happen to be successful either in destroying their enemies or robing them of their horses, or individually stealing the horses of an enemy. these are considered acts of equal heroism among them, and that of killing an enemy without scalping him is considered of no importance; in fact the whole honour seems to be founded in the act of scalping, for if a man happens to slay a dozen of his enemies in action and others get the scalps or first lay their hand on the dead person the honor is lost to him who killed them and devolves on those who scalp or first touch them. Among the Shoshones, as well as all the Indians of America, bravery is esteemed the primary virtue; nor can any one become eminent among them who has not at some period of his life given proofs of his possessing this virtue. with them there can be no preferment without some ware-like achievement.

QUESTIONS FOR READING AND DISCUSSION

1. The ravenous Shoshone who devoured the deer caused Lewis to write that he "did not untill now think that human nature ever presented Itself in a shape so nearly allyed to the brute creation." How did observing behavior that he considered horrifying shape Lewis's other observations of the Shoshone, if at all? Did Lewis consider the Shoshone subhuman?

2. Lewis admired some qualities of the Shoshone and criticized others. What traits did he mention in his journal? What did he say about relations of gender and power among the Indians? To what extent did he believe the Shoshone were different from white Americans?

3. In what ways had whites already influenced the Shoshone? Did Lewis believe the Shoshone were likely to adopt the ways of white Americans? Why or why not?

4. If the Shoshone had recorded an account of white American behavior based on the activities of Lewis and Clark, what might they have noted? How accurate a portrayal would such observations have been? To what extent were Lewis's observations an accurate account of typical Shoshone ideals and actions?

DOCUMENT 10–3

A Slave Demands That Thomas Jefferson Abolish Slavery

In early December 1808, President Thomas Jefferson received a long letter from an unknown person who signed the letter, "A Slave." Internal evidence suggests the author was a man and may have been a well-educated slave, although it is impossible to be certain. The author described the horrors of slavery and called on Jefferson to end it. In the excerpt below, A Slave repeatedly referred to Jefferson's own indictments of slavery in the Declaration of Independence and his Notes on the State of Virginia *and demanded that Jefferson act in accordance with his beliefs. The letter illustrates the enormous power of revolutionary ideals as well as the glaring contradiction of slavery that Jefferson and other major political leaders tried to ignore. Jefferson never answered A Slave's letter.*

A Slave to Thomas Jefferson, November 30, 1808

Our burdens are heavy & call loud for justice! Call loud for mercy! I Therefore, take the liberty Sir, to address you myself upon the subject of slavery, and ask you a few questions. . . . [C]an you plead ignorance in . . . this inhuman slavery? If not, what can be your reasons (since you have been rais'd to the highest office in the government) for suffering us to be used in this brutal manner? Can any man who is not over-aw'd by a tyrant, sway'd by prejudice, in love with slavery & oppression, or who lives himself in idleness, drunkenness & debauchery, say, that there is either, honour, honesty, humanity, piety, charity, virtue, or religion in such

From A Slave to Thomas Jefferson, November 30, 1808, Thomas Jefferson Papers, Library of Congress.

conduct? O! merciful God, is this humanity? is this concistant with thy holy law, and agreeable to thy divine will? . . . Its quite good enough for Negroes, who the sainted pilgrims say, are only a black beast . . . with a flat nose, thick lips, woolly head, ivory teeth; and with a face somewhat resembling the human, but clearly not a human being. To prove our human-nature, sir, and our rights as citizens of these states, we have only to appeal to the Declaration of Independence which says, We hold these truths self-evident; that all men, (not all white men) are created equal; that they are endued by their Creator with inherent & inalienable rights; that among these are life, liberty & the pursuit of happiness. What think you now sir; are we men, or are we beasts. If this is not sufficient to prove our human-nature; our rights and our citizenship, take another section from the original draft of [the Declaration of Independence]. . . . In speaking of the oughtrages commited by the king of England, you say, He has waiged cruel war against humman-nature itself, violating its most sacred rights of life & liberty in the persons of a distant people, who never offended him, captivating and carrying them into slavery in another hemisphere or incur miserable death in their transportation thither: this piratical warfare . . . is the warfare of the Christian king of Great Britain, Determined to keep open a market where MAN shall be bought and sold. This is sufficient one would suppose, to convince any unprejudiced mind; but it seem that it has not carried conviction into the flinty hearts of the sainted pilgrims in America, & I fear nothing will but the sword. . . .

[T]he greatest part of all the manual labour that is done in the southern states is performed by slaves; and . . . they in general git nothing for it (except kicks and curses) and that their haughty lordling masters live in idleness drunkenness and debauchery, and aggrandize themselves and families at the expence of the honest labours of the unfortunate people. . . . What can a nation do more readily to destroy happiness, prosperity and religion, than to enslave her citizens? Is it not a speices of every evil which a nation can be guilty of to destroy all these principles? . . .

Slavery is unjust because it destroys the rites of women & children. It is a mere state of barberism, in which neither the delicacy and chastity of sex, nor the debility & ignorance of little children are regarded. The situation of the female slaves is more deplorable and degrading than that of the untutored savage. For little as savages respect the rights of women & children, their women have exemption from labour, & protection from insult during those delicate & painful periods which are peculiar to their sex; & their children are instructed in all the knowledge which is by them deem either useful or ornamental. The degree of servitude to which savage women are bound, is trifling in comparison with the task of a female slave; and inasmuch as their husbands & children reap the fruits of their labor, & in some measure repay it by acquiring a superior skill in hunting & war their labour becomes rather a pleasure than a burden. But what is to mitigate the labour of the poor female slave, with the precious burden of her affections at her breast. . . .

He who contributes by manual labour to the great stock of wealth, must in justice be entitled to some reward; but in vain does the wretched slave fell the forests, clear the grounds, prepare them for seed; watch & cultivate the tender plant, reap down & geather in the harvest, & bear it to market.

Our inhuman tyrants take the whole to riot in drunkenness & debauchery, & to aggrandize themselves & families, and we who have bourn the heat and burden of the day, git nothing but kicks and curses, for all our labour. "With what execration should the states man be loaded, who permiting one half the citizens thus to trample on the rights of the other, transforms those into despots, & these into enemies, destroys the morals of one part, and the amor patriae [patriotism, love of country] of the other. With the morals of the people, their industry also is destroye'd; for in a warm climate, no man will labour for himself who can make another labour for him." [The quotation is from Jefferson's *Notes on the State of Virginia.*] This sufficiently proves my assertions, and justifies me in saying, that a majority of the American agents in the southern states, are a set of inhuman scoundrils, and ought to be tar'd and feather'd and tyed to the tale end of a dung cart; and horse-whipt throughout the country, from state to state, and forever after banished from human society.

If slavery has become so firmly established in the country, as not to be avoided or garded against, it is such a pleasing object, as to be no longer odious and irreligious, but a source of happiness and prosperity, its high time for America to giv up all pretensions to liberty & freedom. . . .

But we have not lost all hopes; we can't yet believe, sir, that you have become so deprav'd as to be in love with slavery or have done reflecting upon the wrath of a just God, or that his justice cannot sleep forever. Yet there appears to me to be something in your administration, sir, very misterious. What your reasons can be for keeping open that execrable market where MAN shall be bought and sold, which you wrote so warmly against in the year '76, and condemn'd as a mark of disgrace, of the deepist dye in the Christian king of G. Britain, I cannot conceive. Is a crime of this execrable nature any more criminal in the Christian Crown of Britain, than in the Christian Executive of America? If not, what are your reasons, sir, for suffering us since 30th Nov. '81 [the significance of the date is unknown; it might be the birthday of the author of the letter] to be trodden under foot & abused in such an inhuman and bruital matter? Are not Our rites as well secured to use by every law of natures God as any man's in the universe? we think so; therefore, sir we consider ourselves intitled to our yearly wages from that very hour, and no man in the government (except a tyrant) can dispute our demand a single moment. And you m[a]y depend on this sir, that we shall never be reconciled to this government till we git it, & our freedom with it. I think sir, you can't do yourself & your country a greater honour, nor your unfortunate countrymen a greater piece of justice and mercy, then by freeing your slaves & paying them their yearly wages from '81 to this day. And then, if any slave-holder in America shall hereafter refuse or neglect so to do, let him or them be made an example of, and their heads be hung in gibbets [gallows] for an everlasting monument: & a terror to tyrants & evil doers. O! Thomas, you have had a long nap, and spent a great number of years in ease & plenty, upon our hard earned property, while we have been in the mean time, smarting under the cow hide and sweating in the fields to raise provision to nurse tyrants to cut your throat and perpetuate our own bonds. Why you should wish, in a free republick, to nurs, educate and exercise your children in such a tyrannical manner, I cannot conceive, since you so early saw, and confes'd the error; and must ere this most severly have felt the effects of your folly. . . .

It is high time for you, sir, to decide, whether or not you will any longer use us in this bruital manner, or adopt us as brethren, for, in our opinion: on this single circumstance alone, depends the future prosperity, or destruction of these states, and the safty of your own life in perticular. . . .

These are painful truths which no person can deny, who has ever lived three months among slave-holders. This being our unhappy condition, we humbly beseech you, sir, to lay our cause before the agents of this government, & request them to interpose between us & our inhuman tyrants, or other-wise, necessity will ere long oblidge us to seek our own safty, by takeing away the lives of our tyrants, & freeing ourselves at once from such inhuman monsters. . . . Let me once more request you sir, to lay our grievances before the sovreign people of these states— Don't neglect it sir, unless you take delight in tyranny & oppression, or are thursting after blood. . . .

Once more let me repeat it, as no subject can be dwelt upon which borders so strong on justice & mercy as the abolition of slavery; I say, sir, you cannot do your self & country so great an honour, nor your country-men a greater kindness; nor will virtue in no act of your life shine so conspicuous as in the freedom of your slaves, & by reparation for the insult offered them. Such an example, in a cause of so much magnitude to human-nature, must inevitable throw such a luster on your character that no diamond in the universe could outshine it. And I flatter myself, that such an example in a man of your character, would have such an influence on the minds of slave-holders in general in America . . . that they would not only free their own, but would make use of all their influence to effect a general immancipation; and free their country from this inhuman slaviry & disgrace. . . . Your compliance sir, will revive the expiring hopes of two millions of the most miserable of all the human race. . . . We hope at least sir, that you will deign to make known our miserable condition to the agents of the sovreign people of these states, that we may shortly hear whether or not they will interpose between us and our inhuman masters, in order if possable, to mitigate our pains, ease our burdens, & heal our smarting wounds.

QUESTIONS FOR READING AND DISCUSSION

1. What ideas of Thomas Jefferson did A Slave employ to argue against slavery?
2. According to A Slave, why were slaveholders "inhuman tyrants"? Did A Slave consider Jefferson such a tyrant? Why did he claim Jefferson "had a long nap"?
3. How should slaveholders be treated, according to A Slave? Why?
4. What did A Slave mean by asking Jefferson to provide "reparation for the insult offered" his slaves? How would reparation be determined and why?
5. If Jefferson had responded to the arguments of A Slave, what might he have said (see also Document 8–2)?

DOCUMENT 10–4

James Forten Protests Pennsylvania Law Threatening Enslavement of Free African Americans

During the decades after the Revolution, northern states slowly ended slavery, usually by gradual emancipation laws. Pennsylvania led the way with its 1780 abolition law, but by 1812, many whites sought to limit the growing numbers of free blacks by a law prohibiting African Americans from entering the state. James Forten, a freeborn African American who was a wealthy sailmaker in Philadelphia, published an attack on the proposed legislation as a violation of natural rights, the law, the Constitution, and simple humanity. Forten's protest, excerpted here, illustrates both the authority and the limits of revolutionary ideals in defining the freedom of African Americans. The proposed Pennsylvania law never passed, although similar laws passed in other northern states in the years before the Civil War.

Letters from a Man of Colour, on a Late Bill before the Senate of Pennsylvania, 1813

We hold this truth to be self-evident, that GOD created all men equal, and [it] is one of the most prominent features in the Declaration of Independence, and in that glorious fabric of collected wisdom, our noble Constitution. This idea embraces the Indian and the European, the Savage and the Saint, the Peruvian and the Laplander, the white Man and the African, and whatever measures are adopted subversive of this inestimable privilege, are in direct violation of the letter and spirit of our Constitution. . . .

These thoughts were suggested by the . . . late bill, before the Senate of Pennsylvania, to prevent the emigration of people of colour into this state. It was not passed [and] . . . we sincerely hope, the white men, whom we should look upon as our protectors, will become convinced of the inhumanity and impolicy of such a measure. . . . This is almost the only state in the Union wherein the African[s] have justly boasted of rational liberty and the protection of the laws, and shall it now be said they have been deprived of that liberty, and publicly exposed for sale to the highest bidder? Shall colonial inhumanity that has marked many of us with shameful stripes, become the practice of the people of Pennsylvania . . . ? People of Pennsylvania . . . doom us not to the unhappy fate of thousands of our countrymen in the Southern States and the West Indies; despise the traffic in blood, and the blessing of the African will forever be around you. Many of us are men of property, for the security of which, we have hitherto looked to the laws of our blessed state, but should this become a law, our property is jeopardized, since the same power which can expose to sale an unfortunate creature, can wrest from him those estates which years of honest industry have accumulated. . . . We grant there are a number of worthless men belonging to our colour, but there are laws of sufficient rigour for their punishment. . . . Punish the guilty man of colour to the utmost limit of the laws, but sell him not into slavery! . . . If he is too indolent to labour for his own subsistence, compel him to do so; but sell him not into slavery. By selling him you do not make him better, but commit a wrong. . . . Many of our ancestors were brought here more than one hundred years ago; many of our fathers, many of ourselves, have fought and bled for the independence of our country. Do not then expose us to sale. Let not the spirit of the father behold the son robbed of that liberty which he died to establish. . . .

The Constitution of Pennsylvania . . . declared "that all men are born equally free and independent, and have certain inherent and indefeasible rights, among which are those of enjoying life and liberty." . . . Has the God who made the white man and the black, left any record declaring us a different species. Are we not sustained by the same power, supported by the same food, hurt by the same wounds, pleased with the same delights, and propagated by the same means. And should we not then enjoy the same liberty, and be protected by the same laws. . . . It cannot be that the authors of our Constitution intended to exclude us from its benefits, for just emerging from unjust and cruel emancipation, their souls were

From James Forten, *Letters from a Man of Colour, on a Late Bill before the Senate of Pennsylvania* (Philadelphia, n.p., 1813); reprinted in *Pamphlets of Protest: An Anthology of Early African-American Protest Literature, 1790–1860*, eds. Richard Newman, Patrick Rael, and Philip Lapsansky (New York: Routledge, 2001), 67–72.

too much affected with their own deprivations to commence the reign of terrour over others. They knew we were deeper skinned that they were, but they acknowledged us as men, and found that many an honest heart beat beneath a dusky bosom. They felt that they had no more authority to enslave us, than England had to tyrannize over them. They were convinced that if amenable to the same laws in our actions, we should be protected by the same laws in our rights and privileges. Actuated by these sentiments they adopted the glorious fabric of our liberties, and declaring "all men" free, they did not particularize white and black, because they never supposed it would be made a question whether we were men or not. . . .

Let us put a case, in which the law in question operates peculiarly hard and unjust. — I have a brother, perhaps, who, resides in a distant part of the Union, and after a separation of years, actuated by the same fraternal affection which beats in the bosom of a white man, he comes to visit me. Unless that brother be registered in twenty four hours after, and be able to produce a certificate to that effect, he is liable, according to . . . the bill, to a fine of twenty dollars, to arrest, imprisonment and sale. . . . It is to be hoped that in our legislature there is a patriotism, humanity, and mercy sufficient to crush this attempt upon the civil liberty of freemen [who] . . . have been the scorn, and whose calamities have been the jest, of the world for ages. . . .

Are not men of colour sufficiently degraded? Why then increase their degradation. It is a well known fact, that black people, upon certain days of public jubilee, dare not to be seen after twelve o'clock in the day, upon the field to enjoy the times; for no sooner do the fumes of that potent devil, Liquor, mount into the brain, than the poor black is assailed like the destroying Hyena or the avaricious Wolf! I allude particularly to the Fourth of July — Is it not wonderful, that the day set apart for the festival of Liberty, should be abused by the advocates of Freedom, in endeavoring to sully what they profess to adore. If men, though they know that the law protects all, will dare, in defiance of law, to execute their hatred upon the defenceless black, will they not by the passage of this bill, believe him still more a mark for their venom and spleen — Will they not believe him completely deserted by authority, and subject to every outrage brutality can inflict. . . .

By . . . this bill . . . the police officers are authorized to apprehend any black, whether a vagrant or a man of reputable character, who cannot produce a Certificate that he has been registered. He is to be arrayed before a justice, who thereupon is to commit him to prison! The jailor is to advertise a Freeman, and at the expiration of six months, if no owner appears for this degraded black, he is to be exposed to sale, and if not sold to be confined at hard labour for seven years! . . . The Constable, whose antipathy generally against the black is very great, will take the opportunity of hurting his feelings! Perhaps, he sees him at a distance and having a mind to raise the boys in hue and cry against him, exclaims, "Halloa! Stop the Negro!" — The boys, delighting in the sport, immediately begin to hunt him, and immediately from a hundred tongues, is heard the cry — "Hoa, Negro, where is your Certificate!" — Can any thing be conceived more degrading to humanity! Can any thing be done more shocking to the principal of Civil Liberty! — A person arriving from another state, ignorant of the existence of such a law, may fall a victim to its cruel oppression. But he is to be advertised, and if no owner appears — How can an owner appear for a man who is free and belongs to no one! — If no owner appears, he is exposed for sale! — Oh, inhuman spectacle: found in no unjust act, convicted of no crime, he is barbarously sold like the produce off the soil, to the highest bidder, or what is still worse, for no crimes, without the inestimable privilege of a trial by his peers, doomed to the dreary walls of a prison for the term of seven tedious years. . . . Search the legends of tyranny and find no precedent. . . .

The . . . bill . . . prevents freemen from living where they please—Pennsylvania has always been a refuge from slavery, and to this state the Southern black, when freed, has flown for safety. Why does he this! When masters in many of the Southern states, which they frequently do, free a particular black, unless the black leaves the state in so many hours any person resident of the said state, can have him arrested and again sold to Slavery:—The hunted black is obliged to flee or remain and be again a slave. I have known persons of this discription sold three times after being first emancipated. Where shall he go? . . . Is there no spot on earth that will protect him! . . .

It is in vain that we are forming societies of different kinds to ameliorate the condition of our unfortunate brethren, to correct their morals and to render them not only honest but useful members to society. All our efforts by this bill, are despised, and we are doomed to feel the lash of oppression:—As well may we be outlawed, as well may the glorious privileges of the Gospel, be denied us, and all endeavours used to cut us off from happiness. . . . I trust the eloquence of nature will succeed, and the law-givers of this happy Commonwealth will yet remain the Black's friend, and the advocates of Freemen.

QUESTIONS FOR READING AND DISCUSSION

1. What legal principles did James Forten invoke in his criticisms against the Pennsylvania law? What moral principles did he appeal to? What historical experiences? Were the legal, moral, and historical standards compatible? Why or why not?

2. How would the law operate? What was its purpose? What consequences would it have, according to Forten?

3. In what ways were African Americans "degraded," according to Forten? How would the proposed law further degrade free men of color?

4. To whom did Forten appeal to change the law, and why did he believe "the eloquence of nature will succeed"?

DOCUMENT 10–5

James Hamilton's Path to Enlistment during the War of 1812

Americans interpreted liberty in a number of ways, not all of them informed by integrity or morality. James Hamilton enlisted and served in the infantry during the War of 1812, deserting numerous times before being honorably discharged in 1817. About a year later Hamilton reenlisted and at one point became engaged in a dispute with his commander, shooting and killing him. Just before his execution for murder, Hamilton dictated a confession that catalogued his misdeeds. In the excerpt below, Hamilton described the path he followed from his infancy to the army, disclosing experiences common among young men in the early republic who, unlike Hamilton, did not become murderers.

Confession, 1818

My birth, like my death, was the combined effect of infamy and sin. I was the illegitimate offspring of a mother whom I never knew, and of a father of whom I am equally ignorant. . . . The place of my nativity was in the city of New-York, and my birth occurred on the 2d of May, 1791. I was informed that I was nursed by hand, and that my mother died while I was an infant. At four or five years of age I recollect living with one James Hunter, and some time with Susan Griffin and a while with one Polly Blytham. . . .

At the age of ten years I was put, by my supposed father, to one William Cummings, who adopted me as his nephew. . . . He sent me to the house of John Morrison . . . at Little Britain, where I attended the school of one Mr. Ellison, between two and three years, and made some proficiency in learning. With Mr. Morrison I went to New-York and staid a few days with my adopted uncle; from there I was sent to live with Barnabas Manney, in Blooming Grove, and attended the school of one Patrick Fellemyth, where I was whipped almost daily for fighting with, and abusing my school-fellows. At this school I learnt nothing, paying no attention whatever to my book—Conceiving my master was too severe, I engaged ten other boys with myself to seize him one morning upon his coming into school, give him a beating, then throw him on the fire and keep him there until he was severely scorched. This project was luckily prevented by some young children of a Mr. Herod giving information to their father, who, together with other neighbors came to the school-house, and instead of our abusing the master, he, in the presence of the parents, severely flogged us; the marks of which I carried for some time. After this, instead of going into school I would play the truant. Mr. Manney, perceiving my untowardness, took me from school and set me at work. . . . While with Mr. Manney, I was compelled to attend church, but minded little what the minister said. . . . I was at length sent . . . [to] Mr. James Hultz, to Decker Town . . . in the county of Orange—with him I continued about three months, with intent to learn the trade of a tanner and shoe-maker, which trades, Mr. Hultz then pursued, but he being absent one day, left me in the care of an apprentice by the name of Reuben Sergeant, with whom I fought and very severely cut him with my shoe knife; on the return of Mr. Hultz, I was taken to the tan-house, questioned and lied, and was pretty severely chastised with small rods, for which reason, I next evening made my escape to Little Britain, and went to the house of Mr. Morrison. After staying there two days, his sons gave me some money, and I went to a brother of Mr. Manney's, a blacksmith, residing in Pleasant Valley, in the county of Duchess. I intended, with him, to learn the trade of a blacksmith, of which I had always been fond, but he having an apprentice would not take me—this apprentice, (a Mr. Baxter) got me into the shop of one William Hunter, with whom I continued seven or eight months, and made quite a proficiency in the trade; and he being, as I thought, too often absent, I left him and went to work four or five months with a quaker and farmer, named Green, who gave me a good suit of clothes and recommended me to a blacksmith in New-Windsor, by the name of Chauncey Wooden—with him I labored about four months, for which he paid me $32, and I then went to the city of New-York, and here met with

From James Hamilton, *The Life and Dying Confession of James Hamilton, Executed for the Murder of Major Benjamin Birdsall, November 6, 1818, at Albany* (New York, 1819), 3–6.

an acquaintance by the name of Lemuel Minton, who got me employed with him on board a small schooner, belonging to one William Wendell, (a methodist;) with him I continued about six weeks, when Menton and myself, from wrestling commenced fighting, and the captain coming on deck while I had Menton down, struck me, upon which I seized a billet of wood and instantly drove both Menton and my employer off the schooner—I then jumped on the wharf, and a short time after returned with the same cudgel, and drove them off again, went into the cabin, took my clothes and approaching Mr. Wendell, demanded of him instant payment, and threatened, upon his refusal, to pound him to a jelly, whereupon he took out fifteen dollars and handed me—I then left him and went to work for about two months with a Mr. Clark, of Peekskill, a farmer—from thence to Augustus Taylor's, where I stayed about four months, then went with one David Haven to New-York, where I boarded with a widow Odle; here I went to work for a blacksmith named John Johnson for one dollar a day, and for about three weeks paid my board regularly, at the end of which I falsely told Mrs. Odle I could not get my pay from Johnson, and after staying two weeks longer she turned me away. I then went to board with a Mr. Yeomans, and three days after I was arrested at the suit of the widow Odle, and Mr. Johnson became security for the debt; shortly after which I sold my trunk and clothes for thirty dollars to one of his journeymen, paid Mr. Johnson and left him—I then commenced visiting scenes of vice and prostitution. . . . During this time I became acquainted with Hugh M'Clellan, a sailor, and in his company I spent about three months longer, living by gaming, (at which M'Clellan was quite an adept)—by him I was introduced to a decent house kept by the widow Pullis, who had one son and two daughters; with the eldest, named Catherine, then about eighteen, I soon formed an acquaintance; and after a courtship of about three months, married her; but alas, vice had at that time taken such deep root in my bosom, that I could not (although I dearly loved my wife) refrain from visiting prostitutes. I found at length, I was diseased by this course of dissipation, and daring not to visit my wife, I did (unknown to her) ship in a schooner . . . bound to Norfolk, Va. At Norfolk I tarried about two weeks; thence I went to Alexandria; thence to Baltimore and Boston, and thence back to New-York, where I found myself the father of a son (of which I had been informed at Norfolk,) notwithstanding which, I made it a practice, at each port, to visit houses of debauchery. With my wife I continued three or four weeks, and then went again to Alexandria and to Norfolk, and again returned to New-York, where, by my wife's request, I left the schooner and continued about two months doing no business, constantly gambling, drinking and visiting houses of ill fame. I then went with capt. Williams to Alexandria—I there left him and hired myself for some time as an ostler [stableman] to James Brooks, who kept the city hotel—here I wrote several letters to my wife and received three from her . . . which informed me that she had a second child, and a daughter; upon this I became, without cause, very jealous, believing the child not mine, and wrote her for answer, "I did not care." . . . M'Clellan and myself went with one capt. Weeks to Norfolk, where we, together with a young Englishman, shipped on board a brig . . . for Cadiz. . . . On our return to Norfolk, M'Clellan and myself went in a small schooner to Boston, and . . . went to the house of one Richard Connelly, in Tin Pot. . . . Here I became acquainted with a prostitute named Sally Smith; and she, together with one Charlotte Hatch, handsomely supported me, they often contending and fighting on my account.—During my stay in Boston, I received several letters from my wife, and I wrote several in return, professing love and attachment to her, having at this time been satisfied the daughter was my own; but being so long habituated to vice, I continued my old course. M'Clellan here shipped on board the navy, received his three months bounty, and soon after concluded to run away; upon which I started with him to travel through the country. We came to the house of one John Green a little over the mountain; he having formerly been a sea captain, but since, a steady, worthy religious farmer, who kindly took us in. . . . [W]e went to work in a few days with him, and he was so well pleased with me that he offered me twelve dollars per month by the year, and soon after our arrival, proposed going to a store and buying me a long suit of clothes for sunday; but M'Clellan wishing to go to Albany, I accompanied him . . . [and] we went to work for Pliny Miller, chopping wood at seventy-five cents per cord — M'Clelland and myself labored for about three weeks, when I borrowed for [M'Clellan], three dollars [from] Miller, and [M'Clellan] went off, but where I have never heard. . . . I continued with Miller about three months and worked very hard, but he being a tavern keeper, I fell in his debt for rum about thirty dollars. One day when he was attending the court at Troy, (he being also a constable) I left him and came to Albany. . . . [B]ut on going to [a militia] rendezvous . . . and hearing one of the soldiers say "whoever enlists cannot be taken for debt and that clears them for ever," and fearing that Miller would follow me and put me in prison, I instantly consented to enlist and went . . . and took the oath of enlistment. I stayed at the rendezvous one month and was much pleased with the life of a soldier, being kindly treated by my officers, and myself always appearing neat and clean and doing my duty faithfully. One day, however, sergeant Roberts struck a soldier with his rattan [switch] for speaking on parade; upon which I told the sergeant if he were to strike me in that way I would give him a flogging; for this rash declaration I was sent to the guard-house and put in irons. . . . [L]ieut. Bliss called upon me and . . . observed that I was bound by my oath to obey my superior officers and that the sergeant was one. I replied that I never swore to be *whipped* by my officers, and if they should do it I would desert.

QUESTIONS FOR READING AND DISCUSSION

1. What examples did Hamilton give of his "infamy and sin"? To what extent did these result from Hamilton's liberty? According to Hamilton, why did he behave as he did?

2. Hamilton specified the names of many people with whom he lived and worked. What does that suggest, if anything, about relations among people in the early republic? To what extent did those relations influence Hamilton?

3. How would you describe Hamilton's occupation? How do you think he would have described his occupation? What does his pattern of work suggest about the character of employment in the early republic?

4. Hamilton often used and threatened violence, once telling an employer he would "pound him to a jelly." Why did Hamilton resort to violence? What purposes did he seek to achieve? Did his behavior cause problems in the army that he did not confront in civilian life?

5. Hamilton moved around a great deal. How would you describe his home? How do you think he would describe his home? Do you think his experiences were typical of many young American men? If so, which ones?

1. How did Thomas Jefferson's ideas about America compare with those of A Slave and James Forten?

2. To what extent were Jefferson's goals for Native Americans consistent with Meriwether Lewis's observations about the Shoshone? Did Jefferson and Lewis believe that Indians could participate fully and equally in American society? If so, how? If not, why not?

3. To what extent do the documents in this chapter suggest a broad agreement among Americans about the meaning of liberty during these years? To what extent do these documents suggest that Americans significantly disagreed about the meaning of liberty?

4. In what ways do the documents in this chapter provide evidence of the strength of democratic aspirations in the first quarter of the nineteenth century? To what extent did democratic values inform Jeffersonian ideas, A Slave's letter, Forten's protest, and relations with Native Americans? What values competed with democracy?

11 The Expanding Republic

1815–1840

During the 1820s and 1830s, as Americans continued to migrate westward, they disagreed over how social and economic institutions should be influenced by the ideals of liberty, equality, and democracy. Were corporations and banks to be feared as undemocratic concentrations of power, or were they institutions that fostered economic improvement for all? Were families nurseries of good citizens or prisons to which women were sentenced for life? Should Indian lands be reserved for the use of native tribes or opened to white settlers? Should slavery be abolished or preserved and expanded? The following documents illustrate some of the ways Americans grappled with such questions.

DOCUMENT 11–1

President Andrew Jackson's Parting Words to the Nation

As president, Andrew Jackson battled what he considered unconstitutional schemes to expand the powers of the federal government. Determined to defeat the consolidated powers of the monied interests, he championed the many against the few. When Jackson relinquished the presidency to Martin Van Buren in March 1837, he surveyed the political principles that governed Jacksonian Democrats. His farewell address, excerpted here, discloses the suspicion of power felt by many in Jackson's America.

Farewell Address, **March 4, 1837**

We have now lived almost fifty years under the Constitution framed by the sages and patriots of the Revolution. . . . Our Constitution is no longer a doubtful experiment, and at the end of nearly half a century we find that it has preserved

From James D. Richardson, ed., *A Compilation of the Messages and Papers of the Presidents, 1789–1897* (New York: Bureau of National Literature, 1969), 4:1512–27.

unimpaired the liberties of the people, secured the rights of property, and that our country has improved and is flourishing beyond any former example in the history of nations. . . .

In the legislation of Congress also, and in every measure of the general government, justice to every portion of the United States should be faithfully observed. No free government can stand without virtue in the people and a lofty spirit of patriotism, and if the sordid feelings of mere selfishness shall usurp the place which ought to be filled by public spirit, the legislation of Congress will soon be converted into a scramble for personal and sectional advantages. Under our free institutions the citizens of every quarter of our country are capable of attaining a high degree of prosperity and happiness without seeking to profit themselves at the expense of others; and every such attempt must in the end fail to succeed, for the people in every part of the United States are too enlightened not to understand their own rights and interests and to detect and defeat every effort to gain undue advantages over them; and when such designs are discovered it naturally provokes resentments which can not always be easily allayed. Justice — full and ample justice — to every portion of the United States should be the ruling principle of every freeman, and should guide the deliberations of every public body, whether it be state or national.

It is well known that there have always been those amongst us who wish to enlarge the powers of the general government, and experience would seem to indicate that there is a tendency on the part of this government to overstep the boundaries marked out for it by the Constitution. Its legitimate authority is abundantly sufficient for all the purposes for which it was created, and its powers being expressly enumerated, there can be no justification for claiming anything beyond them. Every attempt to exercise power beyond these limits should be promptly and firmly opposed, for one evil example will lead to other measures still more mischievous; and if the principle of constructive powers or supposed advantages or temporary circumstances shall ever be permitted to justify the assumption of a power not given by the Constitution, the general government will before long absorb all the powers of legislation, and you will have in effect but one consolidated government. From the extent of our country, its diversified interests, different pursuits, and different habits, it is too obvious for argument that a single consolidated government would be wholly inadequate to watch over and protect its interests; and every friend of our free institutions should be always prepared to maintain unimpaired and in full vigor the rights and sovereignty of the states and to confine the action of the general government strictly to the sphere of its appropriate duties. . . .

Plain as these principles appear to be, you will yet find there is a constant effort to induce the general government to go beyond the limits of its taxing power and to impose unnecessary burdens upon the people. Many powerful interests are continually at work to procure heavy duties on commerce and to swell the revenue beyond the real necessities of the public service, and the country has already felt the injurious effects of their combined influence. They succeeded in obtaining a tariff of duties bearing most oppressively on the agricultural and laboring classes of society and producing a revenue that could not be usefully employed within the range of the powers conferred upon Congress, and in order to fasten upon the people this unjust and unequal system of taxation extravagant schemes of internal improvement were got up in various quarters to squander the money and to purchase support. Thus one unconstitutional measure was intended to be upheld by another, and the abuse of the power of taxation was to be maintained by usurping the power of expending the money in internal improvements. You can not have forgotten the severe and doubtful struggle through which we passed when the executive department of the government by its veto endeavored to arrest this prodigal scheme of injustice and to bring back the legislation of Congress to the boundaries prescribed by the Constitution. The good sense and practical judgment of the people when the subject was brought before them sustained the course of the Executive, and this plan of unconstitutional expenditures for the purposes of corrupt influence is, I trust, finally overthrown. . . .

But, rely upon it, the design to collect an extravagant revenue and to burden you with taxes beyond the economical wants of the Government is not yet abandoned. The various interests which have combined together to impose a heavy tariff and to produce an overflowing Treasury are too strong and have too much at stake to surrender the contest. The corporations and wealthy individuals who are engaged in large manufacturing establishments desire a high tariff to increase their gains. Designing politicians will support it to conciliate their favor and to obtain the means of profuse expenditure for the purpose of purchasing influence in other quarters; and since the people have decided that the federal government can not be permitted to employ its income in internal improvements, efforts will be made to seduce and mislead the citizens of the several states by holding out to them the deceitful prospects of benefits to be derived from a surplus revenue collected by the general government and annually divided among the states; and if, encouraged by these fallacious hopes, the states should disregard the principles of economy which ought to characterize every republican government, and should indulge in lavish expenditures exceeding their resources, they will before long find themselves oppressed with debts which they are unable to pay, and the temptation will become irresistible to support a high tariff in order to obtain a surplus for distribution. Do not allow yourselves, my fellow-citizens, to be misled on this subject. The federal government can not collect a surplus for such purposes without violating the principles of the Constitution and assuming powers which have not been granted. It is, moreover, a system of injustice, and if persisted in will inevitably lead to corruption, and must end in ruin. The surplus revenue will be drawn from the pockets of the people—from the farmer, the mechanic, and the laboring classes of society; but who will receive it when distributed among the states, where it is to be disposed of by leading state politicians, who have friends to favor and political partisans to gratify? It will certainly not be returned to those who paid it and who have most need of it and are honestly entitled to it. There is but one safe rule, and that is to confine the general government rigidly within the sphere of its appropriate duties. It has no power to raise a revenue or impose taxes except for the purposes enumerated in the Constitution, and if its income is found to exceed these wants it should be forthwith reduced and the burden of the people so far lightened. . . .

Recent events have proved that the paper-money system of this country may be used as an engine to undermine your free institutions, and that those who desire to engross all power in the hands of the few and to govern by corruption or force are aware of its power and prepared to employ it. . . .

But when the charter for the Bank of the United States was obtained from Congress it perfected the schemes of the paper system and gave to its advocates the position they have struggled to obtain from the commencement of the federal government to the present hour. The immense capital and peculiar privileges bestowed upon it enabled it to exercise despotic sway over the other banks in every part of the country. From its superior strength it could seriously injure, if not destroy, the business of any one of them which might incur its resentment; and it openly claimed for itself the power of regulating the currency throughout the United States. In other words, it asserted (and it undoubtedly possessed) the power to make money plenty or scarce at its pleasure, at any time and in any quarter of the Union, by controlling the issues of other banks and permitting an expansion or compelling a general contraction of the circulating medium, according to its own will. . . . The result of the ill-advised legislation which established this great monopoly was to concentrate the whole moneyed power of the Union, with its boundless means of corruption and its numerous dependents, under the direction and command of one acknowledged head, thus organizing this particular interest as one body and securing to it unity and concert of action throughout the United States, and enabling it to bring forward upon any occasion its entire and undivided strength to support or defeat any measure of the government. . . .

The distress and alarm which pervaded and agitated the whole country when the Bank of the United States waged war upon the people in order to compel them to submit to its demands can not yet be forgotten. The ruthless and unsparing temper with which whole cities and communities were oppressed, individuals impoverished and ruined, and a scene of cheerful prosperity suddenly changed into one of gloom and despondency ought to be indelibly impressed on the memory of the people of the United States. . . . No nation but the freemen of the United States could have come out victorious from such a contest; yet, if you had not conquered, the government would have passed from the hands of the many to the hands of the few, and this organized money power from its secret conclave would have dictated the choice of your highest officers and compelled you to make peace or war, as best suited their own wishes. . . .

It is one of the serious evils of our present system of banking that it enables one class of society — and that by no means a numerous one — by its control over the currency, to act injuriously upon the interests of all the others and to exercise more than its just proportion of influence in political affairs. The agricultural, the mechanical, and the laboring classes have little or no share in the direction of the great moneyed corporations, and from their habits and the nature of their pursuits they are incapable of forming extensive combinations to act together with united force. . . .

The planter, the farmer, the mechanic, and the laborer all know that their success depends upon their own industry and economy, and that they must not expect to become suddenly rich by the fruits of their toil. Yet these classes of society form the great body of the people of the United States; they are the bone and sinew of the country — men who love liberty and desire nothing but equal rights and equal laws, and who, moreover, hold the great mass of our national wealth, although it is distributed in moderate amounts among the millions of freemen who possess it. But with overwhelming numbers and wealth on their side they are in constant danger of losing their fair influence in the government, and with difficulty maintain their just rights against the incessant efforts daily made to encroach upon them. . . . [U]nless you become more watchful in your states and check this spirit of monopoly and thirst for exclusive privileges you will in the end find that the most important powers of government have been given or bartered away, and the control over your dearest interests has passed into the hands of these corporations.

The paper-money system and its natural associations — monopoly and exclusive privileges — have already struck their roots too deep in the soil, and it will require all your efforts to check its further growth and to eradicate the evil. The men who profit by the abuses and desire to perpetuate them will continue to besiege the halls of legislation in the general government as well as in the states, and will seek by every artifice to mislead and deceive the public servants. . . .

The progress of the United States under our free and happy institutions has surpassed the most sanguine hopes of the founders of the Republic. Our growth has been rapid beyond all former example in numbers, in wealth, in knowledge, and all the useful arts which contribute to the comforts and convenience of man, and from the earliest ages of history to the present day there never have been thirteen millions of people associated in one political body who enjoyed so much freedom and happiness as the people of these United States. You have no longer any cause to fear danger from abroad; your strength and power are well known throughout the civilized world, as well as the high and gallant bearing of your sons. It is from within, among yourselves — from cupidity, from corruption, from disappointed ambition and inordinate thirst for power — that factions will be formed and liberty endangered. It is against such designs, whatever disguise the actors may assume, that you have especially to guard yourselves. You have the highest of human trusts committed to your care. Providence has showered on this favored land blessings without number, and has chosen you as the guardians of freedom, to preserve it for the benefit of the human race.

QUESTIONS FOR READING AND DISCUSSION

1. What did Jackson cite as the principal dangers to free government? Why were "expressly enumerated" constitutional powers important?

2. How and why had "powerful interests," including "the money power," exercised their influence? In what ways had Jackson dealt with them while he was president?

3. How did Jackson believe freedom could be protected? Why did he expect that the future danger to liberty would be "from within, among yourselves"?

4. To what extent did Jackson envision a future significantly different from the past? What did he identify as the major changes under way in American society? Did he seek largely to restore a golden past or to shape a transformed future?

DOCUMENT 11–2

Cherokees Debate Removal

President Jackson proudly announced to Congress in 1830 that the "benevolent policy of the government . . . in relation to the removal of the Indians beyond the white settlements is approaching to a conclusion." To the Indians being removed, the policy did not appear benevolent. In 1836, Congress ratified the Treaty of New Echota, which provided that the Cherokees would relinquish all claims to land east of the Mississippi in return for land west of the Mississippi, a large cash payment, and help moving to their new homes. The treaty bitterly divided Cherokees. The largest group, led by the principal chief, John Ross, opposed the treaty and insisted that the Cherokees not give up their lands. A minority group, led by Elias Boudinot, signed the treaty and urged other Cherokees to accept its terms. The following selections from letters by Ross and Boudinot reveal the clashing assessments among Cherokees about the threats they confronted and how best to respond to them.

John Ross
Answer to Inquiries from a Friend, 1836

I wish I could acquiesce in your impression, that a Treaty has been made, by which every difficulty between the Cherokees and the United States has been set at rest; but I must candidly say, that I know of no such Treaty. I do not mean to prophesy any similar troubles to those which have, in other cases, followed the failure to adjust disputed points with Indians; the Cherokees act on a principle preventing apprehensions of that nature—their principle is, "endure and forbear"; but I must distinctly declare to you that I believe, the document[1] signed by unauthorized individuals at Washington, will never be regarded by the Cherokee nation as a Treaty. The delegation appointed by the people to make a Treaty, have protested against that instrument "as deceptive to the world and a fraud upon the Cherokee people." . . .

With your impressions concerning the advantages secured by the subtle instrument in question, you will, no doubt, wonder at this opposition. But it possesses not the advantages you and others imagine; and that is the reason why it has encountered, and ever will encounter opposition. You suppose we are to be removed through it from a home, by circumstances rendered disagreeable and even untenable, to be secured in a better home, where nothing can disturb or dispossess us. *Here is the great mystification.* We are not secured in the new home promised to us. We are exposed to precisely the same miseries, from which, if this measure is enforced, the United States' power professes to relieve us, but does so entirely by the exercise of that power, against our will.

If we really had the security you and others suppose we have, we would not thus complain. . . .

One impression concerning us, is, that though we object to removal, as we are equally averse to becoming citizens of the United States, we ought to be forced to remove; to be tied hand and foot and conveyed to the extreme western frontier, and then turned loose among the wild beasts of the wilderness. Now, the fact is, we never have objected to become citizens of the United States and to conform to her laws; but in the event of conforming to her laws, we have required the protection and privileges of her laws to accompany that conformity on our part. We have asked this repeatedly and repeatedly has it been denied. . . .

In conclusion I would observe, that I still strongly hope we shall find ultimate justice from the good sense of the administration and of the people of the United States. I will not even yet believe that either the one or the other would wrong us

---

From John Ross, *Letter in Answer to Inquiries from a Friend*, July 2, 1836; Elias Boudinot, *Letters and Other Papers Relating to Cherokee Affairs: Being a Reply to Sundry Publications by John Ross*, 1837, in *The Cherokee Removal: A Brief History with Documents*, eds. Theda Perdue and Michael D. Green (Boston: Bedford Books, 1995), 147–51, 153–59.

[1] **the document**: The Treaty of New Echota.

with their eyes open. I am persuaded they have erred only in ignorance, and an ignorance forced upon them by the misrepresentation and artifices of the interested. . . . The Cherokees, under any circumstances, have no weapon to use but argument. If that should fail, they must submit, when their time shall come, in silence, but honest argument they cannot think will be forever used in vain. The Cherokee people will always hold themselves ready to respect a *real* treaty and bound to sustain any treaty which they can feel that they are bound to respect. But they are certain not to consider the attempt of a very few persons to sell the country for themselves, as obligatory upon them, and I and all my associates in the regular delegation, still look confidently to the effect of a sense of justice upon the American community, in producing a real settlement of this question, upon equitable terms and with competent authorities. But, on one point, you may be perfectly at rest. Deeply as our people feel, I cannot suppose they will ever be goaded by those feelings to any acts of violence. No, sir. They have been too long inured [accustomed] to suffering without resistance, and they still look to the sympathies and not to the fears, of those who have them in their power. In certain recent discussions in the representative hall at Washington, our enemies made it an objection against me and against others, that we were not Indians, but had *the principles* of white men, and were consequently unworthy of a hearing in the Indian cause. I will own that it has been my pride, as Principal Chief of the Cherokees, to implant in the bosoms of the people, and to cherish in my own, *the principles* of white men! It is to this fact that our white neighbours must ascribe their safety under the smart of the wrongs we have suffered from them. It is in this they may confide for our continued patience. But when I speak of *the principles* of white men, I speak not of such principles as actuate those who talk thus to us, but of those mighty principles to which the United States owes her greatness and her liberty. To principles like these even yet we turn with confidence for redemption from our miseries. When Congress shall be less overwhelmed with business, no doubt, in some way, the matter may be brought to a reconsideration, and when the representatives of the American people have leisure to see how little it will cost them to be just, we are confident they will be true to themselves, in acting with good faith towards us. Be certain that while the Cherokees are endeavouring to obtain a more friendly consideration from the United States, they will not forget to show by their circumspection how well they merit it; and though no doubt there are many who will represent them otherwise, for injurious purposes, I can assure you that the white people have nothing to apprehend, even from our sense of contumely[2] and unfairness, unless it be through the perverse and the treacherous manoeuvres of such agents as they themselves may keep among us.

Elias Boudinot
A Reply to John Ross, 1837

"What is to be done?" was a natural inquiry, after we found that all our efforts to obtain redress from the General Government, *on the land of our fathers*, had been of no avail. The first rupture among ourselves was the moment we presumed to answer that question. To a portion of the Cherokee people it early became evident

---

[2]**contumely**: Humiliating insults.

that the interest of their countrymen and the happiness of their posterity, depended upon an entire change of policy. Instead of contending uselessly against superior power, the only course left, was, to yield to circumstances over which they had no control.

In all difficulties of this kind, between the United States and the Cherokees, the only mode of settling them has been by treaties; consequently, when a portion of our people became convinced that no other measures would avail, they became the *advocates of a treaty*, as the only means to extricate the Cherokees from their perplexities; hence they were called *the treaty party*. Those who maintained the old policy, were known as the *anti-treaty party*. At the head of the latter has been Mr. John Ross. . . .

To advocate a treaty was to declare war against the established habits of thinking peculiar to the aborigines. It was to come in contact with settled prejudices — with the deep rooted attachment for the soil of our forefathers. Aside from these natural obstacles, the influence of the chiefs, who were ready to take advantage of the well known feelings of the Cherokees, in reference to their lands, was put in active requisition against us. . . .

It is with sincere regret that I notice you [John Ross] say little or nothing about the moral condition of this people, as affected by present circumstances. I have searched in vain, in all your late communications, for some indication of your sensibility upon this point. . . . Indeed, you seem to have forgotten that your people are a community of moral beings, capable of an elevation to an equal standing with the most civilized and virtuous, or a deterioration to the level of the most degraded, of our race. . . . Can it be possible that you consider the mere pains and privations of the body, and the loss of a paltry sum of money, of a paramount importance to the depression of the mind and the degradation and pollution of the soul? That the difficulties under which they are laboring, originating from the operation of the State laws, and their absorption by a white population, *will* affect them in that light, I need not here stop to argue with you: that they have *already* affected them, is a fact too palpable, too notorious, for us to deny it: that they will *increase* to affect them, in proportion to the delay of applying the remedy, we need only judge from past experience. How, then, can you reconcile your conscience and your sense of what is demanded by the best interest of your people. . . . How can you persist in deluding your people with phantoms, and in your opposition to that which alone is practicable, when you see them dying a moral death?

To be sure, from your account of the condition and circumstances of the Cherokees, the public may form an idea different from what my remarks may seem to convey. When applied to a portion of our people, confined mostly to whites intermarried among us, and the descendants of whites, your account is probably correct . . . but look at the mass, look at the entire population as it now is, and say, can you see any indication of a progressing improvement, anything that can encourage a philanthropist? You know that it is almost a dreary waste. I care not if I am accounted a slanderer of my country's reputation; every observing man in this nation knows that I speak the words of truth and soberness. In the light that I consider my countrymen, not as mere animals, and to judge of their happiness by their condition as such, which, to be sure, is bad enough, but as moral beings, to be affected for better or for worse by moral circumstances, I say their condition is wretched. Look, my dear sir, around you, and see the progress that vice and immorality have already made! see the spread of intemperance, and the wretchedness and misery it has already occasioned! I need not reason with a man of your sense and discernment, and of your observation, to show the debasing character of that vice to our people; you will find an argument in every tippling shop in the country; you will find its cruel effects in the bloody tragedies that are frequently occurring in the frequent convictions and executions for murders, and in the tears and groans of the widows and fatherless, rendered homeless, naked, and hungry, by this vile curse of our race. And has it stopped its cruel ravages with the lower or poorer classes of our people? Are the higher orders, if I may so speak, left untainted? While there are honorable exceptions in all classes . . . it is not to be denied that, as a people, we are making a rapid tendency to a general immorality and debasement. What more evidence do we need, to prove this general tendency, than the slow but sure insinuation of the lower vices into our female population? Oh! it is heart-rending to think of these things, much more to speak of them; but the world *will* know them, the world *does* know them, and we need not try to hide our shame. . . .

If the dark picture which I have here drawn is a true one, and no candid person will say it is an exaggerated one, can we see a brighter prospect ahead? In another country, and under other circumstances, there is a *better* prospect. Removal, then, is the only remedy, the only *practicable* remedy. By it there *may be* finally a renovation; our people *may* rise from their very ashes, to become prosperous and happy, and a credit to our race. Such has been and is now my opinion, and under such a settled opinion I have acted in all this affair. My language has been; "fly for your lives"; it is now the same. I would say to my countrymen, you among the rest, fly from the moral pestilence that will finally destroy our nation.

What is the prospect in reference to *your* plan of relief, if you are understood at all to have any plan? It is dark and gloomy beyond description. Subject the Cherokees to the laws of the States in their present condition? It matters not how favorable those laws may be, instead of remedying the evil you would only rivet the chains and fasten the manacles of their servitude and degradation. The final destiny of our race, under such circumstances, is too revolting to think of. Its course must be downward, until it finally becomes extinct or is merged in another race, more ignoble and more detested. Take my word for it, it is the sure consummation, if you succeed in preventing the removal of your people. The time will come when there will be only here and there those who can be called upon to sign a protest, or to vote against a treaty for their removal; when the few remnants of our once happy and improving nation will be viewed by posterity with curious and gazing interest, as relics of a brave and noble race. Are our people destined to such a catastrophe? Are we to run the race of all our brethren who have gone before us, and of whom hardly any thing is known but their name, and, perhaps, only here and there a solitary being, waking, "as a ghost over the ashes of his fathers," to remind a stranger that such a race *once* existed? May God preserve us from such a destiny.

QUESTIONS FOR READING AND DISCUSSION

1. For Ross, what did the principle "endure and forbear" suggest the Cherokee should do? In what sense did Ross believe argument was a "weapon"?

2. What was Ross's view of the "*principles* of white men"? How did they differ from the principles of Cherokees?

3. According to Boudinot, why was removal "the only course left"? Why was "the moral condition" of the Cherokees an inducement for removal?

4. According to Boudinot, what would be the result of following Ross's plan and not leaving ancestral lands in the East?

5. How did Ross and Boudinot differ in their views of whites and of state and federal governments? How did they differ in their views of Cherokees? What did each see as the most important sources of security and safety?

DOCUMENT 11–3

Alexis de Tocqueville Describes the Three Races in the United States

In 1831 Alexis de Tocqueville, a young nobleman, came to the United States to study innovative prisons, but he soon became fascinated by the people and institutions of the young nation that seemed strikingly different from his native France. After almost two years of traveling throughout the United States, Tocqueville returned to France and, in 1835, published the first volume of Democracy in America, *his analysis of the distinctive features of American society and government. Tocqueville's work was heralded in Europe and America at the time and has been recognized as a classic work ever since. In the excerpt below, Tocqueville described the "three races" that resided in the United States and sketched his views of their futures. Tocqueville's remarks arose from his firsthand observations during his travels as well as from his numerous conversations with Americans — ranging from President Andrew Jackson to Native Americans and slaves — and from his own outlook as a French aristocrat.*

Democracy in America, 1835

THE PRESENT AND PROBABLE FUTURE CONDITION OF THE THREE RACES THAT INHABIT THE TERRITORY OF THE UNITED STATES

The human beings who are scattered over [the United States] . . . do not form, as in Europe, so many branches of the same stock. Three races, naturally distinct, and, I might almost say, hostile to each other, are discoverable among them at the first glance. Almost insurmountable barriers had been raised between them by education and law, as well as by their origin and outward characteristics, but fortune has brought them together on the same soil, where, although they are mixed, they do not amalgamate, and each race fulfills its destiny apart.

Among these widely differing families of men, the first that attracts attention, the superior in intelligence, in power, and in enjoyment, is the white, or European, the MAN preeminently so called, below him appear the Negro and the Indian. These two unhappy races have nothing in common, neither birth, nor features, nor language, nor habits. Their only resemblance lies in their misfortunes. Both of them occupy an equally inferior position in the country they inhabit; both suffer from tyranny; and if their wrongs are not the same, they originate from the same authors.

If we reason from what passes in the world, we should almost say that the European is to the other races of mankind what man himself is to the lower

From Alexis de Tocqueville, *Democracy in America*, trans. Henry Reeve (London: Longman, 1862), Book 1, chapter 18.

animals: he makes them subservient to his use, and when he cannot subdue he destroys them. Oppression has, at one stroke, deprived the descendants of the Africans of almost all the privileges of humanity. The Negro of the United States has lost even the remembrance of his country; the language which his forefathers spoke is never heard around him; he abjured their religion and forgot their customs when he ceased to belong to Africa, without acquiring any claim to European privileges. But he remains half-way between the two communities, isolated between two races; sold by the one, repulsed by the other; finding not a spot in the universe to call by the name of country, except the faint image of a home which the shelter of his master's roof affords.

The Negro has no family: woman is merely the temporary companion of his pleasures, and his children are on an equality with himself from the moment of their birth. . . . The Negro, plunged in this abyss of evils, scarcely feels his own calamitous situation. Violence made him a slave, and the habit of servitude gives him the thoughts and desires of a slave, he admires his tyrants more than he hates them, and finds his joy and his pride in the servile imitation of those who oppress him. His understanding is degraded to the level of his soul.

The Negro enters upon slavery as soon as he is born, nay, he may have been purchased in the womb, and have begun his slavery before he began his existence. Equally devoid of wants and of enjoyment, and useless to himself, he learns, with his first notions of existence, that he is the property of another, who has an interest in preserving his life, and that the care of it does not devolve upon himself; even the power of thought appears to him a useless gift of Providence, and he quietly enjoys all the privileges of his debasement.

If he becomes free, independence is often felt by him to be a heavier burden than slavery; for, having learned in the course of his life to submit to everything except reason, he is too unacquainted with her dictates to obey them. A thousand new desires beset him, and he has not the knowledge and energy necessary to resist them: these are masters which it is necessary to contend with, and he has learned only to submit and obey. In short, he is sunk to such a depth of wretchedness that while servitude brutalizes, liberty destroys him.

Oppression has been no less fatal to the Indian than to the Negro race, but its effects are different. Before the arrival of white men in the New World, the inhabitants of North America lived quietly in their woods, enduring the vicissitudes and practicing the virtues and vices common to savage nations. The Europeans having dispersed the Indian tribes and driven them into the deserts, condemned them to a wandering life, full of inexpressible sufferings.

Savage nations are only controlled by opinion and custom. When the North American Indians had lost the sentiment of attachment to their country; when their families were dispersed, their traditions obscured, and the chain of their recollections broken; when all their habits were changed, and their wants increased beyond measure, European tyranny rendered them more disorderly and less civilized than they were before. The moral and physical condition of these tribes continually grew worse, and they became more barbarous as they became more wretched. Nevertheless, the Europeans have not been able to change the character of the Indians; and though they have had power to destroy, they have never been able to subdue and civilize them.

The lot of the Negro is placed on the extreme limit of servitude, while that of the Indian lies on the uttermost verge of liberty; and slavery does not produce more fatal effects upon the first than independence upon the second. The Negro has lost all property in his own person, and he cannot dispose of his existence without committing a sort of fraud. But the savage is his own master as soon as he is able to act; parental authority is scarcely known to him; he has never bent his will to that of any of his kind, nor learned the difference between voluntary obedience and a shameful subjection; and the very name of law is unknown to him. To be free, with him, signifies to escape from all the shackles of society. As he delights in this barbarous independence and would rather perish than sacrifice the least part of it, civilization has little hold over him.

The Negro makes a thousand fruitless efforts to insinuate himself among men who repulse him; he conforms to the tastes of his oppressors, adopts their opinions, and hopes by imitating them to form a part of their community. Having been told from infancy that his race is naturally inferior to that of the whites, he assents to the proposition and is ashamed of his own nature. In each of his features he discovers a trace of slavery, and if it were in his power, he would willingly rid himself of everything that makes him what he is.

The Indian, on the contrary, has his imagination inflated with the pretended nobility of his origin, and lives and dies in the midst of these dreams of pride. Far from desiring to conform his habits to ours, he loves his savage life as the distinguishing mark of his race and repels every advance to civilization, less, perhaps, from hatred of it than from a dread of resembling the Europeans. . . .

The Negro, who earnestly desires to mingle his race with that of the European, cannot do so; while the Indian, who might succeed to a certain extent, disdains to make the attempt. The servility of the one dooms him to slavery, the pride of the other to death. . . .

These are great evils; and it must be added that they appear to me to be irremediable. I believe that the Indian nations of North America are doomed to perish, and that whenever the Europeans shall be established on the shores of the Pacific Ocean, that race of men will have ceased to exist. The Indians had only the alternative of war or civilization; in other words, they must either destroy the Europeans or become their equals. . . .

The Indians will perish in the same isolated condition in which they have lived, but the destiny of the Negroes is in some measure interwoven with that of the Europeans. These two races are fastened to each other without intermingling; and they are alike unable to separate entirely or to combine. The most formidable of all the ills that threaten the future of the Union arises from the presence of a black population upon its territory; and in contemplating the cause of the present embarrassments, or the future dangers of the United States, the observer is invariably led to this as a primary fact. . . .

[T]he abstract and transient fact of slavery is fatally united with the physical and permanent fact of color. The tradition of slavery dishonors the race, and the peculiarity of the race perpetuates the tradition of slavery. . . . Thus the Negro transmits the eternal mark of his ignominy [disgrace] to all his descendants; and although the law may abolish slavery, God alone can obliterate the traces of its existence.

The modern slave differs from his master not only in his condition but in his origin. You may set the Negro free, but you cannot make him otherwise than an alien to the European. Nor is this all; we scarcely acknowledge the common features of humanity in this stranger whom slavery has brought among us. His physiognomy is to our eyes hideous, his understanding weak, his tastes low; and we are almost inclined to look upon him as a being intermediate between man and the brutes. The moderns, then, after they have abolished slavery, have three prejudices to contend against, which are less easy to attack and far less easy to conquer than the mere fact of servitude: the prejudice of the master, the prejudice of the race, and the prejudice of color. . . .

The pride of origin, which is natural to the English, is singularly augmented by the personal pride that democratic liberty fosters among the Americans: the white citizen of the United States is proud of his race and proud of himself. But if the whites and the Negroes do not intermingle in the North of the Union, how should they mix in the South? Can it be supposed for an instant that an American of the Southern states, placed, as he must forever be, between the white man, with all his physical and moral superiority, and the Negro, will ever think of being confounded with the latter? The Americans of the Southern states have two powerful passions which will always keep them aloof: the first is the fear of being assimilated to the Negroes, their former slaves; and the second, the dread of sinking below the whites, their neighbors. . . .

The danger of a conflict between the white and the black inhabitants of the Southern states of the Union (a danger which, however remote it may be, is inevitable) perpetually haunts the imagination of the Americans, like a painful dream. . . .

I am obliged to confess that I do not regard the abolition of slavery as a means of warding off the struggle of the two races in the Southern states. The Negroes may long remain slaves without complaining; but if they are once raised to the level of freemen, they will soon revolt at being deprived of almost all their civil rights; and as they cannot become the equals of the whites, they will speedily show themselves as enemies. . . .

When I contemplate the condition of the South, I can discover only two modes of action for the white inhabitants of those States: namely, either to emancipate the Negroes and to intermingle with them, or, remaining isolated from them, to keep them in slavery as long as possible. All intermediate measures seem to me likely to terminate, and that shortly, in the most horrible of civil wars and perhaps in the extirpation of one or the other of the two races. Such is the view that the Americans of the South take of the question, and they act consistently with it. As they are determined not to mingle with the Negroes, they refuse to emancipate them.

QUESTIONS FOR READING AND DISCUSSION

1. According to Tocqueville, how did the three races of America differ from each other? Why did he believe the races were "hostile to each other"?

2. Why did Tocqueville believe that "the European is to the other races of mankind what man himself is to the lower animals"? According to Tocqueville, what made groups of people, such as Europeans, Indians, and Negroes, "a race"?

3. What evidence did Tocqueville offer to support his argument that "the lot of the Negro is placed on the extreme limit of servitude, while that of the Indian lies on the uttermost verge of liberty"?

4. Why, according to Tocqueville, were "three prejudices . . . less easy to attack and far less easy to conquer than the mere fact of servitude: the prejudice of the master, the prejudice of the race, and the prejudice of color"?

5. What future did Tocqueville foresee for Europeans, Indians, and Negroes and why?

DOCUMENT 11–4

David Walker Demands Emancipation

A free African American born in North Carolina in 1785 to a free mother and a slave father, David Walker traveled throughout the United States before settling in Boston in 1827, where he ran a secondhand clothing store. Outraged by slavery and white suprem-acy, Walker wrote an incendiary appeal to other people of color to work for the emancipa-tion of all slaves. Walker lambasted slaveholders, whites, and Christians for accepting slavery and discriminating against people of African descent. He also criticized slaves and free African Americans for accommodating to slavery and failing to work for emancipation. Walker's Appeal, *excerpted below, circulated widely and alarmed many whites with its justification for slaves to rise up against their masters. Walker died under mysterious cir-cumstances in 1830; he may have been poisoned in retaliation for publishing his* Appeal.*

Appeal to the Colored Citizens of the World, 1829

[I promise] ... to demonstrate in the course of ... my Appeal ... that we Coloured People of these United States, are, the most wretched, degraded and abject set of beings that ever lived since the world began, down to the present day, and, that, the white Christians of America, who hold us in slavery, (or, more prop-erly speaking, pretenders to Christianity,) treat us more cruel and barbarous than any Heathen nation did any people whom it had subjected, or reduced to the same condition, that the Americans ... have us. . . .

It is expected that all coloured men, women and children (who are not too deceitful, abject, and servile to resist the cruelties and murders inflicted upon us by the white slave holders, our enemies by nature) of every nation, language and tongue under heaven, will try to procure a copy of this Appeal and read it, or get some one to read it to them, for it is designed more particularly for them. . . .

And as the inhuman system of slavery, is the source from which most of our miseries proceed, I shall begin with that curse to nations, which has spread terror and devastation through so many nations of antiquity, and which is raging to such a pitch at the present day in Spain and in Portugal. It had one tug in England, in France, and in the United States of America. . . . The fact is, the labour of slaves comes so cheap to the avaricious usurpers, and is (as they think) of such great utility to the country where it exists, that those who are actuated by sordid avarice only, overlook the evils, which will as sure as the Lord lives, follow after the good. In fact, they are so happy to keep in ignorance and degradation, and to receive the homage and the labour of the slaves, they forget that God rules in the armies of heaven and among the inhabitants of the earth, having his ears continually open to the cries, tears and groans of his oppressed people; and being a just and holy Being will at one day appear fully in behalf of the oppressed, and arrest the prog-ress of the avaricious oppressors; for although the destruction of the oppressors

From David Walker, *Walker's Appeal in Four Articles; Together with a Preamble, To the Coloured Citizens of the World, but in Particular, and Very Expressly, to Those of the United States of America Written in Boston, State of Massachusetts, September 28, 1829* (Boston: Revised and Published by David Walker, 1830).

God may not effect by the oppressed, yet the Lord our God will bring other destructions upon them—for not unfrequently will he cause them to rise up one against another, to be split and divided, and to oppress each other, and sometimes to open hostilities with sword in hand. . . .

Now I appeal to heaven and to earth, and particularly to the American people themselves, who cease not to declare that our condition is not hard, and that we are comparatively satisfied to rest in wretchedness and misery, under them and their children. Not, indeed, to show me a coloured President, a Governor, a Legislator, a Senator, a Mayor, or an Attorney at the Bar.—But to show me a man of colour, who holds the low office of a Constable, or one who sits in a Juror Box, even on a case of one of his wretched brethren, throughout this great Republic!! . . .

Do they not institute laws to prohibit us from marrying among the whites? I would wish, candidly, however, before the Lord, to be understood, that I would not give a pinch of snuff to be married to any white person I ever saw in all the days of my life. . . .

They think because they hold us in their infernal chains of slavery, that we wish to be white, or of their color—but they are dreadfully deceived—we wish to be just as it pleased our Creator to have made us, and no avaricious and unmerciful wretches, have any business to make slaves of, or hold us in slavery. How would they like for us to make slaves of, and hold them in cruel slavery, and murder them as they do us? . . .

Fear not the number and education of our enemies, against whom we shall have to contend for our lawful right; guaranteed to us by our Maker; for why should we be afraid, when God is, and will continue, (if we continue humble) to be on our side?

The man who would not fight under our Lord and Master Jesus Christ, in the glorious and heavenly cause of freedom and of God—to be delivered from the most wretched, abject and servile slavery, that ever a people was afflicted with since the foundation of the world, to the present day—ought to be kept with all of his children or family, in slavery, or in chains, to be butchered by his cruel enemies. . . .

I therefore ask the whole American people, had I not rather die, or be put to death, than to be a slave to any tyrant, who takes not only my own, but my wife and children's lives by the inches? Yea, would I meet death with avidity far! far!! in preference to such servile submission to the murderous hands of tyrants. . . .

I must observe to my brethren that at the close of the first Revolution in this country, with Great Britain, there were but thirteen States in the Union, now there are twenty-four, most of which are slave-holding States, and the whites are dragging us around in chains and in handcuffs, to their new States and Territories to work their mines and farms, to enrich them and their children—and millions of them believing firmly that we being a little darker than they, were made by our Creator to be an inheritance to them and their children for ever—the same as a parcel of brutes.

Are we MEN!!—I ask you, O my brethren! are we MEN? Did our Creator make us to be slaves to dust and ashes like ourselves? . . .

Read the history particularly of Hayti, and see how they were butchered by the whites, and do you take warning. . . . God will indeed, deliver you through him from your deplorable and wretched condition under the Christians of America. . . .

The whites want slaves, and want us for their slaves, but some of them will curse the day they ever saw us. As true as the sun ever shone in its meridian splendor, my colour will root some of them out of the very face of the earth. They shall have enough of making slaves of, and butchering, and murdering us in the manner which they have. No doubt some may say that I write with a bad spirit, and that I being a black, wish these things to occur. Whether I write with a bad or a good spirit, I say if these things do not occur in their proper time, it is because the world in which we live does not exist. . . .

Hayti, the glory of the blacks and terror of tyrants, is enough to convince the most avaricious and stupid of wretches. . . .

Any man who is curious to see the full force of ignorance developed among the coloured people of the United States of America, has only to go into the southern and western states of this confederacy, where, if he is not a tyrant, but has the feelings of a human being, who can feel for a fellow creature, he may see enough to make his very heart bleed! He may see there, a son take his mother, who bore almost the pains of death to give him birth, and by the command of a tyrant, strip her as naked as she came into the world, and apply the cow-hide to her, until she falls a victim to death in the road! He may see a husband take his dear wife, not unfrequently in a pregnant state, and perhaps far advanced, and beat her for an unmerciful wretch, until his infant falls a lifeless lump at her feet! . . . My observer may see fathers beating their sons, mothers their daughters, and children their parents, all to pacify the passions of unrelenting tyrants. He may also, see them telling news and lies, making mischief one upon another. These are some of the productions of ignorance, which he will see practised among my dear brethren, who are held in unjust slavery and wretchedness, by avaricious and unmerciful tyrants. . . . And when my curious observer comes to take notice of those who are said to be free, (which assertion I deny) and who are making some frivolous pretentions to common sense, he . . . may see some of my brethren in league with tyrants, selling their own brethren into hell upon earth, not dissimilar to the exhibitions in Africa, but in a more secret, servile and abject manner. . . . My observer may see some of those ignorant and treacherous creatures (coloured people) sneaking about in the large cities, endeavouring to find out all strange coloured people, where they work and where they reside, asking them questions, and trying to ascertain whether they are runaways or not, telling them, at the same time, that they always have been, are, and always will be, friends to their brethren; and, perhaps, that they themselves are absconders, and a thousand such treacherous lies to get the better information of the more ignorant!!! There have been and are at this day in Boston, New-York, Philadelphia, and Baltimore, coloured men, who are in league with tyrants, and who receive a great portion of their daily bread, of the moneys which they acquire from the blood and tears of their more miserable brethren, whom they scandalously delivered into the hands of our natural enemies!!!!!! . . .

[W]e are, by our treachery, wickedness and deceit, working against ourselves and our children — helping ours, and the enemies of God, to keep us and our dear little children in their infernal chains of slavery!!! . . .

Men of colour, who are also of sense, for you particularly is my APPEAL designed. Our more ignorant brethren are not able to penetrate its value. I call upon you therefore to cast your eyes upon the wretchedness of your brethren, and to do your utmost to enlighten them. . . . I met a coloured man in the street a short time since, with a string of boots on his shoulders; we fell into conversation, and in course of which, I said to him, what a miserable set of people we are! He asked, why?—Said I, we are so subjected under the whites, that we cannot obtain the comforts of life, but by cleaning their boots and shoes, old clothes, waiting on them, shaving them &c. Said he, (with the boots on his shoulders) "I am completely happy!!! I never want to live any better or happier than when I can get a plenty of boots and shoes to clean!!!" . . . Understand me, brethren, I do not mean to speak against the occupations by which we acquire enough and sometimes scarcely that, to render ourselves and families comfortable through life. I am subjected to the same inconvenience, as you all.—My objections are, to our glorying and being happy in such low employments; for if we are men, we ought to be . . . looking forward with thankful hearts to higher attainments than wielding the razor and cleaning boots and shoes. . . . I advance it therefore to you . . . as an unshaken and for ever immoveable fact, that your full glory and happiness, as well as all other coloured people under Heaven, shall never be fully consummated, but with the entire emancipation of your enslaved brethren all over the world.

QUESTIONS FOR READING AND DISCUSSION

1. According to Walker, how had "the white Christians of America" made the "Coloured People of these United States . . . the most wretched, degraded and abject set of beings"? What was Walker's view of God? What did he believe God would do about slavery? How and why?

2. In what ways, according to Walker, was "slavery . . . the source from which most of our miseries proceed"? How did slavery affect Walker, who was free? How did it affect other free African Americans, in Walker's view? How did it affect slaves?

3. What did Walker believe "Men of colour" should do about slavery? How should they deal with the reality of their poverty and marginality? What should slaves do?

4. Who did Walker see as the enemies of African Americans? Who did he see as allies?

5. What did Walker envision about the future of the United States? What grounds did he have for projecting such a future?

DOCUMENT 11–5

Sarah Grimké on the Status of Women

The ideals of liberty and equality appealed strongly to many American women. Those ideals confronted the strength of male supremacy and of widespread assumptions about the proper domestic role for women. Sarah Grimké took a leading role in attacking the unjust subordination of women in American life. The daughter of a wealthy slaveholder in Charleston, South Carolina, Grimké found slavery repugnant and moved to Philadelphia, where she became a Quaker and a leader for women's rights and abolition. Grimké's Letters on the Equality of the Sexes and the Condition of Women, *published in 1838 and excerpted here, reveals her criticisms of the prevailing inequality of the sexes.*

Letters on the Equality of the Sexes, 1838

During the early part of my life, my lot was cast among the butterflies of the *fashionable* world; and of this class of women, I am constrained to say, both from experience and observation, that their education is miserably deficient; that they are taught to regard marriage as the one thing needful, the only avenue to distinction; hence to attract the notice and win the attentions of men, by their external charms, is the chief business of fashionable girls. They seldom think that men will be allured by intellectual acquirements, because they find, that where any mental superiority exists, a woman is generally shunned and regarded as stepping out of her "appropriate sphere," which, in their view, is to dress, to dance, and to set out to the best possible advantage her person, to read the novels which inundate the press, and which do more to destroy her character as a rational creature, than any thing else. Fashionable women regard themselves, and are regarded by men, as pretty toys or as mere instruments of pleasure; and the vacuity of mind, the heartlessness, the frivolity which is the necessary result of this false and debasing estimate of women, can only be fully understood by those who have mingled in the folly and wickedness of fashionable life; and who have been called from such pursuits by the voice of the Lord Jesus, inviting their weary and heavy laden souls to come unto Him and learn of Him, that they may find something worthy of their immortal spirit, and their intellectual powers; that they may learn the high and holy purposes of their creation, and consecrate themselves unto the service of God; and not, as is now the case, to the pleasure of man.

There is another and much more numerous class in this country, who are withdrawn by education or circumstances from the circle of fashionable amusements, but who are brought up with the dangerous and absurd idea, that marriage is a kind of preferment; and that to be able to keep their husband's house, and render his situation comfortable, is the end of her being. Much that she does and says and thinks is done in reference to this situation; and to be married is too often held up to the view of girls as the sine qua non of human happiness and human existence. For this purpose more than for any other, I verily believe the majority of girls are trained. This is demonstrated by the imperfect education which is bestowed upon them, and the little pains taken to cultivate their minds, after they leave school by the little time allowed them for reading, and by the idea being constantly inculcated, that although all household concerns should be attended to with scrupulous punctuality at particular seasons, the improvement of their intellectual capacities, is only a secondary consideration, and may serve as an occupation to fill up the odds and ends of time. In most families, it is considered a matter of far more consequence to call a girl off from making a pie, or a pudding, than to interrupt her whilst engaged in her studies. This mode of training necessarily exalts, in their view, the animal above the intellectual and spiritual nature, and teaches women to regard themselves as a kind of machinery, necessary to keep the domestic engine in order, but of little value as the *intelligent* companions of men.

Let no one think, from these remarks, that I regard a knowledge of housewifery as beneath the acquisition of women. Far from it: I believe that a complete knowledge of household affairs is an indispensable requisite in a woman's educa-

---

From Sarah Grimké, *Letters on the Equality of the Sexes and the Condition of Women* (Boston: I. Knapp, 1838).

tion,—that by the mistress of a family, whether married or single, doing her duty thoroughly and *understandingly*, the happiness of the family is increased to an incalculable degree, as well as a vast amount of time and money saved. All I complain of is, that our education consists so almost exclusively in culinary and other manual operations. I do long to see the time, when it will no longer be necessary for women to expend so many precious hours in furnishing "a well spread table," but that their husbands will forgo some of their accustomed indulgences in this way, and encourage their wives to devote some portion of their time to mental cultivation, even at the expense of having to dine sometimes on baked potatoes, or bread and butter. . . .

There is another way in which the general opinion, that women are inferior to men, is manifested, that bears with tremendous effect on the laboring class, and indeed on almost all who are obliged to earn a subsistence, whether it be by mental or physical exertion—I allude to the disproportionate value set on the time and labor of men and of women. A man who is engaged in teaching, can always, I believe, command a higher price for tuition than a woman—even when he teaches the same branches, and is not in any respect superior to the woman. This I know is the case in boarding and other schools with which I have been acquainted, and it is so in every occupation in which the sexes engage indiscriminately. As for example, in tailoring, a man has twice, or three times as much for making a waistcoat or pantaloons as a woman, although the work done by each may be equally good. In those employments which are peculiar to women, their time is estimated at only half the value of that of men. A woman who goes out to wash, works as hard in proportion as a wood sawyer, or a coal heaver, but she is not generally able to make more than half as much by a day's work. The low remuneration which women receive for their work, has claimed the attention of a few philanthropists, and I hope it will continue to do so until some remedy is applied for this enormous evil. . . . All these things evince the low estimation in which woman is held. There is yet another and more disastrous consequence arising from this unscriptural notion—women being educated, from earliest childhood, to regard themselves as inferior creatures, have not that self-respect which conscious equality would engender, and hence when their virtue is assailed, they yield to temptation with facility, under the idea that it rather exalts than debases them, to be connected with a superior being.

There is another class of women in this country, to whom I cannot refer, without feelings of the deepest shame and sorrow. I allude to our female slaves. Our southern cities are whelmed beneath a tide of pollution; the virtue of female slaves is wholly at the mercy of irresponsible tyrants, and women are bought and sold in our slave markets, to gratify the brutal lust of those who bear the name of Christians. In our slave States, if amid all her degradation, and ignorance, a woman desires to preserve her virtue unsullied, she is either bribed or whipped into compliance, or if she dares resist her seducer, her life by the laws of some of the slave States may be, and has actually been sacrificed to the fury of disappointed passion. Where such laws do not exist, the power which is necessarily vested in the master over his property, leaves the defenceless slave entirely at his mercy, and the sufferings of some females on this account, both physical and mental, are intense. . . . But even if any laws existed in the United States, as in Athens formerly, for the protection of female slaves, they would be null and void, because the evidence of a colored person is not admitted against a white, in any of our Courts of Justice in the slave States. . . .

Nor does the colored woman suffer alone: the moral purity of the white woman is deeply contaminated. In the daily habit of seeing the virtue of her enslaved sister sacrificed without hesitancy or remorse, she looks upon the crimes of seduction and illicit intercourse without horror, and although not personally involved in the guilt, she loses that value for innocence in her own, as well as the other sex, which is one of the strongest safeguards to virtue. She lives in habitual intercourse with men, whom she knows to be polluted by licentiousness, and often is she compelled to witness in her own domestic circle, those disgusting and heart-sickening jealousies and strafes which disgraced and distracted the family of Abraham. In addition to all this, the female slaves suffer every species of degradation and cruelty, which the most wanton barbarity can inflict; they are indecently divested of their clothing, sometimes tied up and severely whipped, sometimes prostrated on the earth, while their naked bodies are torn by the scorpion lash. . . .

Can any American woman look at these scenes of shocking licentiousness and cruelty, and fold her hands in apathy, and say, "I have nothing to do with slavery"? *She cannot and be guiltless.*

QUESTIONS FOR READING AND DISCUSSION

1. According to Grimké, what were the deficiencies of "the butterflies of the *fashionable* world"?

2. Why were "women being educated, from earliest childhood, to regard themselves as inferior creatures"? In what ways did this sense of inferiority affect women? How should women be educated, according to Grimké? Why did she believe that a "knowledge of housewifery" was "an indispensable requisite in a woman's education"?

3. What were the particular oppressions of slave women? What meanings did Grimké attach to the term *enslaved sister*? Why was "the moral purity of the white woman . . . deeply contaminated" by slavery?

4. How did Grimké propose to promote the equality of the sexes?

COMPARATIVE QUESTIONS

1. How did the vision of the future expressed by John Ross, Elias Boudinot, and David Walker compare with that of Andrew Jackson and Alexis de Tocqueville?

2. How did Jackson's opposition to the concentration of power compare with Sarah Grimké's criticisms of the inequality of the sexes? To what extent would Jackson have agreed with Grimké and vice versa?

3. The Cherokees, Grimké, and Walker confronted powerful, widespread, and hostile attitudes and interests. What methods did they plan to use to change attitudes and overcome opposing interests? What were the principal ideas that both aided and hindered their efforts? How might Tocqueville have responded to their methods and goals?

4. Judging from the documents in this chapter, how did the experiences of the federal government, Cherokees, women, and abolitionists reflect the achievements and limitations of democracy and equality during the 1820s and 1830s?

12 The New West and the Free North

1840–1860

mericans in the 1840s and 1850s celebrated freedom, democracy, and opportunity. Whether clearing land for a farm, moving west to start over, opening a store, or working in a factory, many Americans took advantage of what Abraham Lincoln and others called the free-labor system. Free labor unleashed human potential, its proponents claimed, and made possible the era's impressive economic growth and geographic expansion. The achievements of free labor came at a price, however, as others pointed out. Competition and accumulation stunted human growth. Women, blacks, and others were excluded from enjoying the virtues of free labor. Both the shortcomings and the strengths of free labor were magnified in the frenzy of the California gold rush. Still, according to free-labor proponents like Lincoln, education combined with hard work promised unmatched opportunities for white men.

DOCUMENT 12–1

Abraham Lincoln Explains the Free-Labor System

In 1859, Abraham Lincoln—a prominent Illinois lawyer and Republican Party leader— described to the Wisconsin Agricultural Society the benefits of hard work, free labor, and education. Although Lincoln grew up on small farms in Kentucky, Indiana, and Illinois, he had not worked on a farm in nearly thirty years. Lincoln's speech, excerpted below, portrayed the individual and social progress made possible by the free-labor system. In part, Lincoln silently suggested that his personal career—a poor, uneducated log-cabin farm boy who became a prosperous, educated attorney and politician—was a model that all Americans should aspire to emulate.

Address before the Wisconsin State Agricultural Society, Milwaukee, Wisconsin, September 30, 1859

I presume I am not expected to employ the time assigned me, in the mere flattery of the farmers, as a class. My opinion of them is that, in proportion to numbers, they are neither better nor worse than other people. In the nature of things they are more numerous than any other class; and I believe there really are more attempts at flattering them than any other; the reason of which I cannot perceive, unless it be that they can cast more votes than any other. . . .

But farmers, being the most numerous class, it follows that their interest is the largest interest. It also follows that that interest is most worthy of all to be cherished and cultivated — that if there be inevitable conflict between that interest and any other, that other should yield. . . .

The effect of thorough cultivation upon the farmer's own mind, and, in reaction through his mind, back upon his business, is perhaps quite equal to any other of its effects. Every man is proud of what he does *well*; and no man is proud of what he does *not* do well. With the former, his heart is in his work; and he will do twice as much of it with less fatigue. The latter [he] performs a little imperfectly, looks at it in disgust, turns from it, and imagines himself exceedingly tired. The little he has done, comes to nothing, for want of finishing.

The man who produces a good full crop will scarcely ever let any part of it go to waste. He will keep up the enclosure about it, and allow neither man nor beast to trespass upon it. He will gather it in due season and store it in perfect security. Thus he labors with satisfaction, and saves himself the whole fruit of his labor. The other, starting with no purpose for a full crop, labors less, and with less satisfaction; allows his fences to fall, and cattle to trespass; gathers not in due season, or not at all. Thus the labor he has performed, is wasted away, little by little, till in the end, he derives scarcely anything from it. . . .

The world is agreed that *labor* is the source from which human wants are mainly supplied. There is no dispute upon this point. From this point, however, men immediately diverge. Much disputation is maintained as to the best way of applying and controlling the labor element. By some it is assumed that labor is available only in connection with capital — that nobody labors, unless somebody else, owning capital, somehow, by the use of that capital, induces him to do it. Having assumed this, they proceed to consider whether it is best that capital shall *hire* laborers, and thus induce them to work by their own consent; or *buy* them, and drive them to it without their consent. Having proceeded so far they naturally conclude that all laborers are necessarily either *hired* laborers, or *slaves*. They further assume that whoever is once a *hired* laborer, is fatally fixed in that condition for life; and thence again that his condition is as bad as, or worse than that of a slave. This is the "mud-sill" theory.

But another class of reasoners hold the opinion that there is no *such* relation between capital and labor, as assumed; and that there is no such thing as a freeman being fatally fixed for life, in the condition of a hired laborer, that both these assumptions are false, and all inferences from them groundless. They hold that labor is prior to, and independent of, capital; that, in fact, capital is the fruit of labor, and could never have existed if labor had not *first* existed — that labor can

From Roy P. Basler, ed., *Collected Works of Abraham Lincoln* (New Brunswick: Rutgers University Press, 1953), 3:471–82.

exist without capital, but that capital could never have existed without labor. Hence they hold that labor is the superior—greatly the superior—of capital.

They do not deny that there is, and probably always will be, *a* relation between labor and capital. The error, as they hold, is in assuming that the *whole* labor of the world exists within that relation. A few men own capital; and that few avoid labor themselves, and with their capital, hire, or buy, another few to labor for them. A large majority belong to neither class—neither work for others, nor have others working for them. Even in all our slave States, except South Carolina, a majority of the whole people of all colors, are neither slaves nor masters. In these Free States, a large majority are neither *hirers* nor *hired*. Men, with their families— wives, sons and daughters—work for themselves, on their farms, in their houses and in their shops, taking the whole product to themselves, and asking no favors of capital on the one hand, nor of hirelings or slaves on the other. It is not forgotten that a considerable number of persons mingle their own labor with capital; that is, labor with their own hands, and also buy slaves or hire freemen to labor for them; but this is only a *mixed*, and not a *distinct* class. No principle stated is disturbed by the existence of this mixed class. Again, as has already been said, the opponents of the "mud-sill" theory insist that there is not, of necessity, any such thing as the free hired laborer being fixed to that condition for life. There is demonstration for saying this. Many independent men, in this assembly, doubtless a few years ago were hired laborers. And their case is almost if not quite the general rule.

The prudent, penniless beginner in the world, labors for wages awhile, saves a surplus with which to buy tools or land, for himself; then labors on his own account another while, and at length hires another new beginner to help him. This, say its advocates, is *free* labor—the just and generous, and prosperous system, which opens the way for all—gives hope to all, and energy, and progress, and improvement of condition to all. If any continue through life in the condition of the hired laborer, it is not the fault of the system, but because of either a dependent nature which prefers it, or improvidence, folly, or singular misfortune.

I have said this much about the elements of labor generally, as introductory to the consideration of a new phase which that element is in process of assuming. The old general rule was that *educated* people did not perform manual labor. They managed to eat their bread, leaving the toil of producing it to the uneducated. This was not an insupportable evil to the working bees, so long as the class of drones remained very small. But *now*, especially in these free States, nearly all are educated—quite too nearly all, to leave the labor of the uneducated, in any wise adequate to the support of the whole. It follows from this that henceforth educated people must labor. Otherwise, education itself would become a positive and intolerable evil. No country can sustain, in idleness, more than a small percentage of its numbers. The great majority must labor at something productive. From these premises the problem springs, "How can *labor* and *education* be the most satisfactorily combined?"

By the "mud-sill" theory it is assumed that labor and education are incompatible; and any practical combination of them impossible. According to that theory, a blind horse upon a tread-mill, is a perfect illustration of what a laborer should be—all the better for being blind, that he could not tread out of place, or kick understandingly. According to that theory, the education of laborers, is not only useless, but pernicious, and dangerous. In fact, it is, in some sort, deemed a misfortune that laborers should have heads at all. Those same heads are regarded as explosive materials, only to be safely kept in damp places, as far as possible from that peculiar sort of fire which ignites them. A Yankee who could invent a strong *handed* man without a head would receive the everlasting gratitude of the "mud-sill" advocates.

But Free Labor says "no!" Free Labor argues that, as the Author of man makes every individual with one head and one pair of hands, it was probably intended that heads and hands should co-operate as friends; and that that particular head, should direct and control that particular pair of hands. As each man has one mouth to be fed, and one pair of hands to furnish food, it was probably intended that that particular pair of hands should feed that particular mouth—that each head is the natural guardian, director, and protector of the hands and mouth inseparably connected with it; and that being so, every head should be cultivated, and improved, by whatever will add to its capacity for performing its charge. In one word Free Labor insists on universal education.

I have so far stated the opposite theories of "Mud-Sill" and "Free Labor" without declaring any preference of my own between them. On an occasion like this I ought not to declare any. I suppose, however, I shall not be mistaken, in assuming as a fact, that the people of Wisconsin prefer free labor, with its natural companion, education.

This leads to the further reflection, that no other human occupation opens so wide a field for the profitable and agreeable combination of labor with cultivated thought, as agriculture. I know of nothing so pleasant to the mind, as the discovery of anything which is at once *new* and *valuable*—nothing which so lightens and sweetens toil, as the hopeful pursuit of such discovery. And how vast, and how varied a field is agriculture, for such discovery. The mind, already trained to thought, in the country school, or higher school, cannot fail to find there an exhaustless source of profitable enjoyment. Every blade of grass is a study; and to produce two, where there was but one, is both a profit and a pleasure. And not grass alone; but soils, seeds, and seasons—hedges, ditches, and fences, draining, droughts, and irrigation—plowing, hoeing, and harrowing—reaping, mowing, and threshing—saving crops, pests of crops, diseases of crops, and what will prevent or cure them—implements, utensils, and machines, their relative merits, and [how] to improve them—hogs, horses, and cattle—sheep, goats, and poultry—trees, shrubs, fruits, plants, and flowers—the thousand things of which these are specimens—each a world of study within itself.

In all this, book-learning is available. A capacity, and taste, for reading, gives access to whatever has already been discovered by others. It is the key, or one of the keys, to the already solved problems. And not only so. It gives a relish, and facility, for successfully pursuing the [yet] unsolved ones. The rudiments of science, are available, and highly valuable. Some knowledge of Botany assists in dealing with the vegetable world—with all growing crops. Chemistry assists in the analysis of soils, selection, and application of manures, and in numerous other ways. The mechanical branches of Natural Philosophy, are ready help in almost every-thing; but especially in reference to implements and machinery.

The thought recurs that education—cultivated thought—can best be combined with agricultural labor, or any labor, on the principle of *thorough* work—that careless, half performed, slovenly work, makes no place for such combination. And thorough work, again, renders sufficient, the smallest quantity of ground to each man. And this again, conforms to what must occur in a world less inclined to wars, and more devoted to the arts of peace, than heretofore. Population must increase rapidly—more rapidly than in former times—and ere long the most valuable of all arts, will be the art of deriving a comfortable subsistence from the smallest area of soil. No community whose every member possesses this art, can ever be the victim of oppression in any of its forms. Such community will be alike independent of crowned-kings, money-kings, and land-kings. . . .

Let us hope, rather, that by the best cultivation of the physical world, beneath and around us; and the intellectual and moral world within us, we shall secure an individual, social, and political prosperity and happiness, whose course shall be onward and upward, and which, while the earth endures, shall not pass away.

QUESTIONS FOR READING AND DISCUSSION

1. According to Lincoln, how did the free labor system contrast with "the 'mud-sill' theory"?

2. What evidence did Lincoln offer to show that free labor was "the just and generous, and prosperous system, which opens the way for all—gives hope to all, and energy, and progress, and improvement of condition to all"?

3. What significance did Lincoln attribute to his remark that "heads and hand should co-operate as friends"?

4. Why, according to Lincoln, did many Americans fail to achieve all the benefits of the free-labor system?

5. How might a landless farmer, an immigrant Irish laborer, a female domestic servant, or a free African American tradesman have responded to Lincoln's description of the free-labor system?

DOCUMENT 12–2

The Anxiety of Gain: Henry W. Bellows on Commerce and Morality

The opportunities that the free-labor system offered to striving, disciplined, frugal Americans had far more than economic consequences. Henry W. Bellows, a prominent Unitarian minister in New York City, criticized the personal and moral effects of Americans' desire to get ahead, to do better, to take care of business. In an article published in a Whig journal in 1845, Bellows analyzed a dark side of the free-labor system that its proponents usually ignored.

The Influence of the Trading Spirit upon the Social and Moral Life of America, 1845

All strangers who come among us remark the excessive anxiety written in the American countenance. The widespread comfort, the facilities for livelihood, the spontaneous and cheap lands, the high price of labor, are equally observed, and render it difficult to account for these lines of painful thoughtfulness. It is not poverty, nor tyranny, nor overcompetition which produces this anxiety; that is

---

From Henry W. Bellows, "The Influence of the Trading Spirit upon the Social and Moral Life of America," in *The American Review: A Whig Journal of Politics, Literature, Art, and Science* (1845).

clear. It is the concentration of the faculties upon an object, which in its very nature is unattainable—the perpetual improvement of the outward condition. There are no bounds among us to the restless desire to be better off; and this is the ambition of all classes of society. We are not prepared to allow that wealth is more valued in America than elsewhere, but in other countries the successful pursuit of it is necessarily confined to a few, while here it is open to all. No man in America is contented to be poor, or expects to continue so. There are here no established limits within which the hopes of any class of society must be confined, as in other countries. There is consequently no condition of hopes realized, in other words, of contentment. In other lands, if children can maintain the station and enjoy the means, however moderate, of their father, they are happy. Not so with us. This is not the spirit of our institutions. Nor will it long be otherwise in other countries. That equality, that breaking down of artificial barriers which has produced this universal ambition and restless activity in America, is destined to prevail throughout the earth. But because we are in advance of the world in the great political principle, and are now experiencing some of its first effects, let us not mistake these for the desirable fruits of freedom. Commerce is to become the universal pursuit of men. It is to be the first result of freedom, of popular institutions everywhere. Indeed, every land not steeped in tyranny is now feeling this impulse. But while trade is destined to free and employ the masses, it is also destined to destroy for the time much of the beauty and happiness of every land. This has been the result in our own country. We are free. It is a glorious thing that we have no serfs, with the large and unfortunate exception of our slaves—no artificial distinctions—no acknowledged superiority of blood—no station which merit may not fill—no rounds in the social ladder to which the humblest may not aspire. But the excitement, the commercial activity, the restlessness, to which this state of things has given birth, is far from being a desirable or a natural condition. It is natural to the circumstances, but not natural to the human soul. It is good and hopeful to the interests of the race, but destructive to the happiness, and dangerous to the virtue of the generation exposed to it.

Those unaccustomed, by reading or travel, to other states of society, are probably not aware how very peculiar our manner of life here is. The laboriousness of Americans is beyond all comparison, should we except the starving operatives of English factories. . . . Nay, we are all, no matter what our occupations, more or less, and all greatly, sufferers from the excessive stimulus under which every thing is done. We are all worn out with thought that does not develop our thinking faculties in a right direction, and with feeling expended upon poor and low objects. There is no profession that does not feel it. The lawyer must confine himself to his office, without vacation, to adjust a business which never sleeps or relaxes. The physician must labor day and night to repair bodies, never well from over-exertion, over-excitement, and over-indulgence. The minister must stimulate himself to supply the cravings of diseased moral appetites, and to arouse the attention of men deafened by the noise, and dizzy with the whirl in which they constantly live.

We call our country a happy country; happy, indeed, in being the home of noble political institutions, the abode of freedom; but very far from being happy in possessing a cheerful, light-hearted, and joyous people. Our agricultural regions even are infected with the same anxious spirit of gain. If ever the curse of labor was upon the race, it is upon us; nor is it simply now "by the sweat of thy brow thou shalt earn thy bread." Labor for a livelihood is dignified. But we labor for bread, and labor for pride, and labor for pleasure. A man's life with us does consist of the abundance of the things which he possesseth. To get, and to have the reputation of possessing, is the ruling passion. To it are bent all the energies of nine-tenths of our population. Is it that our people are so much more miserly and earth-born than any other? No, not by any constitutional baseness; but circumstances have necessarily given this direction to the American mind. In the hard soil of our common mother, New England — the poverty of our ancestors — their early thrift and industry — the want of other distinctions than those of property — the frown of the Puritans upon all pleasures; these circumstances combined, directed our energies from the first into the single channel of trade. And in that they have run till they have gained a tremendous head, and threaten to convert our whole people into mere money-changers and producers. Honor belongs to our fathers, who in times of great necessity met the demand for a most painful industry with such manly and unflinching hearts. But what was their hard necessity we are perpetuating as our willing servitude! what they bore as evil we seek as good. . . .

It is said that we are not a happy people. And it is true; for we most unwisely neglect all those free fountains of happiness which Providence has opened for all its children. Blessed beyond any people with the means of living, supplied to an unparalleled extent with the comforts and luxuries of life, our American homes are sombre and cheerless abodes. There is even in the air of comfort which their well-furnished apartments wear something uncomfortable. They are the habitations of those who do not live at home. They are wanting in a social and cheerful aspect. They seem fitted more to be admired than to be enjoyed. The best part of the house is for the occasional use of strangers, and not to be occupied by those who might, day by day, enjoy it, which is but one proof among many that we love to appear comfortable rather than to be so. Thus miserable pride hangs like a millstone about our hospitality. . . . We are ashamed of any thing but affluence, and when we cannot make an appearance, or furnish entertainments as showy as the richest, we will do nothing. Thus does pride close our doors. . . .

It is rare . . . to find a virtuous American past middle life, who does not regard amusements of all sorts either as childish or immoral; who possesses any acquaintance with or taste for the arts, except it be a natural and rude taste for music; or who reads any thing except newspapers, and only the political or commercial columns of those. It is the want of tastes for other things than business which gives an anxious and unhappy turn to our minds. It cannot be many years before the madness of devoting the whole day to the toils of the countinghouse will be acknowledged; before the claim of body and mind to relaxation and cheerful, exhilarating amusement will be seen. We consider the common suspicion which is felt of amusements among thoughtful people to be one of the most serious evils to which our community is exposed. . . . Children are without the protection of their parents in their enjoyments. And thus, too, is originated one of the greatest curses of our social state — the great want of intimacy and confidence between children and their parents, especially between fathers and sons.

Overt sins are more rare here than elsewhere. As far as morality is restrictive in its nature, it has accomplished a great work in America. The vices or sins which are reducible to statute, or known by name, are generally restrained. We have a large class of persons of extraordinary propriety and faultlessness of life. Our view of morals has a tendency to increase this class. Our pursuits are favorable to it. The love of gain is one of the most sober of all desires. The seriousness of a miser surpasses the gravity of a devotee. Did not every commercial city draw a large body of strangers to it, and attract many reckless and vicious persons, it would wear a very solemn aspect. The pleasure-seeking, the gay, the disorderly, are never the trading population. Large commercial cities tend to great orderliness and decency of manners and morals. But they also tend to very low and barren views of moral excellence. And the American spirit of our own day illustrates this. Our moral sense operates only in one direction. Our virtues are the virtues of merchants, and not of men. We run all to honesty, and mercantile honesty. We do not cultivate the graces of humanity. We have more conscience than heart, and more propriety than either. The fear of evil consequences is more influential than the love of goodness. There is nothing hearty, gushing, eloquent, in the national virtue. You do not see goodness leaking out from the full vessel at every motion it feels. Our goodness is formal, deliberate, premeditated. The upright man is not benevolent, and the just man is not generous. The good man is not cheerful. The religious man is not agreeable. In other words, our morals are partial, and there-fore barren. It is not generally understood how great scrupulousness of character may be united with great selfishness, and how, along with a substantial virtue, there may exist the most melancholy deficiencies. This seems to be very common with us, and to be the natural result of our engrossing pursuits. Every one minds his own business, to the extreme peril of his own soul. . . . Our social condition makes us wary, suspicious, slow to commit ourselves too far in interest for others. The shyness of the tradesman communicates itself to the manners of the visitor; we learn to live within ourselves; we grow unsocial, unfraternal in feeling; and the sensibility, the affection, the cordiality, the forth-putting graces of a warm and virtuous heart, die of disuse. For our part, we are ready to say, let us have more faults and more virtues; more weaknesses and more grace; less punctilio [petty formalities], and more affluence of heart. Let us be less dignified and more cordial; less sanctimonious and more unselfish; less thriving and more cheerful; less toil-some and more social.

We want, as a people, a rounder character. Our humanity is pinched; our tastes are not generous. The domestic and social virtues languish. . . . Children grow up unknown to their parents. The mature despise their own youth, and have no sympathy with the romance, the buoyancy, the gayety of their children. Enter-prise is our only enthusiasm. We grow to be ashamed of our best affections. We are afraid to acknowledge that we derive enjoyment from trifles, and make apolo-gies for being amused with any thing. Thus is the beautiful field of life burnt over, and all its spontaneous flowers and fruitage destroyed; a few towering trunks alone redeeming the landscape.

QUESTIONS FOR READING AND DISCUSSION

1. According to Bellows, what were the sources of the "anxious spirit of gain"?
2. Why was there no contentment in America? Why did comfort and morality coexist with narrowness and barrenness? To what extent did ideals of equality produce discontent?
3. What remedies did Bellows propose? Why would those remedies work?
4. Bellows analyzed the costs of Americans' pursuit of happiness. What stan-dards did he use to measure those costs? What alternative standards of happi-ness did he value?
5. Do you think most Americans would have agreed with Bellows? Why or why not?

DOCUMENT 12–3
Gold Fever

California gold epitomized the wealth and success that seemed just beyond the grasp of many Americans during the 1840s and 1850s. The gold rush offered opportunities for gain that years of ordinary toil could never supply. Gold was there for the taking, for the dissolute hustler as well as the upright practitioner of free-labor values. Or so it seemed. Walter Colton kept a diary as the gold fever struck Monterey, California, in the summer of 1849. Born in Vermont in 1797, Colton became a minister and served as a chaplain in the U.S. Navy. Shortly after Americans seized Monterey for the United States in 1846, Colton was appointed alcalde of the city, an office that combined duties of mayor and judge. When rumors of gold reached Monterey, Colton witnessed the contagion of gold fever and charted the spread of the epidemic in his diary, excerpted here.

Walter Colton
California Gold Rush Diary, 1849–1850

Monday, May 29 [1849]. Our town was startled out of its quiet dreams to-day, by the announcement that gold had been discovered on the American Fork. The men wondered and talked, and the women too; but neither believed. . . .

Monday, June 5. Another report reached us this morning from the American Fork. The rumor ran, that several workmen, while excavating for a millrace,[1] had thrown up little shining scales of a yellow ore, that proved to be gold; that an old Sonoranian,[2] who had spent his life in gold mines, pronounced it the genuine thing. Still the public incredulity remained, save here and there a glimmer of faith. . . .

Tuesday, June 6. Being troubled with the golden dream . . . , I determined to put an end to the suspense, and dispatched a messenger this morning to the American Fork. He will have to ride, going and returning, some four hundred miles, but his report will be reliable. We shall then know whether this gold is a fact or a fiction. . . .

Tuesday, June 20. My messenger sent to the mines, has returned with specimens of the gold; he dismounted in a sea of upturned faces. As he drew forth the yellow lumps from his pockets, and passed them around among the eager crowd, the doubts, which had lingered till now, fled. All admitted they were gold, except one old man, who still persisted they were some Yankee invention, got up to reconcile the people to the change of flag. The excitement produced was intense; and many were soon busy in their hasty preparations for a departure to the mines. The family who had kept house for me caught the moving infection. Husband and

---

From Walter Colton, *Three Years in California* (1850; Temecula, CA: Reprint Services Corp., 1992), 242–375.

[1]**millrace**: A channel for water to drive a mill wheel.

[2]**Sonoranian**:A person from the Sonora region of Mexico.

wife were both packing up; the blacksmith dropped his hammer, the carpenter his plane, the mason his trowel, the farmer his sickle, the baker his loaf, and the tapster his bottle. All were off for the mines, some on horses, some on carts, and some on crutches, and one went in a litter. An American woman, who had recently established a boarding-house here, pulled up stakes, and was off before her lodgers had even time to pay their bills. Debtors ran, of course. I have only a community of women left, and a gang of prisoners, with here and there a soldier, who will give his captain the slip at the first chance. I don't blame the fellow a whit; seven dollars a month, while others are making two or three hundred a day! [T]hat is too much for human nature to stand. . . .

Tuesday, July 18. Another bag of gold from the mines, and another spasm in the community. It was brought down by a sailor from Yuba river, and contains a hundred and thirty-six ounces. It is the most beautiful gold that has appeared in the market. . . . My carpenters, at work on the school-house, on seeing it, threw down their saws and planes, shouldered their picks, and are off for the Yuba. Three seamen ran from the Warren, forfeiting their four years' pay; and a whole platoon of soldiers from the fort left only their colors behind. . . .

Thursday, Aug. 16. Four citizens of Monterey are just in from the gold mines on Feather River, where they worked in company with three others. They employed about thirty wild Indians, who are attached to the rancho owned by one of the party. They worked precisely seven weeks and three days, and have divided seventy-six thousand eight hundred and forty-four dollars—nearly eleven thousand dollars to each. . . . [L]et me introduce a man, well known to me, who has worked on the Yuba river sixty-four days, and brought back, as the result of his individual labor, five thousand three hundred and fifty-six dollars. . . . [L]et me introduce another townsman, who has worked on the North Fork fifty-seven days, and brought back four thousand five hundred and thirty-four dollars. . . . Is not this enough to make a man throw down his ledger and shoulder a pick? . . .

Tuesday, Aug. 28. The gold mines have upset all social and domestic arrangements in Monterey; the master has become his own servant, and the servant his own lord. The millionaire is obliged to groom his own horse, and roll his own wheelbarrow; and the hidalgo[3]—in whose veins flows the blood of all the Cortes—to clean his own boots! Here is lady L——, who has lived here seventeen years, the pride and ornament of the place, with a broomstick in her jewelled hand! And here is lady B—— with her daughter—all the way from "old Virginia," where they graced society with their varied accomplishments—now floating between the parlor and kitchen, and as much at home in the one as the other! And here is lady S——, whose cattle are on a thousand hills, lifting, like Rachel of old, her bucket of water from the deep well! And here is lady M. L——, whose honeymoon is still full of soft seraphic [angelic] light, unhouseling a potatoe, and hunting the hen that laid the last egg. And here am I, who have been a man of some note in my day, loafing on the hospitality of the good citizens, and grateful for a meal, though in an Indian's wigwam. Why, is not this enough to make one wish the gold mines were in the earth's flaming centre, from which they sprung? . . .

---

[3]**hidalgo**: A landowner of Spanish descent.

Saturday, Sept. 16 . . . All distinctions indicative of means have vanished; the only capital required is muscle and an honest purpose. I met a man to-day from the mines in patched buckskins, rough as a badger from his hole, who had fifteen thousand dollars in yellow dust, swung at his back. . . . And there is more where this came from. His rights in the great domain are equal to yours, and his prospects of getting it out vastly better. With these advantages, he bends the knee to no man, but strides along in his buckskins, a lord of earth by a higher prescriptive privilege than what emanates from the partiality of kings. . . . Clear out of the way with your crests, and crowns, and pedigree trees, and let this democrat pass. . . .

Wednesday, Oct. 18. We are camped in the centre of the gold mines, in the heart of the richest deposits which have been found, and where there are many hundred at work. I have taken some pains to ascertain the average per man that is got out; it must be less than half an ounce per day. It might be more were there any stability among the diggers; but half their time is consumed in what they call prospecting; that is, looking up new deposits. An idle rumor, or more surmise, will carry them off in this direction or that, when perhaps they gathered nothing for their weariness and toil. . . . I have never met with one who had the strength of purpose to resist these roving temptations. . . .

Thursday, Oct. 19. All the gold-diggers through the entire encampment, were shaken out of their slumbers this morning by a report that a solid pocket of gold had been discovered in a bend of the Stanislaus. In half an hour a motley multitude, covered with crowbars, pickaxes, spades, rifles, and washbowls, went streaming over the hills in the direction of the new deposits. You would have thought some fortress was to be stormed, or some citadel sapped. . . . The most curious feature in this business is, that out of a regiment of gold-hunters, where the utmost apparent confusion prevails, the absence of two men should be noticed. But the motions of every man are watched. Even when he gathers up his traps, takes formal leave, and is professedly bound home, he is tracked for leagues. No disguise can avail him; the most successful war-stratagem would fail here. . . .

Thursday, Nov. 2. Quite a sensation was produced among the gold-diggers this morning by the arrival of a wagon from Stockton, freighted with provisions and a barrel of liquor. The former had been getting scarce, and the latter had long since entirely given out. The prices of the first importation were—flour, two dollars a pound; sugar and coffee, four dollars; and the liquor, which was nothing more nor less than New England rum, was twenty dollars the quart. But few had bottles: every species of retainer was resorted to; some took their quart cups, some their coffee-pots, and others their sauce-pans; while one fellow, who had neither, offered ten dollars to let him suck with a straw from the bung. All were soon in every variety of excitement, from prattling exhilaration, to roaring inebriety. Some shouted, some danced, and some wrestled: a son of Erin [Irishman] poured out his soul on the beauties of the Emerald isle; a German sung the songs of his fatherland; a Yankee apostrophized the mines, which swelled in the hills around; an Englishman challenged all the bears in the mountain glens to mortal combat; and a Spaniard, posted aloft on a beetling crag, addressed the universe. . . .

Wednesday, Nov. 8. Some fifty thousand persons are drifting up and down these slopes of the great Sierra, of every hue, language, and clime, tumultuous and confused as a flock of wild geese taking wing at the crack of a gun, or autumnal leaves strown on the atmospheric tides by the breath of the whirlwind. All are in quest of gold; and, with eyes dilated to the circle of the moon, rush this way and that, as some new discovery, or fictitious tale of success may suggest. Some are with tents, and some without; some have provisions, and some are on their last ration; some are carrying crowbars; some pickaxes and spades; some wash-bowls and cradles; some hammers and drills, and powder enough to blow up the rock of Gibraltar. . . . Such a mixed and motley crowd—such a restless, roving, rummaging, ragged multitude, never before roared in the rookeries of man. . . . Each great camping-ground is denoted by the ruins of shovels and shanties, the bleaching bones of the dead, disinhumed by the wolf, and the skeleton of the culprit, still swinging in the wind, from the limb of a tree, overshadowed by the raven. . . .

Monday, May 14 [1850]. Much has been said of the amounts of gold taken from the mines by Sonoranians, Chilians, and Peruvians, and carried out of the country. As a general fact, this apprehension and alarm is without any sound basis. Not one pound of gold in ten, gathered by these foreigners, is shipped off to their credit: it is spent in the country for provisions, clothing, and in the hazards of the gaming table. It falls into the hands of those who command the avenues of commerce, and ultimately reaches our own mints. I have been in a camp of five hundred Sonoranians, who had not gold enough to buy a month's provisions— all had gone, through their improvident habits, to the capacious pockets of the Americans. To drive them out of California, or interdict their operations, is to abstract that amount of labor from the mines, and curtail proportionably the proceeds. If gold, slumbering in the river banks and mountains of California, be more valuable to us than when stamped into eagles and incorporated into our national currency, then drive out the Sonoranians: but if you would have it here and not there, let those diggers alone. When gold shall begin to fail, or require capital and machinery, you will want these hardy men to quarry the rocks and feed your stampers; and when you shall plunge into the Cinnabar mountains, you will want them to sink your shafts and kindle fires under your great quicksilver retorts. They will become the hewers of wood and drawers of water to American capital and enterprise. But if you want to perform this drudgery yourself, drive out the Sonoranians, and upset that cherished system of political economy founded in a spirit of wisdom and national justice. . . .

Wednesday, June 20. The causes which exclude slavery from California lie within a nut-shell. All here are diggers, and free white diggers wont dig with slaves. They know they must dig themselves: they have come out here for that purpose, and they wont degrade their calling by associating it with slave-labor: self-preservation is the first law of nature. They have nothing to do with slavery in the abstract, or as it exists in other communities; not one in ten cares a button for its abolition, nor the Wilmot proviso either: all they look at is their own position; they must themselves swing the pick, and they wont swing it by the side of negro slaves. That is their feeling, their determination, and the upshot of the whole business. An army of half a million, backed by the resources of the United States, could not shake their purpose. Of all men with whom I have ever met, the most firm, resolute, and indomitable, are the emigrants into California. They feel that they have got into a new world, where they have a right to shape and settle things in their own way. No mandate, unless it comes like a thunder-bolt straight out of heaven, is regarded. . . . They walk over hills treasured with the precious ores; they dwell by streams paved with gold; while every mountain around soars into the heaven. . . . All these belong to them; they walk in their midst; they feel their presence and power, and partake of their grandeur. Think you that such men will consent to swing the pick by the side of slaves? Never! While the stream owns its source, or the mountain its base. You may call it pride, or what you will, but *there* it is—deep as the foundations of our nature, and unchangeable as the laws of its divine Author.

QUESTIONS FOR READING AND DISCUSSION

1. According to Colton, how and why did gold fever upset social and domestic arrangements in Monterey? What did he mean by stating, "All distinctions indicative of means have vanished; the only capital required is muscle and an honest purpose"?
2. How did gold fever influence white miners' attitudes toward other racial and ethnic groups? Why, according to Colton, did miners favor excluding slavery from California?
3. To what extent did the gold rush exemplify the operation of the free-labor system?
4. Was California during the gold rush atypical of American society east of the Mississippi during the 1840s and 1850s? Why or why not?

DOCUMENT 12–4

That Woman Is Man's Equal: The Seneca Falls Declaration

Women did not share the opportunities that the free-labor system made available to white men. In 1848, more than 150 women and 30 men met at Seneca Falls, New York, to protest the male supremacy that prevailed throughout America. This first women's-rights convention adopted the "Declaration of Sentiments," reprinted here, drafted by Elizabeth Cady Stanton. Born in 1815 in a small town in New York, Stanton received a good education and, with her husband, Henry B. Stanton, was an active abolitionist. Stanton's Seneca Falls Declaration appealed to widely shared American ideals in order to demonstrate that drastic changes were necessary if those ideals were to have much meaning for women.

Declaration of Sentiments, 1848

When, in the course of human events, it becomes necessary for one portion of the family of man to assume among the people of the earth a position different from that which they have hitherto occupied, but one to which the laws of nature and of nature's God entitle them, a decent respect to the opinions of mankind requires that they should declare the causes that impel them to such a course.

We hold these truths to be self-evident: that all men and women are created equal; that they are endowed by their Creator with certain inalienable rights; that

From Susan B. Anthony, Elizabeth Cady Stanton, and Matilda Joslyn Gage, eds., *History of Woman Suffrage* (Rochester, NY: S. B. Anthony, 1889).

among these are life, liberty, and the pursuit of happiness; that to secure these rights governments are instituted, deriving their just powers from the consent of the governed. Whenever any form of government becomes destructive of these ends, it is the right of those who suffer from it to refuse allegiance to it, and to insist upon the institution of a new government, laying its foundations on such principles, and organizing its powers in such form, as to them shall seem most likely to effect their safety and happiness. Prudence, indeed, will dictate that governments long established should not be changed for light and transient causes; and accordingly all experience hath shown that mankind are more disposed to suffer, while evils are sufferable, than to right themselves by abolishing the forms to which they were accustomed. But when a long train of abuses and usurpations, pursuing invariably the same object evinces a design to reduce them under absolute despotism, it is their duty to throw off such government, and to provide new guards for their future security. Such has been the patient sufferance of the women under this government, and such is now the necessity which constrains them to demand the equal station to which they are entitled.

The history of mankind is a history of repeated injuries and usurpations on the part of man toward woman, having in direct object the establishment of an absolute tyranny over her. To prove this, let facts be submitted to a candid world.

He has never permitted her to exercise her inalienable right to the elective franchise. He has compelled her to submit to laws, in the formation of which she had no voice. He has withheld from her rights which are given to the most ignorant and degraded men—both natives and foreigners.

Having deprived her of this first right of a citizen, the elective franchise, thereby leaving her without representation in the halls of legislation, he has opposed her on all sides.

He has made her, if married, in the eye of the law, civilly dead.

He has taken from her all right in property, even to the wages she earns.

He has made her, morally, an irresponsible being, as she can commit many crimes with impunity, provided they be done in the presence of her husband. In the covenant of marriage, she is compelled to promise obedience to her husband, he becoming, to all intents and purposes, her master—the law giving him power to deprive her of her liberty, and to administer chastisement.

He has so framed the laws of divorce, as to what shall be the proper causes, and in case of separation, to whom the guardianship of the children shall be given, as to be wholly regardless of the happiness of women—the law, in all cases, going upon a false supposition of the supremacy of man, and giving all power into his hands.

After depriving her of all rights as a married woman, if single, and the owner of property, he has taxed her to support a government which recognizes her only when her property can be made profitable to it.

He has monopolized nearly all the profitable employments, and from those she is permitted to follow, she receives but a scanty remuneration. He closes against her all the avenues to wealth and distinction which he considers most honorable to himself. As a teacher of theology, medicine, or law, she is not known.

He has denied her the facilities for obtaining a thorough education, all colleges being closed against her.

He allows her in Church, as well as State, but in a subordinate position, claiming Apostolic authority for her exclusion from the ministry, and, with some exceptions, from any public participation in the affairs of the Church.

He has created a false public sentiment by giving to the world a different code of morals for men and women, by which moral delinquencies which exclude women from society, are not only tolerated, but deemed of little account in man.

He has usurped the prerogative of Jehovah himself, claiming it as his right to assign for her a sphere of action, when that belongs to her conscience and to her God.

He has endeavored, in every way that he could, to destroy her confidence in her own powers, to lessen her self-respect, and to make her willing to lead a dependent and abject life.

Now, in view of this entire disfranchisement of one-half the people of this country, their social and religious degradation—in view of the unjust laws above mentioned, and because women do feel themselves aggrieved, oppressed, and fraudulently deprived of their most sacred rights, we insist that they have immediate admission to all the rights and privileges which belong to them as citizens of the United States.

In entering upon the great work before us, we anticipate no small amount of misconception, misrepresentation, and ridicule; but we shall use every instrumentality within our power to effect our object. We shall employ agents, circulate tracts, petition the State and National legislatures, and endeavor to enlist the pulpit and the press in our behalf. We hope this Convention will be followed by a series of Conventions embracing every part of the country.

RESOLUTIONS

WHEREAS, The great precept of nature is conceded to be, that "man shall pursue his own true and substantial happiness." [William] Blackstone in his *Commentaries* remarks, that this law of Nature being coequal with mankind, and dictated by God himself, is of course superior in obligation to any other. It is binding over all the globe, in all countries and at all times; no human laws are of any validity if contrary to this, and such of them as are valid, derive all their force, and all their validity, and all their authority, mediately and immediately, from this original; therefore,

Resolved, That such laws as conflict, in any way, with the true and substantial happiness of woman, are contrary to the great precept of nature and of no validity, for this is "superior in obligation to any other."

Resolved, That all laws which prevent woman from occupying such a station in society as her conscience shall dictate, or which place her in a position inferior to that of man, are contrary to the great precept of nature, and therefore of no force or authority.

Resolved, That woman is man's equal—was intended to be so by the Creator, and the highest good of the race demands that she should be recognized as such.

Resolved, That the women of this country ought to be enlightened in regard to the laws under which they live, that they may no longer publish their degradation by declaring themselves satisfied with their present position, nor their ignorance, by asserting that they have all the rights they want.

Resolved, That inasmuch as man, while claiming for himself intellectual superiority, does accord to woman moral superiority, it is pre-eminently his duty to encourage her to speak and teach, as she has an opportunity, in all religious assemblies.

Resolved, That the same amount of virtue, delicacy, and refinement of behavior that is required of woman in the social state, should also be required of man, and the same transgressions should be visited with equal severity on both man and woman.

Resolved, That the objection of indelicacy and impropriety, which is so often brought against woman when she addresses a public audience, comes with a very ill-grace from those who encourage, by their attendance, her appearance on the stage, in the concert, or in feats of the circus.

Resolved, That woman has too long rested satisfied in the circumscribed limits which corrupt customs and a perverted application of the Scriptures have marked out for her, and that it is time she should move in the enlarged sphere which her great Creator has assigned her.

Resolved, That it is the duty of the women of this country to secure to themselves their sacred right to the elective franchise.

Resolved, That the equality of human rights results necessarily from the fact of the identity of the race in capabilities and responsibilities.

Resolved, therefore, That, being invested by the Creator with the same capabilities, and the same consciousness of responsibility for their exercise, it is demonstrably the right and duty of woman, equally with man, to promote every righteous cause by every righteous means; and especially in regard to the great subjects of morals and religion, it is self-evidently her right to participate with her brother in teaching them, both in private and in public, by writing and by speaking, by any instrumentalities proper to be used, and in any assemblies proper to be held; and this being a self-evident truth growing out of the divinely implanted principles of human nature, any custom or authority adverse to it, whether modern or wearing the hoary sanction of antiquity, is to be regarded as a self-evident falsehood, and at war with mankind.

QUESTIONS FOR READING AND DISCUSSION

1. Why do you think that the writers of the Seneca Falls Declaration used the Declaration of Independence as their model?
2. In what ways did men exercise "an absolute tyranny" over women? Why?
3. In what sense were married women "civilly dead" in the eyes of the law? Why was suffrage important for women?
4. What changes did the Seneca Falls Declaration propose? What methods might bring about those changes?
5. How might opponents of the declaration have responded to these arguments? How would the assumptions of opponents be likely to differ from those of the declaration?

DOCUMENT 12–5

A Farmer's View of His Wife

Widespread assumptions about the proper relations between husband and wife emerged from a conversation Eliza Farnham had with a newly married farmer on an Illinois riverboat. Born in New York, Farnham described her conversation in Life in Prairie Land *(1846), a book about her experiences in Illinois in the late 1830s, shortly after her marriage. Farnham's account of the conversation disclosed her own views as well as those of the farmer.*

Eliza Farnham

Conversation with a Newly Wed Westerner, 1846

The strange character of the feeling manifested by [the] husband, made me very desirous of drawing him into an expression of it in words before he left us, and as their landing-place would probably be reached on the third morning, I availed myself of a chance meeting . . . to engage him in conversation. A few words about the height of the water, the timber, and the prairies, served the purpose.

"You are going to become a prairie farmer?" I said.

"No, I've been one afore, I've got a farm up the river hyur that I've *crapped*[1] twice a'ready; there's a good cabin on it, and it's about as good a place, I reckon, as can be found in these diggins."

"Then you built a cage," I said, "and went back for your bird to put in it?"

He looked at me, and his face underwent a contortion, of which words will convey but a faint idea. It was a mingled expression of pride and contempt, faintly disguised by a smile that was intended to hide them.

"Why, I don't know what you Yankees call a bird," he replied, "but I call her a woman. I shouldn't make much account of havin a bird in my cabin, but a good, stout woman I should calculate was worth somethin. She can pay her way, and do a handsome thing besides, helpin me on the farm."

Think of that, ye belles and fair-handed maidens! How was my sentiment rebuked!

"Well, we'll call her a woman, which is, in truth, much the more rational appellation. You intend to make her useful as well as ornamental to your home?"

"Why, yes; I calculate 'taint of much account to have a woman if she ain't of no use. I lived up hyur two year, and had to have another man's woman do all my washin and mendin and so on, and at last I got tired o' totin my plunder back and forth, and thought I might as well get a woman of my own. There's a heap of things beside these, that she'll do better than I can, I reckon; every man ought to have a woman to do his cookin and such like, 'kase it's easier for them than it is for us. They take to it kind o' naturally."

I could scarcely believe that there was no more human vein in the animal, and determined to sound him a little deeper.

"And this bride of yours is the one, I suppose, that you thought of all the while you were making your farm and building your cabin? You have, I dare say, made a little garden, or set out a tree, or done something of the kind to please her alone?"

"No, I never allowed to get a woman till I found my neighbors went ahead of me with 'em, and then I should a got one right thar, but there wasn't any stout ones in our settlement, and it takes so long to make up to a *stranger*, that I allowed I mought as well go back and see the old folks, and git somebody that I know'd thar to come with me."

"And had you no choice made among your acquaintants? was there no one person of whom you thought more than another?" said I.

From Eliza Farnham, *Life in Prairie Land* (New York: Harper and Brothers, 1846).
[1]**crapped**: Planted with a crop.

"Yas, there was a gal I used to know that was stouter and bigger than this one. I should a got her if I could, but she'd got married and gone off over the *Mississippi*, somewhar."

The cold-hearted fellow! it was a perfectly business matter with him.

"Did you select this one solely on account of her size?" said I.

"Why, pretty much," he replied; "I reckon women are some like horses and oxen, the biggest can do the most work, and that's what I want one for."

"And is that all?" I asked, more disgusted at every word. "Do you care nothing about a pleasant face to meet you when you go home from the field, or a soft voice to speak kind words when you are sick, or a gentle friend to converse with you in your leisure hours?"

"Why, as to that," he said. "I reckon a woman ain't none the worse for talk because she's stout and able to work. I calculate she'll mind her own business pretty much, and if she does she won't talk a great deal to me; that ain't what I got her for."

"But suppose when you get home she should be unhappy, and want to see her parents and other friends?"

"Why I don't allow she will; I didn't get her for that. . . . I shall give her enough to eat and wear, and I don't calculate she'll be very *daunsey*[2] if she gets that; if she is she'll git *shet* of it after a while."

My indignation increased at every word.

"But you brought her away from her home to be treated as a human being, not as an animal or machine. Marriage is a moral contract, not a mere bargain of business. The parties promise to study each other's happiness, and endeavor to promote it. You could not marry a woman as you could buy a washing machine, though you might want her for the same purpose. If you take the machine there is no moral obligation incurred, except to pay for it. If you take the woman, there is. Before you entered into this contract I could have shown you a machine that would have answered your purpose admirably. It would have washed and ironed all your clothes, and when done, stood in some out-of-the-way corner till it was wanted again. You would have been under no obligation, not even to feed and clothe it, as you now are. It would have been the better bargain, would it not?"

"Why that would be according to what it cost in the fust place; but it wouldn't be justly the same thing as havin a wife, I reckon, even if it was give to you."

"No, certainly not; it would free you from many obligations that you are under to a wife" (it was the first time, by the way, he had used the word), "and leave you to pursue your own pleasure without seeing any sorrowful or sour faces about you."

"Oh, I calculate sour faces won't be of much account to me. If a woman'll mind her business, she may look as thunderin as a live airthquake, I shan't mind it. . . . I reckon the Yankees may do as they like about them things, and I shall do jist the same. I don't think a woman's of much account anyhow, if she can't help herself a little and me too. If the Yankee women was *raised up like the women* here *aar*, they'd cost a heap less and be worth more."

I turned away, saying that I trusted his wife would agree with him in these opinions, or they might lead to some unpleasant differences.

"Oh, as to that," said he, "I reckon her pinions won't go fur anyhow; she'll think pretty much as I do, or not at all."

---

[2]*daunsey*: An idiom meaning to feel like dancing or celebrating.

QUESTIONS FOR READING AND DISCUSSION

1. Why did the farmer want a wife? What traits did he seek in a wife?
2. What did Farnham mean by saying to the farmer, "you built a cage . . . and went back for your bird to put in it"? How did Farnham's views about wives differ from the farmer's?
3. Did Farnham and the farmer disagree on all points?
4. Farnham stated that she "trusted his [the farmer's] wife would agree with him in these opinions." Why did Farnham think the farmer's wife would agree with him rather than with her? What did Farnham's observations suggest about her own perceptions of what women believed about themselves and why?

COMPARATIVE QUESTIONS

1. How do Abraham Lincoln's view of the free-labor system compare with Henry Bellows's views of the temptations and anxieties of material success, including during the gold rush, as witnessed by Walter Colton?
2. In what ways are the views of men as presented in the Seneca Falls Declaration comparable to those of Lincoln, Bellows, and the prairie farmer interviewed by Eliza Farnham?
3. The prairie farmer, Farnham, and the authors of the Seneca Falls Declaration asserted convictions about what women's rights were in fact and what they should be. What assumptions, if any, did these commentators share? What differences did they express? What arguments might appeal most strongly to the farmer's wife? What might influence her or her husband to reconsider their opinions?
4. Each of the documents in this chapter provides evidence of the achievements and limitations freedom offered Americans in the 1840s and 1850s. To what extent do the documents suggest that the problems of American society could be overcome by expanding freedom?

The Slave South

1820–1860

I n most ways, slavery was king in the South, although white Southerners often claimed that cotton ruled. The southern states produced millions of pounds of cotton, but they also grew huge quantities of tobacco, rice, and sugar. Slaves provided most of the labor for these valuable crops, as well as being forced to do a wide variety of other tasks, ranging from cleaning house and minding children to building houses, sailing boats, managing the labor of other slaves, and even having sex forced upon them by whites. The following documents disclose some of the distinctive tensions that slavery generated among white and black Southerners and between the South and the North.

DOCUMENT 13–1

Madison Hemings Recalls Life as Thomas Jefferson's Enslaved Son

Slave owners often forced their slave women to engage in sexual relations. Recent DNA studies have suggested that Thomas Jefferson fathered children with his slave Sally Hemings. One of those children, Madison Hemings, recounted his experiences as an enslaved son of Jefferson to a newspaper reporter in Pike County, Ohio, in 1873. Hemings's story reveals the stark lines of race and status that structured life on Jefferson's plantation. It also suggests the contours of a half-secret history of sex across the color line in the slave South, a history whites frequently denied in public.

Interview, 1873

I never knew of but one white man who bore the name of Hemings; he was an Englishman and my great grandfather. He was captain of an English trading vessel which sailed between England and Williamsburg, Va., then quite a port. My

From "Life among the Lowly, No. 1," *Pike County (Ohio) Republican*, March 13, 1873.

great-grandmother was a fullblooded African, and possibly a native of that country. She was the property of John Wales, a Welchman. Capt. Hemings happened to be in the port of Williamsburg at the time my grandmother was born, and acknowledging her fatherhood he tried to purchase her of Mr. Wales, who would not part with the child, though he was offered an extraordinarily large price for her. She was named Elizabeth Hemings. Being thwarted in the purchase, and determined to own his own flesh and blood he resolved to take the child by force or stealth, but the knowledge of his intention coming to John Wales' ears, through leaky fellow servants of the mother, she and the child were taken into the "great house" under their master's immediate care. I have been informed that it was not the extra value of that child over other slave children that induced Mr. Wales to refuse to sell it, for slave masters then, as in later days, had no compunctions of conscience which restrained them from parting mother and child of however tender age, but he was restrained by the fact that just about that time amalgamation[1] began, and the child was so great a curiosity that its owner desired to raise it himself that he might see its outcome. Capt. Hemings soon afterwards sailed from Williamsburg, never to return. Such is the story that comes down to me.

Elizabeth Hemings grew to womanhood in the family of John Wales, whose wife dying she (Elizabeth) was taken by the widower Wales as his concubine, by whom she had six children—three sons and three daughters, viz: Robert, James, Peter, Critty, Sally and Thena. These children went by the name of Hemings.

Williamsburg was the capital of Virginia, and of course it was an aristocratic place, where the "bloods" of the Colony and the new State most did congregate. Thomas Jefferson, the author of the Declaration of Independence, was educated at William and Mary College, which had its seat at Williamsburg. He afterwards studied law with Geo. Wythe, and practiced law at the bar of the general court of the Colony. He was afterwards elected a member of the provincial legislature from Albemarle county. Thos. Jefferson was a visitor at the "great house" of John Wales, who had children about his own age. He formed the acquaintance of his daughter Martha (I believe that was her name, though I am not positively sure,) and intimacy sprang up between them which ripened into love, and they were married. They afterwards went to live at his country seat Monticello, and in course of time had born to them a daughter whom they named Martha. About the time she was born my mother, the second daughter of John Wales and Elizabeth Hemings was born. On the death of John Wales, my grandmother, his concubine, and her children by him fell to Martha, Thomas Jefferson's wife, and consequently became the property of Thomas Jefferson, who in the course of time became famous, and was appointed minister to France during our revolutionary troubles, or soon after independence was gained. About the time of the appointment and before he was ready to leave the country his wife died, and as soon after her interment as he could attend to and arrange his domestic affairs in accordance with the changed circumstances of his family in consequence of this misfortune (I think not more than three weeks thereafter) he left for France, taking his eldest daughter with him. He had sons born to him, but they died in early infancy, so he then had but two children—Martha and Maria. The latter was left home, but afterwards was ordered to follow him to France. She was three years or so younger than Martha.

---

[1]**amalgamation**: Refers here to mixed-race children fathered by white men with enslaved women of African descent.

My mother accompanied her as a body servant. When Mr. Jefferson went to France Martha was just budding into womanhood. Their stay (my mother's and Maria's) was about eighteen months. But during that time my mother became Mr. Jefferson's concubine, and when he was called back home she was enciente [pregnant] by him. He desired to bring my mother back to Virginia with him but she demurred. She was just beginning to understand the French language well, and in France she was free, while if she returned to Virginia she would be re-enslaved. So she refused to return with him. To induce her to do so he promised her extraordinary privileges, and made a solemn pledge that her children should be freed at the age of twenty-one years. In consequence of his promise, on which she implicitly relied, she returned with him to Virginia. Soon after their arrival, she gave birth to a child, of whom Thomas Jefferson was the father. It lived but a short time. She gave birth to four others, and Jefferson was the father of all of them. Their names were Beverly, Harriet, Madison (myself), and Eston—three sons and one daughter. We all became free agreeably to the treaty entered into by our parents before we were born. We all married and have raised families.

Beverly left Monticello and went to Washington as a white man. He married a white woman in Maryland, and their only child, a daughter, was not known by the white folks to have any colored blood coursing in her veins. Beverly's wife's family were people in good circumstances.

Harriet married a white man in good standing in Washington City, whose name I could give, but will not, for prudential reasons. She raised a family of children, and so far as I know they were never suspected of being tainted with African blood in the community where she lived or lives. I have not heard from her for ten years, and do not know whether she is dead or alive. She thought it to her interest, on going to Washington, to assume the role of a white woman, and by her dress and conduct as such I am not aware that her identity as Harriet Hemings of Monticello has ever been discovered.

Eston married a colored woman in Virginia, and moved from there to Ohio, and lived in Chillicothe several years. In the fall of 1852 he removed to Wisconsin, where he died a year or two afterwards. He left three children.

As to myself, I was named Madison by the wife of James Madison, who was afterwards President of the United States. Mrs. Madison happened to be at Monticello at the time of my birth, and begged the privilege of naming me, promising my mother a fine present for the honor. She consented, and Mrs. Madison dubbed me by the name I now acknowledge, but like many promises of white folks to the slaves she never gave my mother anything. I was born at my father's seat of Monticello, in Albemarle county, Va., near Charlottesville, on the 18th day of January, 1805. My very earliest recollections are of my grandmother Elizabeth Hemings. That was when I was about three years old. She was sick and upon her death bed. I was eating a piece of bread and asked if she would have some. She replied: "No, granny don't want bread any more." She shortly afterwards breathed her last. I have only a faint recollection of her.

Of my father, Thomas Jefferson, I knew more of his domestic than his public life during his life time. It is only since his death that I have learned much of the latter, except that he was considered as a foremost man in the land, and held many important trusts, including that of President. I learned to read by inducing the white children to teach me the letters and something more; what else I know of books I have picked up here and there till now I can read and write. I was almost 21 1/2 years of age when my father died on the 4th of July, 1826.

About his own home he was the quietest of men. He was hardly ever known to get angry, though sometimes he was irritated when matters went wrong, but even then he hardly ever allowed himself to be made unhappy any great length of time. Unlike Washington he had but little taste or care for agricultural pursuits. He left matters pertaining to his plantations mostly with his stewards and overseers. He always had mechanics at work for him, such as carpenters, blacksmiths, shoemakers, coopers, &c. It was his mechanics he seemed mostly to direct, and in their operations he took great interest. Almost every day of his later years he might have been seen among them. He occupied much of the time in his office engaged in correspondence and reading and writing. His general temperament was smooth and even; he was very undemonstrative. He was uniformly kind to all about him. He was not in the habit of showing partiality or fatherly affection to us children. We were the only children of his by a slave woman. He was affectionate toward his white grandchildren, of whom he had fourteen, twelve of whom lived to manhood and womanhood. His daughter Martha married Thomas Mann Randolph by whom she had thirteen children. Two died in infancy. The names of the living were Ann, Thomas Jefferson, Ellen, Cornelia, Virginia, Mary, James, Benj. Franklin, Lewis Madison, Septemia and Geo. Wythe. . . .

Maria married John Epps, and raised one son—Francis.

My father generally enjoyed excellent health. I never knew him to have but one spell of sickness, and that was caused by a visit to the Warm Springs in 1818. Till within three weeks of his death he was hale and hearty, and at the age of 83 years walked erect and with a stately tread. I am now 68, and I well remember that he was a much smarter man physically, even at that age, than I am.

When I was fourteen years old I was put to the carpenter trade under the charge of John Hemings, the youngest son of my grandmother. His father's name was Nelson, who was an Englishman. She had seven children by white men and seven by colored men—fourteen in all. My brothers, sister Harriet and myself, were used alike. We were permitted to stay about the "great house," and only required to do such light work as going on errands. Harriet learned to spin and to weave in a little factory on the home plantation. We were free from the dread of having to be slaves all our lives long, and were measurably happy. We were always permitted to be with our mother, who was well used. It was her duty, all her life which I can remember, up to the time of father's death, to take care of his chamber and wardrobe, look after us children and do such light work as sewing, &c. Provision was made in the will of our father that we should be free when we arrived at the age of 21 years. We had all passed that period when he died but Eston, and he was given the remainder of his time shortly after. He and I rented a house and took mother to live with us, till her death, which event occurred in 1835.

In 1834 I married Mary McCoy. Her grandmother was a slave, and lived with her master, Stephen Hughes, near Charlottesville, as his wife. She was manumitted[2] by him, which made their children free born. Mary McCoy's mother was his daughter. I was about 28 and she 22 years of age when we married. We lived and labored together in Virginia till 1836, when we voluntarily left and came to Ohio. We settled in Pebble township, Pike County. We lived there four or five years and during my stay in the county I worked at my trade [as a] . . . carpenter.

---

[2]**manumitted**: Freed from slavery.

When we came from Virginia we brought one daughter (Sarah) with us, leaving the dust of a son in the soil near Monticello. We have born to us in this State nine children. Two are dead. . . . All the others are married and raising families.

QUESTIONS FOR READING AND DISCUSSION

1. Hemings was interviewed in Ohio nearly a half century after Jefferson's death in Virginia. Do you think his testimony is credible? Why or why not?
2. Madison Hemings said Thomas Jefferson "was not in the habit of showing partiality or fatherly affection to us children," yet he "was affectionate toward his white grandchildren." What might have accounted for this difference?
3. Why did Hemings gain his freedom, according to his account? Is there any evidence that Hemings was favored by Jefferson?
4. What do Hemings's experiences suggest about the sexual behavior of white slave owners and slave women, as well as the meanings of race and family in the slave South? Do you think Hemings's experiences were typical or atypical? Why or why not?

DOCUMENT 13–2

Plantation Rules

Masters made the rules on their plantations. The rules defined in general terms what the master expected slaves to do and not to do. Rules differed greatly from master to master, and, as circumstances required, they had to be changed. In most cases, masters communicated their rules in face-to-face encounters with their slaves. Some masters recorded their rules for their own reference or the use of an overseer. Bennet Barrow, the owner of nearly 200 slaves on his cotton plantation in Louisiana, noted his plantation rules in his diary on May 1, 1838, the source of the following selection. Barrow's rules illustrate not only his specific concerns but also the underlying question that every master confronted: How best to get slaves to do what their masters wanted?

Bennet Barrow

Highland Plantation Journal, May 1, 1838

No negro shall leave the place at any time without my permission, or in my absence that of the Driver the driver in that case being responsible, for the cause of such absence, which ought never to be omitted to be enquired into—

The Driver should never leave the plantation, unless on business of the plantation

No negro shall be allowed to marry out of the plantation

No negro shall be allowed to sell anything without my express permission I have ever maintained the doctrine that my negroes have no time Whatever, that they are always liable to my call without questioning for a moment the propriety

From Edwin Adams Davis, ed., *Plantation Life in the Florida Parishes of Louisiana, 1836–1846, as Reflected in the Diary of Bennet H. Barrow* (New York: AMS Press, 1943).

of it, I adhere to this on the grounds of expediency and right. The verry security of the plantation requires that a general and uniform control over the people of it should be exercised. Who are to protect the plantation from the intrusions of ill designed persons When evry body is a broad? Who can tell the moment When a plantation might be threatened with destruction from Fire—could the flames be arrested if the negroes are scattered throughout the neighborhood, seeking their amusement. Are these not duties of great importance, and in which evry negro himself is deeply interested to render this part of the rule justly applicable, however, it would be necessary that such a settled arrangement should exist on the plantation as to make it unnecessary for a negro to leave it. . . . You must, therefore make him as comfortable at Home as possible, affording him, What is essentially necessary for his happiness—you must provide for him Your self and by that means creat in him a habit of perfect dependence on you—Allow it ounce to be understood by a negro that he is to provide for himself, and you that moment give him an undeniable claim on you for a portion of his time to make this provision, and should you from necessity, or any other cause, encroach upon his time—disappointment and discontent are seriously felt—if I employ a labourer to perform a certain quantum of work per day and I agree to pay him, a certain amount for the performance of said work When he had accomplished it I of course have no further claim on him for his time or services—but how different is it with a slave—Who can calculate the exact profit or expence of a slave one year with another, if I furnish my negro with evry necessary of life, without the least care on his part—if I support him in sickness, however long it may be, and pay all his expenses, though he does nothing—if I maintain him in his old age, when he is incapable of rendering either himself or myself any service, am I not entitled to an exclusive right to his time good feelings, and a sense of propriety would all ways prevent unnecessary employment on the Sabbath, and policy would check any exaction of excessive labor in common. . . . I never give a negro a Pass to go from home without he first states particularly where he wishes to go, and assigns a cause for his desiring to be absent. if he offers a good reason, I never refuse, but otherwise, I never grant him a Pass, and feel satisfied that no practice is more prejudicial to the community, and to the negros themselves, than that of giving them general Passes to go, Where they please I am so opposed to this plan that I never permit any negro to remain on my plantation, whose Pass does not authorize him expressly to come to it—Some think that after a negro has done his work it is an act of oppression to confine him to the plantation, when he might be strolling about the neighborhood for his amusement and recreation—this is certainly a mistaken humanity. Habit is evry thing—The negro who is accustomed to remain constantly at Home, is just as satisfied with the society on the plantation as that which he would find elsewhere, and the verry restrictions laid upon him being equally imposed on others, he does not feel them, for society is kept at Home for them. . . . No rule that I have stated is of more importance than that relating to negroes marrying out of the plantation it seems to me, from What observations I have made, it is utterly impossible to have any method, or regularity when the men and women are permitted to take wives and husbands indiscriminately off the plantation, negroes are verry much desposed to pursue a course of this kind, and without being able to assign any good reason, though the motive can be readily perceived, and is a strong one with them, but one that tend not in the Least to the benefit of the Master, or their ultimate good. the inconveniences that at once strikes one as arising out of such a practice are these—

First—in allowing the men to marry out of the plantation, you give them an uncontrolable right to be frequently absent

2d—Wherever their wives live, there they consider their homes, consequently they are indifferent to the interest of the plantation to which they actually belong—

3d—it creates a feeling of independance, from being, of right, out of the control of the masters for a time—

4th—They are repeatedly exposed to temptation from meeting and associating with negroes from different directions, and with various habits & vices—

5th—Where there are several women on a plantation, they may have husbands from different plantations belonging to different persons. These men posess different habits are acustomed to different treatment, and have different privileges, so your plantation every day becomes a rendeezvous of a medly of characters. Negroes who have the privilege of a monthly Passes to go where they please, and at any hour that they say they have finished their work, to leave their Master's plan'tn come into yours about midday, When your negroes are at work, and the Driver engaged, they either take possession of houses their wives live—and go to sleep or stroll about in perfect idleness—feeling themselves accessible to every thing. What an example to those at work at the time—can any circumstance be more Intrusive of good order and contentment

Sixthly—When a man and his wife belong to different persons, they are liable to be separated from each other, as well as their children, whether by caprice of either of the parties, or When there is a sale of property—this keeps up an unsettled state of things, and gives rise to repeated new connections. . . . I prefer giving them money of Christmas to their making any thing, thereby creating an interest with you and yours. . . . I furnish my negroes regularly with their full share of allowance weakly. 4 pound & 5 pound of meat to evry thing that goes in the field—2 pound over 4 years 1½ between 15 months and 4 years old—Clear good meat—I give them cloths twice a year, two suits—one pair shoes for winter evry third year a blanket. . . . I supply them with tobacco if a negro is suffered to sell any thing he chooses without any inquiry being made, a spirit of trafficing at once is created. to carry this on, both means and time are necessary, neither of which is he of right possessed. A negro would not be content to sell only What he raises or makes either corn (should he be permitted) or poultry, or the like, but he would sell part of his allowance allso, and would be tempted to commit robberies to obtain things to sell. Besides, he would never go through his work carefully, particularly When other engagements more interesting and pleasing are constantly passing through his mind, but would be apt to slight his work That the general conduct of master has a verry considerable influence on the character and habits of his slave, will be readily admitted. When a master is uniform in his own habits & conduct, his slaves know his wishes, and What they are to expect if they act in opposition to, or conformity with them, therefore, the more order and contentment Exist.

A plantation might be considered as a piece of machinery, to operate successfully, all of its parts should be uniform and exact, and the impelling force regular and steady; and the master, if he pretended at all to attend to his business, should be their impelling force, if a master exhibits no extraordinary interest in the proceedings on his plantation, it is hardly to be expected that any other feelings but apathy, and perfect indifference could exist with his negroes, and it would be unreasonable for him . . . to expect attention and exaction from those, Who have no other interest than to avoid the displeasure of their master. in the different departments on the plantation as much destinction and separation are kept up as possible with a view to create responsibility—The Driver has a directed charge of every thing, but there are subordinate persons, who take the more immediate care of the different departments. For instance, I make one persons answerable for my stock. Horses cattle hogs, &c. another the plantation untensials &c. one the sick—one the poultry. another providing for and taking care of the children whose parents are in the field &c. As good a plan as could be adopted, to establish security and good order on the plantation is that of constituting a watch at night, consisting of two or more men. they are answerable for all trespasses commited during their watch, unless they produce the offender. or give immediate alarm. When the protection of a plantation is left to the negroes generally, you at once percieve the truth of the maxim that what is evry one's business, is no one's business. but when a regular watch is Established, Each in turn performs his tour of duty, so that the most careless is at times, made to be observant and watchful—the very act of organizing a watch bespeaks a care and attention on the part of a master, Which has the due influence on the negro—

Most of the above rules "in fact with the exception of the last" I have adopted since 1833. And with success—get your negroes ounce disciplined and planting is a pleasure—A Hell without it never have an Overseer—Every negro to come up Sunday after their allowance Clean & head well combed—it gives pride to every one, the fact of master feeling proud of them, When clean &c.

Never allow any man to talk to your negroes, nothing more injurious.

Questions for Reading and Discussion

1. Barrow wrote that he considered it a matter of "expediency and right" that his slaves "have no time Whatever, that they are always liable to my call without questioning for a moment the propriety of it." In what ways did this rule influence Barrow's slaves and Barrow himself? Did Barrow's slaves have any free time?

2. Why did Barrow prohibit his slaves from marrying slaves belonging to another master and from selling chickens or corn?

3. What did he believe motivated his slaves? How did he try to influence their motivation? Why did he believe it so important to "furnish my negro with evry necessary of life"?

4. Does the diary offer hints about the degree to which Barrow's slaves followed his rules? Does it provide evidence that his slaves had rules of their own, in conflict with his? If Barrow's slaves had commented on his rules, what might they have said about them to one another?

Document 13–3

Fanny Kemble Learns about Abuses of Slave Women

In 1834, the beautiful and famous English actress, Fanny Kemble, married Pierce Butler, a fabulously wealthy American who owned hundreds of slaves who labored on his family's plantations located on the coast of Georgia. Kemble lived on Butler's plantation from 1838 to 1839 and confronted for the first time the realities of slavery that made possible the luxuries and privileges that she and her husband enjoyed. A journal she kept while on the plantation documented the routine living and working conditions among slave women on Butler's plantations. Kemble divorced Butler in 1849, losing custody of the couple's two daughters, and subsequently published her journal in 1863. In the following selection from her journal, Kemble described what she learned from the slave women who repeatedly came to visit her.

Journal of a Residence on a Georgian Plantation in 1838–1839

This morning I had a visit from two of the [slave] women, Charlotte and Judy, who came to me for help and advice for a complaint, which it really seems to me every other woman on the estate is cursed with, and which is a direct result of the conditions of their existence; the practice of sending women to labor in the fields in the third week after their confinement is a specific for causing this infirmity, and I know no specific for curing it under these circumstances. As soon as these poor things had departed with such comfort as I could give them, and the bandages they especially begged for, three other sable graces introduced themselves, Edie, Louisa, and Diana; the former told me she had had a family of seven children, but had lost them all through "ill luck," as she denominated the ignorance and ill treatment which were answerable for the loss of these, as of so many other poor little creatures their fellows. Having dismissed her and Diana with the sugar and rice they came to beg, I detained Louisa. . . . She had not finished her task one day, when she said she felt ill, and unable to do so, and had been severely flogged by Driver Bran, in whose "gang" she then was. The next day, in spite of this encouragement to labor, she had again been unable to complete her appointed work; and Bran having told her that he'd tie her up and flog her if she did not get it done, she had left the field and run into the swamp. . . .

Yesterday evening I had a visit that made me very sorrowful—if anything connected with these poor people can be called more especially sorrowful than their whole condition; but Mr. ——'s declaration that he will receive no more statements of grievances or petitions for redress through me, makes me as desirous now of shunning the vain appeals of these unfortunates as I used to be of receiving and listening to them. The imploring cry, "Oh missis!" that greets me whichever way I turn, makes me long to stop my ears now; for what can I say or do any more for them? The poor little favors—the rice, the sugar, the flannel— that they beg for with such eagerness, and receive with such exuberant gratitude, I can, it is true, supply, and words and looks of pity and counsel of patience and such instruction in womanly habits of decency and cleanliness, as may enable them to better, in some degree, their own hard lot; but to the entreaty, "Oh missis, you speak to massa for us! Oh missis, you beg massa for us! Oh missis, you tell massa for we, he sure do as you say!"—I cannot now answer as formerly, and I turn away choking and with eyes full of tears from the poor creatures, not even daring to promise any more the faithful transmission of their prayers.

The women who visited me yesterday evening were all in the family-way, and came to entreat of me to have the sentence (what else can I call it?) modified, which condemns them to resume their labor of hoeing in the fields three weeks

From Frances Anne Kemble, *Journal of a Residence on a Georgian Plantation in 1838–1839* (New York: Harper & Brothers Publishers, 1863), 174–75, 182–83, 189–92, 199–200.

after their confinement. They knew, of course, that I cannot interfere with their appointed labor, and therefore their sole entreaty was that I would use my influence with Mr. —— to obtain for them a month's respite from labor in the field after child-bearing. Their principal spokeswoman, a woman with a bright sweet face, called Mary, and a very sweet voice, which is by no means an uncommon excellence among them, appealed to my own experience; and while she spoke of my babies, and my carefully tended, delicately nursed, and tenderly watched confinement and convalescence, [she] implored me to have a kind of labor given to them less exhausting during the month after their confinement. . . . At length I told them that Mr. —— had forbidden me to bring him any more complaints from them, for that he thought the ease with which I received and believed their stories only tended to make them discontented, and that, therefore, I feared I could not promise to take their petitions to him; but that he would be coming down to "the point" soon, and that they had better come then some time when I was with him, and say what they had just been saying to me: and with this, and various small bounties, I was forced, with a heavy heart, to dismiss them, and when they were gone, with many exclamations of, "Oh yes, missis, you will, you will speak to massa for we; God bless you, missis, we sure you will!" I had my cry out for them, for myself, for us. All these women had had large families, and *all* of them had lost half their children, and several of them had lost more. . . .

[Here are] . . . the entries for to-day recorded in a sort of daybook, where I put down very succinctly the number of people who visit me, their petitions and ailments, and also such special particulars concerning them as seem to me worth recording. You will see how miserable the physical condition of many of these poor creatures is; and their physical condition, it is insisted by those who uphold this evil system, is the only part of it which is prosperous, happy, and compares well with that of northern laborers. Judge from the details I now send you; and never forget, while reading them, that the people on this plantation are well off, and consider themselves well off, in comparison with the slaves on some of the neighboring estates.

Fanny has had six children, all dead but one. She came to beg to have her work in the field lightened.

Nanny has had three children, two of them are dead; she came to implore that the rule of sending them into the field three weeks after their confinement might be altered.

Leah, Caesar's wife, has had six children, three are dead.

Sophy, Lewis' wife, came to beg for some old linen; she is suffering fearfully, has had ten children, five of them are dead. The principal favor she asked was a piece of meat, which I gave her.

Sally, Scipio's wife, has had two miscarriages and three children born, one of whom is dead. She came complaining of incessant pain and weakness in her back. This woman was a mulatto daughter of a slave called Sophy, by a white man of the name of Walker, who visited the plantation.

Charlotte, Renty's wife, had had two miscarriages, and was with child again. She was almost crippled with rheumatism, and showed me a pair of poor swollen knees that made my heart ache. I have promised her a pair of flannel trowsers, which I must forthwith set about making.

Sarah, Stephen's wife,—this woman's case and history were, alike, deplorable, she had had four miscarriages, had brought seven children into the world, five of whom were dead, and was again with child. She complained of dreadful pains in the back, and an internal tumor which swells with the exertion of working in the fields; probably, I think, she is ruptured. She told me she had once been mad and ran into the woods, where she contrived to elude discovery for some time, but was at last tracked and brought back, when she was tied up by the arms and heavy logs fastened to her feet, and was severely flogged. After this she contrived to escape again, and lived for some time skulking in the woods, and she supposes mad, for when she was taken again she was entirely naked. She subsequently recovered from this derangement, and seems now just like all the other poor creatures who come to me for help and pity. . . .

Sukey, Bush's wife, only came to pay her respects. She had had four miscarriages, had brought eleven children into the world, five of whom are dead.

Molly, Quambo's wife, also only came to see me; hers was the best account I have yet received; she had had nine children, and six of them were still alive.

This is only the entry for to-day, in my diary, of the people's complaints and visits. Can you conceive a more wretched picture than that which it exhibits of the conditions under which these women live? Their cases are in no respect singular, and though they come with pitiful entreaties that I will help them with some alleviation of their pressing physical distresses, it seems to me marvellous with what desperate patience (I write it advisedly, patience of utter despair) they endure their sorrow-laden existence. Even the poor wretch who told that miserable story of insanity and lonely hiding in the swamps and scourging when she was found, and of her renewed madness and flight, did so in a sort of low, plaintive, monotonous murmur of misery, as if such sufferings were all "in the day's work."

I ask these questions about their children because I think the number they bear as compared with the number they rear a fair gauge of the effect of the system on their own health and that of their offspring. . . .

I have had an uninterrupted stream of women and children flowing in the whole morning to say, "Ha de missis!" Among others, a poor woman called Mile, who could hardly stand for pain and swelling in her limbs; she had had fifteen children and two miscarriages, nine of her children had died; for the last three years she had become almost a cripple with chronic rheumatism, yet she is driven every day to work in the field. She held my hands and stroked them in the most appealing way, while she exclaimed, "Oh my missis! my missis! me neber sleep till day for de pain," and with the day her labor must again be resumed. I gave her flannel and sal volatile [an ointment] to rub her poor swelled limbs with; rest I could not give her—rest from her labor and her pain—this mother of fifteen children.

Another of my visitors had a still more dismal story to tell; her name was Die; she had had sixteen children, fourteen of whom were dead; she had had four miscarriages, one had been caused by falling down with a very heavy burthen on her head, and one from having her arms strained up to be lashed. I asked her what she meant by having her arms tied up; she said their hands were first tied together, sometimes by the wrists, and sometimes, which was worse, by the thumbs, and they were then drawn up to a tree or post, so as almost to swing them off the ground, and then their clothes rolled round their waist, and a man with a cowhide stands and stripes them. I give you the woman's words; she did not speak of this as of anything strange, unusual or especially horrid and abominable; and when I said, "Did they do that to you when you were with child?" she simply replied, "Yes, missis." And to all this I listen—I, an English woman, the wife of the man who owns these wretches, and I cannot say, "That thing shall not be done again; that cruel shame and villany shall never be known here again." I gave the woman meat and flannel, which were what she came to ask for, and remained choking with indignation and grief long after they had all left me to my most bitter thoughts.

QUESTIONS FOR READING AND DISCUSSION

1. Why did slave women come to talk with Fanny Kemble? Why do you think women in particular (instead of men) came to her?
2. What did Kemble mean by observing that the slave women seemed to consider that their "sufferings were all 'in a day's work.'" Do you think her observation was probably accurate? Why or why not?
3. Why did Kemble's husband forbid her "to bring him any more complaints"?
4. Why did the visits of the slave women leave Kemble "choking with indignation and grief"?
5. Do you believe Kemble's claim that the number of children slave women birthed compared to the number they reared was "a fair gauge of the effect of the system on their own health and that of their offspring"? Why or why not?

DOCUMENT 13–4

Nat Turner Explains Why He Became an Insurrectionist

In August 1831, Nat Turner led a slave insurrection in Southampton, Virginia, not far from the small town of Jerusalem. A learned and deeply religious man, Turner, accompanied by a small band of fellow rebels, killed fifty-five whites, more than half of them children, before they themselves were captured and executed by local whites. Turner's insurrection electrified the nation. To white Southerners, it demonstrated the necessity of unrelenting vigilance and unyielding control over slaves. To many people in the free states, it demonstrated slaves' unquenchable desire for freedom and desperate willingness to kill to get it. When Turner was captured, Thomas Gray, a white lawyer from Virginia, interviewed him in his cell shortly before his execution. Gray quickly published Turner's Confessions, *which was read avidly throughout the country. This text must be examined with care to attempt to sift what Turner said and believed—as well as what he may have left unsaid—from what Gray wrote. This selection contains Turner's account of how and why he became an insurrectionist. It discloses Turner's belief in miraculous, supernatural omens that impelled his actions and provides revealing glimpses of slaves' relationships with one another and with their white owners.*

The Confessions of Nat Turner, 1831

You have asked me to give a history of the motives which induced me to undertake the late insurrection, as you call it—To do so I must go back to the days of my infancy, and even before I was born. I was thirty-one years of age the 2nd

---

From *The Confessions of Nat Turner, the Leader of the Late Insurrection in Southampton, Va. As Fully and Voluntarily Made to Thomas R. Gray, in the Prison Where He Was Confined* . . . (Baltimore, 1831).

of October last, and born the property of Benj. Turner, of this county. In my child-hood a circumstance occurred which made an indelible impression on my mind, and laid the ground work of that enthusiasm, which has terminated so fatally to many, both white and black, and for which I am about to atone at the gallows. It is here necessary to relate this circumstance—trifling as it may seem, it was the commencement of that belief which has grown with time, and even now, sir, in this dungeon, helpless and forsaken as I am, I cannot divest myself of. Being at play with other children, when three or four years old, I was telling them some-thing, which my mother overhearing, said it had happened before I was born—I stuck to my story, however, and related some things which went, in her opinion, to confirm it—others being called on were greatly astonished, knowing that these things had happened, and caused them to say in my hearing, I surely would be a prophet, as the Lord had shewn me things that had happened before my birth. And my father and mother strengthened me in this my first impression, saying in my presence, I was intended for some great purpose, which they had always thought from certain marks on my head and breast. . . . My grandmother, who was very religious, and to whom I was much attached—my master, who belonged to the church, and other religious persons who visited the house, and whom I often saw at prayers, noticing the singularity of my manners, I suppose, and my uncommon intelligence for a child, remarked I had too much sense to be raised, and if I was, I would never be of any service to any one as a slave—To a mind like mine, restless, inquisitive and observant of every thing that was passing, it is easy to suppose that religion was the subject to which it would be directed, and although this subject principally occupied my thoughts—there was nothing that I saw or heard of to which my attention was not directed—The manner in which I learned to read and write, not only had great influence on my own mind, as I acquired it with the most perfect ease, so much so, that I have no recollection whatever of learning the alphabet—but to the astonishment of the family, one day, when a book was shewn to me to keep me from crying, I began spelling the names of different objects—this was a source of wonder to all in the neighbor-hood, particularly the blacks—and this learning was constantly improved at all opportunities—when I got large enough to go to work, while employed, I was reflecting on many things that would present themselves to my imagination, and whenever an opportunity occurred of looking at a book, when the school children were getting their lessons, I would find many things that the fertility of my own imagination had depicted to me before; all my time, not devoted to my master's service, was spent either in prayer, or in making experiments in casting different things in moulds made of earth, in attempting to make paper, gun-powder, and many other experiments, that although I could not perfect, yet convinced me of its practicability if I had the means. I was not addicted to stealing in my youth, nor have ever been—Yet such was the confidence of the negroes in the neighborhood, even at this early period of my life, in my superior judgment, that they would often carry me with them when they were going on any roguery, to plan for them. Growing up among them, with this confidence in my superior judgment, and when this, in their opinions, was perfected by Divine inspiration, from the circum-stances already alluded to in my infancy, and which belief was ever afterwards zealously inculcated by the austerity of my life and manners, which became the subject of remark by white and black.—Having soon discovered to be great, I must appear so, and therefore studiously avoided mixing in society, and wrapped myself in mystery, devoting my time to fasting and prayer—by this time, having arrived to man's estate, and hearing the scriptures commented on at meetings, I was struck with that particular passage which says: "Seek ye the kingdom of Heaven and all things shall be added unto you." I reflected much on this passage, and prayed daily for light on this subject—As I was praying one day at my plough, the spirit spoke to me, saying "Seek ye the kingdom of Heaven and all things shall be added unto you." *Question*—what do you mean by the Spirit. *Ans.* The Spirit that spoke to the prophets in former days—and I was greatly astonished, and for two years prayed continually, whenever my duty would permit—and then again I had the same revelation, which fully confirmed me in the impression that I was ordained for some great purpose in the hands of the Almighty. Several years rolled round, in which many events occurred to strengthen me in this my belief. At this time I reverted in my mind to the remarks made of me in my childhood, and the things that had been shewn me—and as it had been said of me in my childhood by those by whom I had been taught to pray, both white and black, and in whom I had the greatest confidence, that I had too much sense to be raised, and if I was, I would never be of any use to any one as a slave. Now finding I had arrived to man's estate, and was a slave, and these revelations being made known to me, I began to direct my attention to this great object, to fulfill the purpose for which, by this time, I felt assured I was intended. Knowing the influence I had obtained over the minds of my fellow servants, (not by the means of conjuring and such like tricks—for to them I always spoke of such things with contempt) but by the communion of the Spirit whose revelations I often communicated to them, and they believed and said my wisdom came from God. I now began to prepare them for my purpose, by telling them something was about to happen that would terminate in fulfilling the great promise that had been made to me—About this time I was placed under an over-seer, from whom I ran away—and after remaining in the woods thirty days, I returned, to the astonishment of the negroes on the plantation, who thought I had made my escape to some other part of the country, as my father had done before. But the reason of my return was, that the Spirit appeared to me and said I had my wishes directed to the things of this world, and not to the kingdom of Heaven, and that I should return to the service of my earthly master—"For he who knoweth his Master's will, and doeth it not, shall be beaten with many stripes, and thus have I chastened you." And the negroes found fault, and murmured against me, saying that if they had my sense they would not serve any master in the world. And about this time I had a vision—and I saw white spirits and black spirits engaged in battle, and the sun was darkened—the thunder rolled in the Heavens, and blood flowed in streams—and I heard a voice saying, "Such is your luck, such you are called to see, and let it come rough or smooth, you must surely bare it." I now withdrew myself as much as my situation would permit, from the intercourse of my fellow servants, for the avowed purpose of serving the Spirit more fully—and it appeared to me, and reminded me of the things it had already shown me, and that it would then reveal to me the knowledge of the elements, the revolution of the planets, the operation of tides, and changes of the seasons. After this revelation in the year of 1825, and the knowledge of the elements being made known to me, I sought more than ever to obtain true holiness before the great day of judgment should appear, and then I began to receive the true knowledge of faith. And from the first steps of righteousness until the last, was I made perfect; and the Holy Ghost was with me, and said, "Behold me as I stand in the Heavens"—and I looked and saw the forms of men in different attitudes—and there were lights in the sky to which the children of darkness gave other names than what they really were—for they were the lights of the Savior's hands, stretched forth from east to west, even as they were extended on the cross on Calvary for the redemption of sinners. And I wondered greatly at these miracles, and prayed to be informed of a certainty of the meaning thereof—and shortly afterwards, while laboring in the field, I discovered drops of blood on the corn as though it were dew from heaven—and I communicated it to many, both white and black, in the neighborhood—and I then found on the leaves in the woods hieroglyphic characters, and numbers, with the forms of men in different attitudes, portrayed in blood, and representing the figures I had seen before in the heavens. And now the Holy Ghost had revealed itself to me, and made plain the miracles it had shown me—For as the blood of Christ had been shed on this earth, and had ascended to heaven for the salvation of sinners, and was now returning to earth again in the form of dew—and as the leaves on the trees bore the impression of the figures I had seen in the heavens, it was plain to me that the Savior was about to lay down the yoke he had borne for the sins of men, and the great day of judgment was at hand. About this time I told these things to a white man, (Etheldred T. Brantley) on whom it had a wonderful effect—and he ceased from his wickedness, and was attacked immediately with a cutaneous eruption, and blood oozed from the pores of his skin, and after praying and fasting nine days, he was healed, and the Spirit appeared to me again, and said, as the Savior had been baptised so should we be also—and when the white people would not let us be baptised by the church, we went down into the water together, in the sight of many who reviled us, and were baptised by the Spirit—After this I rejoiced greatly, and gave thanks to God. And on the 12th of May, 1828, I heard a loud noise in the heavens, and the Spirit instantly appeared to me and said the Serpent was loosened, and Christ had laid down the yoke he had borne for the sins of men, and that I should take it on and fight against the Serpent, for the time was fast approaching when the first should be last and the last should be first. *Ques.* Do you not find yourself mistaken now? *Ans.* Was not Christ crucified? And by signs in the heavens that it would make known to me when I should commence the great work—and until the first sign appeared, I should conceal it from the knowledge of men—And on the appearance of the sign, (the eclipse of the sun last February) I should arise and prepare myself, and slay my enemies with their own weapons. And immediately on the sign appearing in the heavens, the seal was removed from my lips, and I communicated the great work laid out for me to do, to four in whom I had the greatest confidence, (Henry, Hark, Nelson, and Sam)—It was intended by us to have begun the work of death on the 4th July last—Many were the plans formed and rejected by us, and it affected my mind to such a degree, that I fell sick, and the time passed without our coming to any determination how to commence—Still forming new schemes and rejecting them, when the sign appeared again, which determined me not to wait longer.

Since the commencement of 1830, I had been living with Mr. Joseph Travis, who was to me a kind master, and placed the greatest confidence in me; in fact, I had no cause to complain of his treatment to me. On Saturday evening, the 20th of August, it was agreed between Henry, Hark and myself to prepare a dinner the next day for the men we expected, and then to concert a plan, as we had not yet determined on any. Hark, on the following morning, brought a pig, and Henry brandy, and being joined by Sam, Nelson, Will and Jack, they prepared in the woods a dinner, where, about three o'clock, I joined them.

Q. Why were you so backward in joining them?

A. The same reason that had caused me not to mix with them for years before.

I saluted them on coming up, and asked Will how came he there, he answered, his life was worth no more than others, and his liberty as dear to him. I asked him if he thought to obtain it? He said he would, or lose his life. This was enough to put him in full confidence. Jack, I knew, was only a tool in the hands of Hark, it was quickly agreed we should commence at home (Mr. J. Travis') on that night, and until we had armed and equipped ourselves, and gathered sufficient force, neither age nor sex was to be spared, (which was invariably adhered to). We remained at the feast, until about two hours in the night, when we went to the house and found Austin; they all went to the cider press and drank, except myself. On returning to the house, Hark went to the door with an axe, for the purpose of breaking it open, as we knew we were strong enough to murder the family, if they were awakened by the noise; but reflecting that it might create an alarm in the neighborhood, we determined to enter the house secretly, and murder them whilst sleeping.

QUESTIONS FOR READING AND DISCUSSION

1. According to Turner's *Confessions*, in what ways did he consider himself "great," set apart from other slaves? How did he receive confirmation of his special qualities?

2. What did his family and friends think about him? Why did some find fault and murmur against him? What did Turner mean by saying, "Was not Christ crucified?"

3. To what extent does this excerpt from Turner's *Confessions* document the significance of religion among slaves? Can one distinguish the relative significance of Christianity as compared with other religious beliefs? To what degree did religious beliefs encourage or discourage insurrection among slaves?

4. Even though Turner's owner, Joseph Travis, was "a kind master," why did Turner and the other insurrectionists begin by killing him and his family?

5. How might the fact that Turner made his *Confessions* to a white man while in jail awaiting execution have influenced what he said? How might Gray have shaped Turner's testimony? If one assumes, for the sake of argument, that Gray wrote exactly what Turner said, do you think Turner gave an accurate account of his beliefs and motives? Why or why not?

DOCUMENT 13–5

The Proslavery Argument

Slaveholders passionately defended slavery from attacks by abolitionists. Their proslavery arguments not only responded to criticisms of slaveholders but also indicted the character and values of free society. James Henry Hammond, the author of the following letter addressed to an English abolitionist, was a prominent South Carolina planter and politician. Owner of a large plantation and scores of slaves, Hammond had served a term in Congress and had been governor of his state when he wrote this letter, which first appeared in a Columbia, South Carolina, newspaper in 1845.

James Henry Hammond
Letter to an English Abolitionist, 1845

You will say that man cannot hold *property in man.* The answer is, that he can and actually does hold property in his fellow all the world over, in a variety of *forms, and has always done so.* . . .

If you were to ask me whether I am an advocate of Slavery in the abstract, I should probably answer, that I am not, according to my understanding of the question. I do not like to deal in abstractions. It seldom leads to any useful ends. There are few universal truths. I do not now remember any single moral truth universally acknowledged. . . . Justice itself is impalpable as an abstraction, and abstract liberty the merest phantasy that ever amused the imagination. This world was made for man, and man for the world as it is. We ourselves, our relations with one another and with all matter, are real, not ideal. I might say that I am no more in favor of Slavery in the abstract, than I am of poverty, disease, deformity, idiocy, or any other inequality in the condition of the human family; that I love perfection, and think I should enjoy a millennium such as God has promised. But what would that amount to? A pledge that I would join you to set about eradicating those apparently inevitable evils of our nature, in equalizing the condition of all mankind, consummating the perfection of our race, and introducing the millennium? By no means. To effect these things, belongs exclusively to a higher power. And it would be well for us to leave the Almighty to perfect his own works and fulfil his own covenants. Especially, as the history of the past shows how entirely futile all human efforts have proved, when made for the purpose of aiding Him in carrying out even his revealed designs, and how invariably he has accomplished them by unconscious instruments, and in the face of human expectation. Nay more, that every attempt which has been made by fallible man to extort from the world obedience to his "abstract" notions of right and wrong, has been invariably attended with calamities dire, and extended just in proportion to the breadth and vigor of the movement. On Slavery in the abstract, then, it would not be amiss to have as little as possible to say. Let us contemplate it as it is. And thus contemplating it, the first question we have to ask ourselves is, whether it is contrary to the will of God, as revealed to us in his Holy Scriptures—the only certain means given us to ascertain his will. If it is, then Slavery is a sin. And I admit at once that every man is bound to set his face against it, and to emancipate his slaves, should he hold any.

Let us open these Holy Scriptures. . . . You cannot deny that God especially authorized his chosen people to purchase "bondmen forever" from the heathen, as recorded in the twenty-fifth chapter of Leviticus, and that they are there designated by the very Hebrew word used in the tenth commandment. Nor can you deny that a "BONDMAN FOREVER" is a "SLAVE"; yet you endeavor to hang an argument of immortal consequence upon the wretched subterfuge, that the precise word "slave" is not to be found in the translation of the Bible. As if the translators were canonical expounders of the Holy Scriptures, and *their words*, not God's *meaning*, must be regarded as his revelation. . . .

From James Henry Hammond, "Letter to an English Abolitionist" (Columbia, SC: Allen, McCarter and Co., 1845).

It is impossible, therefore, to suppose that Slavery is contrary to the will of God. It is equally absurd to say that American Slavery differs in form or principle from that of the chosen people. *We accept the Bible terms as the definition of our Slavery, and its precepts as the guide of our conduct.* . . .

I think, then, I may safely conclude, and I firmly believe, that American Slavery is not only not a sin, but especially commanded by God through Moses, and approved by Christ through his apostles. And here I might close its defence; for what God ordains, and Christ sanctifies, should surely command the respect and toleration of man. . . .

I endorse without reserve the much abused sentiment . . . that "Slavery is the corner-stone of our republican edifice"; while I repudiate, as ridiculously absurd, that much lauded but nowhere accredited dogma of Mr. Jefferson, that "all men are born equal." No society has ever yet existed . . . without a natural variety of classes. The most marked of these must, in a country like ours, be the rich and the poor, the educated and the ignorant. It will scarcely be disputed that the very poor have less leisure to prepare themselves for the proper discharge of public duties than the rich; and that the ignorant are wholly unfit for them at all. In all countries save ours, these two classes, or the poor rather, who are presumed to be necessarily ignorant, are by law expressly excluded from all participation in the management of public affairs. In a Republican Government this cannot be done. Universal suffrage, though not essential in theory, seems to be in fact a necessary appendage to a republican system. Where universal suffrage obtains, it is obvious that the government is in the hands of a numerical majority; and it is hardly necessary to say that in every part of the world more than half the people are ignorant and poor. Though no one can look upon poverty as a crime, and we do not here generally regard it as any objection to a man in his individual capacity, still it must be admitted that it is a wretched and insecure government which is administered by its most ignorant citizens, and those who have the least at stake under it. Though intelligence and wealth have great influence here, as everywhere, in keeping in check reckless and unenlightened numbers, yet it is evident to close observers, if not to all, that these are rapidly usurping all power in the non-slaveholding States, and threaten a fearful crisis in republican institutions there at no remote period. In the slaveholding States, however, nearly one-half of the whole population, and those the poorest and most ignorant, have no political influence whatever, because they are slaves. Of the other half, a large proportion are both educated and independent in their circumstances, while those who unfortunately are not so, being still elevated far above the mass, are higher toned and more deeply interested in preserving a stable and well ordered government, than the same class in any other country. Hence, Slavery is truly the "corner-stone" and foundation of every well designed and durable "republican edifice." . . .

But the question is, whether free or slave labor is cheapest to us in this country, at this time, situated as we are. And it is decided at once by the fact that we cannot avail ourselves of any other than slave labor. We neither have, nor can we procure, other labor to any extent, or on anything like the terms mentioned. We must, therefore, content ourselves with our dear labor, under the consoling reflection that what is lost to us, is gained to humanity; and that, inasmuch as our slave costs us more than your free man costs you, by so much is he better off. . . . Slavery is rapidly filling up our country with a hardy and healthy race, peculiarly adapted to our climate and productions, and conferring signal political and social advantages on us as a people. . . .

Failing in all your attempts to prove that [slavery] is sinful in its nature, immoral in its effects, a political evil, and profitless to those who maintain it, you appeal to the sympathies of mankind, and attempt to arouse the world against us by the most shocking charges of tyranny and cruelty. You begin by a vehement denunciation of "the irresponsible power of one man over his fellow men." . . . I deny that the power of the slaveholder in America is "irresponsible." He is responsible to God. He is responsible to the world. . . . He is responsible to the community in which he lives, and to the laws under which he enjoys his civil rights. Those laws do not permit him to kill, to maim, or to punish beyond certain limits, or to overtask, or to refuse to feed and clothe his slave. In short, they forbid him to be tyrannical or cruel. . . . Still, though a slaveholder, I freely acknowledge my obligations as a man; and that I am bound to treat humanely the fellow-creatures whom God has entrusted to my charge. I feel, therefore, somewhat sensitive under the accusation of cruelty, and disposed to defend myself and fellow-slaveholders against it. It is certainly the interest of all, and I am convinced that it is also the desire of every one of us, to treat our slaves with proper kindness. It is necessary to our deriving the greatest amount of profit from them. Of this we are all satisfied. . . .

Slaveholders are no more perfect than other men. They have passions. Some of them, as you may suppose, do not at all times restrain them. Neither do husbands, parents and friends. And in each of these relations, as serious suffering as frequently arises from uncontrolled passions, as ever does in that of master and slave. . . . I have no hesitation in saying that our slaveholders are kind masters, as men usually are kind husbands, parents and friends—as a general rule, kinder. A bad master—he who overworks his slaves, provides ill for them, or treats them with undue severity—loses the esteem and respect of his fellow-citizens to as great an extent as he would for the violation of any of his social and most of his moral obligations. . . .

Of late years we have been not only annoyed, but greatly embarrassed in this matter, by the abolitionists. We have been compelled to curtail some privileges; we have been debarred from granting new ones. In the face of discussions which aim at loosening all ties between master and slave, we have in some measure to abandon our efforts to attach them to us, and control them through their affections and pride. We have to rely more and more on the power of fear. We must, in all our intercourse with them, assert and maintain strict mastery, and impress it on them that they are slaves. This is painful to us, and certainly no present advantage to them. But it is the direct consequence of the abolition agitation. We are determined to continue masters, and to do so we have to draw the rein tighter and tighter day by day to be assured that we hold them in complete check. How far this process will go on, depends wholly and solely on the abolitionists. When they desist, we can relax. We may not before. . . . I assure you that my sentiments, and feelings, and determinations, are those of every slaveholder in this country. . . .

Now I affirm, that in Great Britain the poor and laboring classes of your own race and color, not only your fellow-beings, but your *fellow-citizens*, are more miserable and degraded, morally and physically, than our slaves; to be elevated to the actual condition of whom, would be to these, your *fellow-citizens*, a most glorious act of *emancipation*. And I also affirm, that the poor and laboring classes of our older free States would not be in a much more enviable condition, but for our Slavery. . . . [Hammond then quotes from a British report giving examples of the terrible working conditions experienced by some free laborers in England.]

It is shocking beyond endurance to turn over your records, in which the condition of your laboring classes is but too faithfully depicted. Could our slaves but see it, they would join us in lynching the abolitionists, which, by the by, they would not now be loth to do. We never think of imposing on them such labor, either in amount or kind. We never put them to *any work*, under ten, more generally at twelve years of age, and then the very lightest. Destitution is absolutely unknown—never did a slave starve in America; while in moral sentiments and feelings, in religious information, and even in general intelligence, they are infinitely the superiors of your operatives. When you look around you, how dare you talk to us before the world of Slavery? For the condition of your wretched laborers, you, and every Briton who is not one of them, are responsible before God and man. If you are really humane, philanthropic, and charitable, here are objects for you. Relieve them. Emancipate them. Raise them from the condition of brutes, to the level of human beings—of American slaves, at least. . . .

The American slaveholders, collectively or individually, ask no favors of any man or race who tread the earth. In none of the attributes of men, mental or physical, do they acknowledge or fear superiority elsewhere. They stand in the broadest light of the knowledge, civilization and improvement of the age, as much favored of heaven as any of the *sons of* Adam. . . . They cannot be flattered, duped, nor bullied out of their rights or their propriety.

QUESTIONS FOR READING AND DISCUSSION

1. Why did Hammond oppose slavery in the abstract but defend it "as it is" in the South? Why did he refuse to try to end slavery?

2. What did Hammond mean by declaring that "slavery is the corner-stone of our republican edifice"? Why did he consider human equality "ridiculously absurd"?

3. How did abolitionists influence slaveholders? Why were opponents of slavery so misguided, according to Hammond?

4. Hammond argued that white laborers in Britain or the North were "more miserable and degraded" than slaves. Why? How might white laborers and slaves have replied to this assertion?

COMPARATIVE QUESTIONS

1. How did Bennet Barrow's plantation rules compare with the experiences of Madison Hemings and Nat Turner and with the statements about slavery made by James Henry Hammond? Did Barrow, Hemings, Turner, and Hammond express similar views about slaves and their motivations?

2. How did Hammond's account of slavery compare to that of the slave women who visited Fanny Kemble? How might Hammond have responded to Kemble? How might the slave women and Kemble have responded to Hammond?

3. What similarities and differences characterized slaves' experiences on the plantations of Thomas Jefferson (Madison Hemings document), Bennet Barrow, and Pierce Butler (Fanny Kemble document)?

4. Judging from the documents in this chapter, to what extent did the slave South embody values embraced throughout American society? To what extent were the values of black and white Southerners distinctive? Why?

14 The House Divided

1846–1861

Politicians defined the terms of the sectional crisis in speech after speech, grappling with the underlying question of what to do about slavery. Three of the most important answers to that question were presented by Abraham Lincoln, Frederick Douglass, and Jefferson Davis. Hearing and reading their speeches helped Americans to decide what they believed and, ultimately, to choose sides. Beneath the rhetoric and bluster of the politicians, the genuine, day-to-day character of freedom in American life was at stake. The experiences of fugitive slave Margaret Garner and antislavery activist and author Lydia Maria Child illustrate that sectional polarization over slavery and race reached far beyond the realm of electoral politics.

DOCUMENT 14–1
The Kansas–Nebraska Act

The Kansas–Nebraska Act ruptured old political coalitions. For decades, the Whig and Democratic parties had been national parties, with leaders and voters in both free states and slave states. Kansas–Nebraska drove a sectional wedge into each party. The act alienated many Northern Whigs and Democrats. Addressing an audience in Peoria, Illinois, in October 1854, Abraham Lincoln passionately denounced the Kansas–Nebraska Act. In his speech, excerpted here, Lincoln explained the grave danger posed by the act.

Abraham Lincoln
Speech in Peoria, Illinois, October 16, 1854

Preceding the Presidential election of 1852, each of the great political parties, democrats and whigs, met in convention, and adopted resolutions endorsing the compromise of '50; as a "finality," a final settlement . . . of all slavery agitation. . . .

During this long period of time Nebraska had remained, substantially an uninhabited country, but now emigration to, and settlement within it began to

take place. It is about one third as large as the present United States, and its importance so long overlooked, begins to come into view. . . . On January 4th, 1854,
Judge [Stephen A.] Douglas introduces a new bill to give Nebraska territorial government. . . . [A]bout a month after the introduction of the bill, on the judge's own
motion, it is so amended as to declare the Missouri Compromise inoperative and
void; and, substantially, that the People who go and settle there may establish
slavery, or exclude it, as they may see fit. In this shape the bill passed both branches
of congress, and became a law.

This is the *repeal* of the Missouri Compromise. . . . I think, and shall try to
show, that it is wrong; wrong in its direct effect, letting slavery into Kansas and
Nebraska—and wrong in its prospective principle, allowing it to spread to every
other part of the wide world, where men can be found inclined to take it.

This *declared* indifference, but as I must think, covert *real* zeal for the spread
of slavery, I can not but hate. I hate it because of the monstrous injustice of slavery
itself. I hate it because it deprives our republican example of its just influence in
the world—enables the enemies of free institutions, with plausibility, to taunt us
as hypocrites—causes the real friends of freedom to doubt our sincerity, and especially because it forces so many really good men amongst ourselves into an open
war with the very fundamental principles of civil liberty—criticising the Declaration of Independence, and insisting that there is no right principle of action but
self-interest.

Before proceeding, let me say I think I have no prejudice against the Southern
people. They are just what we would be in their situation. If slavery did not now
exist amongst them, they would not introduce it. If it did now exist amongst us,
we should not instantly give it up. This I believe of the masses north and south.
Doubtless there are individuals, on both sides, who would not hold slaves under
any circumstances; and others who would gladly introduce slavery anew, if it
were out of existence. We know that some southern men do free their slaves, go
north, and become tip-top abolitionists; while some northern ones go south, and
become most cruel slave-masters.

When southern people tell us they are no more responsible for the origin of
slavery, than we; I acknowledge the fact. When it is said that the institution exists;
and that it is very difficult to get rid of it, in any satisfactory way, I can understand and appreciate the saying. I surely will not blame them for not doing what
I should not know how to do myself. If all earthly power were given to me, I
should not know what to do, as to the existing institution. My first impulse would
be to free all the slaves and send them to Liberia,—to their own native land.
But a moment's reflection would convince me, that whatever of high hope, (as I
think there is) there may be in this, in the long run, its sudden execution is impossible. If they were all landed there in a day, they would all perish in the next
ten days; and there are not surplus shipping and surplus money enough in the
world to carry them there in many times ten days. What then? Free them all,
and keep them among us as underlings? Is it quite certain that this betters their
condition? I think I would not hold one in slavery, at any rate; yet the point is
not clear enough for me to denounce people upon. What next? Free them, and
make them politically and socially, our equals? My own feelings will not admit

From Roy P. Basler, ed., *The Collected Works of Abraham Lincoln* (New Brunswick,
NJ: Rutgers University Press, 1953), 2:247–82.

of this; and if mine would, we well know that those of the great mass of white people will not. Whether this feeling accords with justice and sound judgment, is not the sole question, if indeed, it is any part of it. A universal feeling, whether well or ill-founded, can not be safely disregarded. We can not, then, make them equals. It does seem to me that systems of gradual emancipation might be adopted; but for their tardiness in this, I will not undertake to judge our brethren of the south.

When they remind us of their constitutional rights, I acknowledge them, not grudgingly, but fully, and fairly; and I would give them any legislation for the reclaiming of their fugitives, which should not, in its stringency, be more likely to carry a free man into slavery, than our ordinary criminal laws are to hang an innocent one.

But all this, to my judgment, furnishes no more excuse for permitting slavery to go into our own free territory, than it would for reviving the African slave trade by law. The law which forbids the bringing of slaves from Africa; and that which has so long forbid the taking them to Nebraska, can hardly be distinguished on any moral principle; and the repeal of the former could find quite as plausible excuses as that of the latter. . . .

Some men, mostly whigs, who condemn the repeal of the Missouri Compromise, nevertheless hesitate to go for its restoration, lest they be thrown in company with the abolitionist. Will they allow me as an old whig to tell them good humoredly, that I think this is very silly? Stand with anybody that stands RIGHT. Stand with him while he is right and PART with him when he goes wrong. Stand WITH the abolitionist in restoring the Missouri Compromise; and stand AGAINST him when he attempts to repeal the fugitive slave law. In the latter case you stand with the southern disunionist. What of that? you are still right. In both cases you are right. In both cases you oppose the dangerous extremes. In both you stand on middle ground and hold the ship level and steady. In both you are national and nothing less than national. This is good old whig ground. To desert such ground, because of any company, is to be less than a whig—less than a man—less than an American.

I particularly object to the NEW position which the avowed principle of this Nebraska law gives to slavery in the body politic. I object to it because it assumes that there CAN be MORAL RIGHT in the enslaving of one man by another. I object to it as a dangerous dalliance for a free people—a sad evidence that, feeling prosperity we forget right—that liberty, as a principle, we have ceased to revere. I object to it because the fathers of the republic eschewed, and rejected it. The argument of "Necessity" was the only argument they ever admitted in favor of slavery; and so far, and so far only as it carried them, did they ever go. They found the institution existing among us, which they could not help; and they cast blame upon the British King for having permitted its introduction. BEFORE the constitution, they prohibited its introduction into the north-western Territory—the only country we owned, then free from it. AT the framing and adoption of the constitution, they forbore to so much as mention the word "slave" or "slavery" in the whole instrument. . . . Thus, the thing is hid away, in the constitution, just as an afflicted man hides away a wen [cyst] or a cancer. . . . Less than this our fathers COULD not do; and MORE they WOULD not do. Necessity drove them so far, and farther, they would not go. But this is not all. The earliest Congress, under the constitution, took the same view of slavery. They hedged and hemmed it in to the narrowest limits of necessity. . . .

Thus we see, the plain unmistakable spirit of that age, towards slavery, was hostility to the PRINCIPLE, and toleration, ONLY BY NECESSITY.

But NOW it is to be transformed into a "sacred right." Nebraska brings it forth, places it on the high road to extension and perpetuity; and, with a pat on its back, says to it, "Go, and God speed you." . . . Little by little, but steadily as man's march to the grave, we have been giving up the OLD for the NEW faith. Near eighty years ago we began by declaring that all men are created equal; but now from that beginning we have run down to the other declaration, that for some men to enslave OTHERS is a "sacred right of self-government." These principles can not stand together. They are as opposite as God and mammon [greed]; and whoever holds to the one, must despise the other. . . .

Let no one be deceived. The spirit of seventy-six and the spirit of Nebraska, are utter antagonisms; and the former is being rapidly displaced by the latter. Fellow countrymen—Americans south, as well as north, shall we make no effort to arrest this? . . . In our greedy chase to make profit of the negro, let us beware, lest we "cancel and tear to pieces" even the white man's charter of freedom.

Our republican robe is soiled, and trailed in the dust. Let us repurify it. Let us turn and wash it white, in the spirit, if not the blood, of the Revolution. Let us turn slavery from its claims of "moral right," back upon its existing legal rights, and its arguments of "necessity." Let us return it to the position our fathers gave it; and there let it rest in peace. Let us re-adopt the Declaration of Independence, and with it, the practices, and policy, which harmonize with it. Let north and south— let all Americans—let all lovers of liberty everywhere—join in the great and good work. If we do this, we shall not only have saved the Union; but we shall have so saved it, as to make, and to keep it, forever worthy of the saving.

QUESTIONS FOR READING AND DISCUSSION

1. In what way did the Kansas–Nebraska Act repeal the Missouri Compromise? Why did Lincoln consider the act the result of "covert *real* zeal for the spread of slavery"?

2. To what extent did Lincoln oppose slavery? Did he believe slaveholders should emancipate their slaves, and if so, what did he believe should happen to them? Would abolitionists have found his arguments convincing? What about slaveholders?

3. What did Lincoln mean by declaring, "I think I have no prejudice against the Southern people"? What strategies did he use to promote national unity?

4. Why did Lincoln believe "our republican robe is soiled, and trailed in the dust"? How did he use the historical legacy of the founders to support his arguments?

DOCUMENT 14–2

The Antislavery Constitution

The political debate between North and South pivoted on the question of what the Constitution permitted—or required—the federal government to do about slavery. Abolitionist William Lloyd Garrison publicly burned the Constitution in 1854 because, he said, by permitting slavery it was "a covenant with death, an agreement with hell." Frederick

Douglass, a former slave and prominent black abolitionist, declared that, on the contrary, the Constitution was opposed to slavery. In countless speeches to northern antislavery audiences, Douglass set forth his views of the Constitution, which he summarized in a pamphlet published in 1860, the source of the following excerpt.

Frederick Douglass

The Constitution of the United States: Is It Proslavery or Antislavery? 1860

I only ask you to look at the American Constitution . . . and you will see with me that no man is guaranteed a right of property in man, under the provisions of that instrument. If there are two ideas more distinct in their character and essence than another, those ideas are "persons" and "property," "men" and "things." Now, when it is proposed to transform persons into "property" and men into beasts of burden, I demand that the law that contemplates such a purpose shall be expressed with irresistible clearness. The thing must not be left to inference, but must be done in plain English. . . .

[Many Americans] are in the habit of treating the negro as an exception to general rules. When their own liberty is in question they will avail themselves of all rules of law which protect and defend their freedom; but when the black man's rights are in question they concede everything, admit everything for slavery, and put liberty to the proof. They reverse the common law usage, and presume the negro a slave unless he can prove himself free. I, on the other hand, presume him free unless he is proved to be otherwise. Let us look at the objects for which the Constitution was framed and adopted, and see if slavery is one of them. Here are its own objects as set forth by itself: "We, the people of these United States, in order to form a more perfect union, establish justice, ensure domestic tranquillity, provide for the common defence, promote the general welfare, and secure the blessings of liberty to ourselves and our prosperity, do ordain and establish this Constitution for the United States of America." . . . These are all good objects, and, slavery, so far from being among them, is a foe of them. But it has been said that negroes are not included within the benefits sought under this declaration. This is said by the slaveholders in America . . . but it is not said by the Constitution itself. Its language is "we the people"; not we the white people, not even we the citizens, not we the privileged class, not we the high, not we the low, but we the people; not we the horses, sheep, and swine, and wheel-barrows, but we the people, we the human inhabitants; and, if negroes are people, they are included in the benefits for which the Constitution of America was ordained and established. . . .

[T]he constitutionality of slavery can be made out only by disregarding the plain and common-sense reading of the Constitution itself; by discrediting and casting away as worthless the most beneficent rules of legal interpretation; by ruling the negro outside of these beneficent rules; by claiming everything for slavery; by denying everything for freedom; by assuming that the Constitution does not mean what it says, and that it says what it does not mean, by disregarding the written Constitution, and interpreting it in the light of a secret understanding. It

---

From Frederick Douglass, *The Constitution of the United States: Is It Pro-Slavery or Anti-Slavery?* (1860).

is in this mean, contemptible, and underhand method that the American Constitution is pressed into the service of slavery. They go everywhere else for proof that the Constitution is pro-slavery but to the Constitution itself. The Constitution declares that no person shall be deprived of life, liberty, or property without due process of law; it secures to every man the right of trial by jury, the privilege of the writ of habeas corpus . . . [and] it secures to every State a republican form of government. Any one of these provisions, in the hands of abolition statesmen, and backed up by a right moral sentiment, would put an end to slavery in America. The Constitution forbids the passing of a bill of attainder: that is, a law entailing upon the child the disabilities and hardships imposed upon the parent. Every slave law in America might be repealed on this very ground. The slave is made a slave because his mother is a slave. But to all this it is said that the practice of the American people is against my view. I admit it. They have given the Constitution a slaveholding interpretation. I admit it. They have committed innumerable wrongs against the negro in the name of the Constitution. Yes, I admit it all; and I go with him who goes farthest in denouncing these wrongs. But it does not follow that the Constitution is in favour of these wrongs because the slaveholders have given it that interpretation. . . .

My argument against the dissolution of the American Union is this: It would place the slave system more exclusively under the control of the slaveholding States, and withdraw it from the power in the Northern States which is opposed to slavery. Slavery is essentially barbarous in its character. It, above all things else, dreads the presence of an advanced civilisation. It flourishes best where it meets no reproving frowns, and hears no condemning voices. While in the Union it will meet with both. Its hope of life, in the last resort, is to get out of the Union. I am, therefore, for drawing the bond of the Union more closely, and bringing the Slave States more completely under the power of the Free States. What they most dread, that I most desire. I have much confidence in the instincts of the slaveholders. They see that the Constitution will afford slavery no protection when it shall cease to be administered by slaveholders. They see, moreover, that if there is once a will in the people of America to abolish slavery, there is no word, no syllable in the Constitution to forbid that result. . . .

The American people in the Northern States have helped to enslave the black people. Their duty will not have been done till they give them back their plundered rights. . . . My position now is one of reform, not of revolution. I would act for the abolition of slavery through the Government. . . . If slaveholders have ruled the American Government for the last fifty years, let the anti-slavery men rule the nation for the next fifty years.

QUESTIONS FOR READING AND DISCUSSION

1. According to Douglass, what were the antislavery provisions of the Constitution? Was Douglass's interpretation a "plain and common-sense reading of the Constitution itself," as he claimed?
2. In his view, why did slavery exist? Why were Americans "in the habit of treating the negro as an exception to general rules"? Why was slavery "essentially barbarous"?
3. Why was Douglass "against the dissolution of the American Union"?
4. What needed to be done to put the antislavery powers of the Constitution into effect? Why did he advocate "reform, not revolution"?

DOCUMENT 14–3

The Proslavery Constitution

Southern politicians argued that the Constitution required the federal government to pro-
tect owners of all forms of property, including slaves. The heated sectional debate about the
scope of federal power and states' rights focused attention on the territories. Could settlers
in a federal territory prohibit slavery or refuse to protect it? Or, regardless of territorial
laws, did the Constitution mandate that slavery in federal territories be protected by fed-
eral laws? In a speech to the U.S. Senate in May 1860, excerpted here, Jefferson Davis
made the case for federal protection. In less than a year, Senator Davis, a wealthy planter
from Mississippi, became president of the Confederacy.

Jefferson Davis
Speech before the U.S. Senate, May 1860

Among the many blessings for which we are indebted to our ancestry, is
that of transmitting to us a written Constitution; a fixed standard to which, in the
progress of events, every case may be referred, and by which it may be mea-
sured. . . . With this . . . to check, to restrain, and to direct their posterity, they
might reasonably hope the Government they founded should last forever; that
it should secure the great purposes for which it was ordained and established; that
it would be the shield of their posterity equally in every part of the country, and
equally in all time to time. . . .

Our fathers were aware of the different interests of the navigating and planting States, as they were then regarded. They sought to compose those difficulties,
and by compensating advantages given by one to the other, to form a Government
equal and just in its operation; and which, like the gentle showers of heaven,
should fall twice blessed, blessing him that gives and him that receives. This beneficial action and reaction between the different interests of the country constituted the bond of union and the motive of its formation. They constitute it to-day,
if we are sufficiently wise to appreciate our interests, and sufficiently faithful to
observe our trust. Indeed, with the extension of territory, with the multiplication
of interests, with the varieties, increasing from time to time, of the products of this
great country, the bonds which bind the Union together should have increased. . . .

The great principle which lay at the foundation of this fixed standard, the
Constitution of the United States, was the equality of rights between the States.
This was essential; it was necessary; it was a step which had to be taken first,
before any progress could be made. It was the essential requisite of the very idea
of sovereignty in the State; of a compact voluntarily entered into between sovereigns; and it is that equality of right under the Constitution on which we now
insist. . . .

We claim protection [of slavery], first, because it is our right; secondly, because
it is the duty of the General Government; and thirdly, because we have entered
into a compact together, which deprives each State of the power of using all the

---

From Dunbar Rowland, ed., *Jefferson Davis, Constitutionalist: His Letters, Papers, and*
Speeches (New York: AMS Press, 1923), 120–30.

means which it might employ for its own defense. This is the general theory of the right of protection. . . . [I]f general protection be the general duty, I ask, in the name of reason and constitutional right—I ask you to point me to authority by which a discrimination is made between slave property and any other. Yet this is the question now fraught with evil to our country. It is this which has raised the hurricane threatening to sweep our political institutions before it. . . .

I have been the determined opponent of what is called squatter sovereignty. I never gave it countenance, and I am now least of all disposed to give it quarter. . . . What right had Congress then, or what right has it now, to abdicate any power conferred upon it as trustee of the States? . . . In 1850, following the promulgation of this notion of squatter sovereignty, we had the idea of non-intervention introduced into the Senate of the United States, and it is strange to me how that idea has expanded. . . . Non-intervention then meant, as the debates show, that Congress should neither prohibit nor establish slavery in the Territories. That I hold to now. Will any one suppose that Congress then meant by non-intervention that Congress should legislate in no regard in respect to property in slaves? Why, sir, the very acts which they passed at the time refute it. There is the fugitive slave law. . . .

By what species of legerdemain[1] this doctrine of non-intervention has come to extend to a paralysis of the Government on the whole subject, to exclude the Congress from any kind of legislation whatever, I am at a loss to conceive. . . . I had no faith in it then; I considered it an evasion; I held that the duty of Congress ought to be performed, that the issue was before us, and ought to be met, the sooner the better; that truth would prevail if presented to the people. . . .

That is what we ask of Congress now. . . . I am not one of those who would willingly see this Congress enact a code to be applied to all Territories and for all time to come. I only ask that . . . when personal and property rights in the Territories are not protected, then the Congress, by existing laws and governmental machinery, shall intervene and provide such means as will secure in each case, as far as may be, an adequate remedy. I ask no slave code, nor horse code, nor machine code. I ask that the Territorial Legislature be made to understand beforehand that the Congress of the United States does not concede to them the power to interfere with the rights of person or property guaranteed by the Constitution, and that it will apply the remedy, if the Territorial Legislature should so far forget its duty, so far transcend its power, as to commit that violation of right. . . .

These are the general views which I entertain of our right of protection and the duty of the Government. They are those which are entertained by the constituency I have the honor to represent. . . . For weal or for woe, for prosperity or adversity, for the preservation of the great blessings which we enjoy, or the trial of a new and separate condition, I trust Mississippi never will surrender the smallest atom of the sovereignty, independence, and equality, to which she was born, to avoid any danger or any sacrifice to which she may thereby be exposed. . . .

We have made no war against [the North]. We have asked no discrimination in our favor. We claim to have but the Constitution fairly and equally administered. To consent to less than this, would be to sink in the scale of manhood; would be to make our posterity so degraded that they would curse this generation for robbing them of the rights their revolutionary fathers bequeathed them.

---

[1]**legerdemain**: Sleight of hand, trickery.

QUESTIONS FOR READING AND DISCUSSION

1. According to Davis, what constitutional principles guaranteed federal protection for slavery? To what extent were those principles enshrined in specific constitutional provisions?

2. How did "the great principle" of "the equality of rights between the States" serve to protect slavery?

3. Why did Davis oppose both "squatter sovereignty" and "non-intervention"?

4. How did he propose to resolve the disputes about slavery?

5. In what sense did Davis believe white Southerners' "manhood" was at stake in the constitutional conflict?

DOCUMENT 14–4

Levi Coffin Describes Margaret Garner's Attempt to Escape Slavery

Margaret Garner and her husband, children, and other family members fled slavery in northern Kentucky by crossing the frozen Ohio River to Cincinnati in January 1856. Garner and her family were soon captured and tried under the provisions of the federal fugitive slave law. Levi Coffin, a prosperous Quaker merchant and abolitionist, tried to help Garner escape, but failed. Coffin recalled Garner's plight in his memoir, published long after slavery was abolished following the Civil War. Coffin's account, excerpted below, illustrates the flesh and blood reality that underlay the abstract constitutional debates about slavery. Garner's experience vividly documents the effectiveness of the fugitive slave law in protecting the property rights of slave owners.

Reminiscences, 1880

Perhaps no case that came under my notice, while engaged in aiding fugitive slaves, attracted more attention and aroused deeper interest and sympathy than the case of Margaret Garner, the slave mother, who killed her child rather than see it taken back to slavery. This happened in the latter part of January, 1856. The Ohio River was frozen over at the time, and the opportunity thus offered for escaping to a free State was embraced by a number of slaves living in Kentucky, several miles back from the river. A party of seventeen, belonging to different masters in the same neighborhood, made arrangements to escape together. There was snow on the ground and the roads were smooth, so the plan of going to the river on a sled naturally suggested itself. The time fixed for their flight was Sabbath night, and having managed to get a large sled and two good horses, belonging to one of their masters, the party of seventeen crowded into the sled and started on their hazardous journey in the latter part of the night. They drove the

From Levi Coffin, *Reminiscences of Levi Coffin, The Reputed President of the Underground Railroad . . .* , 2nd ed. (Cincinnati: Robert Clarke, 1880), 557–67.

horses at full speed, and at daylight reached the river. . . . They left the sled and horses here, and as quickly as possible crossed the river on foot. It was now broad daylight, and people were beginning to pass about the streets [of Cincinnati, Ohio], and the fugitives divided their company that they might not attract so much notice.

An old slave man named Simon, and his wife Mary, together with their son Robert and his wife Margaret Garner and four children, made their way to the house of a colored man named Kite, who had formerly lived in their neighborhood and had been purchased from slavery by his father, Joe Kite. They had to make several inquiries in order to find Kite's house, which was below Mill Creek, in the lower part of the city. This afterward led to their discovery; they had been seen by a number of persons on their way to Kite's, and were easily traced by pursuers. The other nine fugitives were more fortunate. They made their way up town and found friends who conducted them to safe hiding-places, where they remained until night. They were then put on the Underground Railroad, and went safely through to Canada.

Kite felt alarmed for the safety of the party that had arrived at his house, and as soon as breakfast was over, he came to my store, at the corner of Sixth and Elm Streets, to ask counsel regarding them. I told him that they were in a very unsafe place and must be removed at once. I directed him how to conduct them from his house to the outskirts of the city . . . to a settlement of colored people in the western part of the city, where fugitives were often harbored. I would make arrangements to forward them northward, that night, on the Underground Railroad. Kite returned to his house at once, according to my directions, but he was too late; in a few minutes after his return, the house was surrounded by pursuers—the masters of the fugitives, with officers and a posse of men. The door and windows were barred, and those inside refused to give admittance. The fugitives were determined to fight, and to die, rather than to be taken back to slavery. Margaret, the mother of the four children, declared that she would kill herself and her children before she would return to bondage. The slave men were armed and fought bravely. The window was first battered down with a stick of wood, and one of the deputy marshals attempted to enter, but a pistol shot from within made a flesh wound on his arm and caused him to abandon the attempt. The pursuers then battered down the door with some timber and rushed in. The husband of Margaret fired several shots, and wounded one of the officers, but was soon overpowered and dragged out of the house. At this moment, Margaret Garner, seeing that their hopes of freedom were vain seized a butcher knife that lay on the table, and with one stroke cut the throat of her little daughter, whom she probably loved the best. She then attempted to take the life of the other children and to kill herself, but she was overpowered and hampered before she could complete her desperate work. The whole party was then arrested and lodged in jail.

The trial lasted two weeks, drawing crowds to the court-room every day. . . . The counsel for the defense [Jolliffe and Getchell] brought witnesses to prove that the fugitives had been permitted to visit the city at various times previously. It was claimed that Margaret Garner had been brought here by her owners a number of years before, to act as nurse girl, and according to the law which liberated slaves who were brought into free States by the consent of their masters, she had been free from that time, and her children, all of whom had been born since then—following the condition of the mother—were likewise free.

The Commissioner [hearing the case under the fugitive slave law] decided that a voluntary return to slavery, after a visit to a free State, re-attached the conditions of slavery, and that the fugitives were legally slaves at the time of their escape. . . .

Jolliffe said that in the final argument of the case he intended . . . to demonstrate . . . to the Court, that the Fugitive Slave law was unconstitutional, and as part and parcel of that argument he wished to show the effects of carrying it out. It had driven a frantic mother to murder her own child rather than see it carried back to the seething hell of American slavery. . . .

Margaret Garner, the chief actor in the tragedy which had occurred, naturally excited much attention. She was a mulatto, about five feet high, showing one-fourth or one-third white blood. She had a high forehead, her eyebrows were finely arched and her eyes bright and intelligent, but the African appeared in the lower part of her face, in her broad nose and thick lips. On the left side of her forehead was an old scar, and on the cheek-bone, on the same side, another one. When asked what caused them, she said: "White man struck me." That was all, but it betrays a story of cruelty and degradation, and, perhaps, gives the key-note to Margaret's hate of slavery, her revolt against its thralldom, and her resolve to die rather than go back to it.

She appeared to be twenty-two or twenty-three years old. While in the court-room she was dressed in dark calico, with a white handkerchief pinned around her neck, and a yellow cotton handkerchief, arranged as a turban, around her head. The babe she held in her arms was a little girl, about nine months old, and was much lighter in color than herself, light enough to show a red tinge in its cheeks. During the trial she would look up occasionally, for an instant, with a timid, apprehensive glance at the strange faces around her, but her eyes were generally cast down. The babe was continually fondling her face with its little hands, but she rarely noticed it, and her general expression was one of extreme sadness. The little boys, four and six years old, respectively, were bright-eyed, woolly-headed little fellows, with fat dimpled cheeks. During the trial they sat on the floor near their mother, playing together in happy innocence, all unconscious of the gloom that shrouded their mother, and of the fact that their own future liberty was at stake. The murdered child was almost white, a little girl of rare beauty.

The case seemed to stir every heart that was alive to the emotions of humanity. The interest manifested by all classes was not so much for the legal principles involved, as for the mute instincts that mold every human heart—the undying love of freedom that is planted in every breast—the resolve to die rather than submit to a life of degradation and bondage.

A number of people, who were deeply interested in the fugitives, visited them in prison and conversed with them. Old Simon, his wife Mary, and their son Robert, while expressing their longing for freedom, said that they should not attempt to kill themselves if they were returned to slavery. Their trust in God seemed to have survived all the wrong and cruelty inflicted upon them by man, and though they felt often like crying bitterly, "How long, O Lord, how long?" they still trusted and endured. But Margaret seemed to have a different nature; she could see nothing but woe for herself and her children. . . . Those who came to speak words of comfort and cheer felt them die upon their lips, when they looked into her face, and marked its expression of settled despair. Her sorrow was beyond the reach of any words of encouragement and consolation. . . .

Among those who visited Margaret in prison was Lucy Stone, the well-known eloquent public speaker. . . . She said: . . . "When I saw that poor fugitive, took her toil-hardened hand in mine, and read in her face deep suffering and an ardent longing for freedom, . . . I told her that a thousand hearts were aching for her, and that they were glad one child of hers was safe with the angels. Her only reply was a look of deep despair, of anguish such as no words can speak. I thought the spirit she manifested was the same with that of our ancestors to whom we had erected the monument at Bunker Hill—the spirit that would rather let us all go back to God than back to slavery. The faded faces of the negro children tell too plainly to what degradation female slaves must submit. Rather than give her little daughter to that life, she killed it. If in her deep maternal love she felt the impulse to send her child back to God, to save it from coming woe, who shall say she had no right to do so? . . . With my own teeth I would tear open my veins and let the earth drink my blood, rather than to wear the chains of slavery. How then could I blame her for wishing her child to find freedom with God and the angels, where no chains are?" . . .

But . . . the Commissioner remanded the fugitives back to slavery. He said that it was not a question of feeling to be decided by . . . his sympathies; the law of Kentucky and of the United States made it a question of property.

In regard to the claim, plainly established by the evidence, that the fugitives had previously been brought to this State by the consent of their masters, he said: "Had the slaves asserted their freedom, they would have been practically free, but they voluntarily returned to slavery. In allowing them to come to Ohio, the master voluntarily abandoned his claim upon them, and they, in returning, abandoned their claim to freedom." . . .

The fugitives were then delivered to their owners, who conveyed them . . . to the wharf of the Covington ferry-boat. A crowd followed them to the river, but there was no demonstration. The masters were surrounded by large numbers of their Kentucky friends, who had stood by them [the owners] and guarded their interests during the trial, and there was great rejoicing among them, on account of their victory.

The masters kept their slaves in jail in Covington, a few days, then . . . sent . . . [Margaret and her family] down the river [toward New Orleans]. . . . It was reported that on her way down the river [Margaret] sprang from the boat into the water with her babe in her arms; that when she rose she was seized by some of the boat hands and rescued, but that her child was drowned.

QUESTIONS FOR READING AND DISCUSSION

1. According to Coffin's memoir, for what reasons did antislavery supporters of Margaret Garner believe she murdered her daughter? Do you think they were correct? What evidence might suggest Garner's motives?

2. How did Margaret Garner's outlook differ from that of her husband and his parents? What accounts for the differences, according to Coffin and Lucy Stone?

3. What did the commissioner who ruled on the Garner case in Ohio mean by concluding that "the law of Kentucky and of the United States made it a question of property"?

4. To what extent did Garner's case illustrate sectional tensions over the fugitive slave law?

DOCUMENT 14–5

Abolitionist Lydia Maria Child Defends John Brown and Attacks the Slave Power

Some Americans did not limit themselves to making speeches about slavery and the Constitution. John Brown, a militant abolitionist, decided to take matters into his own hands. Brown led a small group of supporters against proslavery men in Pottawatomie, Kansas, in 1856. Three years later, in October 1859, he directed an attack on the U.S. arsenal at Harpers Ferry, Virginia, which resulted in his arrest, trial, and execution for murder and treason. Lydia Maria Child, a prominent antislavery activist and author from Massachusetts, wrote Virginia governor Henry A. Wise, asking for permission to visit Brown and nurse wounds he suffered at Harpers Ferry. The following excerpts from the exchange of letters between Child and Wise illustrate the sympathy Brown's attack evoked among many in the North and the outrage it created among whites in the South. The correspondence reveals the sectional hostility engendered by slavery and what Child calls "the Slave Power."

Correspondence between Lydia Maria Child and Virginia Governor Henry A. Wise, 1859

LYDIA MARIA CHILD TO GOV. WISE

Wayland, Mass., Oct. 26th, 1859

Governor Wise: . . .

I and all my large circle of abolition acquaintances were taken by surprise when news came of Capt. [John] Brown's recent attempt [at Harpers Ferry]; nor do I know of a single person who would have approved of it, had they been apprised of his intention. But I and thousands of others feel a natural impulse of sympathy for the brave and suffering man. Perhaps God, who sees the inmost of our souls, perceives some such sentiment in your heart also. He needs a mother or sister to dress his wounds, and speak soothingly to him. Will you allow me to perform that mission of humanity? If you will, may God bless you for the generous deed!

I have been for years an uncompromising Abolitionist, and I should scorn to deny it or apologize for it as much as John Brown himself would do. Believing in peace principles, I deeply regret the step that the old veteran has taken, while I honor his humanity towards those who became his prisoners. But because it is my habit to be as open as the daylight, I will also say, that if I believed our religion justified men in fighting for freedom, I should consider the enslaved every where as best entitled to that right. Such an avowal is a simple, frank expression of my sense of natural justice. . . .

Yours, respectfully,

L. MARIA CHILD.

From *Anti-Slavery Tracts No. 1, New Series. Correspondence between Lydia Maria Child, and Gov. Wise and Mrs. Mason of Virginia* (New York: American Anti-Slavery Society, 1860).

GOV. WISE TO LYDIA MARIA CHILD

Richmond, Va., Oct. 29th, 1859

Madam: . . .

You ask me . . . to allow you to perform the mission "of mother or sister, to dress his [John Brown's] wounds, and speak soothingly to him." By this, of course, you mean to be allowed to visit him in his cell, and to minister to him in the offices of humanity. Why should you not be so allowed, Madam? Virginia and Massachusetts are involved in no civil war, and the Constitution which unites them in one confederacy guarantees to you the privileges and immunities of a citizen of the United States in the State of Virginia. That Constitution I am sworn to support, and am, therefore, bound to protect your privileges and immunities as a citizen of Massachusetts coming into Virginia for any lawful and peaceful purpose. . . .

I could not permit an insult even to woman in her walk of charity among us, though it to be to one who whetted knives of butchery for our mothers, sisters, daughters and babes. We have no sympathy with your sentiments of sympathy with Brown, and are surprised that you were "taken by surprise when news came of Capt. Brown's recent attempt." His attempt was a natural consequence of your sympathy, and the errors of that sympathy ought to make you doubt its virtue from the effect on his conduct. . . .

Respectfully,
HENRY A. WISE.

LYDIA MARIA CHILD TO GOV. WISE

Wayland, Mass., Nov. 10, 1859

In your civil but very diplomatic reply to my letter, you inform me that I have a constitutional right to visit Virginia, for peaceful purposes, in common with every citizen of the United States. I was perfectly well aware that such was the *theory* of constitutional obligation in the Slave States; but I was also aware of what you omit to mention, viz.; that the Constitution has, in reality, been completely and systematically nullified, whenever it suited the convenience or the policy of the Slave Power. Your constitutional obligation, for which you profess so much respect, has never proved any protection to citizens of the Free States, who happened to have a black, brown, or yellow complexion; nor to any white citizen whom you even suspected of entertaining opinions opposite to your own. . . . This total disregard of constitutional obligation has been manifested not merely by the Lynch Law of mobs in the Slave States, but by the deliberate action of magistrates and legislators. . . . [I]t would seem as if the less that was said about respect for constitutional obligations at the South, the better. Slavery is, in fact, an infringement of all law, and adheres to no law, save for its own purposes of oppression.

You accuse Captain John Brown of "whetting knives of butchery for the mothers, sisters, daughters and babes" of Virginia; and you inform me of the well-known fact that he is "arraigned for the crimes of murder, robbery and treason." I will not here stop to explain why I believe that old hero to be no criminal, but a martyr to righteous principles which he sought to advance by methods sanctioned by his own religious views, though not by mine. . . . I do not see how Gov. Wise can consistently arraign him for crimes he has himself commended. *You* have threatened to trample on the Constitution, and break the Union, if a majority of the legal voters in these Confederated States dared to elect a President unfavorable to the extension of Slavery. Is not such a declaration proof of premeditated treason? . . .

If Captain Brown intended, as you say, to commit treason, robbery and murder, I think I have shown that he could find ample authority for such proceedings in the public declarations of Gov. Wise. And if, as he himself declares, he merely intended to free the oppressed, where could he read a more forcible lesson than is furnished by the State Seal of Virginia? I looked at it thoughtfully before I opened your letter; and though it had always appeared to me very suggestive, it never seemed to me so much so as it now did in connection with Captain John Brown. A liberty-loving hero stands with his foot upon a prostrate despot; under his strong arm, manacles and chains lie broken; and the motto is, "*Sic Semper Tyrannis*"; "Thus be it ever done to Tyrants." And this is the blazon of a State whose most profitable business is the Internal Slave-Trade!—in whose highways coffles of human chattels, chained and manacled, are frequently seen! . . . What if some Vezey,[1] or Nat Turner, should be growing up among those apparently quiet spectators? . . . I know that a slave-holding community necessarily lives in the midst of gunpowder; and, in this age, sparks of free thought are flying in every direction. You cannot quench the fires of free thought and human sympathy by any process of cunning or force. . . .

In your letter, you suggest that such a scheme as Captain Brown's is the natural result of the opinions with which I sympathize. Even if I thought this to be a correct statement, though I should deeply regret it, I could not draw the conclusion that humanity ought to be stifled, and truth struck dumb, for fear that long-successful despotism might be endangered by their utterance. But the fact is, you mistake the source of that strange outbreak. No abolition arguments or denunciations, however earnestly, loudly, or harshly proclaimed, would have produced that result. It was the legitimate consequence of the continual and constantly increasing aggressions of the Slave Power. The Slave States, in their desperate efforts to sustain a bad and dangerous institution, have encroached more and more upon the liberties of the Free States. . . .

The manifested opposition to Slavery began with the lectures and pamphlets of a few disinterested men and women, who based their movements upon purely moral and religious grounds; but their expostulations were met with a storm of rage, with tar and feathers, brickbats, demolished houses, and other applications of Lynch Law. When the dust of the conflict began to subside a little, their numbers were found to be greatly increased by the efforts to exterminate them. They had become an influence in the State too important to be overlooked by shrewd calculators. Political economists began to look at the subject from a lower point of view. They used their abilities to demonstrate that slavery was a wasteful system, and that the Free States were taxed, to an enormous extent, to sustain an institution which, at heart, two-thirds of them abhorred. . . . At last, politicians were compelled to take some action on the subject. It soon became known to all the people that the Slave States had always managed to hold in their hands the political power of the Union, and that while they constituted only one-third of the white population of these States, they held more than two-thirds of all the lucrative, and once honorable offices; an indignity to which none but a subjugated people had ever submitted. The knowledge also became generally diffused, that while the Southern States *owned* their Democracy at home, and voted for them,

---

[1]**Vezey**: Denmark Vesey, a free African American executed in Charleston, South Carolina, in 1822 for planning a slave insurrection.

they also systematically *bribed* the nominally Democratic party, at the North, with the offices adroitly kept at their disposal.

Through these, and other instrumentalities, the sentiments of the original Garrisonian Abolitionist became very widely extended, in forms more or less diluted. But by far the most efficient co-labors we have ever had have been the Slave States themselves. By denying us the sacred Right of Petition, they roused the free spirit of the North . . . [and] forced the Fugitive Slave Law upon us, in violation of all our humane instincts and all our principles of justice. And what did they procure for the Abolitionist by that despotic process? A deeper and wider detestation of Slavery throughout the Free States, and the publication of Uncle Tom's Cabin, an eloquent outburst of moral indignation, whose echoes wakened the world to look upon their shame.

By fillibustering and fraud, they dismembered Mexico, and having thus obtained the soil of Texas, they tried to introduce it as a Slave State into the Union. . . .

Soon afterward, a Southern Slave Administration ceded to the powerful monarchy of Great Britain several hundred thousands of square miles, that must have been made into Free States . . . and then they turned upon the weak Republic of Mexico, and, in order to make more Slave States, wrested from her twice as many hundred thousands of square miles, to which we had not a shadow of right. . . .

Emboldened by continual success in aggression, they made use of the pretence of "Squatter Sovereignty" to break the league . . . by which all the territory of the United States south of 36° 30′ was guaranteed to Slavery, and all north of it to Freedom. Thus Kansas became the battle-ground of the antagonistic elements in our Government. Ruffians hired by the Slave Power were sent thither temporarily, to do the voting, and drive from the polls the legal voters, who were often murdered in the process. . . . in order to establish a Constitution abhorred by the people. This was their exemplification of Squatter Sovereignty. A Massachusetts Senator, distinguished for candor, courtesy, and stainless integrity, was half murdered by slaveholders, merely for having the manliness to state these facts to the assembled Congress of the nation. Peaceful emigrants from the North, who went to Kansas for no other purpose than to till the soil, erect mills, and establish manufactories, schools, and churches, were robbed, outraged, and murdered. For many months, a war more ferocious than the warfare of wild Indians was carried on against a people almost unresisting, because they relied upon the Central Government for aid. And all this while, the power of the United States, wielded by the Slave Oligarchy, was on the side of the aggressors. . . . This was the state of things when the hero of Osawatomie [Pottawatomie] and his brave sons went to the rescue. It was he who first turned the tide of Border-Ruffian triumph, by showing them that blows were to be taken as well as given.

You may believe it or not, Gov. Wise, but it is certainly the truth that, because slaveholders so recklessly sowed the wind in Kansas, they reaped a whirlwind at Harper's Ferry.

The people of the North had a very strong attachment to the Union; but, by your desperate measures, you have weakened it beyond all power of restoration. . . . A majority of them would rejoice to have the Slave States fulfil their oft-repeated threat of withdrawal from the Union. . . . The moral sense of these States is outraged by being accomplices in sustaining an institution vicious in all its aspects; and it is now generally understood that we purchase our disgrace at great pecuniary expense. If you would only make the offer of a separation in serious earnest, you would hear the hearty response of millions,

"Go, gentlemen, and 'Stand not upon the order of your going,
    But go at once!'"
Yours, with all due respect,
L. MARIA CHILD.

QUESTIONS FOR READING AND DISCUSSION

1. To what degree did Child approve of Brown's raid on Harpers Ferry? Why did she cite the Virginia motto, "Thus be it ever done to Tyrants"? How did Child's view of Brown differ from that of Wise?

2. How did Child respond to Wise's argument that Brown's raid "was a natural consequence" of Child's "sympathy" for "one who whetted knives of butchery for our mothers, sisters, daughters and babes"?

3. What did Child mean by "the Slave Power"? What consequences did it have, according to her?

4. To what extent did antislavery activists shape opinion in the North about slavery, according to Child?

5. Why did Child favor the "separation" of the slave states from the Union?

COMPARATIVE QUESTIONS

1. How did Abraham Lincoln's view of the Constitution's position on slavery differ from Frederick Douglass's? In what ways did Lincoln's and Douglass's views differ from Jefferson Davis's and Lydia Maria Child's?

2. What might Levi Coffin and Lydia Maria Child have thought about the constitutional interpretations of Lincoln, Douglass, and Davis? Judging from the documents in this chapter, how would Lincoln, Douglass, and Davis have reacted to Margaret Garner's actions and Child's arguments?

3. How did each of these individuals define the political problem posed by slavery? What was at stake for these individuals and the people they represented in the debate over slavery?

4. To what extent were racial attitudes and assumptions important in these constitutional arguments? To what extent was the meaning of white racial identity at stake? Why?

15 The Crucible of War

1861–1865

The American Civil War began with the dissolution of the Union. The Confederacy seceded from the Union and fought to maintain its independence. The North went to war to defeat the Confederacy and preserve the Union. Before long, the war confronted most Americans with unprecedented, unexpected, and often painful experiences. In the crucible of conflict, Union war aims shifted toward freedom, slaves fought in Yankee blue against their old masters, white Northerners rioted against the draft and black Americans, Union troops struck the hard hand of war against Confederate civilians, and hundreds of thousands of men became casualties, as the following documents illustrate.

DOCUMENT 15–1

President Lincoln's War Aims

Abraham Lincoln became president pledging to prohibit the extension of slavery to new territories and to do nothing about slavery in the states where it already existed. Within weeks, the nation plunged into war. Antislavery activists pressured Lincoln to make freedom a war aim. In 1862, when fellow Republican Horace Greeley, the editor of the New York Tribune, *criticized Lincoln's reluctance to embrace emancipation, Lincoln defended his policy in a public letter, the first selection that follows. Less than five months later, Lincoln issued the Emancipation Proclamation, the second selection. Later in 1863, after the ferocious battle at Gettysburg, Lincoln delivered his famous address at the dedication of the military cemetery. The Gettysburg Address, the third selection, infused the war to save the Union with universal significance.*

From Roy P. Basler, ed., *The Collected Works of Abraham Lincoln* (New Brunswick, NJ: Rutgers University Press, 1953), 5:388–89; 6:28–30; 7:22–23.

Letter to Horace Greeley, August 22, 1862

Executive Mansion,
Washington, August 22, 1862.
Hon. Horace Greely

Dear Sir

I have just read yours of the 19th. addressed to myself through the New-York Tribune. . . . If there be perceptable in it an impatient and dictatorial tone, I waive it in deference to an old friend, whose heart I have always supposed to be right.

As to the policy I "seem to be pursuing" as you say, I have not meant to leave any one in doubt.

I would save the Union. I would save it the shortest way under the Constitution. The sooner the national authority can be restored; the nearer the Union will be "the Union as it was." If there be those who would not save the Union, unless they could at the same time *save* slavery, I do not agree with them. If there be those who would not save the Union unless they could at the same time *destroy* slavery, I do not agree with them. My paramount object in this struggle *is* to save the Union, and is *not* either to save or to destroy slavery. If I could save the Union without freeing *any* slave I would do it, and if I could save it by freeing all the slaves I would do it; and if I could save it by freeing some and leaving others alone I would also do that. What I do about slavery, and the colored race, I do because I believe it helps to save the Union; and what I forbear, I forbear because I do not believe it would help to save the Union. I shall do *less* whenever I shall believe what I am doing hurts the cause, and I shall do *more* whenever I shall believe doing more will help the cause. I shall try to correct errors when shown to be errors; and I shall adopt new views so fast as they shall appear to be true views.

I have here stated my purpose according to my view of official duty; and I intend no modification of my oft-expressed personal wish that all men every where could be free.

The Emancipation Proclamation, January 1, 1863

I, Abraham Lincoln, President of the United States, by virtue of the power in me vested as Commander-in-Chief, of the Army and Navy of the United States in time of actual armed rebellion against authority and government of the United States, and as a fit and necessary war measure for suppressing said rebellion, do, on this first day of January, in the year of our Lord one thousand eight hundred and sixty three, and in accordance with my purpose so to do publicly proclaimed for the full period of one hundred days . . . order and designate as the States and parts of States wherein the people thereof respectively, are this day in rebellion against the United States, the following, to wit:

Arkansas, Texas, Louisiana, (except the Parishes of St. Bernard, Plaquemines, Jefferson, St. Johns, St. Charles, St. James, Ascension, Assumption, Terrebonne, Lafourche, St. Mary, St. Martin, and Orleans, including the City of New-Orleans) Mississippi, Alabama, Florida, Georgia, South-Carolina, North-Carolina, and Virginia, (except the forty-eight counties designated as West Virginia, and also the counties of Berkley, Accomac, Northampton, Elizabeth-City, York, Princess Ann, and Norfolk, including the cities of Norfolk & Portsmouth); and which excepted parts are, for the present, left precisely as if this proclamation were not issued.

And by virtue of the power, and for the purpose aforesaid, I do order and declare that all persons held as slaves within said designated States, and parts of States, are, and henceforward shall be free; and that the Executive government of the United States, including the military and naval authorities thereof, will recognize and maintain the freedom of said persons.

And I hereby enjoin upon the people so declared to be free to abstain from all violence, unless in necessary self-defence; and I recommend to them that, in all cases when allowed, they labor faithfully for reasonable wages.

And I further declare and make known, that such persons of suitable condition, will be received into the armed service of the United States to garrison forts, positions, stations, and other places, and to man vessels of all sorts in said service.

And upon this act, sincerely believed to be an act of justice, warranted by the Constitution, upon military necessity, I invoke the considerate judgment of mankind, and the gracious favor of Almighty God.

In witness whereof, I have hereunto set my hand and caused the seal of the United States to be affixed.

Done at the City of Washington, this first day of January, in the year of our Lord one thousand eight hundred and sixty three, and of the Independence of the United States of America the eighty-seventh.

The Gettysburg Address, November 19, 1863

Four score and seven years ago our fathers brought forth on this continent, a new nation, conceived in Liberty, and dedicated to the proposition that all men are created equal.

Now we are engaged in a great civil war, testing whether that nation, or any nation so conceived and so dedicated, can long endure. We are met on a great battle-field of that war. We have come to dedicate a portion of that field, as a final resting place for those who here gave their lives that that nation might live. It is altogether fitting and proper that we should do this.

But, in a larger sense, we can not dedicate—we can not consecrate—we can not hallow—this ground. The brave men, living and dead, who struggled here, have consecrated it, far above our poor power to add or detract. The world will little note, nor long remember what we say here, but it can never forget what they did here. It is for us the living, rather, to be dedicated here to the unfinished work which they who fought here have thus far so nobly advanced. It is rather for us to be here dedicated to the great task remaining before us—that from these honored dead we take increased devotion to that cause for which they gave the last full measure of devotion—that we here highly resolve that these dead shall not have died in vain—that this nation, under God, shall have a new birth of freedom—and that government of the people, by the people, for the people, shall not perish from the earth.

QUESTIONS FOR READING AND DISCUSSION

1. In his letter to Greeley, how far did Lincoln say he was willing to go to end slavery? What was his paramount goal? What was the significance of his distinction between his "*official* duty" and his "*personal* wish"?

2. To what extent were Lincoln's war aims altered by the Emancipation Proclamation? Why did he specify that the proclamation was "a fit and necessary war measure"? Why did he name specific states, counties, parishes, and cities?

3. In the Gettysburg Address, what did Lincoln say was at stake in the war? What meanings did the address associate with the Union?

4. How might Lincoln's audience have shaped his message? Who was his audience, both locally and throughout the nation?

5. How did Lincoln's views toward slavery and the Union evolve during the war, judging from these documents?

DOCUMENT 15–2

A Former Slave's War Aims

Slaves and most free African Americans did not share Lincoln's constitutional reservations about emancipation. Many sought to fight in uniform to help obtain their freedom, as the following document reveals. This letter from a former slave was picked up by a policeman on a street in New Orleans in early September 1863 and turned over to military authorities, who preserved it. Both parts of the letter are in the same handwriting. (The spelling and punctuation have been faithfully reproduced from the original; if you find a passage puzzling, try reading it aloud. Note in particular that "the" should usually be read as "they.")

Statement from an Anonymous Former Slave, New Orleans, 1863

the president Shall be Commander in Chief of the Army and navy of the united States and of the militia of the Several States when called into the actual Service of the united States

Let See if Slavery was any value . . . the number of Slaves in the Southern States estimated 3,500,000 and the were worth $1200,000,000 in gold which would be a bout $1800,000,000 in Green Backs Eighteen hundred million Dollars the Collored population is not educated but what Great responciblity has been placeed on them the have been Steam boat pilots ingenears and Black Smiths Coopers Carpenters Shoe makers Drivers on plantations Sugar makers porters on Steam boats and at hotels Dineing Servant Porters in Commision houses Grocery Stores Public weighers Carrige Drivers preachers of the Gospel the best Soldiers the united States Can Raise but the tel lies Sometimes and So dos all negro traders the get Drunk and lawiers and merchants Generals and Governors and all Clases the black men has wives and Sweet harts jest like the white men Some white men has Collored wives and Sweet hearts god made all it is not a City rule for Collored

From "Statements of a Colored Man [September 1863]," in *Freedom: A Documentary History of Emancipation, 1861–1867*, Series 2, *The Black Military Experience*, eds. Ira Berlin, Joseph Reidy, and Leslie S. Rowland (Cambridge: Cambridge University Press, 1982), 153–57.

people to ride in the white peoples cars but the bed togeather God mad all the must all Die

it is retten that a man can not Serve two master But it Seems that the Collored population has got two a rebel master and a union master the both want our Servises one wants us to make Cotton and Sugar And the Sell it and keep the money the union masters wants us to fight the battles under white officers and the injoy both money and the union black Soldiers And white officers will not play togeathe much longer the Constitution is if any man rebells against those united States his property Shall be confescated and Slaves declared and henceforth Set free forever when theire is a insurection or rebllion against these united States the Constitution gives the president of the united States full power to arm as many soldiers of African decent as he deems nescesisary to Surpress the Rebellion and officers Should be black or white According to their abillitys the Collored man Should guard Stations Garison forts and mand vessels according to his Compasitys

A well regulated militia being necessary to the cecurity of a free State the right of the people to keep and Bear arms Shall not be infringed

we are to Support the Constitution but no religious test Shall ever be required as a qualification to Any office or public trust under the united States the excitement of the wars is mostly keep up from the Churches the Say god is fighting the battle but it is the people But the will find that god fought our battle once the way to have peace is to distroy the enemy As long as theire is a Slave their will be rebles Against the Government of the united States So we must look out our white officers may be union men but Slave holders at heart the Are allways on hand when theire is money but Look out for them in the battle feild liberty is what we want and nothing Shorter

our Southern friend tells that the are fighting for negros and will have them our union friends Says the are not fighting to free the negroes we are fighting for the union and free navigation of the Mississippi river very well let the white fight for what the want and we negroes fight for what we want there are three things to fight for and two races of people divided into three Classes one wants negro Slaves the other the union the other Liberty So liberty must take the day nothing Shorter we are the Blackest and the bravest race the president Says there is a wide Difference Between the black Race and the white race But we Say that white corn and yellow will mix by the taussels but the black and white Race must mix by the roots as the are so well mixed and has no tausels—freedom and liberty is the word with the Collered people

We the people of the united States in order to form a more perfect union Establish justice insure domestick tranquillity provide for the common defence promote the general wellfare and secure the blessings of liberty to ourselves and our posterity do ordain and establish this Constitution for the united States of America

My Dear union masters and reble masters or friends How are we Slave Population to take hold of a musket under white officers which a great part of them has been in the reble army and the meet to hold a war Consels all to them Selves Dear Sir I heard a federal officer Say after the fall of Port hudson to a Collored Soldier we will not want any more negro Soldiers go home to your master i my Self went to a union lawyer on Some Buiness the first question are you free or Slave Before the fall of porthudson the white Preachers told us we were all free as any white man and in Less time than a month after you weare taking us up and puting in the lockups and Cotton presses giving us nothing to eat nor nothing Sleep on And haveing negro traders for recruting officers Drawing his Sword over us like we were dogs By those means you will Soon have the union north if any union man can deny this i will write no more i am for the union and liberty to all men or nothing Shorter treason against the united States Shall consist only in Levying ware against them or in adhering to theire enemies giving them aid and Comfort no person Shall be convicted of treason unless on the testimoney of two witnesses to the Same overt Act or Confession in open Court the Congress Shall Have power to declare punishment of treason but no attainder of treason Shall work Corruption of blood or forfeiture Except during the life of the person attained

Now let us see whether the Colored population will be turn back in to Slavery and the union lost or not on the 4" of last July it was Said to the colored population that the were all free and on the 4" of August locked up in Cotton presses like Horses or hogs By reble watchmen and Saying to us Gen banks Says you are All free why do you not go to him and get passes And one half of the recruiting officers is rebles taken the oath to get a living and would Sink the Government into ashes the Scrptures says the enemy must Suffer death before we can Have peace the fall of porthudson and vicksburg is nothing the rebles must fall or the union must fall Sure the Southern men Says the are not fighting for money the are fighting for negros the northern men Say the did not com South to free the negroes but to Save the union very well for that much what is the colored men fighting for if the makes us free we are happy to hear it And when we are free men and a people we will fight for our rights and liberty we care nothing about the union we heave been in it Slaves over two hundred And fifty years we have made the contry and So far Saved the union and if we heave to fight for our rights let us fight under Colored officers for we are the men that will kill the Enemies of the Government pleas let me continue

Art 173 [of Louisiana law] the Slave is entirely Subject to the will of his master Who may Correct and Chastise him though not with unusal Rigor nor So as to maim or mutilate him or to expose him to the danger of loss of life or to cause his death

Art 174 the Slave is incapable of making any kind of Contract Except those which relate to own emancipation

Art 175 All that a Slave possesses belongs to his master he Possesses nothing of his own excep his peculium that is to Say the Sum of money or movable estate which his master chooses He Should possess

Art 176 the can transmit nothing by Succession or otherwise but the Succession of free persons related to them which the would have Inherited had the been free may pass through them to such of their descendants as may have acquired their liberty before the Succession opened

A part of the Civil Code of louisiana the united States Shall guarantee to every State in this union a republican form of government and Shall protect each of them a gainst invaison and on Aplication of the legislature. or of the executive when the legislature. can not be convened against Domestic violence

now is the united states government and constitution free or a local Goverment if it is free let us colored population muster in to ams and garison forts guard Station and mand vessels and then we will know wheather we are free people or not then we will know wheather you want to make brest works of us or not or make us fools ornot I heard one of most Ables and distingush lawiers Say that the

Colored population was all free and Had as much liberty in the union as he had in four or five days after I went to him to get him to atend Some buiness for me he Said to me Are you free or Slave Sir Said i am free By your own speeches was you born free no Sir Said i we have been made fools of from the time Butlers fleet landed hear but I have remained At my old Stand and will untill i See what i am dowing I know very well that the white union men cannot put down the rebeles for them that was not rebles Soon will be

i am Sory that I am not able to write good may the union forever Stand with peace and liberty to All good people

A Colored man

the president Shall be commander in chief of the Army and navy of the united States and of the miltia of the Several States when called Into actual Service of the united States

when the president ordered three hundred thousand Colored Soldiers to be mustered into the united States Army on the first Day of last April if So the rebles would have fell like the Surrender of vicksburg and porthudson.

Declare freedom at onc and give us Somting to fight for Black Soldiers Black officers and all white rebles will Soon run them in or out of the union

the writer was born in 18.18 feb 16"

one of the union Colored friends

QUESTIONS FOR READING AND DISCUSSION

1. What did this man mean by writing that "the Collored population has got . . . a rebel master and a union master"? How did he view Union men? In what ways did they differ from Confederates?
2. Why should black soldiers fight? Did this man believe the Constitution authorized Lincoln to arm African Americans and use them as soldiers? What was his view of the claim that "northern men Say the[y] did not com[e] South to free the negroes but to save the union"?
3. What was the significance of his statement that "there are three things to fight for and two races of people divided into three Classes"?
4. Why did this man write these things? Whom did he consider his audience? Do you think this document was forged or that it was an authentic statement by "A Colored man"? What evidence seems persuasive?

DOCUMENT 15–3

The New York Draft Riots

In 1863, Congress instituted a draft to provide soldiers for the Union army. Strongly opposed by Democrats, the draft met resistance in many northern cities, but in New York it sparked nearly a week of deadly riots in mid-July—shortly after Union successes at Gettysburg and Vicksburg—that killed more than one hundred people, mostly black Americans. Racism, ethnic hatreds, job competition, and other forces boiled among white, heavily Irish, and Democratic mobs, causing them to target the city's black population. Immediately after the riots, a group of city merchants collected funds to help African

*Americans who had suffered during the riots. In the excerpt below from the merchants'
detailed report, a portrait of New York's African Americans is combined with accounts
of specific incidents that illustrate the fury of the rioters and the innocence of the victims.
The riots demonstrate the intense hostilities—racial, partisan, ethnic, and economic—
that the Civil War generated in the North.*

Report of the Committee of Merchants for the Relief of Colored People Suffering from the Late Riots in the City of New York, 1863

REPORT OF THE SECRETARY

Driven by the fear of death at the hands of the mob, who the week previous
had, as you remember, brutally murdered, by hanging on trees and lamp posts
several of their number, and cruelly beaten and robbed many others, burning and
sacking their houses and driving nearly all from the streets, alleys and docks upon
which they had previously obtained an honest though humble living—these
people had been forced to take refuge on Blackwell's Island, at Police Stations, on
the outskirts of the city, in the swamps and woods back of Bergen, New Jersey . . .
and in the barns and out-houses of the farmers of Long Island. . . . At these places
were scattered some 5,000 homeless and helpless men, women, and children. . . .

During the month ending August 21st there have been 3,941 women, and
2,443 men, making a total of 6,384 persons of mature age, relieved; full one-third
being heads of families, whose children were included in the relief afforded by
your committee, making a total of 12,782 persons relieved.

Of the 2,443 men relieved, their occupations were as follows:

- 1,267 Laborers and Longshoremen
- 177 Whitewashers
- 176 Drivers for Cartmen
- 250 Waiters
- 124 Porters
- 97 Sailors and Boatmen
- 72 Coachmen
- 45 Cooks
- 37 Barbers
- 34 Chimney Sweepers
- 25 Tradesmen
- 20 Butchers
- 15 Bootblacks
- 11 Ministers or Preachers
- 11 Shoemakers
- 11 Tobacconists
- 11 Wood sawyers
- 8 Carpenters

From *Report of the Committee of Merchants for the Relief of Colored People Suffering
from the Late Riots in the City of New York* (New York: George A. Whitehorne, 1863).

- 7 Basket-makers
- 6 Scavengers
- 5 Carpet shakers
- 4 Tailors
- 3 Artists
- 3 Music Teachers
- 3 Coopers
- 2 Engravers
- 2 Janitors
- 2 Measurers
- 2 Oystermen
- 2 Undertakers
- 1 Landlord
- 1 Flour Inspector
- 1 Teacher
- 1 Copyist
- 1 Farmer
- 1 Botanist
- 1 Physician
- 1 Book-binder
- 1 Tin Smith
- 1 Upholsterer
- 1 Black Smith

Of the 3,941 women, were

- 2,924 Day's work women
- 664 Servants hired by month
- 163 Seamstresses
- 106 Cooks
- 19 Worked in Tobacco factory
- 13 Nurses
- 13 Hucksters
- 4 Teachers
- 1 Artist
- 1 Boarding-house keeper
- 1 Basket-maker
- 32 Infirm

INCIDENTS OF THE RIOT

ABRAHAM FRANKLIN

This young man who was murdered by the mob on the corner of Twenty-seventh St., and Seventh avenue, was a quiet, inoffensive man, 23 years of age, of unexceptional character, and a member of Zion African Church in this city. Although a cripple, he earned a living for himself and his mother by serving a gentleman in the capacity of coachman. A short time previous to the assault upon his person, he called upon his mother to see if anything could be done by him for her safety. The old lady, who is noted for her piety and her Christian deportment, said she considered herself perfectly safe; but if her time to die had come, she was ready to die. Her son then knelt down by her side, and implored the protection of Heaven in behalf of his mother. The old lady was affected to tears, and said to our informant that it seemed to her that good angels were present in the room. Scarcely had the supplicant risen from his knees, when the mob broke down the door, seized him, beat him over the head and face with fists and clubs, and then hanged him in the presence of his mother.

While they were thus engaged, the military came and drove them away, cutting down the body of Franklin, who raised his arm once slightly and gave a few signs of life.

The military then moved on to quell other riots, when the mob returned and again suspended the now probably lifeless body of Franklin, cutting out pieces of flesh and otherwise mutilating it.

AUGUSTUS STUART

Died at the Hospital, Blackwell's Island July 22d, from the effects of a blow received at the hands of the mob, within one block and a half of the State Arsenal, corner 7th Avenue and 35th street, on Wednesday evening, July 15th. He had been badly beaten previously by a band of rioters and was frightened and insane from the effects of the blows which he had received. He was running towards the Arsenal for safety when he was overtaken by the mob from whom he received his death blow.

Mrs. Stuart, his wife, says that some of the rioters declared that at the second attack upon him he had fired a pistol at his pursuers; but she says that if he did, he must have obtained the weapon from some friend after he had left home, a few minutes before, for he had no weapon then, nor was he ever known to have had one. He was a member of the church.

PETER HEUSTON

Peter Heuston, sixty-three years of age, a Mohawk Indian, with dark complexion and straight black hair, who has for several years been a resident of this city, at the corner of Rosevelt and Oak streets, and who has obtained a livelihood as a laborer, proved a victim to the late riots.

His wife died about three weeks before the riots, leaving with her husband an only child, a little girl named Lavinia, aged eight years. . . . Heuston served with the New York Volunteers in the Mexican War, and has always been loyal to our government. He was brutally attacked on the 13th of July by a gang of ruffians who evidently thought him to be of the African race because of his dark complexion. He died within four days at Bellevue Hospital from his injuries.

At the end of the Mexican War Heuston received a land warrant from the government, which enabled him to settle on a tract of land at the West, where he lived but a short time previous to his coming to this city.

JEREMIAH ROBINSON

Mrs. Nancy Robinson, widow of the above, killed in Madison near Catherine street, says that her husband in order to escape dressed himself up in some of her clothes, and in company with herself and one other woman left their residence and went towards one of the Brooklyn Ferries.

Robinson wore a hood, which failed to hide his beard. Some boys seeing his beard, lifted up the skirts of his dress, which exposed his heavy boots. Immediately the mob set upon him and the atrocities they perpetrated upon him are so indecent, they are unfit for publication. They finally killed him and threw his body into the river.

His wife and her companion ran up Madison street and escaped across the Grand street Ferry to Brooklyn.

WILLIAM JONES

A crowd of rioters in pursuit of a negro, who in self defence had fired on some rowdies who had attacked him, met an innocent colored man returning from a bakery with a loaf of bread under his arm. They instantly set upon and beat him and after nearly killing him, hanged him to a lamp-post. His body was left suspended for several hours and was much mutilated.

A sad illustration of the painful uncertainty which hung over the minds of the wives and children of the colored men was found in the fact that two wives and their families, were both mourning the loss of their husbands in the case of this man, for upwards of two weeks after its occurrence. And so great was the fear inspired by the mob that no white person had dared to manifest sufficient interest in the mutilated body of the murdered man while it remained in the neighborhood to be able to testify as to who it was. At the end of two weeks the husband of one of the mourners to her great joy returned, like one recovered from the grave. . . .

WM. HENRY NICHOLS

Died July 16th, from injuries received at the hands of the rioters on the 15th of July.

Mrs. Statts, his mother, tells this story:—

The father of Wm. Henry died some years ago, and the boy has since, by good behavior, with persevering industry, earned his own living; he was a communicant of the Protestant Episcopal Church, in good standing. I had arrived from Philadelphia, the previous Monday evening, before any indications of the riot were known, and was temporarily stopping, on Wednesday, July 15th, at the house of my son, No. 147 East 28th street.

At 3 o'clock of that day the mob arrived and immediately commenced an attack with terrific yells, and a shower of stones and bricks, upon the house. In the next room to where I was sitting was a poor woman, who had been confined with a child on Sunday, three days previous. Some of the rioters broke through the front door with pick axes, and came rushing into the room where this poor woman lay, and commenced to pull the clothes from off her. Knowing that their rage was chiefly directed against men, I hid my son behind me and ran with him through the back door, down into the basement. In a little while I saw the innocent babe, of three days old, come crashing down into the yard; some of the rioters had dashed it out of the back window, killing it instantly. In a few minutes streams of water came pouring down into the basement, the mob had cut the Croton water-pipes with their axes. Fearing we should be drowned in the cellar, (there were ten of us, mostly women and children, there) I took my boy and flew past the dead body of the babe, out to the rear of the yard, hoping to escape with him through an open lot into 29th street; but here, to our horror and dismay, we met the mob again; I, with my son, had climbed the fence, but the sight of those maddened demons so affected me that I fell back, fainting, into the yard; my son jumped down from the fence to pick me up, and a dozen of the rioters came leaping over the fence after him. As they surrounded us my son exclaimed, "save my mother, gentlemen, if you kill me." "Well, we will kill you," they answered; and with that two ruffians seized him, each taking hold of an arm, while a third, armed with a crow-bar, calling upon them to stand and hold his arms apart, deliberately struck him a heavy blow over the head, felling him, like a bullock, to the ground. (He died in the N. Y. hospital two days after). I believe if I were to live a hundred years I would never forget that scene, or cease to hear the horrid voices of that demoniacal mob resounding in my ears. . . .

CASE OF BRUTALITY

At a late hour on Wednesday night, a colored man, named Charles Jackson, was passing along West street, in the neighborhood of Pier No. 5; North river. He was a laboring man, and was dressed in a tarpaulin, a blue shirt, and heavy duck trousers. As he was passing a groggery [tavern] in that vicinity, he was observed by a body of dock men, who instantly set after him. He ran with all the swiftness his fears could excite, but was overtaken before he had gone a block. His persecutors did not know him nor did they entertain any spite against him beyond the fact that he was a black man and a laborer about the docks, which they consider their own peculiar field of labor. Nevertheless they knocked him down, kicked him in the face and ribs, and finally by the hands of their leader, deliberately attempted to *cut his throat*. The body, dead they supposed it, was then thrown into the water and left to sink. Fortunately life was not extinct and the sudden plunge brought the poor fellow to his senses, and being a good swimmer he was enabled instinctively to seek for the net work of the dock. This he soon found, but was so weak from the loss of blood and so faint with pain that he could do no more than hold on and wait for day. The day after, Messrs. Kelly and Curtis, of Whitehall, discovered him lying half dead in the water.

QUESTIONS FOR READING AND DISCUSSION

1. What conclusions about black New Yorkers can be drawn from the list of people offered relief by the merchants' committee? What might account for the merchants' relief efforts?

2. Why do you think the rioters attacked African Americans? What accounts for the savage violence of the rioters?

3. To what extent do you think the Civil War was responsible for the riots? Do you think the recently announced Emancipation Proclamation might have influenced the rioters? Why or why not?

DOCUMENT 15–4

Susie King Taylor Describes Her Wartime Experiences

Susie King Taylor, a young slave girl in Savannah, Georgia, escaped with her family to Union lines on St. Simons Island in 1862. Well educated, Taylor organized a school for slave children on the island. When the Union army enlisted a regiment of black soldiers, she worked with them for the duration of the war as a nurse and laundress and continued to teach. In a memoir of her wartime experiences, excerpted here, King describes slaves'

*keen anticipation of freedom at the outset of the war, the sacrifices of black soldiers and
their officers, and the soldiers' sense of achievement by war's end.*

Reminiscences of My Life in Camp, 1902

I was born under the slave law in Georgia, in 1848, and was brought up by
my grandmother in Savannah. There were three of us with her, my younger sister
and brother. My brother and I being the two eldest, we were sent to a friend of my
grandmother . . . to learn to read and write. She was a free woman [of color] and
lived . . . about half a mile from my house. We went every day about nine o'clock,
with our books wrapped in paper to prevent the police or white persons from
seeing them. We went in, one at a time, through the gate, into the yard to the . . .
kitchen, which was the schoolroom. She had twenty-five or thirty children whom
she taught, assisted by her daughter. . . . The neighbors would see us going in
sometimes, but they supposed we were there learning trades, as it was the custom
to give children a trade of some kind. . . . I remained at her school for two years
or more, when I was sent to . . . [another teacher], where I continued until May,
1860, when she told my grandmother she had taught me all she knew, and grandmother had better get some one else who could teach me more, so I stopped my
studies for a while. . . .

I often wrote passes for my grandmother, for all colored persons, free or
slaves, were compelled to have a pass; free colored people having a [white] guardian in place of a master. . . . Every [black] person had to have this pass, for at nine
o'clock each night a bell was rung, and any colored persons found on the street
after this hour were arrested by the watchman, and put in the guard-house until
next morning, when their owners would pay their fines and release them. I knew
a number of persons who went out at any time at night and were never arrested,
as the watchman knew them so well he never stopped them, and seldom asked to
see their passes, only stopping them long enough, sometimes, to say "Howdy,"
and then telling them to go along.

About this time I had been reading so much about the "Yankees" I was very
anxious to see them. The whites would tell their colored people not to go to the
Yankees, for they would harness them to carts and make them pull the carts
around, in place of horses. I asked grandmother, one day, if this was true. She
replied, "Certainly not!" that the white people did not want slaves to go over to
the Yankees, and told them these things to frighten them. . . . I wanted to see these
wonderful "Yankees" so much, as I heard my parents say the Yankee was going to
set all the slaves free. Oh, how those people prayed for freedom! I remember, one
night, my grandmother went out into the suburbs of the city to a church meeting,
and they were fervently singing this old hymn,—

"Yes, we all shall be free,
Yes, we all shall be free,
Yes, we all shall be free,
When the Lord shall appear,"—

From Susie King Taylor, *Reminiscences of My Life in Camp with the 33d United States
Colored Troops Late 1st S. C. Volunteers* (Boston: Pub. by author, 1902), 5–49.

—when the police came in and arrested all who were there, saying they were planning freedom, and sang "the Lord," in place of "Yankee," to blind any one who might be listening. Grandmother never forgot that night, although she did not stay in the guard-house, as she sent to her [white] guardian, who came at once for her. . . .

About the first of June [1862] we were told that there was going to be a settlement of the war. Those who were on the Union side would remain free, and those in bondage were to work three days for their masters and three for themselves. It was a gloomy time for us all, and we were to be sent to Liberia. . . . However, the Confederates would not agree to the arrangement, or else it was one of the many rumors flying about at the time, as we heard nothing further of the matter. . . .

There were about six hundred [black] men, women, and children [nearly all of them slaves] on St. Simon's [island under Union Army control], the women and children being in the majority, and we were afraid to go very far from our own quarters in the daytime, and at night even to go out of the house for a long time, although the men were on the watch all the time; for there were not any soldiers on the island, only the marines who were on the gunboats along the coast. The rebels, knowing this, could steal by them under cover of the night, and getting on the island would capture any persons venturing out alone and carry them to the mainland. . . .

The latter part of August, 1862, Captain C. T. Trowbridge [a white officer in the Union army] . . . came to St. Simon's . . . to get all the men possible to finish filling his regiment [of black men] which he had organized in March, 1862. . . . I was enrolled as laundress.

The first suits worn by the boys were red coats and pants, which they disliked very much, for, they said, "The rebels see us, miles away."

The first colored troops did not receive any pay for eighteen months, and the men had to depend wholly on what they received from the commissary. . . . A great many of these men had large families, and as they had no money to give them, their wives were obliged to support themselves and children by washing for the officers of the gunboats and the soldiers, and making cakes and pies which they sold to the boys in camp. Finally, in 1863, the government decided to give them half pay, but the men would not accept this. They wanted "full pay" or nothing. They preferred rather to give their services to the state, which they did until 1864, when the government granted them full pay, with all the back pay due.

I remember hearing Captain Heasley [a white officer] telling his company, one day, "Boys, stand up for your full pay! I am with you, and so are all the officers." . . .

I had a number of relatives in this regiment,—several uncles, some cousins, and a husband in Company E, and a number of cousins in other companies. . . .

On the first of January, 1863, we held services for the purpose of listening to the reading of President Lincoln's proclamation. . . . It was a glorious day for us all, and we enjoyed every minute of it, and as a fitting close and the crowning event of this occasion we had a grand barbecue. A number of oxen were roasted whole, and we had a fine feast. . . . The soldiers had a good time. They sang or shouted "Hurrah!" all through the camp, and seemed overflowing with fun and frolic. . . .

Some mornings I would go along the picket line,[1] and I could see the rebels on the opposite side of the river. Sometimes as they were changing pickets they would call over to our men and ask for something to eat, or for tobacco, and our men would tell them to come over. Sometimes one or two would desert to us, saying, they "had no negroes to fight for." . . .

I learned to handle a musket very well while in the regiment, and could shoot straight and often hit the target. I assisted in cleaning the guns and used to fire them off, to see if the cartridges were dry, before cleaning and reloading, each day. I thought this great fun. I was also able to take a gun all apart, and put it together again. . . .

Fort Wagner being only a mile from our camp, I went there two or three times a week, and would go up on the ramparts to watch the gunners send their shells into Charleston . . . . Outside of the fort were many skulls lying about; I have often moved them [to] one side out of the path. The comrades and I would have quite a debate as to which side the men fought on. Some thought they were the skulls of our boys; others thought they were the enemy's; but as there was no definite way to know, it was never decided which could lay claim to them. They were a gruesome sight, those fleshless heads and grinning jaws, but by this time I had become accustomed to worse things and did not feel as I might have earlier in my camp life. . . .

*   *   *

Colonel Trowbridge . . . [issued] the following "General Orders" . . . and the regiment mustered out [after the war]. . . .

"Comrades: The hour is at hand when we must separate forever, and nothing can take from us the pride we feel, when we look upon the history of the 'First South Carolina Volunteers,' the first black regiment that ever bore arms in defense of freedom on the continent of America.

"On the 9th day of May, 1862, at which time there were nearly four millions of your race in bondage, sanctioned by the laws of the land and protected by our flag,—on that day, in the face of the floods of prejudice that well-nigh deluged every avenue to manhood and true liberty, you came forth to do battle for your country and kindred.

"For long and weary months, without pay or even the privilege of being recognized as soldiers, you labored on, only to be disbanded and sent to your homes without even a hope of reward, and when our country, necessitated by the deadly struggle with armed traitors, finally granted you the opportunity again to come forth in defense of the nation's life, the alacrity with which you responded to the call gave abundant evidence of your readiness to strike a manly blow for the liberty of your race. And from that little band of hopeful, trusting, and brave men who gathered at Camp Saxton, on Port Royal Island, in the fall of '62, amidst the terrible prejudices that surrounded us, has grown an army of a hundred and forty thousand black soldiers, whose valor and heroism has won for your race a name which will live as long as the undying pages of history shall endure; and by whose efforts, united with those of the white man, armed rebellion has been conquered, the millions of bondsmen have been emancipated, and the fundamental law of the

---

[1]**picket line**: Line of soldiers placed in front of armies to warn of advances by the enemy.

land has been so altered as to remove forever the possibility of human slavery being established within the borders of redeemed America. The flag of our fathers, restored to its rightful significance, now floats over every foot of our territory, from Maine to California, and beholds only free men! The prejudices which formerly existed against you are well-nigh rooted out.

"Soldiers, you have done your duty and acquitted yourselves like men who, actuated by such ennobling motives, could not fail; and as the result of your fidelity and obedience you have won your freedom, and oh, how great the reward! . . .

"Now that you are to lay aside your arms, I adjure you, by the associations and history of the past, and the love you bear for your liberties, to harbor no feelings of hatred toward your former masters, but to seek in the paths of honesty, virtue, sobriety, and industry, and by a willing obedience to the laws of the land, to grow up to the full stature of American citizens. The church, the school-house, and the right forever to be free are now secured to you, and every prospect before you is full of hope and encouragement. The nation guarantees to you full protection and justice, and will require from you in return that respect for the laws and orderly deportment which will prove to every one your right to all the privileges of freemen."

QUESTIONS FOR READING AND DISCUSSION

1. What rumors did Taylor and other slaves in Savannah hear at the outset of the war? How did the rumors influence their encounters with white people in Savannah?

2. How did the black soldiers from the regiment in which Taylor worked respond to receiving less pay than white soldiers?

3. What sacrifices did black soldiers make, according to Taylor?

4. According to Colonel Trowbridge, the white officer in charge of the regiment, what did his black soldiers achieve by their military service? How did he believe those achievements would be rewarded? Do you think his soldiers probably agreed with his assessment?

DOCUMENT 15–5

General William T. Sherman Explains the Hard Hand of War

During the Civil War, both Union and Confederate leaders targeted not only the armies of their enemies but also the will of the civilian populations to support their armies. General William T. Sherman's capture of Atlanta and subsequent March to the Sea in late 1864 epitomized the Union's policy of demoralizing Confederate civilians by demonstrating the inability of Confederate soldiers to defend southern citizens. After seizing Atlanta, Sherman ordered the evacuation of the city's civilian population, for reasons he explained to his superior, General Henry W. Halleck. Sherman's evacuation order elicited protests from Confederate General John Bell Hood and from the mayor and city council of Atlanta, which Sherman answered with justifications of the war and its inherent cruelty. The following correspondence contrasts Sherman's views of the war with those of Hood and the city's white residents.

Correspondence, 1864

Atlanta, Georgia, September 20, 1864

Major-General Halleck, Chief of Staff, Washington, D.C.
GENERAL:

I have the honor herewith to submit copies of a correspondence between General Hood, of the Confederate Army, the Mayor of Atlanta, and myself, touching the removal of the inhabitants of Atlanta.

In explanation of the tone which marks some of these letters, I will only call your attention to the fact that, after I had announced my determination, General Hood took upon himself to question my motives. I could not tamely submit to such impertinence; and I have also seen that, in violation of all official usage, he has published in the Macon [Georgia] newspapers such parts of the correspondence as suited his purpose. This could have had no other object than to create a feeling on the part of the people; but if he expects to resort to such artifices, I think I can meet him there too.

It is sufficient for my Government to know that the removal of the inhabitants has been made with liberality and fairness, that it has been attended with no force, and that no women or children have suffered, unless for want of provisions by their natural protectors and friends.

My real reasons for this step were:

We want all the houses of Atlanta for military storage and occupation.

We want to contract the lines of defense, so as to diminish the garrison to the limit necessary to defend its narrow and vital parts, instead of embracing, as the lines now do, the vast suburbs. This . . . will make it necessary to destroy the very houses used by families as residences.

Atlanta is a fortified town, was stubbornly defended, and fairly captured. As captors, we have a right to it.

The residence here of a poor population would compel us, sooner or later, to feed them or to see them starve under our eyes.

The residence here of the families of our enemies would be a temptation and a means to keep up a correspondence dangerous and hurtful to our cause; a civil population calls for provost-guards, and absorbs the attention of officers in listening to everlasting complaints and special grievances that are not military.

These are my reasons; and, if satisfactory to the Government of the United States, it makes no difference whether it pleases General Hood and *his* people or not. I am, with respect, your obedient servant,

W. T. SHERMAN, Major-General commanding.

Atlanta, Georgia, September 7, 1864

General Hood, commanding Confederate Army.
GENERAL:

I have deemed it to the interest of the United States that the citizens now residing in Atlanta should remove, those who prefer it to go south, and the rest

---

From William T. Sherman, *Memoirs of General William T. Sherman,* 2 vols. (New York: D. A. Appleton & Co., 1886).

north. For the latter I can provide food and transportation to points of their election in Tennessee, Kentucky, or farther north. For the former I can provide transportation by cars as far as Rough and Ready, and also wagons; but, that their removal may be made with as little discomfort as possible, it will be necessary for you to help the families from Rough and Ready to the [railroad] cars. . . . If you consent, I will undertake to remove all the families in Atlanta who prefer to go south to Rough and Ready, with all their movable effects, viz., clothing, trunks, reasonable furniture, bedding, etc., with their servants, white and black, with the proviso that no force shall be used toward the blacks, one way or the other. If they want to go with their masters or mistresses, they may do so; otherwise they will be sent away, unless they be men, when they may be employed by our quartermaster. Atlanta is no place for families or non-combatants, and I have no desire to send them north if you will assist in conveying them south. If this proposition meets your views, I will consent to a truce . . . stipulating that any wagons, horses, animals, or persons sent . . . for the purposes herein stated, shall in no manner be harmed or molested. . . .

W. T. SHERMAN, Major-General commanding.

September 9, 1864

Major-General W. T. Sherman, commanding United States Forces in Georgia.
GENERAL:
. . . I do not consider that I have any alternative in this matter [of a truce]. I therefore accept your proposition to declare a truce of two days, or such time as may be necessary to accomplish the purpose mentioned, and shall render all assistance in my power to expedite the transportation of citizens in this direction. . . .

And now, sir, permit me to say that the unprecedented measure you propose transcends, in studied and ingenious cruelty, all acts ever before brought to my attention in the dark history of war.

In the name of God and humanity, I protest, believing that you will find that you are expelling from their homes and firesides the wives and children of a brave people. I am, general, very respectfully, your obedient servant,

J. B. HOOD, *General.*

Atlanta, Georgia, September 10, 1864

General J. B. Hood, commanding Army of Tennessee, Confederate Army.
GENERAL:
. . . You style the measures proposed "unprecedented," and appeal to the dark history of war for a parallel, as an act of "studied and ingenious cruelty." It is not unprecedented. . . . Nor is it necessary to appeal to the dark history of war, when recent and modern examples are so handy. You yourself burned dwelling-houses along your parapet, and I have seen to-day fifty houses that you have rendered uninhabitable because they stood in the way of your forts and men. You defended Atlanta on a line so close to town that every cannon-shot and many musket-shots from our line of investment, that overshot their mark, went into the habitations of women and children. . . . I have not accused you of heartless cruelty, but merely instance these cases of very recent occurrence, and could go on and

enumerate hundreds of others, and challenge any fair man to judge which of us has the heart of pity for the families of a "brave people."

I say that it is kindness to these families of Atlanta to remove them now, at once, from scenes that women and children should not be exposed to, and the "brave people" should scorn to commit their wives and children to the rude barbarians who thus, as you say, violate the laws of war, as illustrated in the pages of its dark history.

In the name of common-sense, I ask you not to appeal to a just God in such a sacrilegious manner. You who, in the midst of peace and prosperity, have plunged a nation into war—dark and cruel war—who dared and badgered us to battle, insulted our flag, seized our arsenals and forts that were left in the honorable custody of peaceful ordnance-sergeants, seized and made "prisoners of war" the very garrisons sent to protect your people against negroes and Indians, long before any overt act was committed by the (to you) hated Lincoln Government; tried to force Kentucky and Missouri into rebellion, [in] spite of themselves; falsified the vote of Louisiana; turned loose your privateers to plunder unarmed ships; expelled Union families by the thousands, burned their houses, and declared, by an act of your Congress, the confiscation of all debts due Northern men for goods had and received! Talk thus to the marines, but not to me, who have seen these things, and who will this day make as much sacrifice for the peace and honor of the South as the best-born Southerner among you! If we must be enemies, let us be men, and fight it out as we propose to do, and not deal in such hypocritical appeals to God and humanity. God will judge us in due time, and he will pronounce whether it be more humane to fight with a town full of women and the families of a brave people at our back, or to remove them in time to places of safety among their own friends and people. I am very respectfully, your obedient servant,

W. T. SHERMAN, Major-General commanding.

September 12, 1864

Major-General W. T. Sherman, commanding Military Division of the Mississippi
GENERAL:

I have the honor to acknowledge the receipt of your letter. . . .

I see nothing in your communication which induces me to modify the language of condemnation with which I characterized your order. It but strengthens me in the opinion that it stands "preëminent in the dark history of war for studied and ingenious cruelty." Your original order was stripped of all pretenses; you announced the edict for the sole reason that it was "to the interest of the United States." This alone you offered to us and the civilized world as an all sufficient reason for disregarding the laws of God and man. . . .

[Your letter] opens a wide field for the discussion of questions which I do not feel are committed to me. I am only a general of one of the armies of the Confederate States, charged with military operations in the field, under the direction of my superior officers, and I am not called upon to discuss with you the causes of the present war, or the political questions which led to or resulted from it. These grave and important questions have been committed to far abler hands than mine, and I shall only refer to them so far as to repel any unjust conclusion which might be drawn from my silence. You charge my country with "daring and badgering you to battle." The truth is, we sent commissioners to you, respectfully offering a peaceful separation, before the first gun was fired on either side. You say we insulted your flag. The truth is, we fired upon it, and those who fought under it, when you came to our doors upon the mission of subjugation. You say we seized upon your forts and arsenals, and made prisoners of the garrisons sent to protect us against negroes and Indians. The truth is, we, by force of arms, drove out insolent intruders and took possession of our own forts and arsenals, to resist your claims to dominion over masters, slaves, and Indians, all of whom are to this day, with a unanimity unexampled in the history of the world, warring against your attempts to become their masters. You say that we tried to force Missouri and Kentucky into rebellion in spite of themselves. The truth is, my Government, from the beginning of this struggle to this hour, has again and again offered, before the whole world, to leave it to the unbiased will of these States, and all others, to determine for themselves whether they will cast their destiny with your Government or ours; and your Government has resisted this fundamental principle of free institutions with the bayonet, and labors daily, by force and fraud, to fasten its hateful tyranny upon the unfortunate freemen of these States. You say we falsified the vote of Louisiana. The truth is, Louisiana not only separated herself from your Government by nearly a unanimous vote of her people, but has vindicated the act upon every battle-field from Gettysburg to the Sabine, and has exhibited an heroic devotion to her decision which challenges the admiration and respect of every man capable of feeling sympathy for the oppressed or admiration for heroic valor. You say that we turned loose pirates to plunder your unarmed ships. The truth is, when you robbed us of our part of the navy, we built and bought a few vessels, hoisted the flag of our country, and swept the seas, in defiance of your navy, around the whole circumference of the globe. You say we have expelled Union families by thousands. The truth is, not a single family has been expelled from the Confederate States, that I am aware of; but, on the contrary, the moderation of our Government toward traitors has been a fruitful theme of denunciation by its enemies and well-meaning friends of our cause. You say my Government, by acts of Congress, has confiscated "all debts due Northern men for goods sold and delivered." The truth is, our Congress gave due and ample time to your merchants and traders to depart from our shores with their ships, goods, and effects, and only sequestrated the property of our enemies in retaliation for their acts—declaring us traitors, and confiscating our property wherever their power extended, either in their country or our own. Such are your accusations, and such are the facts known of all men to be true.

You order into exile the whole population of a city; drive men, women, and children from their homes at the point of the bayonet, under the plea that it is to the interest of your Government, and on the claim that it is an act of "kindness to these families of Atlanta." . . . You issue a sweeping edict, covering all the inhabitants of a city, and add insult to the injury heaped upon the defenseless by assuming that you have done them a kindness. This you follow by the assertion that you will "make as much sacrifice for the peace and honor of the South as the best-born Southerner." And, because I characterize what you call a kindness as being real cruelty, you presume to sit in judgment between me and my God; and you decide that my earnest prayer to the Almighty Father to save our women and children from what you call kindness, is a "sacrilegious, hypocritical appeal."

You came into our country with your army, avowedly for the purpose of subjugating free white men, women, and children, and not only intend to rule over them, but you make negroes your allies, and desire to place over us an inferior race, which we have raised from barbarism to its present position, which is the highest ever attained by that race, in any country, in all time. I must, therefore, decline to accept your statements in reference to your kindness toward the people of Atlanta, and your willingness to sacrifice every thing for the peace and honor of the South, and refuse to be governed by your decision in regard to matters between myself, my country, and my God.

You say, "Let us fight it out like men." To this my reply is—for myself, and I believe for all the true men, ay, and women and children, in my country—we will fight you to the death! Better die a thousand deaths than submit to live under you or your Government and your negro allies!

Having answered the points forced upon me by your letter . . . I close this correspondence with you; and, notwithstanding your comments upon my appeal to God in the cause of humanity, I again humbly and reverently invoke his almighty aid in defense of justice and right. Respectfully, your obedient servant,

J. B. HOOD, General.

Atlanta, Georgia, September 11, 1864

Major-General W. T. Sherman
SIR:

We the undersigned, Mayor and two of the Council for the city of Atlanta . . . ask leave most earnestly but respectfully to petition you to reconsider the order requiring them to leave Atlanta.

At first view, it struck us that the measure would involve extraordinary hardship and loss, but since we have seen the practical execution of it so far as it has progressed, and the individual condition of the people, and heard their statements as to the inconveniences, loss, and suffering attending it, we are satisfied that the amount of it will involve in the aggregate consequences appalling and heart-rending.

Many poor women are in advanced state of pregnancy, others now having young children, and whose husbands for the greater part are either in the army, prisoners, or dead. Some say: "I have such a one sick at my house; who will wait on them when I am gone?" Others say: "What are we to do? We have no house to go to, and no means to buy, build, or rent any; no parents, relatives, or friends, to go to." Another says: "I will try and take this or that article of property, but such and such things I must leave behind, though I need them much." . . .

[H]ow is it possible for the people still here (mostly women and children) to find any shelter? And how can they live through the winter in the woods—no shelter or subsistence, in the midst of strangers who know them not, and without the power to assist them much, if they were willing to do so?

This is but a feeble picture of the consequences of this measure. You know the woe, the horrors, and the suffering, cannot be described by words; imagination can only conceive of it, and we ask you to take these things into consideration. . . .

Respectfully submitted:
JAMES M. CALHOUN, Mayor.

Atlanta, Georgia, September 12, 1864

James M. Calhoun, Mayor . . . , representing City Council of Atlanta
GENTLEMEN:
I have your letter . . . in the nature of a petition to revoke my orders removing all the inhabitants from Atlanta. I have read it carefully, and give full credit to your statements of the distress that will be occasioned, and yet shall not revoke my orders, because they were not designed to meet the humanities of the case, but to prepare for the future struggles in which millions of good people outside of Atlanta have a deep interest. We must have peace, not only at Atlanta, but in all America. To secure this, we must stop the war that now desolates our once happy and favored country. To stop war, we must defeat the rebel armies which are arrayed against the laws and Constitution that all must respect and obey. To defeat those armies, we must prepare the way to reach them in their recesses, provided with the arms and instruments which enable us to accomplish our purpose. Now, I know the vindictive nature of our enemy, that we may have many years of military operations from this quarter; and, therefore, deem it wise and prudent to prepare in time. The use of Atlanta for warlike purposes is inconsistent with its character as a home for families. There will be no manufactures, commerce, or agriculture here, for the maintenance of families, and sooner or later want will compel the inhabitants to go. Why not go now, when all the arrangements are completed for the transfer, instead of waiting till the plunging shot of contending armies will renew the scenes of the past month? Of course, I do not apprehend any such thing at this moment, but you do not suppose this army will be here until the war is over. I cannot discuss this subject with you fairly, because I cannot impart to you what we propose to do, but I assert that our military plans make it necessary for the inhabitants to go away, and I can only renew my offer of services to make their exodus in any direction as easy and comfortable as possible.
You cannot qualify war in harsher terms than I will. War is cruelty, and you cannot refine it; and those who brought war into our country deserve all the curses and maledictions a people can pour out. I know I had no hand in making this war, and I know I will make more sacrifices to-day than any of you to secure peace. But you cannot have peace and a division of our country. If the United States submits to a division now, it will not stop, but will go on until we reap the fate of Mexico, which is eternal war. The United States does and must assert its authority, wherever it once had power; for, if it relaxes one bit to pressure, it is gone, and I believe that such is the national feeling. This feeling assumes various shapes, but always comes back to that of Union. Once admit the Union, once more acknowledge the authority of the national Government, and, instead of devoting your houses and streets and roads to the dread uses of war, I and this army become at once your protectors and supporters, shielding you from danger, let it come from what quarter it may. I know that a few individuals cannot resist a torrent of error and passion, such as swept the South into rebellion, but you can point out, so that we may know those who desire a government, and those who insist on war and its desolation.
You might as well appeal against the thunder-storm as against these terrible hardships of war. They are inevitable, and the only way the people of Atlanta can hope once more to live in peace and quiet at home, is to stop the war, which can only be done by admitting that it began in error and is perpetuated in pride.

We don't want your negroes, or your horses, or your houses, or your lands, or any thing you have, but we do want and will have a just obedience to the laws of the United States. That we will have, and, if it involves the destruction of your improvements, we cannot help it.

You have heretofore read public sentiment in your newspapers, that live by falsehood and excitement; and the quicker you seek for truth in other quarters, the better. I repeat then that, by the original compact of Government, the United States had certain rights in Georgia, which have never been relinquished and never will be; that the South began war by seizing forts, arsenals, mints, custom-houses, etc., etc., long before Mr. Lincoln was installed, and before the South had one jot or tittle of provocation. I myself have seen in Missouri, Kentucky, Tennessee, and Mississippi, hundreds and thousands of women and children fleeing from your armies and desperadoes, hungry and with bleeding feet. In Memphis, Vicksburg, and Mississippi, we fed thousands upon thousands of the families of rebel soldiers left on our hands, and whom we could not see starve. Now that war comes home to you, you feel very different. You deprecate its horrors, but did not feel them when you sent car-loads of soldiers and ammunition, and moulded shells and shot, to carry war into Kentucky and Tennessee, to desolate the homes of hundreds and thousands of good people who only asked to live in peace at their old homes, and under the Government of their inheritance. But these comparisons are idle. I want peace, and believe it can only be reached through union and war, and I will ever conduct war with a view to perfect and early success.

But, my dear sirs, when peace does come, you may call on me for any thing. Then will I share with you the last cracker, and watch with you to shield your homes and families against danger from every quarter.

Now you must go, and take with you the old and feeble, feed and nurse them, and build for them, in more quiet places, proper habitations to shield them against the weather until the mad passions of men cool down, and allow the Union and peace once more to settle over your old homes at Atlanta. Yours in haste,

W. T. SHERMAN, Major-General commanding.

QUESTIONS FOR READING AND DISCUSSION

1. How do Sherman's and Hood's justifications of war differ? What did Sherman consider Hood's "impertinence"? Why did Hood consider Sherman's order an act of "studied and ingenious cruelty"?

2. Why did Sherman believe it was "kindness" to expel Atlanta's residents? How did Atlanta citizens reply to his orders?

3. In what ways, according to Hood, did Sherman "make negroes your allies"? Did Sherman agree?

4. Did Sherman acknowledge any limits to his declaration that "war is cruelty"? Who was to blame for the horrors of war? According to Sherman, what did the Union want from Confederate civilians?

COMPARATIVE QUESTIONS

1. How did Abraham Lincoln's war aims differ from those of the ex-slave in New Orleans and the black soldiers in whose regiment Susie King Taylor worked?

2. How did General William T. Sherman's views of war compare with those of Abraham Lincoln? How did Sherman's views compare with those of Colonel Trowbridge, the white commander of the black soldiers from Document 15–4?

3. To what extent were the views Lincoln expressed in the Gettysburg Address shared by the New York draft rioters? How would you account for the differences?

4. Given the war aims defined by Lincoln and the contrasting experiences of war illustrated by the other documents, what justified the immense sacrifices made by so many people?

5. War has been termed the continuation of politics by other means. Judging from the documents in this chapter, what key political conflicts shaped the course and outcome of the Civil War?

16 Reconstruction
1863–1877

D uring the turbulent years of Reconstruction, the character of freedom for former slaves was the subject of intense debate within the South and across the nation. Most southern whites sought the most limited form of freedom for African Americans. Most former slaves strove to exercise their liberty to the fullest, as they sought to reunite families and claim their independence from their former masters as much as possible. White vigilantes resorted to murder, lynching, and other acts of brutality to force blacks to limit their horizons. In the end, most northern white Republicans concluded that once former slaves had the vote, the South—not the North or the federal government—should determine how best to define freedom and preserve order.

DOCUMENT 16–1

Carl Schurz Reports on the Condition of the Defeated South

In the summer of 1865, President Andrew Johnson sent Carl Schurz to investigate conditions in the defeated Confederacy. Born in Germany in 1829, Schurz immigrated to the United States in 1852 and became a leader in the Republican Party in Wisconsin. During the Civil War Schurz served as a general in the Union army, commanding troops at Gettysburg and other major battles. Schurz traveled throughout the South immediately after the war and spoke to hundreds of people to gauge the sentiment of leaders and ordinary people about their loyalty to the Union and their attitudes toward emancipation and the men and women recently emancipated from bondage. Schurz's report, excerpted below, discloses the views of southern whites toward the federal government and former slaves in the months following Confederate defeat. Those views shaped the course and consequences of federal efforts to reconstruct the former Confederacy.

From Carl Schurz, *Report on the Condition of the South*, 39th Cong., 1st Sess., Senate Ex. Doc. No. 2 (Washington, 1865).

Report on the Condition of the South, 1865

[A]ll organized attacks upon our military forces stationed in the south have ceased; but there are still localities where it is unsafe for a man wearing the federal uniform or known as an officer of the government to be abroad outside of the immediate reach of our garrisons. The shooting of single soldiers and government couriers was not unfrequently reported while I was in the south. . . . But no instance has come to my notice in which the people of a city or a rural district cordially fraternized with the army. Here and there the soldiers were welcomed as protectors against apprehended dangers; but general exhibitions of cordiality on the part of the population I have not heard of. . . . [U]pon the whole, the soldier of the Union is still looked upon as a stranger, an intruder—as the "Yankee," "the enemy." . . .

While the generosity and toleration shown by the [U.S.] government to the people lately in rebellion has not met with a corresponding generosity shown by those people to the government's friends, it has brought forth some results which, if properly developed, will become of value. It has facilitated the re-establishment of the forms of civil government, and led many of those who had been active in the rebellion to take part in the act of bringing back the States to their constitutional relations. . . . There is, at present, no danger of another insurrection against the authority of the United States on a large scale, and the people are willing to reconstruct their State governments, and to send their senators and representatives to Congress.

But as to the moral value of these results, we must not indulge in any delusions. There are two principal points to which I beg to call your attention. In the first place, the rapid return to power and influence of so many of those who but recently were engaged in a bitter war against the Union, has had one effect which was certainly not originally contemplated by the government. Treason does, under existing circumstances, not appear odious in the south. The people are not impressed with any sense of its criminality. And, secondly, there is, as yet, among the southern people an utter absence of national feeling. I made it a business, while in the South, to watch the symptoms of "returning loyalty" as they appeared not only in private conversation, but in the public press and in the speeches delivered and the resolutions passed at Union meetings. Hardly ever was there an expression of hearty attachment to the great republic, or an appeal to the impulses of patriotism; but whenever submission to the national authority was declared and advocated, it was almost uniformly placed upon two principal grounds: That, under present circumstances, the southern people could "do no better;" and then that submission was the only means by which they could rid themselves of the federal soldiers and obtain once more control of their own affairs. . . .

In speaking above of the improbability of an insurrectionary movement on a large scale, I did not mean to say that I considered resistance in detail to the execution of the laws of Congress and the measures of the government impossible. . . . [M]ost of the conversations I had with southerners upon this subject led me to apprehend that they . . . are rather inclined to ask money of the government as compensation for their emancipated slaves, for the rebuilding of the levees on the Mississippi, and various kinds of damage done by our armies for military purposes, than, as the current expression is, to "help paying the expenses of the whipping they have received." In fact, there are abundant indications in newspaper articles, public speeches, and electioneering documents of candidates, which render it eminently probable that on the claim of compensation for their emancipated slaves the southern States, as soon as readmitted to representation in Congress, will be almost a unit. In the Mississippi convention the idea was broached by Mr. Potter, in an elaborate speech, to have the late slave States relieved from taxation "for years to come," in consideration of "debt due them" for the emancipated slaves; and this plea I have frequently heard advocated in private conversations. . . .

In at least nineteen cases of twenty the reply I received to my inquiry about their views on the new [labor] system was uniformly this: "You cannot make the negro work, without physical compulsion." I heard this hundreds of times, heard it wherever I went, heard it in nearly the same words from so many different persons, that at last I came to the conclusion that this is the prevailing sentiment among the southern people. . . .

I found but few people who were willing to make due allowance for the adverse influence of exceptional circumstances. By a large majority of those I came in contact with, and they mostly belonged to the more intelligent class, every irregularity that occurred was directly charged against the system of free labor. If negroes walked away from the plantations, it was conclusive proof of the incorrigible instability of the negro, and the impracticability of free negro labor. If some individual negroes violated the terms of their contract, it proved unanswerably that no negro had, or ever would have, a just conception of the binding force of a contract, and that this system of free negro labor was bound to be a failure. If some negroes shirked, or did not perform their task with sufficient alacrity, it was produced as irrefutable evidence to show that physical compulsion was actually indispensable to make the negro work. If negroes, idlers or refugees crawling about the towns, applied to the authorities for subsistence, it was quoted as incontestably establishing the point that the negro was too improvident to take care of himself, and must necessarily be consigned to the care of a master. I heard a Georgia planter argue most seriously that one of his negroes had shown himself certainly unfit for freedom because he impudently refused to submit to a whipping. . . . It frequently struck me that persons who conversed about every other subject calmly and sensibly would lose their temper as soon as the negro question was touched. . . .

A belief, conviction, or prejudice, or whatever you may call it, so widely spread and apparently so deeply rooted as this, that the negro will not work without physical compulsion, is certainly calculated to have a very serious influence upon the conduct of the people entertaining it. It naturally produced a desire to preserve slavery in its original form as much and as long as possible . . . remember the admission made by one of the provisional governors, over two months after the close of the war, that the people of his State still indulged in a lingering hope slavery might yet be preserved — or to introduce into the new system that element of physical compulsion which would make the negro work. Efforts were, indeed, made to hold the negro in his old state of subjection, especially in such localities where our military forces had not yet penetrated, or where the country was not garrisoned in detail. Here and there planters succeeded for a limited period to keep their former slaves in ignorance, or at least doubt, about their new rights; but the main agency employed for that purpose was force and intimidation. In many instances negroes who walked away from the plantations, or were found upon the roads, were shot or otherwise severely punished, which was calculated to produce the impression among those remaining with their masters that an attempt to escape from slavery would result in certain destruction. A large proportion of the many acts of violence committed is undoubtedly attributable to this motive. . . .

The conviction, however, that slavery in the old form cannot be maintained has forced itself upon the minds of many of those who ardently desired its preservation. But while the necessity of a new system was recognized as far as the right of property in the individual negro is concerned, many attempts were made to introduce into that new system the element of physical compulsion, which . . . is so generally considered indispensable. This was done by simply adhering, as to the treatment of the laborers, as much as possible to the traditions of the old system, even where the relations between employers and laborers had been fixed by contract. The practice of corporal punishment was still continued to a great extent, although, perhaps, not in so regular a manner as it was practiced in times gone by. . . . The habit is so inveterate with a great many persons as to render, on the least provocation, the impulse to whip a negro almost irresistible. It will continue to be so until the southern people will have learned, so as never to forget it, that a black man has rights which a white man is bound to respect.

Here I will insert some remarks on the general treatment of the blacks as a class, from the whites as a class. It is not on the plantations and at the hands of the planters themselves that the negroes have to suffer the greatest hardships. Not only the former slaveholders, but the non-slaveholding whites, who, even previous to the war, seemed to be more ardent in their pro-slavery feelings than the planters themselves, are possessed by a singularly bitter and vindictive feeling against the colored race since the negro has ceased to be property. The pecuniary value which the individual negro formerly represented having disappeared, the maiming and killing of colored men seems to be looked upon by many as one of those venial offences which must be forgiven to the outraged feelings of a wronged and robbed people. Besides, the services rendered by the negro to the national cause during the war, which make him an object of special interest to the loyal people, make him an object of particular vindictiveness to those whose hearts were set upon the success of the rebellion. The number of murders and assaults perpetrated upon negroes is very great; we can form only an approximative estimate of what is going on in those parts of the south which are not closely garrisoned, and from which no regular reports are received, by what occurs under the very eyes of our military authorities. . . .

So far, the spirit of persecution has shown itself so strong as to make the protection of the freedman by the military arm of the government in many localities necessary — in almost all, desirable. It must not be forgotten that in a community a majority of whose members is peaceably disposed, but not willing or not able to enforce peace and order, a comparatively small number of bold and lawless men can determine the character of the whole. . . .

Aside from the assumption that the negro will not work without physical compulsion, there appears to be another popular notion prevalent in the south, which stands as no less serious an obstacle in the way of a successful solution of the problem. It is that the negro exists for the special object of raising cotton, rice and sugar for the whites, and that it is illegitimate for him to indulge, like other people, in the pursuit of his own happiness in his own way. Although it is admitted that he has ceased to be the property of a master, it is not admitted that he has a right to become his own master. As Colonel Thomas, assistant commissioner of the Freedmen's Bureau in Mississippi, in a letter addressed to me, very pungently expresses it: "The whites esteem the blacks their property by natural right, and, however much they may admit that the relations of masters and slaves have been destroyed by the war and by the President's emancipation proclamation, they still have an ingrained feeling that the blacks at large belong to the whites at large, and whenever opportunity serves, they treat the colored people just as their profit, caprice or passion may dictate."

QUESTIONS FOR READING AND DISCUSSION

1. What did Schurz see as "some results" that "will become of value" in reconstructing the South? What was his view of the "moral value of these results"?

2. What significance did Schurz give to white Southerners' demand for "compensation for emancipated slaves"? What did this demand suggest about the meaning of defeat and emancipation to slaveholders?

3. How did the racial views of white Southerners influence their responses to emancipation? Why did they almost universally insist that "You cannot make the negro work, without physical compulsion"?

4. Schurz reported that white Southerners had "a desire to preserve slavery in its original forms as much and as long as possible." What evidence of that desire did Schurz report?

5. What evidence did Schurz find of the "ingrained feeling that the blacks at large belong to the whites at large"? To what degree was this feeling influential in shaping southern whites' responses to emancipation? To what extent was it influential in shaping federal policy toward Reconstruction?

DOCUMENT 16–2

Black Codes Enacted in the South

After the Civil War, the legal status of former slaves was defined by state legislatures throughout the South. In the months following General Robert E. Lee's surrender at Appomattox, white legislators devised laws to regulate and control former slaves. Known as black codes, these laws defined freedom for African Americans in terms that resembled slavery in many respects, as revealed in the following provisions of the Mississippi Black Code, enacted in November 1865.

Mississippi Black Code, November 1865

AN ACT to confer Civil Rights on Freedmen, and for other purposes.

Be it enacted by the Legislature of the State of Mississippi. That all freedmen, free negroes and mulattoes may sue and be sued, . . . in all the courts of law and equity of this State, and may acquire personal property . . . by descent or purchase, and may dispose of the same, in the same manner . . . that white persons may: Provided that the provisions of this section shall not be so construed as to allow any freedman, free negro or mulatto, to rent or lease any lands or tenements,

---

From W. L. Fleming, ed., *Laws of Mississippi Documentary History of Reconstruction*, 2 vols. (Cleveland: A. H. Clark, 1865), 281–90.

except in incorporated towns or cities in which places the corporate authorities shall control the same. . . .

That all freedmen, free negroes and mulattoes may intermarry with each other. . . . That all freedmen, free negroes and mulattoes, who do now and have heretofore lived and cohabited together as husband and wife shall be taken and held in law as legally married, and the issue shall be taken and held as legitimate for all purposes. That it shall not be lawful for any freedman, free negro or mulatto to intermarry with any white person; nor for any white person to intermarry with any freedman, free negro or mulatto; and any person who shall so intermarry shall be deemed guilty of felony, and on conviction thereof, shall be confined in the State penitentiary for life. . . .

That . . . freedmen, free negroes and mulattoes are now by law competent witnesses . . . in civil cases . . . and they shall also be competent witnesses in all criminal prosecutions where the crime charged is alleged to have been committed by a white person upon or against the person or property of a freedman, free negro or mulatto. . . .

That every freedman, free negro and mulatto, shall, on the second Monday of January, one thousand eight hundred and sixty-six, and annually thereafter, have a lawful home or employment, and shall have written evidence thereof; as follows, to wit: if living in any incorporated city, town or village, a license from the mayor thereof; and if living outside of any incorporated city, town or village, from the member of the board of police of his beat, authorizing him or her to do irregular and job work, or a written contract . . . which licenses may be revoked for cause, at any time, by the authority granting the same. . . .

That all contracts for labor made with freedmen, free negroes and mulattoes, for a longer period than one month shall be in writing and in duplicate, attested and read to said freedman, free negro or mulatto, by a beat, city or county officer, or two disinterested white persons of the county in which the labor is to be performed . . . and if the laborer shall quit the service of the employer, before expiration of his term of service, without good cause, he shall forfeit his wages for that year, up to the time of quitting. . . .

That every civil officer shall, and every person may arrest and carry back to his or her legal employer any freedman, free negro or mulatto, who shall have quit the service of his or her employer before the expiration of his or her term of service without good cause, and said officer and person, shall be entitled to receive for arresting and carrying back every deserting employee aforesaid, the sum of five dollars, and ten cents per mile from the place of arrest to the place of delivery, [to] be paid by the employer. . . .

AN [A]CT to regulate the relation of Master and Apprentice, as related to Freedmen, Free Negroes, and Mulattoes.

Be it enacted by the Legislature of the State of Mississippi:

That it shall be the duty of all sheriffs, justices of the peace, and other civil officers of the several counties in this State, to report to the probate courts of their respective counties, semi-annually, at the January and July terms of said courts, all freedmen, free negroes and mulattoes, under the age of eighteen, within their respective counties, beats or districts, who are orphans, or whose parent or parents have not the means, or who refuse to provide for and support said minors, and thereupon it shall be the duty of said probate court, to order the clerk of said court to apprentice said minors to some competent and suitable person, on such terms as the court may direct. . . . Provided, that the former owner of said minors shall have the preference. . . .

That . . . the said court shall require the said master or mistress to execute bond and security, payable to the State of Mississippi, conditioned that he or she shall furnish said minor with sufficient food and clothing, to treat said minor humanely, furnish medical attention in case of sickness; [and to] teach or cause to be taught him or her to read and write, if under fifteen years old. . . . Provided, that said apprentice shall be bound by indenture, in case of males until they are twenty-one years old, and in case of females until they are eighteen years old. . . .

That in the management and control of said apprentices, said master or mistress shall have power to inflict such moderate corporeal chastisement as a father or guardian is allowed to inflict on his or her child or ward at common law. . . .

That if any apprentice shall leave the employment of his or her master or mistress, without his or her consent, said master or mistress may pursue and recapture said apprentice, and bring him or her before any justice of the peace of the county, whose duty it shall be to remand said apprentice to the service of his or her master or mistress; and in the event of a refusal on the part of said apprentice so to return, then said justice shall commit said apprentice to the jail of said county. . . .

That if any person entice away any apprentice from his or her master or mistress, or shall knowingly employ an apprentice, or furnish him or her food or clothing, without the written consent of his or her master or mistress, or shall sell or give said apprentice ardent spirits, without such consent, said person so offending shall be deemed guilty of a high misdemeanor, and shall, on conviction thereof before the county court, be punished as provided for the punishment of persons enticing from their employer hired freedmen, free Negroes or mulattoes. . . .

AN ACT to amend the Vagrant Laws of the State.

Be it further enacted,

That all freedmen, free negroes and mulattoes in this State, over the age of eighteen years, found on the second Monday in January, 1866, or thereafter, with no lawful employment or business, or found unlawfully assembling themselves together either in the day or night time, and all white persons so assembling with [them] on terms of equality, or living in adultery or fornication with a freedwoman, free negro, or mulatto, shall be deemed vagrants, and on conviction thereof, shall be fined in the sum of not exceeding, in the case of a freedman, free negro or mulatto, fifty dollars, and a white man two hundred dollars, and imprisoned at the discretion of the court, the free negro not exceeding ten days, and the white man not exceeding six months. . . .

That . . . in case any freedman, free negro or mulatto, shall fail for five days after the imposition of any fine or forfeiture upon him or her for violation of any of the provisions of this act, to pay the same, that it shall be, and is hereby made the duty of the sheriff of the proper county to hire out said freedman, free negro or mulatto, to any person who will, for the shortest period of service, pay said fine or forfeiture and all costs: Provided, a preference shall be given to the employer, if there be one, in which case the employer shall be entitled to deduct and retain the amount so paid from the wages of such freedman, free negro or mulatto, then due or to become due. . . .

AN ACT to punish certain offences. . . .

Be it enacted by the Legislature of the State of Mississippi:

That no freedman, free negro or mulatto . . . shall keep or carry fire-arms of any kind, or any ammunition, dirk or bowie knife, and on conviction thereof, in the county court, shall be punished by fine, not exceeding ten dollars, and pay the costs of such proceedings, and all such arms or ammunition shall be forfeited to the informer, and it shall be the duty of every civil and military officer to arrest any freedman, free negro or mulatto found with any such arms or ammunition, and cause him or her to be committed for trial in default of bail. . . .

That any freedman, free negro or mulatto, committing riots, routs, affrays, trespasses, malicious mischief, cruel treatment of animals, seditious speeches, insulting gestures, language or acts, or assaults on any person, disturbances of the peace, exercising the function of a minister of the Gospel, without a license from some regularly organized church, vending spirituous or intoxicating liquors, or committing any other misdemeanor . . . shall, upon conviction thereof, in the county court, be fined, not less than ten dollars, and not more than one hundred dollars, and may be imprisoned, at the discretion of the court, not exceeding thirty days. . . .

That if any white person shall sell, lend or give to any freedman, free negro or mulatto, any firearms, dirk or bowie-knife, or ammunition, or any spirituous or intoxicating liquors, such person or persons so offending, upon conviction thereof, in the county court of his or her county, shall be fined, not exceeding fifty dollars, and may be imprisoned, at the discretion of the court, not exceeding thirty days. . . .

That all the penal and criminal laws now in force in this State, defining offences and prescribing the mode of punishment for crimes and misdemeanors committed by slaves, free negroes or mulattoes, be and the same are hereby re-enacted, and declared to be in full force and effect, against freedmen, free negroes and mulattoes, except so far as the mode and manner of trial and punishment have been changed or altered by law. . . .

That if any freedman, free negro or mulatto, convicted of any of the misde-meanors provided against in this act, shall fail or refuse, for the space of five days after conviction, to pay the fine and costs imposed, such person shall be hired out by the sheriff or other officer, at public outcry, to any white person who will pay said fine and all costs, and take such convict for the shortest time.

QUESTIONS FOR READING AND DISCUSSION

1. What civil rights, if any, did these laws confer on freed black men and women?

2. Why did the laws repeatedly refer to "freedmen, free negroes and mulattoes"?

3. In what ways did these laws limit the freedom of African Americans in Missis-sippi? Were these laws different from the laws governing slaves? If so, how and why?

4. Did former masters exercise any control over their former slaves? To what extent did these laws limit the freedom of white Mississippians?

5. What do these laws suggest about white Southerners' anxieties and fears regarding the end of slavery? In what ways did the laws envision postemanci-pation society differing from antebellum slavery?

Document 16–3

Former Slaves Seek to Reunite Their Families

With freedom, former slaves tried to reunite families slavery had separated. Some freed people traveled far and wide searching for kinfolk. Others appealed for help from the Freedmen's Bureau or enlisted literate friends to write letters of inquiry. But hundreds of former slaves placed advertisements in newspapers, asking for help in locating lost family members. The advertisements below appeared in the Christian Recorder, *the weekly newspaper of the African Methodist Episcopal Church in Philadelphia. The ads provide a glimpse of the scars of slavery and the meanings of freedom for millions of former slaves.*

Advertisements from the Christian Recorder, 1865–1870

January 25, 1865

INFORMATION WANTED

Jacob Brown wishes to find his sister and friends, from whom he was sold about eight years ago. He belonged to George Fisher, of Hardy County, Va., near Morefield. His sister Louisa, who was sold with him into Louisiana, has been back home once. She left three children, named respectively Peter, Isaac, and Moses. She is in New Orleans, and is anxious to hear of them. Another sister remained, named Arena or "Arenir," whose husband was named Paul Peterson. His uncles were Richard and Jacob Cassam, owned by McCoy.

Any person knowing any thing of them will confer a great favor upon the undersigned, who is their young brother, and who escaped from imprisonment in the jail, at Winchester, Va., by writing such information as shall unite those separated by slavery.

Respectfully,
Jacob Brown,
Baton Rouge, Louisiana

July 29, 1865

INFORMATION WANTED

Information is wanted of Cayrel Robinson, who left Liberty, Clay County, Missouri, about four years ago, to join the Union army at Wyandotte, Kansas; and he has not been heard from since. Any information of his whereabouts will be thankfully received by his wife.

Mrs. Fannie Robinson
Care of P. C. Cooper
Box 1129
Davenport, Iowa

From *Christian Recorder*, 1865–1870.

August 5, 1865

INFORMATION WANTED

Edith Chappel left Columbia, South Carolina, on February 20th, 1865, with the army of Gen. Sherman, from the residence of Mrs. Henry Lyons. Her aunt, Fannie Bostick, can be found with

Mr. A. L. Hart
827 Lombard St.
Philadelphia

November 18, 1865

NOTICE

Information wanted of my two brothers Nelson, and Wesley Smothers, and my six sisters, Mary Ann Russell, Harriet, Matilda, Elizabeth, Henrietta, and Cornelia Smothers.

They formerly belonged to Ruth Rigla, who resided two miles from the Old Harper's Ferry Road, Frederick County, Md.

In 1837, we were all sold to South Carolina. I have not seen them since. Any information will be thankfully received by

Rev. Cyrus Boey
Oswego, N.Y.

March 10, 1866

INFORMATION WANTED

By a mother concerning her children. Mrs. Elizabeth Williams, who now resides in Marysville, California, was formerly owned, together with her children viz.: Lydia, William, Allen, and Parker, by one John Petty, who lived about six miles from the town of Woodbury, Franklin County, Tennessee. At that time she was the wife of Sandy Rucker, and was familiarly known as Betsy, sometimes called Betsy Petty.

About twenty-five years ago, the mother was sold to Mr. Marshal Stroud, by whom some twelve or fourteen years later, she was, for the second time since purchased by him, taken to Arkansas. She has never seen the above named children since. Any information given concerning them, however, will be very gratefully received by one whose love for her children survives the bitterness and hardships of many long years spent in slavery.

Preachers in the neighborhood of Woodbury, Tennessee, are especially requested to make inquiry, and communicate any information they may deem valuable either by letter or through the columns of the "Recorder."

April 7, 1866

INFORMATION WANTED

Of the children of Hagar Outlaw, who went from Wake Forest. Three of them, (their names being Cherry, Viny, and Mills Outlaw,) were bought by Abram Hester. Noah Outlaw was taken to Alabama by Joseph Turner Hillsborough. John Outlaw was sold to George Vaughan. Eli Outlaw was sold by Joseph Outlaw. He acted as watchman for old David Outlaw. Thomas Rembry Outlaw was taken away by Wm. Outlaw. Julia Outlaw was sold in New Orleans by Dr. Outlaw. I live in Raleigh, and I hope they will think enough of their mother to come and look for her, as she is growing old, and needs help. She will be glad to see them again at [illegible word]. The place is healthy, and they can all do well here. As the hand of time steals over me now so rapidly, I wish to see my dear ones once more clasped to their mother's heart as in days of yore. Come to the capital of North Carolina, and you will find your mother there, eagerly awaiting her loved ones.

Hugh Outlaw, if you should find any or all of my children, you will do me an incalculable favor by immediately informing them that their mother still lives.

May 5, 1866

INFORMATION WANTED

Of the oldest daughter Jane's children. One son by the name of Andrew, another by the name of Ransom, and another by the name of George, who were taken from me and sold when they were very small.

Also two others, (twins) one called Martha Ann and the other had no name. The name of the father of these children is Washington. He belonged to a man in Franklinton, Ky., whose name was Joseph Kearney.

The mother of these children belonged to a man in Franklin Co., Ky., by the name of Seth Ward, her name is Charity Ward, wife of Washington Kearney, who was killed by a fall from a wagon. Any information concerning any of the above will be thankfully received by addressing

W. A. Bookram
Franklinton, North Carolina

June 9, 1866

INFORMATION WANTED

Charles Metts wishes to hear from his family. His wife's name is Jane, and his children are named Margaret, Drucilla, Elizabeth, and Chas. Henry. He has not seen them for ten years. The last he heard from them was when in the Rebel Army. They were at Columbia, S.C. He could not get a chance to go to see them. He came on to Philadelphia, and is now living here.

Baptist ministers at Columbia, S.C., will please make inquiry concerning the above family. All information will be thankfully received by addressing

Chas. Metts
Care of R. A. Black
"Christian Recorder" Office.
Philadelphia, Pa.

July 14, 1866

INFORMATION WANTED

Lewis Wade wishes to learn the whereabouts of his wife, Lucy, and three children, named respectively, Benjamin, Harriet and Charlotte. He left them in 1850, they then being in Rockbridge county, Virginia. He belonged to Wm. Thompson, while his wife and children belonged to James Watts. Any information respecting them will be thankfully received by the subscriber at Chatham, Canada West, — and Heaven will bless the hand that guides the wanderers home.

Chatham, Canada West

August 11, 1866

INFORMATION WANTED

Phoebe Ann Jackson, formerly Phoebe Nichols is desirous of informing her brother, Thomas G. Nichols, of Galveston, Texas, of her location in Richmond, Va.

Her proper name was Nichols. She was called Robertson, her eldest brother being known by that name.

In the family, beside father and mother, there were twelve brothers and three sisters. Nancy and Peter Robertson were sold to New Orleans; Brother Samuel went to Georgia. Mother could only learn that Francis and Thomas were on the same boat. Mother and father have since died, as also our stepfather, whose name was Africa Hanes.

Address
Phoebe Ann Jackson
1015 Marshall street, corner 11th
Richmond, Va.

September 22, 1866

INFORMATION WANTED

Information wanted of the whereabouts of my husband, Richard Jones, and my two sons, John and Thomas. We were separated in the woods, near a place called Alleywhite, in November, 1862. I was carried back to Suffolk by the Union troops. I have heard nothing of them since.

We were owned by Birven Jones, of Smithfield, Suffolk County, Virginia. I am the granddaughter of old Tom Peet Wilson. I am much in want at this time. Ministers will please read this notice in the churches.

Matilda Jones
Direct to Anthony Bowen
Agent, *Christian Recorder*
No. 85 E St., betw'n 9th and 10th (Island)
Washington, D.C.

November 17, 1866

INFORMATION WANTED

Information wanted of Silvey Lynch, wife of Sandy Lynch, who was carried away from Carolina county, Virginia, by her "master," Wm. Goodman, in 1862. Her maiden name is Silvey Wilkins. She took with her three children. The name of the eldest is Jane; the next eldest is Henrietta; and the youngest is a boy named Alexander.

When my wife was taken away, I was in the army, performing the duties of a servant. My wife was formerly claimed as the property of one Nicholas Wilkins. She is of the Baptist persuasion. Any information concerning her whereabouts will be thankfully received from any one who will please address a letter to

Sandy Lynch
Care of Rev. J. R. V. Thomas
Box 90
Portsmouth, Virginia

March 23, 1867

INFORMATION WANTED

Information wanted of John and Lavinia Teamer, or Teamoh, who were sold in 1853, from Richmond, Va., by one John Lindsay, formally of Fortress Monroe, Va. John was nine years old, and Lavinia eight, at the time of the sale. Their mother Sarah was sold by the same party to Rosinfield, of Richmond, Va. It was thought they were sold to Texas. Ministers of the Christian Church will please inquire, as any information of the parties, will be thankfully received by their father.

Geo. Teamoh
Portsmouth, Va.
P.O. Box 152

November 2, 1867

INFORMATION WANTED
Canton, Ind., Oct. 19, 1867

John Grantson and Albert Thurston Robinson, brothers, aged respectvely about 16 and 13 years, were sent from Missouri to Kentucky in the year 1863. Andrew Robinson, of Clay County, Missouri, was the owner of the boys' father, Coyed Robinson, whose wife, Frances was owned by Whiton Drew, of the same County and State, and after his death fell to his son, Dalphin Drew, who, in 1860, sold her to a man by the name of Pitcher, the former owner of her mother. This man formerly lived in Platt city, Platt county, Missouri. Albert, the youngest boy, was brought to Kentucky in August, 1863, by Dalphin Drew's wife, as nurse for her babe. John the elder boy, and his sister, Mary Eliza, with several others, were sent there a few months later to the care of Washington Gordon, Logan County, Kentucky. From thence they came back here a few months since, intending to get back to Missouri as soon as possible; but the parents may be elsewhere now. A kind, elderly colored man, by the name of Peter Garland, has voluntarily taken charge of them, and placed them in comfortable, but transient homes, but they wish very much to be united to their relatives.

Susan Trueblood

P.S. If any one should wish further information, they can write to me, and I will give it, if possible. My address is Canton, Washington, Co., Indiana.

May 8, 1869

INFORMATION WANTED

Of my son Charles Blackwell. He was sold from me in Lancaster county, Virginia, ten years ago, when quite young. He was sold from the estate of Mr. Joseph Beacham to Mr. Lewis Dix, and then taken to Mississippi. I am an old man and need the companionship of my son. Any assistance in securing information of his whereabouts will be thankfully received. Ministers in Mississippi and throughout the entire country will please read in their churches. Address information to my address,

Lewis Blackwell
Lancaster Court House, Virginia

April 2, 1870

INFORMATION WANTED

Information wanted of Sarah Williams, who I left at Halifax Court House, Va., about 25 years ago. She belonged to a man whose name was William Early, who kept a dry-goods store. Any information of her will be thankfully received by her sister, Martha Ann Good, who was taken away from Nathan Dexter, who kept a hotel at Halifax, at 12 o'clock at night, when quite small, and sold in Alabama, but who now lives at 225 Currant Alley, Philadelphia, Pa.

N.B. Ministers in the South, please read in your churches.

July 2, 1870

INFORMATION WANTED

Of my sisters, Jennette, Eliza, Caroline, America, and Elizabeth, and of my brother Harry. Also of our mother, whose name was Dinah Hickson. They were sold from Liberty, Mo., over 30 years ago, and the last time I heard of them they were on Red River. They belonged to Andy Hickson, and were sold to a man named Francis Benware. Any information of these parties will be gladly received by Moses Hickson,

Now Moses Sisseney
St. Joseph, Mo., Box 507

N.B. Pastors of churches will please read this.

December 10, 1870

INFORMATION WANTED

Of my mother Isabella, my sister Sallie, and of my grandmother, named Minna. I left them in Georgia about thirty years ago. They belonged to a man named Joe Marshall; my mother belonged to a man named Wm. Bell. They lived near Green Brier Meeting House. Any information address, Jas. Bell, Helena, Ark.

QUESTIONS FOR READING AND DISCUSSION

1. How did the people who placed these ads expect readers to recognize their lost family members?
2. What audiences did the people who placed these ads intend to reach? What was the significance of statements such as, "Ministers in Mississippi and throughout the entire country will please read in their churches?"
3. What do these ads suggest about slavery? What do these ads suggest about family relationships among slaves?
4. Do you think such ads actually helped to reunite families? Why or why not? What do these ads suggest about the meanings of freedom for former slaves?

DOCUMENT 16–4

Planter Louis Manigault Visits His Plantations and Former Slaves

For many years before the Civil War, Louis Manigault owned two large and very profitable rice plantations located on Argyle Island in the Savannah River, not far from the city of Savannah, Georgia. He abandoned the plantations when General Sherman's army approached in 1864. His numerous slaves remained on the plantations without white supervision through the end of the war, and more or less made them their own. After emancipation, most of the freed men and women stayed on Manigault's land, where they made contracts with a white man who rented the plantations from Manigault. In 1867 Manigault decided to return to his plantations for the first time since he left in 1864. In his plantation journal, excerpted below, he recorded what he discovered. His observations illustrate the mind-boggling changes the war and emancipation brought to plantations, as well as certain unexpected continuities. As you read Manigault's comments about his former slaves, try to imagine how the freedmen and women viewed their former master.

A Narrative of a Post–Civil War Visit to Gowrie and East Hermitage Plantations, March 22, 1867

I conversed with several Negroes from plantations in our vicinity, from them I received some River News and likewise sent word to some of our former Negroes that I was in Savannah and would visit them. . . .

Some six miles from Savannah we came in sight of the Charleston and Savannah Rail Road, which had not been touched since the advance of Sherman's Army but the twisted and ruined Rails remained as left by the Yankees. . . . The vestiges of former Encampments of large Bodies of Troops were still perceptible on either side of the road. . . . The cruel hand of War was now clearly to be seen; in fact most startling was the change on every side since my last visit here in Dec'r 1864. The large Rice Pounding Mill with its Wheel in the centre similar to the Gowrie Mill was burnt down. This was also the case with the fine wooden Barn close at hand. . . . With far deeper pain however did I contemplate the Ruins of Mr James Potter's handsome Residence. As a Country House it was superior to any on the River, and had been built by Mr Potter about the year of 1854 and with its furniture cost about Twenty Thousand Dollars. Many a time had I spent a pleasing hour at this hospitable Gentleman's House, surrounded by his family of charming Young Ladies not forgetting to mention "Miss Gilby" the English Governess. . . .

General Harrison [who rented Manigault's plantations] was soon pointed out to me. He was in his black-smith Shop overlooking the repair of some Plantation Utensil.

I advanced and introduced myself. He is a Man of commanding appearance, upwards of six feet in heighth, about fifty years of age, married; with five Children . . . and very fine looking, who had served in a [Confederate] Cavalry Regiment throughout the War. The General said he had not visited [Manigault's plantations on] Argyle Island for two or three days and would be happy to accompany me. His Canoe, with old Negro and paddle, was soon in readiness, and with our horse and buggy placed in charge of the Servant to be taken to the Stable we pushed off in the River. . . .

Proceeding now on foot along the Canal Bank . . . we took our nearest course towards Gowrie Settlement. When about half across the Island our progress was impeded by the freshet water knee deep over the check banks. The General pushed on, and Louis [Manigault's son] and I were soon soaked from knees down as we followed; the water becoming deeper still, it was determined he should endeavour to reach Gowrie Settlement and send us some Negro Man to take us on his back. After some delay I recognized our former Cooper "George" approaching, delighted to meet us and calling me "Maussa" as of yore. He [carried us on his back and] placed us in safety on dry land and we walked up to the Settlement. Reaching Gowrie Settlement I placed Louis in charge of (the above mentioned) George's Wife "Betty" a woman I had known for many years and who always bore a good character. She made a fire for him in her house, dried his shoes and stockings and as I learnt afterwards boiled several eggs for him to his great delight. . . .

From Louis Manigault, Manigault Plantation Journal (manuscript), pp. 56–71. Manigault Papers, Southern Historical Collection, University of North Carolina, Chapel Hill.

Not having visited the Plantation since the Advance of Sherman's Army in December 1864 my present visit was one of painful interest. [On my] . . . final visit to the plantation in Dec'r 1864 . . . although the sound of Musketry from the advancing Pickets grew more and more distinct from hour to hour, still up to the very last moment our Negroes behaved well and I left the entire Gang unloading the flat of rice, still pleased to see me, and singing as they bore the heavy loads on their heads from the flat to the Stacks in the Barn Yard. Standing near the ruins of my former dwelling I contemplated the spot. Where once stood this Country House could alone now be seen a few scattering brick, and the tall chimney to denote that spot. Here the most happy period of my boyish days, together with the early years of my married life had been spent. No remnant of my Kitchen, Fine Stable, both built just previous to the War, remained; not even a brick to mark the spot, as all of these had been stolen by the Negroes and sold in Savannah at $5 whilst the Market value was $18. . . .

Trees, Plants, Shrubs, Fences, not a vestige remained, not even the stumps of the trees being visible, all had been used as fire-wood by the Negroes. . . .

The Change in the appearance of Gowrie Settlement is, I may say, from a Village to a Wilderness. There remain in this Gowrie Settlement Four large double Negro Houses, all new, having been built by myself just previous to the War upon high brick foundations elevating them beyond the reach of . . . [flooding]. With the exception of these the Settlement is a barren waste and presents a most abandoned and forlorn appearance. About a half a dozen Negroes crawled out of their houses as we approached, dirty and sluggish in appearance and stupefied by sleep, not knowing whether under the new regime, it would be proper to meet me politely or not, but in every case I advanced and shook hands, calling each by name, which seemed to please them highly. I thought it best to appear but little concerned at the marked change in my situation and joked with them as was my former habit. Five or six were talking to me in this Settlement when one of them remarked "My God, Maussa! Wha mek You trow we side so long; Wha mek You no come back?" My answer amused them highly. Smiling, and turning to the tall chimney of my former happy Home, alone standing to indicate the spot where stood the House; I remarked "Lord! a Massy! You tink I can lib in de Chimney?" which they for the first time appeared to consider true. . . .

Proceeding in front of General Harrison and followed by some of his "Foremen" (none other than our former Negroes "Driver John" [who, before emancipation, supervised the labor of other slaves], "George" Cooper [who built rice barrels], "Big Hector," and "Charles" the Trunk Minder [who supervised sluices for flooding and draining rice fields]) I imagined myself for the moment a Planter once more as if followed by Overseer and Driver. The weather was most beautiful, not a cloud on the Horizon, and so clear and pure the atmosphere that the Presbyterian Church Steeple in Savannah loomed up as if one half its distance. I wished my horse with me to ride over the entire Tract as of yore. But these were only passing momentary thoughts, and soon dispelled by the sad reality of affairs. . . .

Passing through the Settlement and about leaving we were met by Twelve of our former Negroes. They all seemed pleased to see me, calling me "Maussa" the Men still showing respect by taking off their caps. It was singular that after an absence of two and a half years from the Plantation I should now return to visit the place just after the Death of one of three Original Negroes purchased with Gowrie, January 1833. A Woman Known by the Name of "Currie Binah" . . . died yesterday and was buried this morning. Two of the Original Negroes now remain, both as cunning as Negroes can be. These are "Charles the Trunk Minder"; and "Capt'n Hector" for Thirty Years our chief Boat Hand, always spoiled both by my Father and Myself, greatly indulged, and one of the first to give trouble upon the out-break of the War. Amongst the twelve Negroes who advanced to meet me at East Hermitage was, strange to say, the greatest Villain on the Plantation, the most notoriously bad character and worst Negro of the place. Tall, black, lousy, in rags, and uncombed, kinky, knotty-hair approached "Jack Savage." This Negro was bought in 1839. . . . He was an exceedingly lazy Man, although quite smart and our best plantation Carpenter. He was always giving trouble and ever appeared dissatisfied. He was the only Negro ever in our possession who I considered capable of Murdering me, or burning my dwelling at night, or capable of committing any act. The Trunks [sluice gates for flooding and draining rice fields] built by Jack Savage . . . were perfect, and his large Flood-Gates were all that one could desire and specimens of good work. This Man we sold in 1863, he causing trouble on the place, and I had not seen him since 1862. As we met I gave him my hand and made a few friendly remarks. I always gave him many presents such as bacon, and tobacco and rice. Even now I felt sad in contemplating his condition, as in fact was the case with all of them. . . . That former mutual and pleasing feeling of Master towards Slave and vice versa is now as a dream of the past. Our "Northern Brethren" inform us that we Southerners "knew nothing of the Negro Character." This I have always considered perfectly true, but they further state that They (the Yankees) have always known the true Character of the Negro which I consider entirely false in the extreme. So deceitful is the Negro that as far as my own experience extends I could never in a single instance decipher his character. Here at present the last one I should have dreamt of, advances to greet me; whilst sitting idly upon the Negro-House steps dirty and sluggish, I behold young Women to whom I had most frequently presented Ear-Rings, Shoes, Calicos, [and] Kerchief . . . formerly pleased to meet me, but now not even lifting the head as I passed. In former days also fear in a great measure guided the action of the Negro and we Planters could never get at the truth. I am of opinion that very many Negroes are most unhappy in their changed condition, but this however they do not care to admit. . . .

At last I put the simple question to [General Harrison], "out of curiosity, could you give me an idea of [how] you make a 'Contract' with the Negroes, and how do you work the Plantation from your experience as a Planter, since the 'Termination of the War?'" His reply was as follows; and his Plan as far as I can judge, appears to me quite good. "Contract" The portion of the Plantation rented to General Harrison contains 390 Acres. This is divided into 5 Divisions, each Division containing 78 Acres. An intelligent Negro, and one experienced in Rice Culture is chosen. The new appellation of "Foreman" is given him, and he takes full charge of One Division (of in this case 78 Acres). The "Foreman" is to cultivate and in every respect superintend his Division, until his [rice] Crop is threshed, and ready for Market. For this purpose He selects or procures his own Hands, which in this instance requires about 10 for each "Foreman." A "Contract" is signed in Savannah between Gen'l Harrison and his "Foreman" . . . and for this purpose they two appear at the Government [Freedmen's] Bureau where the transaction is effected in proper form established by Law. Little or no intercourse is thus held between Gen'l Harrison and the Mass of the Negroes, and provided the Work is performed it is immaterial what Hands are employed whether the same or others. . . .

All [about the visit] had passed off in a most satisfactory manner, with the exception that upon reaching Savannah I found that the Gen'l's Servant (who had taken charge of horse and buggy up at the place) had stolen nearly every thing I had in the buggy, but I have never thought it worth my while to mention it to the General, as I have no doubt he has from his contact with Negroes annoyance enough.

QUESTIONS FOR READING AND DISCUSSION

1. What evidence did Manigault discover of the "cruel hand of War"?
2. What was responsible for what Manigault called the "change in appearance" of his Gowrie plantation "from a Village to a Wilderness"?
3. How did Manigault's former slaves behave toward him on his visit? How did he account for their behavior? How would you explain their behavior?
4. Why did Manigault believe that, "So deceitful is the Negro that as far as my own experience extends I could never in a single instance decipher his character?" How might his former slaves have described Manigault?
5. Manigault confirmed for himself "the sad reality of affairs" on his visit to his plantations. How, specifically, might his former slaves have described the reality of affairs on his plantations in 1867?

DOCUMENT 16–5

Klan Violence against Blacks

White vigilantes often terrorized African Americans after emancipation. The campaign of terror intensified with congressional Reconstruction and the mobilization of black voters in the Republican Party. The violence attracted the attention of Congress, which held committee hearings throughout the South in 1871 to investigate the Ku Klux Klan. The following testimony of Elias Hill—a black preacher and teacher who lived in York County, South Carolina—illustrates the tactics and purposes of white vigilantes.

Elias Hill

Testimony before Congressional Committee Investigating the Ku Klux Klan, 1871

[The committee included a brief description of Hill.] Elias Hill is a remarkable character. He is crippled in both legs and arms, which are shriveled by rheumatism; he cannot walk, cannot help himself, has to be fed and cared for personally by others; was in early life a slave, whose freedom was purchased, his father buying his mother and getting Elias along with her, as a burden of which his master was glad to be rid. Stricken at seven years old with disease, he never was afterward able to walk, and he presents the appearance of a dwarf with the limbs of a

From U.S. Congress, *Report of the Joint Select Committee to Inquire into the Condition of Affairs in the Late Insurrectionary States* (Washington, DC, 1872), 1:44–46.

child, the body of a man, and a finely developed intellectual head. He learned his letters and to read by calling the school children into the cabin as they passed, and also learned to write. He became a Baptist preacher, and after the war engaged in teaching colored children, and conducted the business correspondence of many of his colored neighbors. He is a man of blameless character, of unusual intelligence, speaks good English, and we put the story of his wrongs in his own language:

On the night of the 5th of last May, after I had heard a great deal of what they had done in that neighborhood, they came. It was between 12 and 1 o'clock at night when I was awakened and heard the dogs barking, and something walking, very much like horses. As I had often laid awake listening for such persons, for they had been all through the neighborhood, and disturbed all men and many women, I supposed that it was them. They came in a very rapid manner, and I could hardly tell whether it was the sound of horses or men. At last they came to my brother's door, which is in the same yard, and broke open the door and attacked his wife, and I heard her screaming and mourning. I could not understand what they said, for they were talking in an outlandish and unnatural tone, which I had heard they generally used at a negro's house. I heard them knocking around in her house. I was lying in my little cabin in the yard. At last I heard them have her in the yard. She was crying and the Ku-Klux were whipping her to make her tell where I lived. I heard her say, "Yon is his house." She has told me since that they first asked who had taken me out of her house. They said, "Where's Elias?" She said, "He doesn't stay here; yon is his house." They were then in the yard, and I had heard them strike her five or six licks when I heard her say this. Some one then hit my door. It flew open. One ran in the house, and stopping about the middle of the house, which is a small cabin, he turned around, as it seemed to me as I lay there awake, and said, "Who's here?" Then I knew they would take me, and I answered, "I am here." He shouted for joy, as it seemed, "Here he is! Here he is! We have found him!" and he threw the bedclothes off of me and caught me by one arm, while another man took me by the other and they carried me into the yard between the houses, my brother's and mine, and put me on the ground beside a boy. The first thing they asked me was, "Who did that burning? Who burned our houses?" — gin-houses, dwelling houses and such. Some had been burned in the neighborhood. I told them it was not me; I could not burn houses; it was unreasonable to ask me. Then they hit me with their fists, and said I did it, I ordered it. They went on asking me didn't I tell the black men to ravish all the white women. No, I answered them. They struck me again with their fists on my breast, and then they went on, "When did you hold a night-meeting of the Union League,[1] and who were the officers? Who was the president?" I told them I had been the president, but that there had been no Union League meeting held at that place where they were formerly held since away in the fall. This was the 5th of May. They said that Jim Raney, that was hung, had been at my house since the time I had said the League was last held, and that he had made a speech. I told them that he had not, because I did not know the man. I said, "Upon honor." They said I had no honor, and hit me again. They went on asking me hadn't I been writing to Mr. A. S. Wallace, in Congress, to get letters from him. I told them I had. They asked what I had been writing about? I told them, "Only tidings." They said,

---

[1]**Union League**: Republican organization that helped mobilize African American voters.

with an oath, "I know the tidings were d——d good, and you were writing something about the Ku-Klux, and haven't you been preaching and praying about the Ku-Klux?" One asked, "Haven't you been preaching political sermons?" Generally, one asked me all the questions, but the rest were squatting over me—some six men I counted as I lay there, Said one, "Didn't you preach against the Ku-Klux," and wasn't that what Mr. Wallace was writing to me about? "Not at all," I said. "Let me see the letter," said he; "what was it about?" I said it was on the times. They wanted the letter. I told them if they would take me back into the house, and lay me in the bed, which was close adjoining my books and papers, I would try and get it. They said I would never go back to that bed, for they were going to kill me. "Never expect to go back; tell us where the letters are." I told them they were on the shelf somewhere, and I hoped they would not kill me. Two of them went into the house. . . . They staid in there a good while hunting about and then came out and asked me for a lamp. I told them there was a lamp somewhere. They said "Where?" I was so confused I said I could not tell exactly. They caught my leg—you see what it is—and pulled me over the yard, and then left me there, knowing I could not walk nor crawl, and all six went into the house. I was chilled with the cold lying in the yard at that time of night, for it was near 1 o'clock, and they had talked and beat me and so on until half an hour had passed since they first approached. After they had staid in the house for a considerable time, they came back to where I lay and asked if I wasn't afraid at all. They pointed pistols at me all around my head once or twice, as if they were going to shoot me, telling me they were going to kill me; wasn't I ready to die, and willing to die? Didn't I preach? That they came to kill me—all the time pointing pistols at me. This second time they came out of the house, after plundering the house, searching for letters, they came at me with these pistols, and asked if I was ready to die. I told them that I was not exactly ready; that I would rather live; that I hoped they would not kill me that time. They said they would; I had better prepare. One caught me by the leg and hurt me, for my leg for forty years has been drawn each year, more and more year by year, and I made moan when it hurt so. One said "G——d d——n it, hush!" He had a horsewhip, and he told me to pull up my shirt, and he hit me. He told me at every lick, "Hold up your shirt." I made a moan every time he cut with the horsewhip. I reckon he struck me eight cuts right on the hip bone; it was almost the only place he could hit my body, my legs are so short—all my limbs drawn up and withered away with pain. I saw one of them standing over me or by me motion to them to quit. They all had disguises on. I then thought they would not kill me. One of them then took a strap, and buckled it around my neck and said, "Let's take him to the river and drown him." . . . After pulling the strap around my neck, he took it off and gave me a lick on my hip where he had struck me with the horsewhip. One of them said, "Now, you see, I've burned up the d——d letter of Wallace's and all," and he brought out a little book and says, "What's this for?" I told him I did not know; to let me see with a light and I could read it. They brought a lamp and I read it. It was a book in which I had keep an account of the school. I had been licensed to keep a school. I read them some of the names. He said that would do, and asked if I had been paid for those scholars I had put down. I said no. He said I would now have to die. I was somewhat afraid, but one said not to kill me. They said "Look here! Will you put a card in the paper next week like June Moore and Sol Hill?" They had been prevailed on to put a card in the paper to renounce all republicanism and never vote. I said, "If I had the money to pay the expense, I could." They said I could borrow, and gave me another lick. They asked me, "Will you quit preaching?" I told them I did not know. I said that to save my life. They said I must stop that republican paper that was coming to Clay Hill. It has been only a few weeks since it stopped. The republican weekly paper was then coming to me from Charleston. It came to my name. They said I must stop it, quit preaching, and put a card in the newspaper renouncing republicanism, and they would not kill me; but if I did not they would come back the next week and kill me. With that one of them went into the house where my brother and my sister-in-law lived, and brought her to pick me up. As she stooped down to pick me up one of them struck her, and as she was carrying me into the house another struck her with a strap. She carried me into the house and laid me on the bed. Then they gathered around and told me to pray for them. I tried to pray. They said, "Don't you pray against Ku-Klux, but pray that God may forgive Ku-Klux. Don't pray against us. Pray that God may bless and save us." I was so chilled with cold lying out of doors so long and in such pain I could not speak to pray, but I tried to, and they said that would do very well, and all went out of the house.

QUESTIONS FOR READING AND DISCUSSION

1. What did the Klan want from Hill? Why did they not kill him?
2. The Klan was concerned about Hill's preaching, teaching, and newspaper reading. Why?
3. Why did the Klan use such brutal violence against Hill and his relatives? According to Hill, how had others been treated by the Klan? Does it appear that the Klan randomly chose people to terrorize? Why or why not?
4. What significance, if any, should be attributed to the Klan's demand that Hill "pray that God may forgive Ku-Klux"? For what did they seek forgiveness? Why?

COMPARATIVE QUESTIONS

1. How do the views of southern whites as reported by Carl Schurz differ from those expressed by Louis Manigault? To what extent do they contrast with the meanings of freedom documented in the advertisements from the *Christian Recorder*?
2. To what extent did the black codes and the Klan's campaign of terror against black Republicans like Hill confirm or contradict the report of Schurz? How did the activities of Hill and other Republicans compare with the freedmen and women on Manigault's plantations?
3. In what ways did Schurz's conclusions about the South differ from those of black and white Southerners in the other documents in this chapter? What explains the differences?
4. Documents in this chapter provide evidence that Reconstruction profoundly challenged fundamental assumptions among Northerners and Southerners, whites and blacks. Judging from these documents, what assumptions were challenged, and how, if at all, did those assumptions change during Reconstruction?

Acknowledgments

Chapter 1 1–1. Geoffrey Symcox and Luciano Formisano, eds. *Italian Reports on America, 1492–1522: Accounts by Contemporary Observers*, trans. by Theodore J. Cachey Jr. and John C. McLucas. Repertorium Columbianum 12 (Turnhout, Belgium: Brepols, 2002), 63–68. Reproduced by permission of Brepols Publishers.

1–4. Aristotle, *The Politics*, translated by Ernest Barker (1995), 8–20. By permission of Oxford University Press.

Chapter 2 2–1. Louis Jadin and Mireille Decorato, *Correspondance de Dom Afonso, roi du Congo, 1506–1543*. (Brussels: Académie Royale des Sciences d'Outre Mer, 1974), 154–62, 166–69. English translation by Marianna Dantas. Reprinted by permission Royal Academy for Overseas Sciences.

2–2. Oliver Dunn and James E. Kelley Jr., eds. and trans. *The Diario of Christopher Columbus's First Voyage to America, 1492–1493*, American Exploration and Traveler Series, vol. 70, 65–109. Copyright © 1989. Reprinted by permission of University of Oklahoma Press. The Diario of Christopher Columbus's first voyage to America, 1492–1493 by COLUMBUS, CHRISTOPHER Reproduced with permission of UNIVERSITY OF OKLAHOMA PRESS in the format Republish in a book via Copyright Clearance Center.

2–3. From *The Conquest of New Spain* by Bernal Díaz, translated with an introduction by J. M. Cohen. (Penguin Classics, 1963), 214–235. Copyright © J. M. Cohen, 1963.

2–4. James Lockhart, ed. and trans., *We People Here: Nahuatl Accounts of the Conquest of Mexico*. Mexican Accounts of Conquest from the Florentine Codex. Reprinted with permission from the Author.

Chapter 3 3–3. From *The Old Dominion in the Seventeenth Century: A Documentary History of Virginia, 1606–1689*, edited by Warren M. Billings. Published for the Omohundro Institute of Early American History and Culture. Copyright © 1974 by the University of North Carolina Press. Used by permission of the publisher.

3–4. From *The Old Dominion in the Seventeenth Century: A Documentary History of Virginia, 1606–1689*, edited by Warren M. Billings. Published for the Omohundro Institute of Early American History and Culture. Copyright © 1974 by the University of North Carolina Press. Used by permission of the publisher.

Chapter 4 4–2. Roger Williams, *A Key into the Language of America*. London: Gregory Dexter, 1643. Edited by John Teunissen and Evelyn J. Hinz (Detroit: 1973). Reprinted by permission.

4–3. Paul Royster, ed. John Easton, "A Relation of the Indian War, 1675," in Charles Henry Lincoln, *Narratives of the Indian Wars, 1675–1699* (New York: Charles Scribner's Sons, 1913), 7–17. Copyright © Paul Royster. Reprinted by permission.

Chapter 5 5–3. From *The Carolina Backcountry on the Eve of the Revolution: The Journal and Other Writings of Charles Woodmason, Anglican Itinerant*, edited by Richard J. Hooker. Copyright © 1953 by the University of North Carolina Press, renewed 1981 by Richard J. Hooker. Published for the Omohundro Institute of Early American History and Culture. Used by permission of the publisher. www.uncpress .unc.edu

5–5. Christian George Andreas Oldendorp, *History of the Evangelical Brethren's Mission on the Caribbean Islands of St. Thomas, St. Cross, and St. John* (Leipzig, 1777), trans. from German in Soi-Daniel W. Brown, "From the Tongues of Africa: A Partial Translation of Oldendorp's Interviews," *Plantation Society*, II (1983), 37–61.

Chapter 7 7–2. Reprinted by permission of the publisher from *The Adam Papers: Adams Family Correspondence, Volumes a and II:* December 1761–March 1778, edited by L.H. Butterfield, Cambridge, Mass.: The Belknap Press of Harvard University Press, Copyright © 1963 by the Massachusetts Historical Society.

Chapter 9 9–4. Althéa de Puech Parham. Excerpt from *My Odyssey: Experiences of a Young Refugee from Two Revolutions by a Creole of Saint Domingue*. Copyright © 1959 by Althéa de Puech Parham. Reprinted by permission of Duncan de Puech Parham, Executor in trust of the Estate of Althéa de Puech Parham.

Chapter 10 10–2. Gary E. Moulton, ed., *The Journals of the Lewis and Clark Expedition*, vol. 5, July 28–November 1, 1805. Copyright © Lincoln: University of Nebraska Press, 1988, 103–59. The journals of the Lewis & Clark Expedition by LEWIS, MERIWETHER; CLARK, WILLIAM Reproduced with permission of UNIVERSITY OF NEBRASKA PRESS in the format Republish in a book via Copyright Clearance Center.

Chapter 12 12–1. Abraham Lincoln, "Address before the Wisconsin State Agricultural Society, Milwaukee, Wisconsin, September 30, 1859," in Roy P. Basler, ed. *The Collected Works of Abraham Lincoln*. New Brunswick, NJ: Rutgers University Press, 1953: vol. 3, 471–82. All rights reserved. Reproduced by permission of The Abraham Lincoln Association.

Chapter 14 14–1. Abraham Lincoln, "Speech in Peoria, Illinois, October 16, 1854," in Roy P. Basler, ed., *The Collected Works of Abraham Lincoln*. New Brunswick, NJ: Rutgers University Press, 1953: vol. 2, 247–82. All rights reserved. Reproduced by permission of The Abraham Lincoln Association.

Chapter 15 15–1. Abraham Lincoln, "Letter to Horace Greeley, August 22, 1862; Emancipation Proclamation, January 1, 1863; Gettysburg Address, November 19, 1863" in Roy P. Basler, ed., *The Collected Works of Abraham Lincoln*. New Brunswick, NJ: Rutgers University Press, 1953: vol. 5: 388–89, 6:28–30, 7: 22–23. All rights reserved. Reproduced by permission of The Abraham Lincoln Association.

15–2. Ira Berlin, Joseph Reidy, and Leslie S. Rowland, eds. "Statements of a Colored Man [September 1863]," in *Freedom: A Documentary History of Emancipation, 1861–1867*, Series 2, *The Black Military Experience*. Copyright © Cambridge: Cambridge University Press, 1982, 153–57.

Chapter 16 16–4. Louis Manigault, Manigault Plantation Journal (manuscript). Manigault Papers, Southern Historical Collection, 56–71. Copyright © Southern Historical Collection, Wilson Library, The University of North Carolina at Chapel Hill.